ELABORATIONS ON EMPTINESS

ELABORATIONS ON EMPTINESS

USES OF THE *HEART SŪTRA*

Donald S. Lopez, Jr.

PRINCETON UNIVERSITY PRESS PRINCETON, NEW JERSEY

Published by Princeton University Press, 41 William Street,
Princeton, New Jersey 08540
In the United Kingdom: Princeton University Press, Chichester, West Sussex

Library of Congress Cataloging-in-Publication Data

Lopez, Donald S., 1952–
Elaborations on emptiness : uses of the Heart Sūtra / Donald S. Lopez.
p. cm.
Includes bibliographical references and index.
ISBN 0-691-02732-3 (cloth : alk. paper)
1. Tripiṭaka. Sūtrapiṭaka. Prajñāpāramitā. Hṛdaya—
Commentaries. I. Tripiṭaka. Sūtrapiṭaka. Prajñāpāramitā.
Hṛdaya. English. II. Title.
BQ1967.L66 1996
294.3'85—dc20 95-44449 CIP

This book has been composed in Sabon

Princeton University Press books are printed on acid-free paper
and meet the guidelines for permanence and durability of the
Committee on Production Guidelines for Book Longevity of the
Council on Library Resources

Printed in the United States of America by Princeton Academic Press

10 9 8 7 6 5 4 3 2 1

For Laura

The Heart Sūtra

The Bhagavatī Heart of the Perfection of Wisdom Sūtra

Bhagavatīprajñāpāramitāhṛdayasūtra

Thus did I hear. At one time the Bhagavan was abiding at Vulture Peak in Rājagṛha with a great assembly of monks and a great assembly of bodhisattvas. At that time, the Bhagavan entered into a samādhi on the categories of phenomena called "perception of the profound." Also at that time, the bodhisattva, the *mahāsattva*, the noble Avalokiteśvara beheld the practice of the profound perfection of wisdom and saw that those five aggregates also are empty of intrinsic existence. Then, by the power of the Buddha, the venerable Śāriputra said this to the bodhisattva, the *mahāsattva*, the noble Avalokiteśvara, "How should a son of good lineage who wishes to practice the profound perfection of wisdom train?" He said that and the bodhisattva, the *mahāsattva*, the noble Avalokiteśvara said this to the venerable Śāriputra, "Śāriputra, a son of good lineage or a daughter of good lineage who wishes to practice the profound perfection of wisdom should perceive things in this way: form is empty; emptiness is form. Emptiness is not other than form; form is not other than emptiness. In the same way, feeling, discrimination, conditioning factors, and consciousnesses are empty. Therefore, Śāriputra, all phenomena are empty, without characteristic, unproduced, unceased, stainless, not stainless, undiminished, unfilled. Therefore, Śāriputra, in emptiness there is no form, no feeling, no discrimination, no conditioning factors, no consciousness, no eye, no ear, no nose, no tongue, no body, no mind, no form, no sound, no odor, no taste, no object of touch, no phenomenon, no eye constituent up to and including no mental consciousness constituent, no ignorance, no extinction of ignorance, no aging and death up to and including no extinction of aging and death. In the same way, no suffering, origin, cessation, path, no wisdom, no attainment, no nonattainment. Therefore, Śāriputra, because bodhisattvas have no attainment, they rely on and abide in the perfection of wisdom; because their minds are without obstruction, they have no fear. They pass completely beyond error and go to the fulfillment of nirvāṇa. All the buddhas who abide in the three times have fully awakened into unsurpassed, complete, perfect enlightenment in dependence on the perfection of wisdom. Therefore, the mantra of the perfection of wisdom is the mantra of great knowledge, the unsurpassed mantra, the mantra equal to the unequaled, the mantra that completely pacifies all suffering. Because it is not false, it should be known to be true. The mantra of the perfection of wisdom is stated thus: *[oṃ] gate gate pāragate pārasaṃgate bodhi svāhā*. Śāriputra, a bodhisattva *mahāsattva* should train in the profound perfection of wisdom in that way." Then the Bhagavan rose from samādhi and said, "Well done" to the bodhisattva, the *mahāsattva*, the noble Avalokiteśvara. "Well done, well done, child of good lineage, it is like that. It is like that; the practice of the profound perfection of wisdom is just as you have taught it. Even the tathāgatas admire it." The Bhagavan having so spoken, the venerable Śāriputra, the bodhisattva, the *mahāsattva*, the noble Avalokiteśvara, and all those surrounding, and the entire world, the gods, humans, demigods, and *gandharvas*, admired and praised the speech of the Bhagavan.[1]

[1] The edition of the sūtra translated here is the one that appears in the Peking edition (P 160, vol. 6, 166.1.7–166.4–5). The sūtra is translated from the Tibetan rather than the Sanskrit because one of the translators of the sūtra from Sanskrit to Tibetan was Vimalamitra. The best study of the *Heart Sūtra* in Tibetan is the superb monograph by Jonathan Silk, *The Heart Sūtra in Tibetan: A Critical Edition of Recension A and Recension B of the Kanjur Text* (Wien: Arbeitskreis für Tibetische und Buddhistische Studien Universität Wien, 1994). The fullest study of the Sanskrit text of the sūtra in English remains Edward Conze, "The Prajñāpāramitā-hṛdaya Sūtra," in his *Thirty Years of Buddhist Studies* (Columbia: University of South Carolina Press, 1968), pp. 148–67. See also Jan Nattier, "The *Heart Sūtra*: A Chinese Apocryphal Text," *Journal of the International Association of Buddhist Studies* 15, no. 2 (1992): 153–223. A Sanskrit edition of the sūtra is also available in P. L. Vaidya, ed., *Mahāyānasūtrasaṃgraha* (Darbhanga, India: The Mithila Institute, 1961), pt. 1, pp. 98–99. For a brief survey of Japanese scholarship on the text of the sūtra, see Hajime Nakamura, *Indian Buddhism: A Survey with Bibliographical Notes* (Delhi: Motilal Banarsidass, 1987), p. 164, n. 47.

Contents

Technical Note and Acknowledgments

IN TRANSLATING the eight commentaries, I made use of two editions: the reprint edition of the Peking (*Peking Tibetan Tripiṭika* [Tokyo and Kyoto: Tibetan Tripiṭaka Research Foundation, 1957]) and the Derge (sDe dge) edition published by the Sixteenth Karma pa (Delhi: Delhi Karmapae Choedhey, Gyalwae Sungrab Partun Khang, 1985). The Peking (also known as Otani, indicated here by P) and Tohoku (for the Derge edition, rendered here as Toh.) catalogue numbers of the eight commentaries (by author) are as follows: Vimalamitra (P 5217, Toh. 3818), Jñānamitra (P 5218, Toh. 3819), Vajrapāṇi (P 5219, Toh. 3820), Praśāstrasena (P 5220, Toh. 3821), Kamalaśīla (P 5221, not in Derge), Atiśa (P 5222, Toh. 3823), Śrīmahājana (P 5223, Toh. 3822), and Śrīsiṃha (or Vairocana) (P 5840, Toh. 4353). Because the Derge has become the more widely available edition, I have provided the Derge page numbers in the body of the translation (with the exception of Kamalaśīla, which does not appear in Derge; I provide the Peking page numbers instead). In the Derge, the commentaries of Vimalamitra, Jñānamitra, Vajrapāṇi, Praśāstrasena, Atiśa, and Śrīmahājana are all in the Shes phyin section, volume ma, 267b1–317a7 (Kamalaśīla is found only in Peking). The commentary of Śrīsiṃha is found in the sNa tshogs section, volume co, 205b7–209b7. In the notes to the translation, I have noted those variants that seem most significant to the translation of the text, following what I judge to be the best reading. Unfortunately, it was not possible to include all variants in spelling and punctuation. A critical edition of the Indian commentaries remains a desideratum for a number of reasons, including the fact that variants in the editions of the *Heart Sūtra* used by the commentators (even if known from memory) may shed light on the vexed question of the date of the *Heart Sūtra*. Nakamura Hajime, in his *Indian Buddhism: A Survey with Bibliographical Notes* (Delhi: Motilal Banarsidass, 1987, p. 160) dates it from the second century of the Common Era. Conze, in his *The Prajñāpāramitā Literature* (The Hague: Mouton, 1960, p. 9) dates it around C.E.350. More recently, Jan Nattier has suggested the possibility that it is a Chinese apocryphon translated into Sanskrit in the seventh century ("The *Heart Sūtra*: A Chinese Apocryphal Text," *Journal of the International Association of Buddhist Studies* 15, no. 2 [1992]: 153–223).

In reading some of the more difficult passages of the commentaries,

I received great assistance from Geshe Yeshe Thapke of the Central Institute of Higher Tibetan Studies in Sarnath, India. I took some small comfort in the fact that the passages that seemed most intractable to me sometimes posed problems for him as well. I also am grateful to Steven Collins for many helpful comments on the essays.

Buddhist terminology that appears in *Webster's Third New International Dictionary* has not been italicized.

ELABORATIONS ON EMPTINESS

Introduction

THE JAPANESE STORY "Miminashi Hōichi" tells the tale of Hōichi, a blind boy with the rare ability to recite the epic *Tale of Heike* in a beautiful voice, accompanying himself on the *biwa*, a stringed instrument. He lived in the temple of Amidaji near the town of Shimonoseki in southern Honshu, the site of the decisive sea battle in which the Heike clan met its demise. Late one summer night, Hōichi was sitting outside playing the *biwa* when he heard someone call his name. From the sound of the footsteps, he determined that the visitor was a samurai in full armor, who told Hōichi that his lord was passing through the area and wished to have performed for him the portion of the epic which tells of that final battle. He was led to what seemed an opulent villa where the women spoke in the language of the court. He was given a kneeling cushion and began to sing the mournful song of the battle. His performance was so poignant that the whispered praise he overheard soon changed to sobs and wails from what must have been a large audience. The lord was so moved that he invited Hōichi to return for the next six nights. The soldier then led him back to the temple before dawn.

The next night, the soldier came once again at the appointed hour and led him away. This time, however, some servants of the monastery followed. They lost Hōichi in the evening fog but eventually heard his song, which led them to the cemetery of Amidaji, where Hōichi sat alone. They led him back to the monastery, where one of the monks realized what had happened. Hōichi was in grave danger, for he had not been taken to a villa each night but to a cemetery, where he had performed not for a noble family but for the ghosts of the Heike clan. On the night when he completed the tale, he would be killed.

That night, the abbot devised a plan to protect him. The monks took calligraphy brushes and ink and wrote the words of the *Heart Sūtra* over Hōichi's entire body. This would render him invisible. If Hōichi remained silent and did not betray his presence with his voice when the soldier came to fetch him, the ghost would be unable to find him. The next morning the monks discovered Hōichi sitting in the monastery's garden, alive. But blood was flowing from holes on either side of his head, holes where his ears had been. The monks had forgotten to write the sūtra on his ears, which alone had remained visible to the ghost, who tore them off to present to his lord. From then on, the famous singer of the *Heike Monogatori* was known as Miminashi Hōichi, "Hōichi the Earless."[1]

This is perhaps the most graphic of the many uses to which the *Heart Sūtra* has been put throughout the many centuries of its history across Asia. Here, Hōichi's salvation (rather than his crime, as in Kafka's penal colony) is inscribed on his blind body, rendering it invisible to the dead. But this salvation comes with a cost, because the monks failed to write the words of the sūtra that begins, "Thus did I hear," on his ears. As a result, the outer organs of hearing, all that remains visible of the blind boy, are left unwritten and are therefore lost.

Although the uses of the *Heart Sūtra* studied in this volume are less immediately visceral, one finds here nonetheless related themes of speech and writing, of performance and protection. The Indian commentators whose works are considered here found in the *Heart Sūtra* something that elicited exegesis, an exegesis that attempted to find in this most terse of sūtras vast elaborations of Indian Buddhist thought and practice. They took it as their task, in a sense, to write the *Heart Sūtra* over this great corpus of doctrine.

In 1988 I published a book entitled *The Heart Sūtra Explained: Indian and Tibetan Commentaries*. This book was an extended multilevel explanation of the sūtra that proceeded through the text word by word, quoting at length from the seven extant Indian commentaries, those quotations in turn explained by me. At times I simply defined technical terms, identified allusions, and provided lists; at other times I reported explanations from the dGe lugs pa tradition of Tibetan exegesis. In the years since the publication of the book, I have had occasion to regret the choice of the title, *The Heart Sūtra Explained*, often at the time of a public lecture, because the person introducing me would inevitably, after announcing the title of my recent book, say wistfully to the audience, "as if the *Heart Sūtra* could ever be explained." Apart from these moments, however, I have felt that the title was appropriate because the book is very much an explanation, in the sense of a leveling, of the seven Indian commentaries that are its primary focus. Because I decided to follow the words of the sūtra, I was constrained to employ only those parts of the Indian commentaries that spoke directly to the meaning of these words. I therefore omitted from consideration those large portions of the commentaries in which the authors would depart from the text to a tangential concern, despite the fact that these frequent excurses were often more revealing than the more prosaic progression through the sūtra. Further-

[1] The story of Hōichi appears in Lafcadio Hearn's *Kwaidan*. See *The Writings of Lafcadio Hearn,* vol. 11, *Kottō and Kwaidan*, large paper edition (Boston: Houghton Mifflin, 1922), pp. 161–75. A film version was included in Masaki Kobayashi's 1965 *Kwaidan*.

more, because seven comments on every word seemed excessive, I often tried to choose one or two passages on a term or phrase that seemed the most interesting or representative. The result was not really a representation of the seven commentaries (less than a third of which ended up being translated in the book) but rather was my own commentary, which homogenized the Indian commentaries into a digest, where discrepancies and idiosyncracies were flattened by generally being ignored, resulting in a commentary that was much more my own than that of any of the seven *paṇḍitas*.

Since completing that book, I have found an eighth Indian commentary to the sūtra, one that has not been placed along with the seven others in the various Tibetan canons, a work attributed to the tantric master Śrīsiṃha (discussed below). These eight works seemed to deserve full translation for a variety of reasons, including that of the value of allowing readers to appreciate the contours in such a range of commentaries, noting how some points are stressed by one author, ignored by another. One of the purposes of the present volume is to offer full translations of these eight works. Another purpose, evident throughout but discussed explicitly in the final chapter, is to explore the role of commentary, both of the traditional Buddhist exegete and of the modern Western scholar.

Perhaps no other Buddhist text, in either speech or writing, has been more popular than the *Heart Sūtra*. The *Lotus* and the *Sukhāvatīvyūha* have been more influential in East Asia in the inspiration of doctrine and art. But the presence of the *Heart Sūtra* has been more pervasive. It is recited daily in Tibetan, Chinese, Japanese, and Korean temples and monasteries, and we have evidence of its recitation in India (see below). Its "form is emptiness, emptiness is form" is among the most famous lines in Buddhist literature.[2] In the Tibetan cultural region, it forms the center of a widely practiced exorcism ritual (discussed in chapter 9). In Japan, as we have seen, it was once written on bodies, and today can be found in many temple shops inscribed on fans, coffee mugs, and neckties. It has elicited more commentaries than any other sūtra. In China, "there is no other single text—nor any single group of scriptures—that has been interpreted by such a long and virtually unbroken list of illustrious au-

[2] It is noteworthy that, at least as preserved in Tibetan translation, all eight of the Indian commentators read the line not as "form is emptiness, emptiness is form," but as "form is empty, emptiness is form." (Kamalaśīla does not cite the line directly, but refers to "consciousness is empty.") In the available Sanskrit editions, both versions appear: *rūpaṃ śūnyatā śūnyataiva rūpaṃ* and *rūpaṃ śūnyaṃ śūnyataiva rūpaṃ*. The latter seems to be better known to the Indian commentators, and is translated literally as "form is empty" in the chapters that follow, despite the wide currency and fame in English of "form is emptiness." There would seem to be a difference philosophically between saying "form is emptiness" and "form is empty." However, during an audience in 1984, His Holiness (H. H.) the Dalai Lama told me that there is no significant difference in meaning.

thorities."[3] A similar claim could be made about Japan. Among the Indian works preserved in the various Tibetan canons, we find not only that the *Heart Sūtra* figures in two tantric sādhanas (discussed in chapter 5), but that it has been the subject of more commentaries (eight) than any other sūtra.[4] No Buddhist text has been so widely deployed for such a diverse range of uses. This volume considers some of the remarkable uses to which the *Heart Sūtra* has been put, within a much more circumscribed time and place, the time of the Pāla Dynasty (the eighth through the twelfth centuries of the Common Era) and the place of India, moving in the ninth chapter to Tibet.

The work of the Western scholar of Buddhism almost always begins with translation, the attempt to render the chosen text(s) as accurately as possible. That was also the case with this project. Especially in works such as these commentaries, one of the tasks of the translator is to identify the many allusions that the authors employ, allusions to often unidentified sūtras, and, more often, to a particular scholastic category or organizing list. These identifications are usually relegated to endnotes, where they are often supplemented by the translator's comments on how another author of another text understood a passage differently or used another scholastic category to make his point. When, as in the case of this volume, we are dealing with eight commentaries to a single sūtra, the points of contact and contrast are greatly multiplied, and, when the translator is moved, rightly or wrongly, to relate these various points to "larger issues," the endnotes swell to overwhelm the translation. The translator is then confronted with the question of priority, that is, which should come first? The translation began as the body of the text, the notes as its appendage. Now the appendage has grown larger than the body; the parasite has overwhelmed the host. If it is necessary to remedy this imbalance, the endnotes must be brought to the foreground and recast from disconnected references into a narrative—in effect, into yet another commentary. The translations are now pushed into the background, into an appendix at the back of the book, their purpose now to provide instantiations and testimonies to points made in the narrative, now divided into chapters and raised to the status of essays.

[3] John McRae, "Ch'an Commentaries on the *Heart Sūtra*: Preliminary Inferences on the Permutation of Chinese Buddhism," *Journal of the International Association of Buddhist Studies* 11, no. 2 (1988): 87.

[4] There are two for the *Vajracchedikā* (attributed to Vasubandhu and Kamalaśīla), three for the *Daśabhūmika*, two for the *Laṅkāvatāra*, two for the *Saptaśatikāprajñāpāramitā*, four for the *Saṃcayagathā*, and four for the *Saṃdhinirmocana*; only two are by Indian authors, one complete by Asaṅga, one partial by Jñānagarbha. The two other commentators are the Tibetan Byang chub rdzu 'phrul (generally identified as the eighth-century translator Cog ro kLu'i rgyal mtshan) and the Sinicized Korean Yuance (Wonch'uk, 613–696).

I have followed a different strategy here, alternating essays and translations. The translations are meant to provide a point of entry into a number of problems of broader theoretical interest, considered in the essays. At the same time, the translations serve as vehicles for bringing the reader back after each essay into the problematics and styles of the Pāla Dynasty commentators, before moving ahead to confront another of the larger issues in the next essay.

The translation of the commentaries was often a difficult task, because these are Indian commentaries originally composed (with the possible exception of that by Śrīsiṃha) in Sanskrit, and then translated into Tibetan, sometimes with the collaboration of the author, sometimes not. The original Sanskrit commentaries have been lost. What I am providing, then, is a translation of a translation. This is a particular problem with these texts, because they belong to a genre of Indian scholastic literature that makes extensive use of various forms of wordplay, drawing elaborate meanings from a very laconic text through paronomasia, exploiting the homonymy of Sanskrit roots, as discussed in the final chapter. Puns do not translate easily. Furthermore, some of the commentaries assume a fairly sophisticated knowledge of Buddhist doctrine; the commentaries are generally scholastic works written for other scholastics. I have not attempted to explain every technical term and phrase. I also do not pretend that the commentaries somehow "stand alone" outside of a rich and variegated scholastic setting (about which we know something) and a political and social setting (about which we know very little). To draw out the thread of a single term in the sūtra draws out not only every other term in the sūtra but also the weave of the vast intertextual web that is late Indian Buddhist scholasticism. My own lassitude prevents me from undertaking so daunting a task, although I provide some guidance to the perplexed in notes and bracketed glosses. Otherwise, I have tried simply to provide "accurate" translations, in full cognizance that the storied precision of the Tibetan rendering of Sanskrit works is best regarded as a story. The translations of the eight Indian commentaries have been interspersed with and embedded among my own essays, essays inspired by the commentaries.

The first of those essays forms the first chapter, and is motivated by the Indian commentators' concern with the identity of the compiler or rapporteur (*saṃgītikartṛ*) of the sūtra: when the sūtra begins, "Thus did I hear" (*evaṃ mayā śrutam*), who is speaking, who is the "I"? Most of the commentators seem compelled to answer this question, suggesting that the issue of the legitimacy of the Mahāyāna sūtras as the authentic word of the Buddha (*buddhavacana*) remained a contested one, even a millennium after the rise of the Mahāyāna and until the end of Buddhism in India. To address the question of who heard the *Heart Sūtra* is to seek to rebut the apparently persistent charges that the Mahāyāna sūtras are spurious, and each answer implies a different point. To say that the *saṃgītikartṛ* is one of the great bodhisattvas, such as Mañjuśrī or Vajrapāṇi, is to imply that the Mahāyāna sūtras are exclusive teachings not intended for the Hīnayāna disciples of the Budddha, the śrāvakas, and thus purposefully delivered in their absence. From this perspective, the Buddha's attendant, the śrāvaka Ānanda, is not and cannot be the *saṃgītikartṛ* because he was not permitted to be present to hear the *Heart Sūtra*. To say, as other Mahāyāna commentators do, that the *saṃgītikartṛ* was Ānanda is to attempt incorporation, that just as the earlier and commonly accepted discourses, the Nikāyas, were heard and reported by Śākyamuni's attendant, so also were the Mahāyana sūtras. An important variant of this position is to say that the *saṃgītikartṛ* was Ānanda, but that he was magically empowered by the Buddha to perform the task and that, even then, he merely heard but did not understand what he would later report. Such a position attempts to have it both ways: preserving the Mahāyāna as the highest teaching, beyond the capacity of śrāvakas, but still to be counted among the discourses heard in the physical presence of Śākyamuni. Finally, to leave the *saṃgītikartṛ* unnamed is to allow sūtras to be heard by anyone with the qualifications of faith, an important concession in a movement with an ever-growing canon of sacred texts. These questions of authority are related intimately to questions of hearing. Why did works that were composed in writing seek to maintain the pretense of speech, as records of something heard? The opening chapter moves to address this question by examining recent theories of the role of orality in the formation of Indian religious texts, both Vedic and Buddhist.

The first chapter is followed by two commentaries, those of Vimalamitra and Atiśa. These two commentaries, the second composed more than two centuries after the first, are placed first for several reasons. First, Vimalamitra and Atiśa are the two commentators among the eight who address the question of the *saṃgītikartṛ* and his qualifications most fully; it is an analysis of their positions that comprises the opening section of the first chapter. Second, Atiśa's commentary (the second shortest of the eight) is clearly a subcommentary on Vimalamitra, elaborating on only a few selected points while deferring to Vimalamitra's extensive commentary on the greater part of the sūtra.

Vimalamitra's commentary is the longest and most thorough of the eight. Its author is a somewhat shadowy figure about whom very little can be said with certainty. He is revered in Tibet as one of the chief Indian figures in the transmission of the rDzogs chen ("great completeness") teachings of the rNying ma sect, especially of the "heart drop" (*snying thig*) tradition. He is said to have been invited (when he was already two hundred years old) to come to Tibet by King Khri srong lde btsan, arriving either before or after the king's death in 797.[5] Vimalamitra remained in Tibet for thirteen years, before leaving for China.[6] While in Tibet, he collaborated in the translation of a number of texts from Sanskrit into Tibetan, including the *Heart Sūtra*. The works attributed to him preserved in the Tibetan canons are all "tantric" in subject matter, with two exceptions: a commentary on the *Perfection of Wisdom in 700 Stanzas* (*Saptaśatikāprajñāpāramitā*) and a commentary on the *Heart Sūtra*. Both are quite straightforward exegetical works, causing the Tibetan historian 'Gos lo tsa ba to report in his *Blue Annals* that they were not the product of the tantric master revered in rNying ma, that there had been, in fact, two Vimalamitras.[7] Regardless, his commentary, apparently composed in Tibet, is clearly the work of a scholastic virtuoso, an expansive yet rather close word-by-word exegesis, ranging widely over the great expanse of Indian philosophical discourse, both Buddhist and non-Buddhist, and replete with citations from numerous sūtras, tantras, and śāstras (Madhyamaka, Yogācāra, and Prāmāṇika) in support of his points. He moves methodically through the sūtra, but at a level of detail greater than that of the other commentators. He goes to especial lengths, for example, to argue that the litany of negations in the sūtra should not be understood to obviate the practice of the bodhisattva path in all of its elaborate detail.

The commentary of Atiśa is among the briefest. Atiśa is well known for his role in the revival of Buddhism in Tibet in the middle of the eleventh century, known as the "latter dissemination" (*spyi dar*). While in Tibet (where he arrived in 1042) he composed his most famous work, the *Lamp for the Path to Enlightenment* (*Bodhipathapradīpa*), as well as his commentary on the *Heart Sūtra*. If we can accept the following story, however, Atiśa's interest in the sūtra antedated his arrival in Tibet. The Tibetan translator Nag tsho Tshul khrims rgyal ba of Gung thang had been sent on a royal mission to India and the great monastery of Vikramaśīla, expressly to invite Atiśa to Tibet. In his account of his journey, he tells of his first meeting with the monk he would later identify as Atiśa:

> I was reciting the *Heart Sūtra* at one of the gates of the monastery. At the point [in the sūtra] where I said, "Form *ha*, feeling *ha*," other paṇḍitas did not say

[5] See Samten G. Karmay, *The Great Perfection: A Philosophical and Meditative Teaching of Tibetan Buddhism* (Leiden: E. J. Brill, 1988), pp. 27–28, 34.

[6] For accounts of Vimalamitra's life and lineage, see Dudjom Rinpoche, *The Nyingma School of Buddhism: Its Fundamentals and History*, vol. 1, trans. and ed. Gyurme Dorje (Boston: Wisdom, 1991), passim (see index in vol. 2). Also see Tarthang Tulku, *Crystal Mirror*, vol. 5 (Berkeley: Dharma, 1977), pp. 191–95; and Eva M. Dargyay, *The Rise of Esoteric Buddhism in Tibet* (Delhi: Motilal Banarsidass, 1977), chap. 2.

[7] This position is evaluated and rejected by Flemming Faber in his article "Vimalamitra—One or Two?" *Studies in Central and East Asian Religions* 2 (1989): 19–26.

> anything. But once the Lord [Atiśa] was walking by. He smiled and stopped, "Thank you, venerable one. But that is the vulgar pronunciation. Say, 'form *a*, feeling *a*.'" I [not realizing that he was Atiśa] thought, "This kind paṇḍita seems special. He is gentle, humble, clear, and whatever he says is spoken with the wish to be helpful. If I cannot invite the Lord [Atiśa], I must invite him [to come to Tibet]. In the morning, I was saying, "form *a*, feeling *a*" when the Lord smiled and said, "Venerable one, even that comes out sounding harsh. This is the speech of the protector Avalokita, there's nothing wrong with it. It is fine to say, 'no form, no feeling.'"[8]

This same Tshul khrims rgyal ba would eventually collaborate with Atiśa in the translation of Atiśa's commentary on the *Heart Sūtra* into Tibetan. As mentioned above, Atiśa assumes a knowledge of Vimalamitra's commentary as he concentrates on only a few points. Almost a third of his work is devoted to the question of the rapporteur and his qualifications, where he contrasts the positions of Dignāga and Vimalamitra. He also glosses the term "viewing" at length (as in "Avalokiteśvara was viewing the five aggregates"), explaining this in terms of four levels of increasingly nonconceptual vision derived from the *Saṃdhinirmocana Sūtra*. Like a number of other commentators, he is determined to find in the sūtra the standard fivefold path to buddhahood.[9] Atiśa also offers an interesting reading of the presence of the mantra in the sūtra, explaining that the teaching of the sūtra up to the point where the mantra occurs is intended for bodhisattvas of less acute intelligence, while the syllables of the mantra set forth the entire path for bodhisattvas who have the capacity to understand it.

[8] Unfortunately, the meaning of the story (apart from the fact that it suggests that the *Heart Sūtra* was recited at Vikramalaśīla and that Atiśa was kind) is unclear. Assuming that Nag tsho was reciting the sūtra in Sanskrit, Atiśa appears to be correcting his pronunciation from *ha rūpa ha vedanā* to *a rūpa a vedanā* to, finally, the more familiar *na rūpa na vedanā*, saying of this latter pronunciation that because it is the speech of Avalokita, there is nothing wrong with saying *na*.

The story appears in *Jo bo rje'i rnam thar lam yig chos kyi 'byung gnas zhes bya ba 'Brom ston pa rgyal ba'i 'byung gnas kyis mdzad pa*, published in Lokesh Chandra, ed., *Biography of Atisha and His Disciple HBrom-ston, Zhö edition*, 2 vols. (New Delhi: International Academy of Indian Culture, 1982), vol. 1, pp. 252–53. Thanks to Hubert Decleer for the reference. The story appears in an abbreviated version in Se ra rJe btsun pa's *Go lan*. See Se ra rJe btsun pa (rJe btsun chos kyi rgyal mtshan), *Zab mo stong pa nyid kyi lta ba la log rtog 'gog par byed pa'i bstan bcos lta ba ngan pa'i mun sel zhes bya ba bshes gnyen chen po go bo rab 'byams pa bsod nams seng ge ba la gdam pa bzhugs so*. The work has been published in India under the abbreviated title *lTa ngen mun sel*, vol. 2. (New Delhi: Champa Chogyal, 1969), pp. 26–27.

[9] See chap. 9 of Donald S. Lopez, Jr., *The Heart Sūtra Explained* (Ithaca, N.Y.: State University of New York Press, 1988) for a detailed discussion of the various ways in which the commentators divide the sūtra into the five paths.

Following the commentaries of Vimalamitra and Atiśa, there is a second essay, which serves as a prologemenon to a consideration of the question of whether the *Heart Sūtra* should be regarded as a sūtra or a tantra; it is classed as one, or the other, or both in the various Tibetan canons. In order to address this question, it is of course important to have a working definition of the term "tantra." Yet "tantra" seems to bear a certain resemblance to time, of which Augustine remarked in his *Confessions* (Book 11.14 [17]), "What then is time? Provided that no one asks me, I know. If I want to explain it to an inquirer, I do not know." Chapter 3 considers some of the vicissitudes encountered in delineating the term "tantra" by both traditional Indian and Tibetan exegetes and by modern scholars from India and the West. Can tantra be defined straightforwardly or should it instead be approached through polythetic classification? Is it a late development or does it form the substratum of Indian religion? Should tantra be understood to be subsequent or prior to sūtra? For whatever reason, tantra seems to suffer more than the usual arbitrariness of the sign.

This essay is followed in chapter 4 by another pair of commentaries. Unlike those of Vimalamitra and Atiśa, these two short commentaries were probably composed within a few decades of one another, but the second is not a subcommentary on the first. Indeed, among the eight commentaries there are no two more different than the commentaries of Kamalaśīla and Śrīsiṃha. Kamalaśīla (c. 740–795) was the famed disciple of Śāntarakṣita and commentator on his teacher's compendium of Buddhist and non-Buddhist doctrine, the *Tattvasaṃgraha* (Compendium of Principles). Kamalaśīla was also the author of the compendium of Mahāyāna philosophy and practice, the *Madhyamakāloka* (Illumination of the Middle Way). Śāntarakṣita had traveled to Tibet, where he joined Padmasambhava in founding the first Buddhist monastery at bSam yas (c. 779) shortly before his death. According to Tibetan histories, when the morality of Tibet was threatened by the teachings of the Chinese Chan master Mo-ho-yen, the king of Tibet (following instructions in Śāntarakṣita's will) invited Kamalaśīla to come to Tibet to counter the Chinese threat. The precise sequence and content of the resulting confrontation (known as the Council of Tibet, the Council of Lhasa, or the Council of bSam yas) are difficult to determine. According to most Tibetan histories, however, Kamalaśīla and his party were declared by the king to have prevailed and the teachings of the Chan master were proscribed.[10] Ka-

[10] The classic studies of the debate remain Paul Demiéville, *Le Concile de Lhasa,* Bibliothèque de l'Institut des Hautes Études Chinoises, no. 7 (Paris: Imprimerie Nationale de France, 1952) and Giuseppe Tucci, *Minor Buddhist Texts*, pt. 2, *First Bhāvanākrama of Kamalaśīla* (Rome: Istituto Italiano per il Medio ed Estremo Oriente, 1958). The most

malaśīla set forth the Mahāyāna path in three works, all entitled *Bhāvanākrama* (Stages of Meditation); the last of them may represent his argument against Mo-ho-yen. Kamalaśīla was apparently assassinated shortly thereafter.

Kamalaśīla's commentary on the *Heart Sūtra* is the shortest of the eight and is concerned exclusively with demonstrating how the myriad categories and subdivisions of the bodhisattva path can be derived from the words of the sūtra. For the Indian Mahāyāna scholastics, the most important śāstra for the exposition of the path was the *Abhisamayālaṃkāra* (Ornament of Realization) of Maitreyanātha. Traditionally considered as a commentary on the *Pañcaviṃśatisāhasrikāprajñāpāramitā-sūtra* (Perfection of Wisdom in 25,000 Stanzas), it is little more than a series of terms drawn from the sūtra, from which commentators sought to construct the components of the bodhisattva's path, the "hidden teaching" of the Perfection of Wisdom sūtras. Apart from emphasizing the necessity of an inferential understanding of emptiness before direct realization can be gained, Kamalaśīla's commentary is largely a matching of terms in the sūtra with categories from the *Abhisamayālaṃkāra*. Indeed, one might suggest that Kamalaśīla attempts to undo the sūtra by reinsinuating the kinds of categories that the sūtra, with its litany of negations, appears to overthrow.

The commentary that follows Kamalaśīla's is that of Śrīsiṃha, a tantric master about whom we know very little. According to Tibetan accounts, he was born in China and studied tantra on Mount Wutai before traveling to India. There he unearthed tantric texts that had been sealed inside the Buddha's seat in Bodhgāyā.[11] Śrīsiṃha is remembered in Tibet as the teacher of Vairocana, one of the most important figures in the earlier dissemination of Buddhism to Tibet. Vairocana was one of the first seven Tibetans ordained as Buddhist monks by Śāntarakṣita at the monastery of bSam yas and soon became an illustrious translator. He is said to have been a disciple of Padmasambhava and a participant on the Indian side in

useful study and analysis of the debate is Luis O. Gómez, "Purifying Gold: The Metaphor of Effort and Intuition in Buddhist Thought and Practice," in Peter Gregory, ed., *Sudden and Gradual: Approaches to Enlightenment in Chinese Thought* (Honolulu: University of Hawaii Press, 1987), pp. 67–165. Gómez's extensive notes contain references to his previous work as well as to the Japanese scholarship on the subject. See also Samten G. Karmay, *The Great Perfection: A Philosophical and Meditative Teaching of Tibetan Buddhism* (Leiden: E. J. Brill, 1988), pp. 86–106; David Snellgrove, *Indo-Tibetan Buddhism* (Boston: Shambala, 1987), pp. 430–436; and especially David Seyfort Ruegg, *Buddha-nature, Mind and the Problem of Gradualism in a Comparative Perspective: On the Transmission and Reception of Buddhism in India and Tibet* (London: School of Oriental and African Studies, 1989).

[11] See Dudjom Rinpoche, *Nyingma School*, vol. 1, pp. 497–501.

the dispute with Mo-ho-yen. After Padmasambhava's departure from Tibet, the king required a fuller exposition of tantra and sent Vairocana to India to obtain further tantric instructions. After many trials, he arrived in India, where he was instructed by Śrīsiṃha. Fearing that the Indian masters would object to his imparting the precious esoteric teachings to a foreigner, Śrīsiṃha insisted that he study sūtras and less esoteric tantric texts with other teachers during the day, receiving the most secret teachings from him under the cover of darkness. It is for the transmission of these secret teachings that Vairocana is best remembered; he is credited with bringing the Great Completeness (*rdzogs chen*) teachings from India to Tibet. When he returned to Tibet, Vairocana is said to have instructed King Khri srong lde btsan. Following the example of his teacher, he taught the king ordinary doctrines, such as the law of karma, during the day and the secret teachings of the Great Completeness at night.[12]

Among the esoteric teachings given by Śrīsiṃha to Vairocana, which he in turn gave to the king (the colophon may suggest that it was during the night), is Śrīsiṃha's tantric commentary on the *Heart Sūtra*, further testimony to its wide appeal in Pāla India, even among tantric yogins. The commentary moves methodically through the sūtra, employing the device of trilevel explication; it gives the outer, inner, and secret meanings of the words of the sūtra. The commentary, which says at the outset that it is not intended for logicians (*tārkika*, *rtog ge ba*), is filled with terms familiar from the Great Completeness, speaking of the great wisdom of self-awareness (*rang rig pa'i ye shes*), the state of nonexertion (*rtsol ba dang bral ba*), the self-arisen state (*rang chas su gnas pa*), and natural liberation (*rang bzhin gyis grol*).

The question of whether the *Heart Sūtra* should be considered a sūtra or a tantra, implicitly contested by Kamalaśīla and Vairocana, is further complicated by the presence in the Tibetan canon of two sādhanas ("means of achievement") based on the *Heart Sūtra*. In Indian Buddhist tantric literature, a sādhana is a ritual text that provides detailed instructions for putting into (usually daily) practice the often unsystematic or cryptic teachings of a specific tantra so as to acquire both mundane and supramundane powers (*siddhi*). Sādhanas generally prescribe a set sequence of procedures to be followed by the meditator, carried out via visualization, such as making offerings to buddhas, bodhisattvas, and various deities, and then inviting them to inhabit a visualized maṇḍala, wherein various identifications are established, often sanctified by the

[12] On Vairocana, see ibid., pp. 538–40 et passim (see index); and especially Karmay, *Great Perfection*, pp. 17–37 et passim. Karmay's work on Vairocana's biography supersedes that found in the doctoral dissertation of A. W. Hanson-Barber, *The Life and Teachings of Vairocana* (University of Wisconsin, 1984).

recitation of mantras. In some sādhanas, the meditator will imagine himself or herself as one of the deities inhabiting the maṇḍala (usually as the central figure); in other cases the meditator imagines himself or herself as a spectator.

As far as I have been able to determine, the *Heart Sūtra* may be the only sūtra (if it be a sūtra) to have a sādhana associated with it. The longer of those two sādhanas is translated in full in chapter 5, with many of the allusions generated by the text noted. Next, there is a general discussion of the various uses to which visualization has been put in Buddhist meditation. I then return to the sādhana, the centerpiece of which is a maṇḍala inhabited by the principal figures of the sūtra. In the center is the embodiment of the perfection of wisdom, the goddess Prajñāpāramitā. She is surrounded by the four speakers of the sūtra: Śākyamuni Buddha, Avalokiteśvara, Śāriputra, and Ānanda (the narrator of the sūtra who says, "Thus did I hear"). Once the maṇḍala has been set in visualization, a series of displacements occurs, which I read from a variety of perspectives.

The next two commentaries, forming chapter 6, are those of Jñānamitra and Praśāstrasena. The colophon of Jñānamitra's commentary reveals nothing about the circumstances of its authorship. He is listed in the catalogues of the Peking and Derge editions of the Tibetan canon as the author of only one other work (a commentary on the *Prajñāpāramitānayaśatapañcāśatikā*). Jñānamitra's is the most straightforward and prosaic of the commentaries. He remains dutifully close to the words of the sūtra, devoting one or two sentences to each word or phrase, explaining, for example, that the title of the sūtra is given at the beginning of the text so that one might know which sūtra it is. His interest in the sūtra does not seem merely scholastic, however. In glossing the epithet of the mantra, "the mantra that thoroughly pacifies all suffering," he writes, "It should be known as the *mantra that completely pacifies all suffering*: upholding the perfection of wisdom, reading about it, reciting it, keeping it properly in mind, and explaining it to others destroys all diseases, such as diseases of the eye, and brings protection because one is protected by the buddhas of the ten directions, by gods, nāgas, and so forth." This would suggest that the "cult of the book" that appears to have been so important in the early stages of what is called the Mahāyāna remained strong in the Pāla Dynasty.

Praśāstrasena's commentary is also quite straightforward and a good deal more expansive. We have no other works by him and know nothing about his life. The commentary is the work of an erudite scholar, fully conversant with the philosophical categories of the late Indian Yogācāra-Mādhyamika synthesis, and with a certain penchant for tripartite categorizations: the author sets forth the three types of wisdom, the three types of perfection, the three types of views. He moves through the sūtra in a systematic but not mechanical fashion, pausing at length over a number of statements, notably the "form is empty, emptiness is form" line, where he is able to provide a soteriological reading. He argues that were the sūtra to say simply "form is empty" it would succeed in dissuading sentient beings from being attached to form. However, they might conclude that form is utterly negated by emptiness, that only emptiness is in any way real, disposing them to the quietism of the Hīnayāna. It would be like telling a blind person walking down a road with thorns on one side and a ravine on the other only that there are thorns on the right but not revealing the presence of the ravine on the left. To counter this danger, the sūtra says that "emptiness is form," indicating that emptiness is not to be found apart from form, thereby moving the blind person to the middle way.

The most famous and most widely recited Buddhist mantra is the mantra that occurs at the end of the *Heart Sūtra*, *gate gate pāragate pārasaṃgate bodhi svāhā*. Both Jñānamitra and Praśāstrasena gloss the epithets of the mantra but neither explains the mantra itself; Praśāstrasena provides it without commentary, Jñānamitra does not even reproduce it. Their treatment of the mantra suggests a certain dis-ease among the commentators as to how precisely to deal with the mantra. The problematics of the mantra are considered at length in chapter 7. The mantra seems to mean "Gone, gone, gone beyond, gone completely beyond, enlightenment, *svāhā*." But mantras are very rarely translated. On the most practical level, a mantra is often untranslated simply because, measured against the model of classical Sanskrit as the perfected language, the mantra has suffered sufficient deformation as to render it grammatically illegible. Further, as an element of ritual discourse, a mantra is as much an event as a denotative statement and as such resists translation or transference from its structural moment. And from the Indian perspective, a mantra can only be in Sanskrit and must remain so in order to retain its potency as speech (*vac*), with its traditional originary primacy over the derivations of script. Indeed, not only should a mantra not be translated from Sanskrit into another language; it should also not be transferred from its natural medium to some other, from sound to writing.

Yet the mantra of the *Heart Sūtra* seems to confound these issues of writing and translation in that it is a mantra that *is* written, but written as the representation of sound. Buddhism, which spread far beyond the confines of the Indian subcontinent, was faced with the task of translating its scriptures. Yet the Tibetan, Chinese, and Japanese translators of the *Heart Sūtra*, did not translate the mantra but transliterated it, in an effort to duplicate and thereby preserve the sound of the speaker's (in this case not the Buddha's, but Avalokiteśvara's) voice. They translated the rest of the sūtra but left the mantra, in sound if not form, in Sanskrit. We must recognize, then, that the experience of reciting the *Heart Sūtra* would be very different for a Tibetan monk than it would be for an Indian monk. The Indian monk, reciting the sūtra in Sanskrit, would intone a Sanskrit mantra. The Tibetan monk, reciting along in Tibetan, would come to a phrase marked by its incomprehensibility, reading a transliteration to produce sounds that were clearly not Tibetan. This, apparently, was the intention of the Indian *paṇḍita*s who collaborated in the translation of the *Heart Sūtra* and its commentaries into Tibetan, all of whom render the mantra in transliteration.

The mantra is not translated but rather transferred, representing neither the meaning of the words (the semantic content) nor their Sanskrit orthography, but their sound. The transliteration of the mantra marks the transportation of the original to another time and another place, offering an image of the timeless, bringing the past into the present, valuing that presence for its form rather than its content, allowing the original to persist through repetition. The translators of the *Heart Sūtra* thus opt for transference rather than translation, leaving the mantra untouched by translation and the apparent limitation that that would entail, leaving the mantra unreconciled with the tongue of the reader but protected as event, an event that communicates nothing.

The final two Indian commentaries, found in chapter 8, are those of Mahājana (or Śrīmahājana) and Vajrapāṇi, whose approaches to the sūtra are as dissimilar to each other as those of Kamalaśīla and Śrīsiṃha. Mahājana's commentary is the only work ascribed to him in the Tibetan canons; he is listed as the translator of nine works, suggesting that he visited Tibet, probably in the late eleventh or early twelfth century.[13] His commentary reflects an author of a decidely Yogācāra persuasion, beginning from its paean to Asaṅga at the beginning to its reading of the "form is empty" line in terms of the doctrine of the three natures (*trisvabhāva*). Like Kamalaśīla, Mahājana takes great pains to extract the elaborate structure of the bodhisattva path (as derived from the *Abhisamayālaṃkāra* and its commentaries) from the taciturn sūtra, but unlike Kamalaśīla, he provides much greater detail. For example, he finds the sixteen moments of forbearance (*kṣānti*) and knowledge (*jñāna*) of the path of vision in the words of the sūtra ("empty, without characteristic, unproduced, unceased, stainless, not stainless, undiminished, unfilled") and he finds the progression through the five paths in the five words of the mantra (minus *svāhā*).

[13] The colophon of his commentary states that he collaborated in its translation with Seng ge rgyal mtshan, who was a student of Ngog bLo ldan shes rab (1059–1109).

In sharp contrast to what some might consider the obsessive scholasticism of Mahājana is the commentary of Vajrapāṇi (born 1019), a tantric master of *mahāmudrā* and disciple of Maitrīpa who was instrumental in the transmission of the lineage of tantric songs (*dohā*) of Saraha to Tibet.[14] The *Blue Annals* reports in some detail seven of his miracles, such as producing fruit from the dung of a red cow.[15] Among the seven works ascribed to his authorship in the Tibetan canons (he was involved in the translation of some twenty-nine works), only his commentary on the *Heart Sūtra* is devoted to a text that is not explicitly "tantric," perhaps suggesting that for Vajrapāṇi the *Heart Sūtra* was also a tantric text. The commentary seems to have been delivered orally and extemporaneously under circumstances that might be described as serendipitous. According to the colophon:

> In the past, some Tibetan virtuous friends asked for teachings from the excellent venerable guru Vajrapāṇi at Lalitapattana in Nepal. One day before the time for the excellent guru to teach the doctrine had arrived, the Tibetan virtuous friends recited a sūtra. The excellent guru asked the translator, "What was that they recited?" The translator said, "The *Heart of the Perfection of Wisdom.*" [Vajrapāṇi said], "Oh, if the *Heart of the Perfection of Wisdom* has spread to Tibet, the Buddha's prophecy is true." He asked whether they knew the instructions on meaning of the *Heart Sūtra.* The translator answered that they had not sought them. "Well then," he said, "I will give you the instructions."

And indeed, there is a certain spontaneity about Vajrapāṇi's commentary, the most free and least methodical of the eight. He passes over ostensibly key passages in the sūtra (including the "form is empty" line) with almost no comment but expands at length on others. His commentary is filled with the tropes and phrasing familiar from Saraha and the *mahāmudrā* cycles; he focuses particularly on the state of "nonmindfulness" or "nonmemory" (*asmṛti, dran pa med pa*).[16]

[14] See Herbert V. Guenther, *Ecstatic Spontaneity* (Berkeley, Calif.: Asian Humanities Press, 1993), pp. 12–13.

[15] See George N. Roerich, trans., *The Blue Annals* (Delhi: Motilal Banarsidass, 1979), pp. 855–60.

[16] For a discussion of this key term in the *mahāmudrā* tradition, see Guenther, *Ecstatic Spontaneity*, pp. 32–40. A survey of occurrences of the term in Indian sūtras and śāstras is provided by Dwag po bKra shis rnam rgyal (1513–87) in his *Nges don phyag rgya chen po'i sgom rim shes bya pa'i legs bshad zla pa'i 'od zer* (Shamar ed.), 246a1–268a5. For an unfortunately unreliable translation of this important work, see Takpa Tashi Namgyal, *Mahāmudrā: The Quintessence of Mind and Meditation*, trans. Lobsang P. Lhalungpa (Boston: Shambala, 1986). For a discussion of the term *dran pa med pa* in the rDzogs chen tradition of the rNying ma pa, see Matthew Kapstein, "The Amnesic Monarch and the Five Mnemic Men: 'Memory' in Great Perfection (Rdzogs-chen) Thought," in Janet Gyatso, ed.,

The protean uses to which the *Heart Sūtra* has been put, however, extend beyond the scholastic categories of Mahājana and the sublime mindfulnessless states of Vajrapāṇi. Chapter 9 is devoted to a description of the most common application of the *Heart Sūtra* in Tibet, as an exorcism text. There are many versions of a ritual manual called the *Sher snying bdud zlog* ("Repelling Demons [with] the *Heart Sūtra*") and it is employed by all four major sects of Tibetan Buddhism. The ritual involves inviting demons called the four *māra*s from their invisible states and causing them to enter dough images. They are then offered various foods and gifts, the most important of which is an effigy of the person who is suffering under their affliction. Throughout the ritual, the *Heart Sūtra* is repeated scores of times, functioning as a long mantra whose power turns the demons away, taking the gift of the effigy in exchange for releasing the afflicted person from their power. After a detailed description of the ritual, the chapter goes on to consider a range of more general problems raised by the text, problems that continue to haunt Ritual Studies and Buddhist Studies, problems that take the form of oppositions —between gift and sacrifice, ostracism and scapegoat, magic and religion, Lamaism and Buddhism, Buddhism and Bön.

To study a text is to study the effects of the text in different periods. This history is to be found, among other places, in commentaries—the texts that the text produced. The volume concludes with a chapter on the function of commentary, first among the traditional commentators on the *Heart Sūtra*, then proceeding to consider modern exegetes who bring this and other Buddhist texts into the fray of what is sometimes termed "comparative philosophy," and moving finally to consider the problems and possibilities of commentary on ancient texts in the current age. The links among these three commentators (the ancient, the modern, and, for want of a better term, the postmodern) lie in an articulation of the notion of association, the way in which one thing, whether aurally or metaphorically, "sounds like" another, whether they be two Sanskrit words or two texts separated by time and topography. It is through exploring these various forms of association that the location of the commentator, who often seeks the transparency of Hōichi's inscribed body, can be brought into relief.

In the Mirror of Memory: Reflections on Mindfulness and Remembrance in Indian and Tibetan Buddhism (Albany: State University of New York Press, 1992), pp. 239–68.

One

Who Heard the *Heart Sūtra*?

> By being transmitted via so many spokesmen, the Saddharma ran the greatest of dangers. From the beginning, it should have been enclosed in a code of authentic writings, recognised by all the members of the Community unanimously; however, the Buddhists only belatedly perceived the necessity of a codification of the Dharma; moreover, the oral transmission of the Doctrine rendered such a task, if not impossible, at least very difficult.
> —*Étienne Lamotte*

IT MAY SEEM SURPRISING that as late as the eleventh century Indian commentators still felt compelled to discuss the referent of the "I" of "Thus did I hear" (*evaṃ mayā śrutam*) at the beginning of Mahāyāna sūtras. Perhaps they were simply performing their roles as commentators in explaining the meaning of every word. Still, one might expect that by that date there would at least have been some agreement among them. But a survey of the Pāla Dynasty commentaries on the *Heart Sūtra* displays a wide range of opinion on the issue. Some of the commentators make a remark only in passing as they gloss the terms of the sūtra, but others, notably Vimalamitra and Atiśa, dwell on the question of the qualifications of the *saṃgītikartṛ* and on what it means to have heard (*śruta*). The term *saṃgītikartṛ* is perhaps best rendered as rapporteur. *Saṃgīti* most often means "song" or anything that is sung or chanted in chorus. In Buddhist texts, it can be a pronouncement of the Buddha or the rehearsal by others of such a pronouncement. But it can also mean a council of monks, gathered to settle questions of doctrine and establish the text of a sūtra. The *kartṛ* is the "maker" or agent of any of these activities. Hence, *saṃgītikartṛ* carries a range of connotations, from the maker of the Buddha's word, to the leader of its public recitation, to the convener of a

A shorter version of this essay appeared as "Authority and Orality in the Mahāyāna," *Numen* 42, no. 1 (January 1995).

council to determine its content, that is, from speaker, to reciter, to redactor. It was rendered in Tibetan as *bka' sdud pa po*, the gatherer of the Buddha's word.

Only the author of the single tantric commentary on the sūtra, the *mahāmudrā* master Vajrapāṇi, remains above the fray, transliterating rather than translating *evaṃ mayā*, calling those four letters (apparently drawing on the *Guhyasamājatantra*) "the source of the 84,000 collections of doctrine and the foundation of all success." The Mādhyamika commentator Jñānamitra states unequivocally that all of the Mahāyāna sūtras were heard and compiled by Mañjuśrī, the bodhisattva of wisdom. The latest of the commentators, Śrīmahājana, reports that according to Dignāga, the *saṃgītikartṛ* was Vajrapāṇi, the bodhisattva of power, but Vimuktasena opts for Ānanda, based on the closing passages of the *Aṣṭasāhasrikāprajñāpāramitā* (Perfection of Wisdom in 8,000 Stanzas) in which the Buddha entrusts the sūtra to Ānanda's care. He also mentions that in the opinion of Ratnākaraśānti, the *saṃgītikartṛ* was Ānanda "empowered by the Buddha."[1] It is significant that Śrīmahājana implies a distinction between Ānanda as rapporteur and Ānanda empowered by the Buddha as rapporteur. This distinction seems also to be at play in the judgments of the final two commentators, Praśāstrasena and Kama laśīla, neither of whom names the *saṃgītikartṛ*; but they do provide a hint in their gloss of *śrutam*. Praśāstrasena states that the term "heard" means that the dharma was apprehended by the consciousness of an ear sense organ, noting that it only means that the dharma was heard; it does not imply that the meaning was understood. Kamalaśīla says nothing on the issue in his *Heart Sūtra* commentary, but in both his commentary on the *Vajracchedikā* (Diamond Cutter) and that on the *Saptaśatikā* (Perfection of Wisdom in 700 Stanzas), he makes the same point: "'Heard' [means] experienced by the ear consciousness; it does not mean understood because no one other than the Tathāgata has the power to comprehend such a doctrine."[2] For Praśāstrasena to say and for Kamalaśīla to imply that the sūtra was heard without being understood (a point to which I will return later) may imply that the *saṃgītikartṛ* was Ānanda, the traditional rapporteur of the Buddha's words, but who, as a śrāvaka, was unable to understand them. This is the position of Haribhadra in his *Abhisamayālaṃkārālokā*, where he reminds his readers how Ānanda, through the practice of *buddhānusmṛti*, was able to overcome his ab-

[1] At least in one work, however, Ratnākaraśānti casts his vote for Vajrapāṇi as the *saṃgītikartṛ* of the Mahāyāna sūtras. See his *Āryāṣṭasāhasrikāprajñāpāramitāpañjikāsārottamā,* P 5200, vol. 92 3.5.6–4.1.2.

[2] Kamalaśīla, Toh. 3815, Derge, Shes phyin ma, 89b3–4.

sence of introspection and say with eloquence, "Thus did I hear."[3] In fact, Vimalamitra claims in his commentary that the grammar of the statement confirms that the words were only heard and not understood: "It says, 'I' [literally 'by me']. Therefore, the third [case ending, the instrumental,] indicates only the hearing of the sounds of the letters just as they are; because it is a consciousness arisen from hearing, it completely eliminates the possibility of it being [the rapporteur's] own realization [of the profound meaning of the sūtra: it is rather just an understanding of the words]. Otherwise, 'heard by me' would be in the sixth [case, the genitive] because of meaning ['my] understanding.' . . . In order to establish his own validity, when the [rapporteur] bears witness to the place, the time, and the audience, and to having witnesses, he is saying, 'I understand that I am a valid speaker; I do not understand the great things of which I speak.'"

It is only in the commentaries of Vimalamitra and Atiśa that the topic of the *saṃgītikartṛ* is actually engaged; the comments of the other exegetes are made more or less in passing. I will focus here on Atiśa because he includes Vimalamitra's position in the course of his discussion. Atiśa notes that the *saṃgītikartṛ* does not simply begin his recitation of a sūtra after declaring "*evaṃ mayā śrutam*" but also provides a setting (*nidāna*, *gleng gzhi*) describing where the sūtra was delivered and who was present. The purpose of such description, he says, is to establish the *saṃgītikartṛ* as reliable (*prāmāṇya*). This, he says, is the position of Dignāga (c. C.E. 480–540), and he cites a passage from the *Prajñāpāramitāpiṇḍārtha* (Condensed Meaning of the Perfection of Wisdom, also known as the *Prajñāpāramitāsaṃgraha*) (3–4) in which the qualifications of the *saṃgītikartṛ* are directly addressed: "In order to establish his validity, the *saṃgītikartṛ* indicates the teacher, the audience, the witness, the time, and the place as factors [causing] the faithful to enter [the teaching], just as in the world, if someone has a witness indicating the place and the time, he is authoritative."[4] Unfortunately, neither Dignāga nor his commentator, Triratnadāsa, makes any mention of what might distinguish the witness (*sākṣin*) from the audience (*parṣad*), with Triratnadāsa merely equating the two: "Because the audience is the bodhisattvas, etc., they should be understood as the witnesses."[5]

[3] For the Sanskrit, see U. Wogihara, ed., *Abhisamayālaṃkār'āloka Prajñāpāramitāvyākhyā: The Work of Haribhadra* (Tokyo: The Toyo Bunko, 1932, 1973), p. 6.

[4] For Sanskrit and Tibetan editions of the passage, see Giuseppe Tucci, "Minor Buddhist Texts on the Prajñāpāramitā: Diṅnāga's Prajñā-pāramitā-Piṇḍārtha," *Journal of the Royal Asiatic Society* (1947): 56, 68.

[5] P 5208, vol. 94, 3.1.5.

Atiśa then notes that Dignāga's assertion that the *saṃgītikartṛ* must have a witness to establish his validity is rejected by Vimalamitra, whose refutation of Dignāga he goes on to explain. He does not alert us to the fact that Vimalamitra does not offer his objections in his commentary to the *Heart Sūtra*, which Atiśa cites liberally on other points, but is to be found instead in Vimalamitra's commentary to the *Saptaśatikā*. In fact, Vimalamitra does not mention Dignāga by name. Instead he says: "It is said that in order for someone to prove himself to be valid, [his identification of] the place and the time are the proof [of his presence] and the audience is the witness, as in the case of a disputed contract. That is not my understanding; [the faithful] go everywhere [to hear sūtras] and if [it were necessary] to ask a witness, it would be a long [time] before those incapable of going there could determine the meaning of the sūtra. [And in the case of sūtras] in which the name of the audience is not indicated, whom should one ask?"[6]

Atiśa discerns two objections here. The first has to do with the function of the witness. According to Atiśa's reading of Dignāga, the purpose of the *saṃgītikartṛ*'s statement of pedigree is to inspire his audience to enter into the dharma. A witness is rarely called upon at the moment of testimony, but rather at some later date, when doubts begin to arise. Dignāga's insistence on the witness therefore is problematic because by the time the doubts arise, the witnesses may have died or gone elsewhere. To prove the peripatetic nature of those who seek the dharma, he cites an unidentified sūtra, "Those who desire to hear the jewel of the profound and limitless sūtras go everywhere for the welfare of all the worldly realms." And in some cases, like that of Mahākāśyapa, who is said to reside inside a mountain, the witnesses may still be alive, but it is our ill fortune that they remain inaccessible to us.

Atiśa's more intriguing gloss of Vimalamitra is what he has to say about Vimalamitra's statement above, that, if having a witness is a requirement, then those who were unable to go to the place where the sūtra is delivered could not determine the meaning of the sūtra. In Atiśa's reading, these people are not ordinary persons prevented by circumstance from traveling to distant lands, but instead those who have attained the powers of clairaudience that are achieved with *ṛddhi* (magical power) and *abhijñā* (superknowledge), which allow them to hear the words of the buddhas from extraordinary distances. What Atiśa seems to take Vimalamitra to be saying is that physical presence in an audience is not required for one to qualify as a *saṃgītikartṛ*; there are other means available for hearing the *buddhavacana*.

[6] Vimalamitra, *Āryasaptaśatikāprajñāpāramitāṭīkā*, Toh. 3814, Derge, Shes phyin ma, 10b1–3.

The second objection to Dignāga discerned by Atiśa is that if one insists on the presence of witnesses in order to prove that what is reported is the word of the Buddha, then sūtras in which there is no mention of the names of the members of the audience, sūtras such as the *Heart Sūtra* in fact, could not be considered *buddhavacana*. The *Heart Sūtra*, of course, mentions Avalokiteśvara and Śāriputra, but they, as interlocutors, seem not to count as witnesses, and none of the others in attendance are mentioned by name. Atiśa seems, then, to reject Dignāga's understanding of the *saṃgītikartṛ* and accepts that of Vimalamitra. And in his own commentary to the *Heart Sūtra*, Vimalamitra makes it clear that being a *saṃgītikartṛ* has little to do with having witnesses, but is much more the result of proper practice:

> The three words [*evaṃ mayā śrutam*], "Thus . . ." form the opening. What "I heard" was "thus"; not something else. Because this removes [the possibility of anything] being left out or added, it is a promise as to the accuracy of what was heard. It expresses the fact that having been heard once, what was taken in and retained is correctly and fully set forth. The correct compilation [comes about through] the ripening of roots of virtue created in relation to the Buddha by one who has the protection of a virtuous friend. These should be known to be practices such as revering the Buddha, asking properly, giving, and ethics. Otherwise, hearing the primary [expression] of the meaning of the perfection of wisdom in this way does not take place.

Thus, that Vimalamitra leaves the *saṃgītikartṛ* unnamed seems to imply more than a nod to Ānanda. His discussion of the topic (with Atiśa's gloss) suggests that anyone who has engaged in the proper practices may develop the capacity to hear a sūtra, perhaps even by magical means. But he also makes it clear that such revelation is of the words alone, to be duly recited; that the event of revelation implies no realization of the profound meaning of the words revealed, such realization remaining the exclusive possession of the absent Buddha.

What, then, is at stake in the identification of the *saṃgītikartṛ*? To claim that the *saṃgītikartṛ* is Vajrapāṇi or Mañjuśrī or Samantabhadra, or to say it is Ānanda, or to leave the *saṃgītikartṛ* unnamed is to add one's voice to one of the most persistent choruses in Indian Mahāyāna literature, the defense of the Mahāyāna sūtras as the word of the Buddha. We find "proofs" of the authenticity of the Mahāyāna in the works of major and minor śāstra authors, as early as Nāgārjuna in the second century[7] in his *Ratnāvalī* (Jeweled Garland) and as late as Abhayākara-

[7] For a discussion of Nāgārjuna's dates, see David Seyfort Ruegg, "Towards a Chronology of the Madhyamaka School," in L. A. Hercus et al., eds., *Indological and Buddhist Studies* (Canberra: Faculty of Asian Studies, 1982), pp. 505–30.

gupta in the twelfth century in probably the last major Buddhist śāstra composed in India, the *Munimatālaṃkāra* (Ornament of the Sage's Mind). In the intervening millennium, Asaṅga in the *Bodhisattvabhūmi* (The Bodhisattva Stage) lists the repudiation of the *bodhisattvapiṭaka* (the Mahāyāna sūtras) as one of four transgressions (*pārājayīka*) of the bodhisattva vow;[8] much of the first chapter the *Mahāyānasūtrālaṃkāra* (Ornament of the Mahāyāna Sūtras) is concerned with proving that the Mahāyāna is the word of the Buddha;[9] and in the *Tarkajvāla*, Bhāvaviveka devotes a large portion of the fourth chapter to a defense of the Mahāyāna, but only after listing the charges brought against it by the śrāvakas: the Mahāyāna sūtras were not included in either the original or subsequent compilations of the *tripiṭaka*; by teaching that the Tathāgata is permanent, the Mahāyāna contradicts the dictum that all conditioned phenomena are impermanent; because the Mahāyāna teaches that the tathāgatagarbha (buddha-nature) is all-pervasive, it does not relinquish the belief in self; because the Mahāyāna teaches that the Buddha did not pass into nirvāṇa, it suggests that nirvāṇa is not the final state of peace; the Mahāyāna contains prophecies that the great śrāvakas will become buddhas; the Mahāyāna belittles the arhats; the Mahāyāna praises bodhisattvas above the Buddha; the Mahāyāna perverts the entire teaching by claiming that Śākyamuni was an emanation; the statement in the Mahāyāna sūtras that the Buddha was constantly in meditative absorption (*samāhita*) is infeasible; by teaching that great sins can be completely absolved, the Mahāyāna teaches that actions have no effects, contradicting the law of karma. "Therefore, the Buddha did not set forth the Mahāyāna; it was created by beings who were certainly demonic in order to deceive the obtuse and mislead those with evil minds."[10]

Thus, to address the question of who heard the *Heart Sūtra* is to seek to rebut these charges, and each answer implies a different point. To say that the *saṃgītikartṛ* is Mañjuśrī or Vajrapāṇi is to imply that the Mahāyāna sūtras are secret teachings not intended for śrāvakas and thus purposefully delivered in their absence; Ānanda is not the *saṃgītikartṛ* because he was not there to hear the sūtras. To say that the *saṃgītikartṛ* was

[8] The *śīla* chapter of Asaṅga's *Bodhisattvabhūmi* has been translated by Mark Tatz in a volume entitled *Asaṅga's Chapter on Ethics with the Commentary of Tsong-kha-pa* (Lewiston, N.Y.: Edwin Mellen, 1986). The relevant passage occurs on p. 64. For the Sanskrit, see Nalinaksha Dutt, *Bodhisattvabhūmi* (Patna: Jayaswal, 1966), p. 112. On the *bodhisattvapiṭaka*, see Ulrich Pagel, *The Bodhisattvapiṭaka*, Buddhica Britannica, no. 5 (Tring, United Kingdom: Institute of Buddhist Studies, 1995).

[9] For the Sanskrit, see Swami Dwarika Das Shastri, ed., *Mahāyānasūtrālaṃkāra by Ārya Asanga* (Vārānasī: Bauddha Bhāratī, 1985).

[10] Translated from the Tibetan; Derge edition of the bsTan 'gyur, Toh. 3856, dBu ma, vol. dza, 155b6–156a7.

Ānanda is to attempt incorporation, that just as the Nikāyas were heard and reported by Śākyamuni's attendant, so also were the Mahāyāna sūtras. And to say that the *saṃgītikartṛ* was Ānanda, but that he was empowered by the Buddha to perform the task and that, even then, he merely heard but did not understand what he would later report, is to attempt to have it both ways, preserving the Mahāyāna as the most profound of teachings, beyond the ken of śrāvakas, but still to be counted among the discourses heard in the physical presence of Śākyamuni. Finally, to leave the *saṃgītikartṛ* unnamed is to allow sūtras to be heard by anyone with the qualifications of faith, for as the *Samādhirāja* says, "When the Buddha, the *dharmarāja*, the proclaimer of all doctrines, the *muni* appears, the refrain that phenomena do not exist arises from the grass, bushes, trees, plants, stones, and mountains."[11]

In pursuing the question of the authenticity of the Mahāyāna further, we may move away from the texts for the moment, to consider recent theories of the origins of the Mahāyāna, by positing two admittedly rather amorphous periods of Indian Mahāyāna, the period of the sūtras and the period of the śāstras. The first, following the work of Gregory Schopen[12] and Andrew Rawlinson,[13] would be placed around the beginning of the Common Era, with the rise of a disparate collection of cults centered around newly composed texts and their charismatic expositors, the *dharmabhāṇaka*. Some of these texts, like the *Lotus*, in addition to proclaiming their own unique potency as the means to salvation, would also praise the veneration of stūpas. Others, like much of the early *prajñāpāramitā* corpus, would proclaim their superiority to stūpas, declaring themselves to be substitutes for the body and speech of the Buddha, equally worthy of veneration and equally efficacious in result. These early sūtras seem to have functioned in mutual independence, with each sūtra deemed complete unto itself, representing its own world.

The commentaries on the *Heart Sūtra* fall into the second phase of Indian Mahāyāna. The period of the śāstras seems to have been a self-conscious scholastic entity that thought of itself as the Mahāyāna and devoted a good deal of energy to surveying what was by then a rather large corpus of sūtras and then attempting, through a variety of her-

[11] Louis de la Vallée Poussin, ed., *Mūlamadhyamakakārikas de Nāgārjuna avec la Prasannapadā Commentaire de Candrakīrti* (Osnabrück: Biblio Verlag, 1970), p. 367.

[12] See, for example, Gregory Schopen, "The Phrase 'sa pṛthivīpradeśaś caityabhūto bhavet' in the Vajracchedikā: Notes on the Cult of the Book in the Mahāyāna," *Indo-Iranian Journal* 17 (1975: 147–181).

[13] See, for example, Andrew Rawlinson, "The Problem of the Origin of the Mahāyāna," in Peter Slater and Donald Wiebe, eds., *Traditions in Contact and Change: Selected Proceedings of the XIVth Congress of the International Association for the History of Religions* (Waterloo, Canada: Wilfred Laurier, 1983), pp. 163–70.

meneutical machinations, to craft the myriad doctrines contained there into a system. The worlds of the individual sūtras were fragmented into repositories from which commentators could extract citations in support of their systems. In short, it is in this latter period that the sūtras, which seem at first to have been recited and worshiped, became the object also of scholastic reflection.

There are obvious problems with such a typology. For example, we have one of the key scholastic defenders of the Mahāyāna, Nāgārjuna, writing in its defense during the period of the composition of the sūtras. Indeed, he sought to provide a schematic overview of Mahāyāna practice by compiling a compendium of quotations from sixty-eight Mahāyāna sūtras, the *Sūtrasamuccaya* (Compendium of Sūtras). That a single author had that many works available to him in the second century indicates the literary energies of their anonymous authors. And the period of the śāstras is no less ambiguous; some sūtras composed in this period attempt to deal with apparent contradictions among the Mahāyāna sūtras, the most famous case being the *Saṃdhinirmocana* (Explanation of the Intention). Indeed, one of the sūtras that Nāgārjuna cites in his *Sūtrasamuccaya*, the *Laṅkāvatāra* (Journey to Sri Lanka) in an apparently interpolated passage, contains a retrospective prophecy of Nāgārjuna's birth, having the Buddha say: "Mahāmati, you should know that after the Sugata has passed away there will appear after some time one who will uphold the ways. In the south, in the land of Veda, a monk renowned as Śrīman, called by the name of Nāga, will destroy the positions of existence and nonexistence. He will fully explain to the world, my vehicle, the unsurpassed Mahāyāna. He will then achieve the Joyful Stage (*pramuditābhūmi*) and go to Sukhāvatī."[14] Thus it would be a mistake to suppose that the apparent unsystematic milieu of the period of the sūtras implies that the authors of those sūtras were unaware or unconcerned with the question of the legitimation of their compositions. In the *Aṣṭasāhasrikāprajñāpāramitā*, for example, there are repeated warnings to regard as demonic those who would dispute that the perfection of wisdom is the word of the Buddha. The *Lotus* takes up the more difficult question of why, if the bodhisattva vehicle is indeed the most sublime path and buddhahood the highest goal, the Buddha taught the śrāvaka vehicle leading to the nirvāṇa of the arhat. The claim to primacy of the earlier tradition is usurped by the Mahāyāna by explaining that what the Buddha had taught before was in fact a lie, that there is no such thing as the path of the arhat, no such thing as nirvāṇa. There is only the Ma-

[14] On the possible identity of this Nāgāhvaya, see David Seyfort Ruegg, *The Literature of the Madhyamaka School of Philosophy in India* (Wiesbaden: Otto Harrassowitz, 1981), pp. 56–57.

hāyāna, which the Buddha intentionally misrepresents out of his compassionate understanding that there are many among his disciples who are incapable of assimilating so far-reaching a vision.

It remained, however, for the *Lotus* to account for those disciples of the Buddha who are reported in the Nikāyas to have become arhats, to have passed into nirvāṇa. What of their attainment? In an ingenious device found also in other Mahāyāna sūtras, the great heroes of the Hīnayāna are drafted into the Mahāyāna by the Buddha's prophecies that even they will surpass the trifling goal of nirvāṇa and go on to follow the Mahāyāna path to eventual buddhahood. The first such prophecy is for the wisest of the early disciples, Śāriputra: "Śāripūtra, in a time to come, having upheld the excellent dharma of several thousands of myriads of millions of buddhas, having made various types of offerings, and having completed these deeds of bodhisattvas during incalculable, limitless inconceivable aeons, you shall arise in the world as a *bhagavan* buddha named Padmaprabha, a tathāgata, an arhat, a complete and perfect buddha, accomplished in knowledge and deed, a *sugata*, understanding the world, a peerless guide taming beings, teacher of gods and humans."[15] Afterwards, hundreds of arhats tacitly denounce their own path by rather indecorously clamoring for prophecies that they also will become buddhas someday, requests that the Buddha happily obliges. The Mahāyāna sūtras thus respond to challenges to their own authenticity by appropriation. Śāriputra, the monk renowned in the Hīnayāna as the wisest of the Buddha's disciples, is transformed into a stock character in the Mahāyāna sūtras, one who is oblivious to the higher teaching. When his ignorance is revealed to him, he desires to learn more, coming to denounce as parochial the wisdom that he had once deemed supreme. Thus, the champion of the Hīnayāna is shown to reject it and embrace that which many adherents of the earlier tradition judged to be spurious.

The early history of the movement, already highly mythologized into a sacred history, was fictionalized further in the Mahāyāna sūtras, creating eventually another sacred history; to legitimate these newly appearing texts, their authors claimed the principal figures of the earlier collection, indeed its very codifiers (Śāriputra, Maudgalyāyana, Kāśyapa, Subhūti) as converts to the Buddha's true (but previously unrevealed) teaching and as central characters in its drama.[16] In doing so they added the theme of

[15] Translated from the Tibetan of the Derge edition of the bKa' 'gyur (Toh. 113), mDo sde, vol. ja, 26b6–27a1. For a translation from Kumārajīva's Chinese, see Leon Hurvitz, *Scripture of the Lotus Blossom of the Fine Dharma (The Lotus Sūtra)* (New York: Columbia University Press, 1976), p. 53.

[16] These elaborate strategies of legitimation that abound in the Mahāyāna sūtras suggest that the authors of these texts hoped to convey the impression that the events recounted in the sūtras were "historical" to the extent that historical personages known to have been

reconciliation, associated with comedy since Aristotle, to the standard romantic emplotment of the Buddhist path narrative. What we have, then, is a case of revisionist myth presented as revisionist history. The early story of Gautama Buddha and his disciples that we find preserved, for example, in the Pāli *suttas*, already accepted as a historical account by the "pre-Mahāyāna" traditions, is radically rewritten in the *Lotus* in such a way as to glorify the *Lotus* itself as the record of what really happened. Such rewriting recurs throughout the history of the Buddhist tradition in the perpetual attempt to recount "what the Buddha taught." At the same time, this rewriting in a certain sense displaces what was for the Mahāyāna a problematic question, the question of origins, by introducing a different frame of reference in which tales lead back not to events, but to other tales.[17]

It would be a mistake, however, to assume that the development of strategies of legitimation in Indian Buddhism coincided with the rise of the Mahāyāna. Criteria to be employed in determining what should be counted as *buddhavacana* seem to have been developed well before the appearance of the Mahāyāna sūtras. Even the earliest formulations do not suggest that the dharma is limited to what was spoken by the Buddha. The Mahāsaṃghikas and Mūlasarvāstivādins counted both what the Buddha himself said as well as discourses delivered by a disciple of the Buddha and certified by him as being true. In the Pāli *Vinaya*, the dharma is what is proclaimed by the Buddha, by śrāvakas, by sages (*ṛṣi*) such as Āraka, and by gods such as Indra. To this list of four, the Sarvāstivādin *Vinaya* adds the category of spontaneously born beings (*upapāduka*).[18] A second set of criteria considered not the speaker but what was said. These are the four *mahāpadeśa*, much discussed by

disciples of the Buddha are given central roles. This weighs against Graeme MacQueen's claim that "It takes little reflection to realize that when the early Mahāyānists defend their *sūtras* as *buddhavacana* they do not mean by this that these texts are speech of the 'historical Buddha.'" Indeed, sūtras like the *Lotus* as well as the *prajñāpāramitā* corpus attempt to legitimate their claim to being *buddhavacana* by adopting a wider historical perspective, toward both the past and the future, than was acknowledged by the earlier tradition. Such a perspective is not, therefore, "transhistorical," as MacQueen suggests but remains very much obsessed with history, as evidenced by the "historical" figures, such as Śāriputra and Subhūti, who populate the Mahāyāna sūtras. MacQueen's point appears in his article, "Inspired Speech in Early Mahāyāna Buddhism II," *Religion* 12 (1982): pp. 49–65.

[17] This point is drawn from Peter Brooks's discussion of Freud's Wolf Man case. See his *Reading for the Plot* (New York: Random House, 1984), p. 277.

[18] See Étienne Lamotte, "La Critique d'authenticitie dans le Bouddhisme," in *India Antiqua* (Leiden: E. J. Brill, 1947). Here and throughout, I cite Sara Boin Webb's translation, "The Assessment of Textual Authenticity in Buddhism," *Buddhist Studies Review* 1 (1984): p. 4–15. The relevant passage occurs on p. 6.

others,[19] which appear as early as the *Dīghanikāya* (2.123) and as late as Prajñākaramati's commentary on the *Bodhicaryāvatāra* (commenting on 9.42). Tests are provided for determining whether the words that a monk reports to have heard from one of four authorities are the teaching of the Buddha: the words (1) of the Buddha, (2) of a community (saṃgha) of elders, (3) of a smaller group of learned elders, and (4) of a single learned monk. When someone claims to have heard a teaching directly from one of these four sources, the saṃgha may determine whether it is the word of the Buddha by seeing whether it fits into the sūtras (*sutte oranti*) and is in agreement with the vinaya (*vinaye sandissanti*). If it does, it is to be accepted; if it does not, it is to be rejected. The Sanskrit versions, both Hīnayāna (in the *Abhidharmakośabhāṣya*[20]) and Mahāyāna, add a third criterion to conformity with the sūtras and with the vinaya: that the words not go against the way things are (*dharmatām na vilomayati*).[21] It is unclear precisely what is added by this third criterion, since it would appear inappropriate for a doctrine to be found to be in accordance with the sūtra and the vinaya, yet contradict the *dharmatā*. As a strategy for determining textual authority the *mahāpadeśa* is highly conservative, effectively sanctioning only those doctrines and practices that are already accepted. It appears to be the product of a community simultaneously lamenting the loss of teachings already forgotten and hence seeking to discover and preserve whatever still remained, while at the same time wary of the introduction of innovation. Thus, even a considerable laxity in the enforcement of these criteria would seem insufficient to account for whatever sparked the explosion of texts that would become the Mahāyāna sūtras.

Before considering that question, however, let us briefly survey the criteria for textual authenticity developed by the Mahāyāna. The long argument in the *Mahāyānasūtrālaṃkāra* has already been delineated in an

[19] See, for example, ibid., pp. 9–13; Ronald M. Davidson, "An Introduction to the Standards of Scriptural Authenticity in Indian Buddhism," in Robert Buswell, ed., *Chinese Buddhist Apocrypha* (Honolulu: University of Hawaii Press, 1990), pp. 300–303; Steven Collins, "On the Very Idea of the Pali Canon," *Journal of the Pali Text Society* 15 (1990): 109–10, n. 18; Lance Cousins, "Pali Oral Literature," in Philip Denwood and Alexander Piatigorsky, eds., *Buddhist Studies: Ancient and Modern* (London: Curzon, 1983), pp. 2–3; James P. McDermott, "Scripture as the Word of the Buddha," *Numen* 31 (1984): 22–39; and Paul J. Griffiths, *On Being Buddha: The Classical Doctrine of Buddhahood* (Albany: State University of New York Press, 1994), pp. 51–56.

[20] See P. Pradhan, ed., *Abhidharmakośabhāṣyam of Vasubandhu* (Patna: Jayaswal Research Institute, 1975), p. 466.

[21] See Lamotte, "La Critique," p. 11; and Walpola Rahula, "Wrong Notions of *Dhammatā* (*Dharmatā*)," in Lance Cousins et al., eds., *Buddhist Studies in Honour of I. B. Horner* (Dordrecht: D. Reidel, 1974), pp. 181–91.

article by Ronald Davidson.[22] Here, we will mention only what is sometimes read as a licentious Mahāyāna twist on the innocuous statement in Aśoka's rock edict at Bhairāt, "All that the *bhagavan* Buddha has spoken is well spoken."[23] The twist is the statement from the *Adhyāśayasañcodanasūtra* (Admonition to Adhyāśaya), "All which is well spoken, Maitreya, is spoken by the Buddha."[24] This chiasmatic reversal would seem to remove all restrictions from admission into *buddhavacana*; but the sūtra, not unexpectedly, qualifies the meaning of *subhāṣita*, of what it means to be well spoken. All inspired speech should be known to be the word of the Buddha if it is meaningful and not meaningless, if it is principled and not unprincipled, if it brings about the extinction and not the increase of the afflictions, and if it sets forth the qualities and benefits of nirvāṇa and not the qualities and benefits of saṃsāra.[25]

There is ostensibly nothing new or controversial here[26] when compared to the *mahāpadeśa*. There are, however, two significant shifts in emphasis. First, unlike the four *mahāpadeśa*, we find in the four criteria above no concern whatsoever with the source of the doctrine; it need not be heard directly from a saṃgha or a learned monk. Second, again unlike the four *mahāpadeśa*, the words are not judged to be the word of the Buddha based on their conformity with already accepted discourses but based instead on their function: to destroy the afflictions and lead to nirvāṇa. This is certainly the most traditional of Buddhist aims, but in the absence of an omniscient arbiter, the Buddha, it is impossible to judge. Mahāyāna exegetes are eager to point out that the mere fact that the Hīnayāna schools dispute the authenticity of the Mahāyāna sūtras signifies nothing since the eighteen śrāvaka schools cannot even agree among

[22] See Davidson, "Introduction," pp. 309–12.

[23] *E kechi bhaṇte bhagavatā budhena bhasite savve se subhāsite vā*. See Lamotte, "La Critique," p. 5.

[24] *Yat kiṃcinmaitreya subhāṣitam sarvaṃ tadbuddhabhāṣitam*. Cited in Prajñākaramati's commentary to the *Bodhicaryāvatāra*. See P. L. Vaidya, ed., *Bodhicaryāvatāra of Śāntideva with the Commentary Pañjikā of Prajñākaramati*, Buddhist Sanskrit Texts, no. 12 (Darbhanga, India: The Mithila Institute, 1960), p. 205, ll. 14–15. See also David Snellgrove, "Notes on the *Adhyāśayasaṃcodanasūtra*," *Bulletin of the School of Oriental and African Studies* 21 (1958): 620–23. It is important to note that the phrase "whatever is well spoken is spoken by the Buddha" also occurs in the Pāli canon at *Aṅguttara Nikāya* A IV, 162–166. See Collins, "On the Very Idea," pp. 94–95.

[25] See Vaidya, ed., *Bodhicaryāvatāra*, p. 205, ll. 10–12; and Davidson, "Introduction," p. 310. The term *subhāṣita* is glossed further by Vasubandhu in his *Vyākhyāyukti*. For a discussion of his ten criteria by Bu-ston, see E. Obermiller, trans., *History of Buddhism (Chos-ḥbyung) by Bu-ston*, pt. 1, *The Jewelry of Scripture* (Heidelberg: Institut für Buddhismus-Kunde, 1931), pp. 25–28.

[26] Davidson ("Introduction," p. 310) notes the presence of first two in the *Mahāvagga*. The last two are quite similar to what appears in the *Nettiprakaraṇa*; see Lamotte, "La Critique," p. 13.

themselves as to which discourses should be accepted as the word of the Buddha. They then shift to the question of the function of the sūtras, claiming that it is the Mahāyāna sūtras that more effectively set forth the path to buddhahood for all beings, a goal, of course, set forth only in the Mahāyāna sūtras.[27] But if there is no Buddha and everything is permitted, why do the commentators continue to cogitate over the identity of the *saṃgītikartṛ*? The attempt to address that question requires us first to return to the deferred question: what took place that sparked the explosion of texts that would become the Mahāyāna sūtras?

In a recent article,[28] Richard Gombrich has speculated that the rise of the Mahāyāna is due to the use of writing. The *Lotus Sūtra* recommends enshrining books in stūpas, as one would a relic, and Gregory Schopen has postulated the presence of a "cult of the book" in the early Mahāyāna, noting the common references in the *prajñāpāramitā* corpus to the merit to be accrued through copying, reciting, and venerating the book.[29] To claim that the rise of the Mahāyāna can be attributed to the new technology of writing is, of course, to also claim that prior to this moment in Buddhist history, the Nikāyas were preserved orally, and the bulk of Gombrich's article is devoted to showing that this was indeed the case.

The first reference to the *tipiṭaka* and its commentary being committed to writing occurs in the *Dīpavaṃsa*, in which it is stated that during the reign of Vaṭṭagāmanī Abhaya (29–17 B.C.E.) the monks who remembered the canon wrote it down, apparently fearing that otherwise it may be lost as a result of war, famine, or infighting among monasteries.[30] In arguing against the existence of a written recension of the Nikāyas prior to this date, Gombrich (expanding on an argument made in an article by Lance Cousins[31]) speculates that the Buddha's words were crafted into

[27] See Davidson, "Introduction," p. 312; and *Bodhicaryāvatāra* 9.42–56 (Vaidya, ed., pp. 204–12). Regarding *Bodhicaryāvatāra* 9.45a, Davidson remarks that Śāntideva defines "the doctrine of the Buddha as that which has its basis in the condition of a fully ordained monk" (p. 312). However, Prajñākaramati's commentary indicates that Śāntideva is defining bhikṣu in a very limited and polemical sense here, as an arhat who has understood the Mādhyamika emptiness; see Vaidya, ed., pp. 206–07. For a discussion of the positions of Nāgārjuna and Candrakīrti on the need for śrāvakas to understand the Mādhyamika emptiness in order to become arhats, see Donald S. Lopez, Jr., "Do Śrāvakas Understand Emptiness?" *Journal of Indian Philosophy* 16 (1988): 65–105.

[28] Richard F. Gombrich, "How the Mahāyāna Began," in Tadeusz Skorupski, ed., *The Buddhist Forum*, vol. 1 (London: School of Oriental and African Studies, 1990), pp. 21–30.

[29] Gregory Schopen, "The Phrase 'sa pṛthivīpradeśaś caityabhūto bhavet' in the Vajracchedikā: Notes on the Cult of the Book in the Mahāyāna," *Indo-Iranian Journal* 17 (1975).

[30] K. R. Norman, *Pāli Literature* (Wiesbaden: Otto Harrassowitz, 1983), pp. 10–11. For a very useful discussion of the possible circumstances leading to this event, see Collins, "On the Very Idea," pp. 96–99.

[31] See Cousins and K. R. Norman, "The Pāli Language and Scriptures," in Tadeusz Skorupski, ed., *The Buddhist Heritage* (Tring, United Kingdom: Institute of Buddhist Stud-

oral texts designed with the aim of mnemonic preservation, employing techniques such as redundancy, versification, and the arrangement of works according to length, all methods known to the monks from the Vedas. The saṃgha was organized toward the task of preservation, with the four Nikāyas representing four traditions of memorization; we find reference, for example, to the Dīghabhāṇakas ("reciters of the long discourses") and the Majjhimabhāṇakas ("reciters of the medium-length discourses"). In addition to the "oral" quality of the Pāli *sutta*s, Gombrich notes that the few references to writing in the *Vinaya* (Monastic Code) are to writing as a means of message sending and public notification (such as the wanted poster described in *Vinaya* 1.43) but never as a means of preserving the canon. Gombrich concludes, following Oldenberg and Rhys Davids, that had the inscription of the canon been an activity of the saṃgha, there would have been some mention of it in the *Vinaya*.[32]

Two lines of argument, not unrelated to each other, require scrutiny here. The first is the claim that the Buddhist canon meets the criteria set for what has come to be called "oral literature"; the second, that the Buddhist oral canon was modeled on the Vedas. Gombrich's argument for the oral quality of the Pāli *sutta*s develops a position put forth by Lance Cousins. Cousins, based on his reading of Albert Lord's analysis of tape-recorded performances by Serbo-Croatian epic singers,[33] argues that the Pāli Nikāyas and Abhidhamma are oral literature. Upon comparing recorded versions, Lord found considerable variation among songs, even those performed by the same singer. Thus, Cousins accounts for variations (such as locations and names of speakers) that occur among the various versions of the Nikāyas by arguing that the discourses of the Buddha were preserved solely in the monks' memories, to be recited publicly for edification and entertainment. He finds further support for his view in the presence of mnemonic formulas and in the fact that the same episode will often appear in separate texts within the Pāli canon.

That Buddhist monks recited sūtras is not at issue. The question is whether the sūtras are the end products of an oral society. A great deal of scholarship has appeared on oral cultures since the work of Milman Parry on the Homeric epics during the 1920s and even since the publica-

---

ies, 1989). For a useful demonstration of the persistence of the oral in Theravāda, see Steven Collins, "Notes on Some Oral Aspects of Pāli Literature," *Indo-Iranian Journal* 35 (1992): 121–35.

[32] Gombrich, "How the Mahāyāna Began," pp. 27–28.

[33] Albert B. Lord, *The Singer of Tales* (Cambridge: Harvard University Press, 1960). For a useful survey of scholarship on the orality issue as it pertains to Homer, see Hugh Lloyd-Jones, "Becoming Homer," *New York Review of Books* 39, no. 5 (March 5, 1992): 52–57.

tion of Lord's work in 1960, much of it usefully summarized by Walter Ong in his 1982 work, *Orality and Literacy*.[34]

Ong provides a laundry list of nine characteristics of oral culture. (1) The works of oral cultures are additive rather than subordinative. They are marked by pragmatics, such as simple grammatical constructions linked by identical conjunctions; written structures, in contrast, place greater emphasis on the organization of the discourse itself, which is separate from the needs of a speaker, employing subordinate clauses rather than conjunctions. (2) The works of oral societies tend to be aggregative rather than analytic, employing a variety of mnemonic aids such as epithets, formulas, and stock phrases, often lacking the sense of individual words as discrete units. (3) Such works are highly redundant, repeating what has been said in order to allow the often distracted listener to follow the narrative.

From these more or less formal observations about orality, Ong next moves to characterizations of oral societies, noting that (4) they are conservative or traditionalist, in that they inhibit intellectual experimentation and speculation. (5) They conceptualize knowledge, in his phrase, "close to the human lifeworld," in that they lack elaborate analytic categories that would structure knowledge apart from lived experience. And in a statement that should set off an alarm in the brain of any student of Buddhism, he declares that "An oral culture has no vehicle so neutral as a list."[35] It is instead literate cultures that devise lists, outside the context of human action. (6) The works of oral cultures are agonistically toned, marked by exaggerated vituperation and extravagant praise and descriptions of what otherwise might be termed graphic violence, thereby situating knowledge within a context of struggle. Writing, on the other hand, "fosters abstractions that disengage knowledge from the arena where human beings struggle with one another."[36] The remaining characteristics are so many variations on what is by now a familiar theme. (7) Orality is empathetic and participatory, bringing about a close communal identification with the known. (8) It is homeostatic in that it remains concerned with the present, allowing memories of what has been irrelevant to fade from communal consciousness. (9) Finally, it is situational rather than abstract, unavoidably using concepts but again within situational frames of reference that are "minimally abstract." For this last point Ong draws on the research of the famous Soviet neurologist A. R. Luria among Russian peasants in the 1930s, noting that illiterates lack articulate self-

[34] Walter J. Ong, *Orality and Literacy: The Technologizing of the Word* (London: Methuen, 1982).

[35] Ibid., p. 42.

[36] Ibid., pp. 43–44.

analysis because it requires "a demolition of situational thinking."[37] For Ong, then, oral cultures are fixed and formulaic, while writing frees the mind for original and abstract thought, a fact (if it indeed be a fact) that Ong seems to report with a certain nostalgic regret.

In his discussion of what he calls the psychodynamics of orality, Ong makes inevitable mention of the claims to orality concerning the Vedas. However, his comments are made in passing and amount to the cautious observation that the traditional assertions that works of such length were orally composed and retained verbatim over many centuries in an oral society (and thus by purely oral means) cannot be taken at face value, asking such questions as whether what was retained was the original composition by the author or some later and revised version.[38]

A more sustained analysis of the claim to Vedic orality has been made by the anthropologist Jack Goody, who devotes a chapter to the issue in his 1987 work, *The Interface between the Written and the Oral*.[39] He argues that the Vedas are not the product of an oral society based on the discrepancies he discerns between the Vedas and verified products of oral societies. For example, unlike other cases of oral recitation, such as the Serbian epics studied by Lord, in which the work is maintained by illiterate or semiliterate singers, in India the responsibility for the oral tradition is confined to a literate caste of specialists. Investigators have also found little evidence of long poems among oral cultures; hence the extreme length of the Vedic corpus also weighs against its orality. The claims to invariant transmission are also reason for suspicion when compared to the considerable variation noted between tape-recorded performances of a single work among oral societies where it is not a poem that is transmitted, but rather its substance and technique.[40] S. Dow has gone so far as to declare, "Verbatim oral transmission of a poem composed orally and not written down is unknown."[41] Instead, Goody sees the Veda as a written tradition passed down, for the most part, by oral means. The brahmans' storied verbatim recall serves as evidence of the existence of writing because a fixed text can be copied and consulted for correction in ways that an oral text cannot. The graphic device of the table used to organize the Sanskrit alphabet, the highly abstract formulas found in Pāṇini, and even the *kramapāṭha* (ab, bc, cd), the *jaṭāpāṭha* (ab, ba, ab, bc, cb, bc, cd, dc, cd), and *ghanapāṭha* (ab, ba, abc, cba, abc) texts de-

[37] Ibid., p. 54.

[38] Ibid., p. 66.

[39] Jack Goody, *The Interface between the Written and the Oral* (Cambridge: Cambridge University Press, 1987).

[40] Ibid., p. 84.

[41] S. Dow, cited in ibid., p. 82.

scribed by Staal in *Nambudiri Veda Recitation* all point, says Goody, to a level of schematization and abstraction impossible without writing. The Vedas are what he calls parallel products of a literate society.[42]

Having argued that the Vedas represent an originally written tradition, Goody must account for the strong claims to the contrary, by both the conservators of the Vedas themselves and their western counterparts. The written Veda would have been preserved orally because of the great difficulty of making and maintaining manuscripts. It would also have been in the brahmans' interests to restrict the instruction of the Veda to the oral medium; as Goody puts it, "by retaining control over the process of transmission, we render our jobs more secure."[43] This is a variation on the familiar "greedy brahman" theory, by which access to the sacred formulas is jealously guarded in order to maintain a monopoly on the fees charged for the performance of rites, a charge that dates back at least to the Cārvākas, the ancient "materialist" school.[44] Goody offers no thoughts on why, if the Vedas are indeed the product of a written tradition, the claim to their oral nature has so long been accepted by Western Sanskritists.

One such Sanskritist, Harry Falk, has reviewed Goody's argument and demonstrated the ways in which Goody has misread and misrepresented a limited group of secondary sources in order to make his case for the written origin of the Vedas, all in an effort to support the thesis that motivates so much of his work: that there is a universal link between writing and "scientific thinking." That we are unable to conceive of the development of a system as abstract as Pāṇini's without writing is no proof of Pāṇini's use of writing; as Falk notes, "this is our fault and not Pāṇini's."[45] Frits Staal concedes the role of a written text at some point in the history of the Indian epics, a genre of literature that more closely fits Goody's thesis. But for Staal the Vedas are something quite apart, con-

[42] Ibid., p. 188. In an impressive essay, Frits Staal argues strongly that not only the Vedas but even Pāṇini's grammar were composed and preserved without recourse to writing. See his *The Fidelity of Oral Tradition and the Origins of Science*, Mededelingen der Koninklijke Nederlandse, Akademie van Wetenschappen, Afd. Letterkunde, Nieuwe Reeks, Deel 49, no. 8 (Amsterdam/Oxford/New York: North-Holland, 1986).

[43] Goody, *Interface*, p. 119.

[44] See Richard P. Hayes, "The Question of Doctrinalism in the Buddhist Epistemologists," *Journal of the American Academy of Religion* 52, no. 4 (1984): 651.

[45] See Harry Falk, "Goodies for India: Literacy, Orality, and Vedic Culture," in Wolfgang Raible, ed., *Erscheinungsformen kultureller Prozesse* (Tübingen: Gunter Narr Verlag, 1990), pp. 103–20. The passage cited here occurs on p. 110. I am grateful to Steven Collins for both alerting me to the existence of this article and kindly providing me with a photocopy. For another critique of Goody, see John Halverson, "Goody and the Implosion of the Literacy Thesis," *Man*, n.s. 27 (1992): 301–17.

veyed secretly with an insistence on formal accuracy to the exclusion of meaning, apparently a unique achievement in human history.[46]

It is not necessary to reproduce Falk's and Staal's refutations of Goody here. A summary of the argument for the oral origin of the Vedas will suffice. The four Saṃhitās (*Ṛg Veda*, *Sāma Veda*, *Yajur Veda*, *Atharva Veda*) are generally thought to have reached their present form by 1000 B.C.E. The possession of writing by foreign traders may have been known in northwest India at the time of the Buddha, where its use was limited to commercial matters. Its alien and hence polluting nature is evidenced in the *Aitareya Āraṇyaka* (5.5.3), which states that the disciple "should not learn [i.e., recite the Veda] when he has eaten flesh, or seen blood, or a dead body, or done what is unlawful, . . . or had intercourse, or written, or obliterated writing."[47] The earliest archaeological evidence of writing in India in an Indian language, after the still undeciphered Harappan seals, are the inscriptions of the rock edicts of Aśoka in Brahmī script, dated circa 258 B.C.E. The Greek ambassador Megasthenes found no evidence of writing among his hosts at the Maurya court in Patna around 300 B.C.E.[48] Although Indologists continue to debate how long before Aśoka the Brahmī script was developed,[49] there is general consensus that

[46] See Staal, *Fidelity of Oral Tradition.*

[47] A. B. Keith, ed. and trans., *The Aitareya Āraṇyaka* (Oxford: Clarendon, 1969), pp. 301–2.

[48] See Falk, "Goodies for India," p. 105. On the date of the Buddha's death and its relation to Aśoka's ascension to the throne, see Hirakawa Akira, *A History of Indian Buddhism from Śākyamuni to Early Mahāyāna*, trans. and ed. Paul Groner (Honolulu: University of Hawaii Press, 1990), pp. 22–23; and Heinz Bechert, "The Date of the Buddha Reconsidered," *Indologica Taurinensia* 10 (1982): 29–36.

[49] Some Sanskritists, such as Falk, hold that the errors, variants, and development of punctuation present in the rock edicts point to a script only newly invented. He thus concludes that "anyone able to distinguish facts from fiction would come to the conclusion that writing in India practised by Indians in Indian scripts can not be much older than 258 B.C." (p. 105). However, other distinguished scholars have reached different conclusions. K. R. Norman finds in the same variations in the Aśokan inscriptions evidence that the script had been in existence in the form that we know it for some time prior to Aśoka, not later than the end of the fourth century B.C.E. See K. R. Norman, "The Development of Writing in India and Its Effect upon the Pāli Canon," *Wiener Zeitschrift für die Kunde Südasiens* 36, Supplementband (1992): 239–49. J. Bronkhorst has suggested that the Padapāṭha of the Ṛgveda was written down at the time of its composition, not later than the sixth century B.C.E. See his "Some Observations on the Padapāṭha of the Ṛgveda," *Indo-Iranian Journal* 24 (1982): 181–89.

For sources on the question of the origins of writing in India, see William A. Graham, *Beyond the Written Word: Oral Aspects of Scripture in the History of Religion* (Cambridge: Cambridge University Press, 1987), p. 199, n. 3. See also Oskar von Hinüber, *Der Beginn der Schrift und frühe Schriftlichkeit in Indien*, Abhandlungen der Geistes und Sozialwissenschaftlichen Klasse, no. 11 (Mainz: Akademie der Wissenschaften und der Literatur, 1990).

the Vedas, long revered as *vāc* (speech), *śabda* (sound), and *śrūti* (heard), were composed orally and then preserved as sound through elaborate oral mnemotechnics, assiduously maintaining the form with little concern for the content.[50]

This fixation on the word was elaborated into the famous Mīmāṃsaka doctrine of the Veda as eternal and uncreated speech. In their doctrine of the Veda as *śabdapramāṇa* (reliable sound) the Mīmāṃsakas argue that were the injunctions in the Vedas dependent on an author, they would be subject to error because humans are subject to error. However, because they do not emanate from a person and are not subject to variations of time, place, and person, instead producing understanding of their own meaning, they are infallible.[51] The Vedas are also eternal because there is no record of their authorship or their composition. Rather, their order has always been established and they are always repeated in the same form. Kumārila says in his *Ślokavārttika*, "The idea in the mind of every speaker is always that, 'I am uttering words that have been used by other persons'; this in itself makes them eternal."[52] Thus, the Vedas are like the sun that reliably provides light for the entire world. Any who do not accept this fact are as owls, blinded by the light by which all others see.[53]

By owls, the Mīmāṃsakas mean the Buddhists, and indeed none of the *tīrthika darśanas* (non-Buddhist schools) seems to provoke such spleen among the *bauddhas* as does Mīmāṃsā and its doctrine of the eternal, uncreated Veda. For example, the eighth-century Yogācāra-Mādhyamika scholar Śāntarakṣita devotes almost half of his massive compendium and refutation of non-Buddhist doctrines, the *Tattvasaṃgraha*, to Mīmāṃsā, with 845 ślokas given over just to the issue of the Vedas as an uncreated and eternal source of knowledge. In his attack on this position, Śāntarakṣita initially concedes the uncreated nature of the Vedas in order to argue that the truth or falsity of a text is to be judged entirely on the basis of the truth or falsity of its author: a person controlled by desire and hatred speaks falsely; a person endowed with wisdom and compassion speaks truly. Because the Vedas lack an author, the claim that they are true can-

[50] See Frits Staal, "The Concept of Scripture in the Indian Tradition," in Mark Juergensmeyer and N. Gerald Barrier, eds., *Sikh Studies: Comparative Perspectives on a Changing Tradition* (Berkeley: Graduate Theological Union, 1979), pp. 121–24.

[51] *Tattvasaṃgraha* ślokas 2346–50. For the Sanskrit, see Dvārikādāsa Śāstri, ed., *Tattvasaṇgraha*, 2 vols. (Varanasi: Bauddha Bharati, 1968). This edition also contains Kamalaśīla's *Tattvasaṃgrahapañjikā*. For an English translation of both works, described by their translator as "rather disappointing; it is purely and almost entirely polemical," see Ganganatha Jha, trans., *The Tattvasaṅgraha of Shāntarakṣita with the Commentary of Kamalashīla*, 2 vols., reprint edition (Delhi: Motilal Banarsidass, 1986).

[52] Cited in *Tattvasaṃgraha* 2291; see also 2286–88.

[53] Ibid., 2351.

not be proven.[54] Furthermore, the Vedas do not possess the capacity to provide knowledge without being explained by persons—persons who, because the Mīmāṃsakas deny the possibility of enlightenment, may be fallible and thus provide faulty explanations. Therefore, even though the Vedas may be uncreated, this provides no support whatsoever about the claim that they are infallible.[55]

But in the end, Śāntarakṣita wants to argue that the Vedas are authored works. If they were eternal and unchanging, all the words would exist at the same moment, would pervade space, and would always remain unmanifest. However, because the words of the Veda appear in ordered sequence, over specific moments of time, and are manifested through particularities of speech, they must have a cause, an author.[56] The fact that the Vedas are difficult to pronounce and understand is no proof of their uncreated nature. That they set forth techniques for curing poison proves nothing; such cures are found in other texts as well. Further proof of their human authorship is their prescription of perverted sexual practices and animal sacrifice.[57]

Of course, Śāntarakṣita cannot stop with this refutation but must eventually go on to demonstrate that although the Vedas are not a valid source of knowledge, the word of the Buddha is. In order to do this, he must establish the possibility of a person achieving omniscience, something that Mīmāṃsā rejects.[58] He begins with the logical point that the mere fact that the Mīmāṃsakas have never perceived an omniscient person does not establish that it is impossible that such a person exists; indeed the omniscient person can only be apprehended by another omniscient person.[59] From here, the argument becomes predictable: an omniscient person is to be judged by his or her knowledge of the truth. Apparently reversing the position he used against Mīmāṃsā, Śāntarakṣita claims here that the Buddha is omniscient not because of who he was but because of what he taught, anātman, a doctrine unique among all teachings.[60] From here, we find a fairly standard Mahāyāna litany of the qualities of the Buddha and his extraordinary pedagogical skills: he teaches

[54] Ibid., 2353–57. It is noteworthy that, following strategies used by both Āryadeva at *Catuḥśataka* 12.5 and Dharmakīrti in the *svārthanumāna* chapter of the *Pramāṇavārttika*, Śāntarakṣita rejects this very argument in his subsequent proof of the omniscience of the Buddha, where he claims that the teachings of the Buddha are infallible not because their teacher is compassionate, but that the teacher is infallible because the teaching is true.

[55] Ibid., 2365–78, 2394–97.

[56] Ibid., 2421–22.

[57] Ibid., 2787–89.

[58] For their refutation of omniscience in general and of the Buddha in particular, see ibid., 3128–61.

[59] Ibid., 3268–76.

[60] Ibid., 3322–44.

the dharma without the slightest operation of thought, like a wheel set in motion;[61] he is not subject to the faults of mortal beings because he is beyond saṃsāra and thus immortal;[62] the scriptures attributed to him need not have been actually spoken by him but sometimes even emanate from walls. Hence, he is not to be regarded as the author of the sūtras; they are rather set forth under his supervision.[63] Finally, he comprehends everything that exists in a single instant, without the necessity that he know them sequentially, unless that is his wish.[64]

Despite or perhaps because of the stridency of the Buddhist attack, the long-held assumption that the Mīmāṃsakas and the Buddhists stand at the antipodes on the question of the nature of scripture requires reexamination. Stcherbatsky may, in fact, have been wrong when he wrote that "There is hardly a single point in philosophy in which both these systems would not represent the one just the reverse of the other."[65] Both would claim that their scriptures are infallible because they are not the product of human authorship, but rather embody a truth that exists without being contingent on human agency. In fact, in the *Saṃyuktāgama*, the Buddha says, "I did not create the twelvefold dependent origination nor was it created by anyone else";[66] the Vaibhāṣikas assert that the words of the Buddha are *apauruṣeya,* that is, with no author, human or divine.[67] Whether the Buddhists hold the words of the Buddha to be sound or a conditioning factor, they hold them to be impermanent and here, at least verbally, would differ with the Mīmāṃsā. However, when the Mīmāṃsakas describe the Vedas as eternal, they explain that this means that they have no beginning in the sense of having no author and they have no end in that they are not destroyed,[68] just as the oft-cited passage from the *Saṃyutta Nikāya* (2.25) states that whether or not the tathāgathas appear, the nature of dharmas remains the same. Both employ identical arguments against those who would deny the infallibility of their scriptures: the Mīmāṃsakas argue that someone who has no connection with the Veda (that is, who is not entitled to study it) and is hostile to it could never be truthful about the infallibility of the Veda.[69] Śāntarakṣita says that it is impossible for ignorant beings like the Mīmāṃsakas to draw

[61] Ibid., 3368–69.

[62] Ibid., 3550–51.

[63] Ibid., 3606–11.

[64] Ibid., 3627–29.

[65] F. Th. Stcherbatsky, *Buddhist Logic*, vol. 1 (New York: Dover, 1962), p. 23.

[66] See Étienne Lamotte, *Le Traité de la grande vertu de sagesse de Nāgārjuna*, tome 5 (Louvain: Institut Orientaliste, 1980), p. 2191.

[67] See Padmanabh S. Jaini, "The Vaibhāṣika Theory of Words and Meanings," *Bulletin of the School of Oriental and African Studies* 22 (1959): 107.

[68] *Tattvasaṃgraha* 2103.

[69] Ibid., 2088–95.

any conclusions about the possibility of omniscience.[70] And the same argument can be used against one's coreligionists, for the author of the *Mahāyānasūtrālaṃkāra* (1.16) proclaims that the only way the adherents of the *śrāvakayāna* could prove that the Mahāyāna sūtras are not the word of the Buddha would be if they themselves had attained the omniscience of a buddha whereby they could perceive things in distant times and places.[71] For a monk to falsely claim such an ability is an offense requiring expulsion from the order. Finally, both speak of the sounds being heard without the need to understand the meaning.

The rhetorical affinities between the Mīmāṃsakas and the Buddhists in their description of scripture are thus clearly present. From another perspective, however, they appear to be quite different: when the Mīmāṃsakas speak of the eternal and unauthored nature of the Vedas, they are speaking of a self-identity of sound; when the Buddhists speak of the eternal nature of dharmas as dependently arisen, they are speaking of a self-identity of reality, that what we are dealing with is an issue of form versus content. Staal explains: "There is no tradition [among the brāhmans] for the preservation of the meaning [of the Veda], a concern regarded as a mere individualistic pastime. The brāhmans' task is more noble: to preserve the sound for posterity, maintain it in its purity, and keep it from contamination by outsiders. Thus it is saved from the unchecked spread and vulgarization which attaches to the written word."[72] A more materialist purpose for the preservation of sound is offered by Falk, who notes that "a priest gets paid for participating in sacrifices. The oral instruction is not a transfer of meaning but a transfer of tools without which the future priest would not be able to practise and earn his livelihood."[73]

The Buddhists, on the other hand, seem more concerned with meaning, if we are to draw the usual conclusion from the famous account of the Buddha forbidding two brahman converts from rendering his teaching in *chandas*, warning that to do so would constitute an infraction of the vinaya, that each disciple was instead to teach the word of the Buddha in his own dialect. The term *chandas* has been widely interpreted, but it seems to mean a method of chanting employed for the Vedas that involved melody (*sāman*) and prolonged intonation (*āyatasvara*).[74] What

[70] Ibid., 3394–96.

[71] See Vaidya, ed., *Bodhicaryāvatāra*, p. xx; and Davidson, "Introduction," p. 312.

[72] Staal, "Concept of Scripture," p. 122.

[73] Falk, "Goodies for India," p. 118.

[74] *Vinaya* 2.139.14–16. For a discussion of the story and its variants in other vinaya texts, as well as a survey of opinion on the meaning of *chandas*, see Étienne Lamotte, *History of Indian Buddhism: From the Origins to the Śaka Era*, trans. Sara Webb-Boin (Louvain: Peeters, 1988), pp. 552–56.

might this distinction—that the *śrotriya*s (the Vedic listeners) were concerned with the precise preservation of the sounds of the Vedas whereas the śrāvakas (the Buddhist listeners) were concerned with the preservation of the meaning of the Buddha's word in the vernacular—imply about the issue of committing the Vedas and the sūtras to writing?

Regardless of one's position on when the writing took place, of whether Goody is right or wrong (and the available evidence points strongly in the direction of his being wrong), it is highly probable that the existence of writing was known to both monks and brahmans by the time of Aśoka, and perhaps a century earlier. The possible significance of the notions of convertibility and totalization suggested by the coincidence in India during the fourth and third centuries B.C.E. of this use of the Brahmī script, the establishment of the Mauryan Empire, the minting of coins, and the delineation of the Abhidharma remains to be explored. The question to which we now turn is why the societies of priests, both Vedic and Buddhist, seem to have rejected the use of writing for the preservation of their knowledge until the late dates that have come down to us (late first century B.C.E. in the case of the Buddhists; as late as the eighth century in the case of the brahmans), whether they, like the utopian society described in *Dao de jing*, "knew writing but returned to the use of the knotted rope, " or were like King Thamus of Thebes, who, as Plato recounts in the *Phaedrus*, refused the gift of writing from the god Theuth: "If men learn this, it will implant forgetfulness in their souls; they will cease to exercise memory because they rely on that which is written, calling things to remembrance no longer from within themselves, but by means of external marks." Socrates concurs, but for other reasons: "And once a thing is placed in writing, the composition, whatever it may be, drifts all over the place, getting into the hands not only of those who understand it, but equally those who have no business with it; it doesn't know how to address the right people, and not address the wrong."[75] Laozi seems to long for a return to an oral culture with no need for writing and the displacements it introduces, where all that is needed is a knotted rope for counting things. Plato sees writing as a dangerous technology, capable of inducing the loss of knowledge and the rise of chaos.

The dangers of writing in the case of the Vedas are obvious. For a tradition that bases itself on the power of the word (in an increasingly unintelligible language, Vedic), that power being invested in those who can speak it, the introduction of writing breaks the unbroken lineage of authenticity of the recital and repetition of the word, disrupts the self-perpetuation of

[75] Edith Hamilton and Huntington Cairns, eds., *Plato: The Collected Dialogues*, Bollingen series, no. 71 (Princeton: Princeton University Press, 1961), pp. 520–21.

both truth and society where authority is passed from father to son. Writing permits the absence of the speaker and the sound and, as Socrates warns, allows dissemination of knowledge among those from whom it should be restricted.

Writing here is not only a technology in its more narrow sense (as used by Goody) of a mechanism that leads to new intellectual practices and hence new ways of producing consciousness in society, as important as this is in the Indian context. Writing is also technology in the wider sense, as a more amorphous, pervasively deployed, institutional practice. It is in this wider sense that Derrida would argue that even if the Vedas were not inscribed in palm leaf they were already written. If writing is seen as "the durable institution of a sign," as a means for recording speech so that it can be repeated in the absence of the original speaker and without knowledge of the speaker's intention, then all linguistic signs are a form of writing.[76] And it is indeed the very fact of its repeatability that the Mīmāṃsakas put forth as a proof for the eternal nature of the Veda. But there seems to be something else at stake, for in the case of the Veda, we do not find speech standing at a remove from self-present truth from which writing is yet a further deviation; rather the sound is itself the truth. The relation of word and meaning is not a matter of convention; the signifying power of the word is eternal, innately conveying its meaning. No arbitrariness of the sign here, where language is claimed not to operate through difference. The identity of speech and truth, of spoken word and meaning, serves to make writing even more suspicious. There is all the more reason for the brahmans to regard writing as a poison.

The Buddhist case is somewhat different. Given the reported wish of the Buddha that his word be disseminated in the vernacular and the apparent Buddhist rejection of caste restrictions, one might wonder what caused the Buddhists to refrain (according to their records) from committing the sūtras to writing for at least four centuries after the Buddha's death. An ideology of the self-presence of speech again provides one possible direction, which points back to the myth of the Buddha's enlightenment, something described as so profound that he only belatedly, and at the urging of the god Brahmā, decided to speak at all. The dharma, as we have seen, was represented not as something that he created but as something that he found, the ancient city at the end of the ancient path through the great forest.[77] His discovery of this truth provided him with the authority to speak, and all subsequent teachings were merely repetitions of what had been heard from him. Thus, the *Heart Sūtra* commen-

[76] Jacques Derrida, *Of Grammatology*, trans. Gayatri Chakravorty Spivak (Baltimore: Johns Hopkins University Press, 1976), p. 44.

[77] *Saṃyutta Nikāya* 12.65.

tators specify that what was heard by the *saṃgītikartṛ* was simply the words; the form was received but the content was not understood because that content remains the pristine possession of the Buddha. The notion of origin from an uncreated truth is as much at play here as it is with the Vedas; so, too, is the power of lineage, of hearing from the teacher what he heard from his teacher, often couched in the rhetoric of father and son, of inheritance and birthright, traced back ultimately to the Buddha. It is this line of legitimation that accounts for the obsession with genealogy that one encounters, for example, in Chan and Zen and throughout Tibetan Buddhism. Thus, we find in many texts, both Hīnayāna and Mahāyāna, the so-called four reliances: "Rely on the dharma, not on the person. Rely on the meaning, not on the letter. Rely on the definitive meaning, not on the provisional meaning. Rely on knowledge (jñāna), not on [ordinary] consciousness (*vijñāna*)."[78] In each opposed pair, the former is the privileged term, the latter is the debased counterpart. Writing stands even further removed, the re-presentation of the word detached from the voice of the lineage. It is to signal participation in that lineage that the sūtras begin, "*evaṃ mayā śrutam.*"

Whether or not the Vedas and sūtras were written down before the tradition reports that they were, we have sufficient reason to suspect why writing would have remained hidden. For it would seem that what Derrida discerned in the history of metaphysics in the West also pertains to India, where writing was "a debased, lateralized, repressed, displaced theme, yet exercising a permanent and obsessive pressure from the place where it remains held in check. A feared writing must be cancelled because it erases the presence of the self-same [*propre*] within speech."[79] If writing was poison for the brahmans, it was chemotherapy for the early Buddhists, accepted only in order to postpone the demise of the dharma; the *Dīpavaṃsa* reports that the monks in Sri Lanka first had the *tipiṭaka* written down when they saw the decay (*hāni*) of sentient beings.[80] Yet the brahmans and the Buddhists seem to be repulsed by two distinguishable dangers of writing. The aversion of the brahmans appears to derive from a recognition of the danger discerned by Plato, where writing leads to uncontrolled diffusion and dispersion of the word, out of the memory and into the world. Thus, the unintelligible sounds of the Veda must be precisely preserved in the mind. The Buddhists, on the other hand, hail the dispersion of the dharma in the vernacular, relying not on the word

[78] On the four reliances (*catuḥpratisaraṇa*), see Étienne Lamotte, "The Assessment of Textual Interpretation in Buddhism," in Donald S. Lopez, Jr., ed., *Buddhist Hermeneutics* (Honolulu: University of Hawaii Press, 1988), pp. 11–27.

[79] Derrida, *Of Grammatology*, p. 270.

[80] Cited by Collins, "On the Very Idea," p. 97.

but on the meaning, despite the concern with monastic maintenance of the *buddhavacana* suggested by the *mahāpadeśas*. They thus seem closer to the Romantic view of writing that we associate with Rousseau, in which the written word is the dead letter, removed from the self-presence of enlightenment and its already inadequate reflection in speech.

All of which makes the virtual explosion of texts by which we mark the rise of the Mahāyāna all the more intriguing, a "movement," which despite its prodigious literature may never have moved beyond the minority during its millennium in India. It is probably premature to provide a narrative "explanation" of the origin of the Mahāyāna, if such will ever be possible. Yet lacking a linear tale to tell, there are certain suggestions to be made. One can begin by observing that the Mahāyāna sūtras have many of the qualities of the Nikāyas (redundancy, stock phrases, reliance on lists)—the very features that lead Cousins and Gombrich to judge the Nikāyas to be oral. The Mahāyāna sūtras differ from the earlier works, however, in their self-consciousness and frequent exaltation of their status as books, as physical objects, with many works being devoted almost entirely to descriptions of benefits to be gained by reciting, copying, and worshiping them.[81] If, as Schopen has suggested, the early Mahāyāna should be viewed as a group of distinct revivalist movements, often centered around a single text, which cannot be easily traced directly from an existing school (e.g., Mahāsaṃghika) or group (monk or lay), then the importance of the writing of the sūtras may have less to do with what the sūtras say than with what they do. Like the Vedas, the form may have been more important than the content, but unlike the Vedas it was not the verbal form so much as the physical form that was the key. The animosity expressed toward the stūpa cult that Schopen has pointed out in many of the earliest Mahāyāna sūtras and the repeated presence of the phrase *sa pṛthivīpradeśaś caityabhūto bhavet* ("that spot of earth [where the sūtra is set forth] becomes a truly sacred place") suggest that what these early movements wanted was not so much new teachings as new centers for worship. Just as the *bodhimaṇḍa* in Bodhgāyā is a sacred place because it is the site of the Buddha's enlightenment, so wherever the perfection of wisdom is set forth also becomes a sacred place because the perfection of wisdom is the cause of the Buddha's enlightenment.[82] With stūpas under the control of more established groups, the new groups required a cultic focal point. The book could then function as a substi-

[81] Gregory Schopen, "The Phrase 'sa pṛthivīpradeśaś caityabhūto bhavet' in the Vajracchedikā: Notes on the Cult of the Book in the Mahāyāna," *Indo-Iranian Journal* 17 (1975): 159.

[82] Ibid., pp. 172–73.

tute for the absent founder, fulfilling the desire for restored presence, physically standing for his speech, manifest as the body of his teaching, a dharmakāya. Sūtras may have been written (down) before, but here was a new reason for their writing. While writing might be condemned as derivative and displaced from the animation of speech (and, in this sense, dead), these dead letters could be also valued precisely because they were dead, the leftover, dispersed (and dispersable) remnants of the living Buddha, suitable for framing in a stūpa, as the *Lotus* recommends. What had made books dangerous is what makes them appealing: they are dead. In order for the supplement to function as a substitute, it must resemble what it replaces; the new sūtras must begin, "*evaṃ mayā śrutam.*"

The moment of origin may be unimaginable, as Derrida claims. Even the attempt at imagination creates a certain sense of shame, of violation, of transgression. In his *Homer and the Origin of the Greek Alphabet*, B. B. Powell postulates that an ancient Greek, his name now lost, was so moved by Homer's recitation that he invented the Greek alphabet for the very purpose of preserving the *Iliad* and the *Odyssey*. The reviewer in the *Times Literary Supplement* identified the many problems with such a theory, but refrained from cruelly spoiling what was at least a lovely thought by not pointing out that this would have required Homer to dictate the *Iliad* and the *Odyssey* twice (and both times very slowly)—once for the recording of the works and again to insure that the transcription (which only the transcriber could read) was correct.[83] A similar sense of dis-ease attends our imagination of an unknown Indian writing down the Veda or the *Vajracchedikā*. The Mahāyāna seems to have remained ambivalent about the word, continuing to produce sūtras but making it a minor transgression of the bodhisattva vow to divert support away from meditators to those who only recite sūtras. The question of the identity of the *saṃgītikartṛ*, then, is the question of where authority should lie—in what is written or in the testimony as to what had been heard? If there is to be resolution, it would seem to come in the moment that is so difficult to imagine, when a monk put stylus to palm leaf and penned the words, *evaṃ mayā śrutam eksasmin samaye bhagavan rājagṛhe viharati sma. . . .*

In the temple called Rokuharamitsuji in Kyoto there is a famous statue of the Heian monk Kūya (903–972), an eccentric devotee of Amitābha. The statue depicts Kūya dressed in rags, with a gong suspended around his

[83] Barry B. Powell, *Homer and the Origin of the Greek Alphabet* (Cambridge: Cambridge University Press, 1991), reviewed by J. T. Hooker in *Times Literary Supplement*, June 14, 1991, p. 29.

neck; he carries a hammer in one hand and a staff topped with antlers in the other. His mouth is open and from it protrudes a wire to which are attached what appear to be six liṅgams. On closer inspection, they are seen to be six identical standing buddhas, one for each of the syllables: *Na-mu-a-mi-da-butsu* (Homage to Amitābha Buddha). Here speech does not pass immediately into silence, but instead, always material and already silent, is preserved behind glass, for us to see.

Two

The Commentaries of Vimalamitra and Atiśa

Vast Explanation of the Noble Heart of the Perfection of Wisdom

Āryaprajñāpāramitāhṛdayaṭīkā

VIMALAMITRA

Homage to the bodhisattva *mahāsattva*, the noble Avalokiteśvara, endowed with great compassion.

Paying homage to all the conquerors and bodhisattvas, the sole friends of transmigrators, I will explain the essence of the mother of conquerors, the supreme primary [expression] of the meaning of the *Śatasāhasrikāprajñāpāramitā* (Perfection of Wisdom in 100,000 Stanzas), and so on.

The factors to be set forth are summarized [as follows]: the opening, the occasion, those gathered to be included in the teaching, the setting, the question, the eleven-part answer, the agreement, and the admiration are included in eight parts, because it is correct to include the praise by the audience there.

The three words [*evaṃ mayā śrutam*], *Thus* . . . form the opening.[1]

[1] Two terms require some discussion here: *gleng slong*, which I translate as "opening," and *gleng bzhi*, which I translate as "setting." The Sanskrit for these terms appear to be *upodghāta* and *nidāna*, respectively, and are glossed by Haribhadra in the *Abhisamayālaṃkārāloka*. Discussing "Thus did I hear" (*evaṃ mayā śrutam*), he says, "Such is the opening (*upodghātaṃ*). Now, one might ask, 'When, from whom, where, and with whom did you hear this precious sūtra?' In order to indicate that one is a reliable person, one sets forth the setting (*nidāna*)—the place, the time, the teacher, the marvelous retinue that [together] are the cause of [the sūtra] being taught—saying, 'At one time.'" For the Sanskrit, see U. Wogihara, ed., *Abhisamayālaṃkār'āloka Prajñāpāramitāvyākhyā: The Work of Haribhadra* (Tokyo: The Toyo Bunko, 1932, 1973), p. 6. Thus, according to Haribhadra, Vimalamitra (both here and in his commentary to the *Saptaśatikāprajñāpāramitā*, Toh. 3814, Shes phyin ma 6b7–7a2), and Atiśa (in his commentary translated below), the opening (*upodghāta, gleng slong*) seems to be only the words, "Thus did I hear" (*evaṃ mayā śrutam*), while the setting (*nidāna, gleng gzhi*) appears to be the setting of the scene, "At one time the Bhagavan was abiding at Vulture Peak in Rājagṛha with a great assembly of monks and a great assembly of bodhisattvas." In his commentary below, Atiśa speaks of a common setting and a special setting. The common setting, found also in other sūtras, is, "At one time the Bhagavan was abiding at Vulture Peak in Rājagṛha with a great assembly

What *I heard* was *thus*; not something else. Because this removes [the possibility of anything] being left out or added, it is a promise as to the accuracy of what was heard. It expresses the fact that having been heard once, what was taken in and retained is correctly and fully set forth. The correct compilation [comes about through] the ripening of roots of virtue created in relation to the Buddha by one who has the protection of a virtuous friend. These should be known to be practices such as revering the Buddha, asking properly, giving, and ethics. Otherwise, hearing the primary [expression] of the meaning of the perfection of wisdom in this way does not take place. As Maitreyanātha says: "Exalting the buddhas, creating roots of virtue with regard to them, together with the protection of the virtuous friend make one a vessel for hearing this. The wise understand that by the practices of revering the Buddha, asking properly,[2] giving, ethics, and so forth, [one becomes] a vessel for receiving and retaining [the teaching]." These produce such things as clarity, undistractedness, and respect in disciples.

---

of monks and a great assembly of bodhisattvas." The special setting, unique to the *Heart Sūtra*, is, "At that time, the Bhagavan entered into a samādhi on the categories of phenomena called, 'perception of the profound.'"

Unfortunately, the commentators are not consistent in the use of the terms, or perhaps the Tibetan translators were not consistent in their renderings of them. Thus, Kamalaśīla, in his commentary on the *Vajracchedikā*, writes: "The setting (*gleng gzhi*) is the cause for the arising of the sūtra; it begins, 'Thus did I hear.' . . . The opening (*gleng bslang*) provides the circumstances in order that the meaning of the sūtra can be explained." See his *Āryaprajñāpāramitāvajracchedikāṭīkā*, Toh. 3817, Shes phyin ma 204b3–4. Praśāstrasena, in his commentary (translated in chap. 6), assigns the terms to different parts of the sūtra. For him the setting (*gleng gzhi*) comes first as, "Thus did I hear. At one time the Bhagavan was abiding at Vulture Peak in Rājagṛha with a great assembly of monks and a great assembly of bodhisattvas." This is followed eventually by the opening (*gleng bslang*), which for him is, "Also at that time, the bodhisattva the *mahāsattva* the noble Avalokiteśvara beheld the practice of the profound perfection of wisdom and saw that those five aggregates also are empty of intrinsic existence." A further complication is found in the *Bhagavadratnaguṇasaṃcayagāthāpañjikā*, which makes the same distinction between the two parts of the beginning of the sūtra that he makes above, but designates both by the same term "setting" (*gleng bzhi*). See Toh. 3792, Shes phyin ja, 2b1–2.

Regardless, this distinction between the opening and the setting sheds considerable light on a question that has long vexed scholars of Buddhism, that is, how one is to read the statement that begins most sūtras, *evam mayā śrutam ekasmin samaye*. Is it, "Thus did I hear. At one time . . . " or is it "Thus did I hear at one time"? It is clear from the above that a number of Buddhist commentators followed the former reading. For a survey of previous scholarship, see Brian Galloway, "'Thus Have I Heard: At One Time . . . ,'" *Indo-Iranian Journal* 34 (1991): 87–104. A further piece of evidence in support of the former reading is a statement from the *Dharmasaṃgīti Sūtra* that traditional exegetes seem so fond of citing, in which the Buddha says, "Monks, you should compile the excellent dharma, with 'Thus did I hear.'"

[2] Derge reads *mang dag* instead of *yang dag*.

It says, *I* [literally, "by me"]. [268a] Therefore, the third[3] [case, the instrumental] indicates only the hearing of the sounds of the letters just as they are; because it is a consciousness arisen from hearing,[4] it completely eliminates the possibility of it being [the rapporteur's] own realization [of the profound meaning of the sūtra; it is rather just an understanding of the words]. Otherwise, *heard by me* would be in the sixth [case, the genitive] because of meaning ["my"] understanding. Now, [in the sūtra] the entity of hearing is being set forth. *At one time* constitutes the occasion; the time is the time, such as autumn. This *at one* [and] this *time* make the *time* specific. It also refers to *abiding*.

He is the Bhagavan because he has destroyed the four *māra*s [of death, the afflictions, the aggregates, and the deity Māra]; he acts as the teacher of transmigrators; his qualities and actions are limitless and sublime. From the viewpoint of his qualities, he is already endowed with limitless [auspicious] marks. However, they are set forth as being appropriate for the simultaneous refuge of those in the audience of the third vehicle who have taken on the welfare of themselves and others [i.e., bodhisattvas]. The reason that the term "Bhagavan" is used is in order to put an end to causes of fear. Therefore, the word "Bhagavan" is used on all occasions of explanation.

Rājagṛha is a certain city in the land of Magadha. In one direction is a mountain called *Pile of Vultures*, which is a permanent abode of the buddhas; they remain there. It should be understood that because the Bhagavan stayed on Vulture Mountain it became a stūpa and is indestructible even by such things as fire. This is stated in the *Bodhisattvapiṭaka*. Similarly, [sūtras] such as the noble *Candrapradīpa* (Moon Lamp) say, "This [place] to the east of Rājagṛha saw ten billion buddhas. Thus, in the presence of all the conquerors, samādhi, this sublime peace, is received." [It] is the place where the Tathāgata, who is free from all faults of investigation and analysis, abides in any of the four postures [standing, sitting, walking, lying down]. How could what has arisen through the power of the Tathāgata be destroyed through disintegration? [268b] The excellent abidings of gods, nobles (āryan), and Brahmā primarily have the character of the fourth concentration, of emptiness, and of great compassion. Therefore, they abide with those three abidings. The meaning of the term is *was abiding*. Thus, the abiding of the Bhagavan [on Vulture Peak] had passed at the time of the correct compilation of the doctrine. Specifying of *at one time* indicates that the teacher of transmigrators who engages in great compassion abided in

[3] Derge reads *gsum pas ni*; Peking reads *gsum pa ni*.

[4] Derge reads *thos pa las byung ba'i shes pa yin bas*; Peking reads *thos pa las byung ba'i shes pa*.

other places at other times. Therefore, other students of the Bhagavan should also abide in the three excellences [of the fourth concentration, emptiness, and great compassion]; they should not act in any other way.

A great assembly of monks indicates those gathered to be included in the teaching.[5] Regarding that, because they have destroyed the afflictions, they are *monks*. Because many of them congregated without division, they are an *assembly*. It is *great* because of being a large group or because of their wisdom, emanations, and so forth. Similarly, [*great* with regard to] the *great*[6] *assembly of bodhisattva mahasāttvas* indicates the three greatnesses [mentioned at *Abhisamayālaṃkāra* 1.42]: the great intention [that makes one] the supreme of all sentient beings (*sarva-sattva-agratā-citta-mahattva*), the great abandonment (*prahāṇa-mahattva*), and the great realization (*adhigama-mahattva*). *Together with* is a term meaning concurrently. Because [those who] abide are concurrent, together is marked with the third case [the instrumental].

Regarding this term, "those gathered to be included," it might be asked who it is that is included. The included are [those whose] roots of virtue, produced earlier, have fully ripened to establish the perception of hearing such a doctrine; it is a term for those who have the fortune to hear the doctrine, and so on.

In order to establish his own validity,[7] when [the rapporteur] bears witness to the place, the time, and the audience, and to having witnesses, he is saying, "I understand that I am a valid speaker; I do not understand the great things of which I speak." A determination of the meaning of the sūtra [269a] by those who are incapable is far-fetched, [even] if they go to those places and ask the witnesses. Furthermore, without indicating the names of the audience for such a sūtra, how can one say who the witnesses are?

Because they are low, the audience of monks is set forth before; because they are high, the audience of bodhisattvas is set forth later. Some [texts] set up a progression from low [to high], such as "the merit of transmigrators of the ten directions, learners, nonlearners, and pratyekabuddhas." Some state a progression from high [to low], such as "buddhas and bodhisattvas." Others hold that because they are always in the audience, the audience of monks is stated first [and] because they are not always there, the audience of bodhisattvas is stated second. [However,] it is not appropriate to say that that which is invariable is to be stated earlier and that which is other is later. It is explained that the setting is that setting with which the teaching begins.

[5] Derge reads *nyan pa* rather than *bstan pa*.

[6] Peking omits *chen po*.

[7] Derge reads *mtshan ma* rather than *tshad ma*.

The statement *At that time* indicates that the roots of virtue of the audience had ripened. That time is the time when the Bhagavan was absorbed in samādhi. Therefore, it says *at that time* because the Bhagavan is the knower of time. *Phenomena* are the aggregates, and so on; [a phenomenon] is asserted to be that which bears[8] its own defining characteristic. Because this is comprehended, realized, and known completely, fully, and in every way and because this comprehends, realizes, and knows completely, fully, and in every way, it says *enumerations of phenomena. The profound* is emptiness, and so forth. That which appears and is perceived in sequence from the perspective of oneself and others is the *perception of the profound.* As it is said [in the *Abhisamayālaṃkara* 4.52], "The profound is emptiness, and so forth. That which is free from the extremes of superimposition and derogation is the profound." It is that which is free from the extremes of superimposition and derogation or is beyond the extremes[9] of existence and nonexistence. Therefore, the master Nāgārjuna said: "The mind that is beyond existence and nonexistence and is unlocated meditates on the meaning of those profundities [269b] through an object that is unobserved." The defining characteristic of samādhi is a one-pointedness of mind. Setting [the mind] properly [and] abiding in the nature of that is called being *absorbed.*

In this way, all of the deeds of buddhas and bodhisattvas are primarily for the welfare of others. Therefore, the Bhagavan's absorption in this samādhi makes it possible for the minds of all the members of the assembly to ripen individually in accordance with [his] demonstration of the meaning of the samādhi. It is to be understood in that way. Here is the source for the Bhagavan's understanding of the absence of the afflicted: "When I saw the nonexistence of the afflicted among those with afflictions,[10] the afflicted in humans was completely abandoned. The nonexistence of the afflicted among conquerors severs the afflicted of those in cities, and so on." The meaning of this is explained below.

It says, *Also at that time. At that time* is the time when the Bhagavan was absorbed in samādhi. The term *also* denotes emphasis. Therefore, it means "at that time only." Or, it says *also* because of inclusion; it serves to include the teaching of the act of absorption and the act of viewing [by Avalokiteśvara] that appears below. Regarding this explanation, only the time of the full ripening of the roots of virtue of the assembly is being referred to. It is correct to include it in that way, not otherwise.

[8] Peking omits *'dzin*, reading simply *rang gi mtshan nyid pa.*

[9] Peking omits *mtha'*.

[10] Derge reads *nyan thos rnams* instead of *nyon mongs pa rnams.*

Sattva[11] [is so-called] because the intention is for enlightenment or because the mind itself is enlightenment. Because of their entry into buddhahood, it is suitable as an etymology for those who have attained empowerment. What is this enlightenment? Enlightenment is of the nature of space; all thought has been abandoned. As it says in the *Vairocanābhisaṃbodhi* (Enlightenment of Vairocana), "Enlightenment has the nature of space. It is the abandonment of all thought." One who wishes to understand that is a *bodhisattva*; it says so there. [270a] *Mahāsattva* in the [sūtra] is an indication of the three [greatnesses], such as the great intention that [makes one] supreme among sentient beings and is due to the great perfection of abiding on a great stage (*bhūmi*). Therefore, he is a *mahāsattva*. As the *Prajñāpāramitāratnaguṇasaṃcayagathā* (Condensed Verses on the Precious Qualities of the Perfection of Wisdom) [1.18] says, "[They have] great giving, great awareness, great power; they abide in the supreme Mahāyāna of the conquerors; they wear great armor and subdue hosts of demons. Therefore, they are called *mahāsattvas*."[12]

Because he has cast afar sinful, nonvirtuous phenomena and has gone far from them, he is called *noble* (*ārya*). By looking down, he [endows] sentient beings with power. He is the lord who wields power without employing the causes of fear and suffering. [Hence], he is so-called. Because he is superior and is the lord who looks down, he is called the "Noble Lord Who Looks Down" (Āryāvalokiteśvara).

Because it is knowledge of the various aspects or is the supreme knowledge, it is called *wisdom*. The nature of excellence is excellence itself; it is only excellence. That which nothing in the world[13] surpasses is explained to be excellent. The excellence of wisdom is the *perfection of wisdom*. Therefore, this is said: Because of the factor of the emptiness of own entity, and so on, it becomes the excellent knowledge; that which is endowed with great supremacy is the perfection of wisdom. As the *Aṣṭasāhasrikāprajñāpāramitā* (Perfection of Wisdom in 8,000 Stanzas) says:

> "Ānanda, if one completely dedicates one's roots of virtue to unsurpassed, perfect, complete enlightenment with wisdom, is that [wisdom] excellent or not?" Ananda replied, "Bhagavan, it is excellent. Sugata, it is excellent." The Bhagavan said, "Therefore, because it is excellent, it wins the name, 'perfection.'"

[11] Derge reads *sems dpa'*, Peking simply *sems*.

[12] The Sanskrit (as edited by Yuyama) is: *mahā-dāyako mahatā-buddhi mahānubhavo mahāyāna uttamu jīnana samābhirūḍho / mahatā-sanaddhu namuciṃ śaṭhu dharṣayiṣye mahāsattva tena hi pravucyati kāraṇena*. See Akira Yuyama, ed., *Prajñā-pāramitā-ratnaguṇa-saṃcaya-gāthā* (Cambridge: Cambridge University Press, 1976), p. 13.

[13] Derge reads *'jigs rten gang la*; Peking reads *'jigs rten na gang la*.

Etymologies other than that are not correct and the joining of sounds is difficult;[14] it would contradict the etymology [provided] by the Bhagavan. The ultimate perfection of wisdom [270b] is the dharmakāya, which has the nature of complete purity. [The perfection of wisdom] that is other than that is the nature of a cause, having the characteristic of the creation of the aspiration (*cittotpāda*), and the achievement of armor (*saṃnāha-pratipatti*), entry (*prasthāna-pratipatti*), collection (*saṃbhāra-pratipatti*), and definite emergence (*niryāṇa-pratipatti*).[15] The meaning of *profound* has already been explained. If one takes [the perfection of wisdom] at that time to refer to the causal perfection of wisdom, it is a locative of place. If [the perfection of wisdom] at that time refers to the fruitional perfection of wisdom, it is a locative of reason.[16]

Regarding that, *practice* is of many types. The path of preparation on the stage of common beings is the practice of belief (*adhimukti*). Six [stages of the ten stages (*bhūmi*) of the bodhisattva path], the second [through seventh] is the practice of achievement. On the eighth stage, it is the practice of certainty. Regarding that, the practice of belief is threefold: for one's own welfare, for one's own and others' welfare, and for others' welfare. Each of these has divisions, such as the small of the small, making eighty-one.[17] Thus, there are twenty-seven types of belief. Regarding the practice of achievement, the three practices, such as ethics, have a nature of purity. By purifying the practice of ethics, [one achieves]

[14] Derge reads *dka' ba*, Peking *dka' la*. Vimalamitra derives pāramitā from *parama*, "excellent." Here, he seems to express his disapproval of the widely adopted folk etymology pāram-ita, "gone to the other side."

[15] These are five of the ten elements characterizing the omniscience (*sarvākarajñatā*), the last four being the four Mahāyāna practices (*pratipatti*). For a study of these and other categories of the path, see E. Obermiller, *Doctrine of the Prajñāpāramitā as Exposed in the Abhisamayālaṃkāra of Maitreya* (Heidelberg: Acta Orientalia, 1932). This work has been reprinted under the misleading title of E. Obermiller, *Prajñāpāramitā in Tibetan Buddhism*, ed. Harcharan Singh Sobti (Delhi: Motilal Banarsidass, 1988).

[16] Vimalamitra is offering two readings of the locative case of *prajñāpāramitā* in the phrase *prajñāpāramitāyāṃ caryāṃ caramāṇa*, literally, "practicing in the practice of the perfection of wisdom." If the perfection of wisdom is causal, that is, a teaching or text that brings about the perfection of wisdom, then the locative is a locative of place, "practicing in the perfection of wisdom." If it is a fruitional perfection of wisdom, the actual perfection of wisdom of a buddha, it is a locative of reason, what Sanskrit grammarians call the *nimitta-saptamī*, "the seventh case that refers to cause or purpose," meaning perhaps, "practicing because of [having achieved] the perfection of wisdom." This latter reading is tentative.

[17] Nine levels are enumerated here: three practices of belief plus the second through the eighth stages of the bodhisattva path. Each of these is itself divided into nine sublevels: the great of the great, the intermediate of the great, the small of the great, the great of the intermediate, the intermediate of the intermediate, the small of the intermediate, the great of the small, the intermediate of the small, and the small of the small. This results in a total of eighty-one, twenty-seven of which are types of belief, that is, these nine for belief for one's own welfare, belief for one's own and others' welfare, and belief for others' welfare.

the second stage. By purifying the training of mind [i.e., the training in samādhi], [one achieves] the third stage. By purifying the training in wisdom, [the achievement] is eightfold; it includes the remaining eight stages.[18] Regarding that, through purifying the training in wisdom that is fully endowed with the categories of enlightenment, the four[19] noble truths, dependent arising, striving, and that which abides in the signless, [one achieves] the four stages, the Radiant, and so on [the fourth through seventh bodhisattva stages]. Thus, the six aspects are the practice of achievement. Regarding the practice of certainty, by purifying the training in wisdom, which is spontaneous and signless, [one attains] the eighth stage. Because it is certain that one will practice in a pure land of a buddha according to one's wish, it is called the practice of certainty. Here [in the sūtra], no specifics are referred to because practice itself encompasses everything. *Practice* means activity, that is, doing. Or, belief itself is practice because it is on the stage of undertaking. It is with this very thing that one undertakes the eleven stages, such as [the first stage] the Joyous. [271a] Other [qualities, such as] attainment, consummation, and purity are established through the remainder of the stages.

The very practice that has that object or that purpose is *viewing*; it abides in accordance with the deed of the Bhagavan [i.e., going into samādhi on emptiness] and does nothing else. This is the meaning [of viewing]. The other members of the audience were abiding in the deed of the Tathāgata [i.e., viewing emptiness]. However, because the noble Avalokiteśvara is the expositor, [the sūtra specifically] indicates that he was engaged [in viewing] in that way. Therefore, Śāriputra is the questioner. *Viewing* means that he saw the various aspects, such as being empty of its own entity, and thought about them individually. Some editions say "thus" (*evam*). Saying "thus" at that point is said to specify the viewing of aspects that appear below, such as the emptiness of the thing itself, signlessness, and nonproduction. For that very reason, the fact [that he viewed these] various [aspects] is expressed through the addition of the term *vyava* [hence, *vyavalokayati*]. In order to indicate how many objects were viewed, it says *the five aggregates*. The term "aggregates" implies the sources[20] and constituents as well because those are also mentioned at the end [i.e., later in the sūtra]. Or, the term *also* [means] that he viewed the sources and constituents. By saying that he saw that those *are empty of intrinsic existence*, it indicates the way they exist; it means that

[18] That is, the seven remaining stages of the bodhisattva path and the stage of buddhahood.

[19] Peking reads *bzhin* instead of *bzhi*.

[20] Derge adds *phung po lnga* prior to *skye mched*.

they are empty of intrinsic existence, devoid, and selfless. This also implies that they are signless and unproduced.

Then in this context means immediately. The power of the deed of the Buddha is *by the power of the Buddha*; it is a term that means by the blessings and power performed by the Bhagavan. This means that the courage for the question to the noble Avalokiteśvara was provided by the Bhagavan; [271b] it would not otherwise be in Śāriputra's purview. Because he is endowed with life from the standpoint of being worthy of praise, due to his abandonment of afflictions, he is called *venerable*. Regarding *Śāriputra*, because he is the son of a woman born into the Śaradvata family, he is Śāriputra.

Said this is what is expressed below. *Said* means said. *Child of good lineage* indicates praise; by receiving empowerment, one has the distinction of being a child of the conquerors. Therefore, this is the form of address. *Whoever* indicates that it is without specificity. *Practice* means to practice and to achieve correctly with care. *Wish* is to aspire to this. [He] *said that*. Some editions say "wish to do the practice." "Do" and "achieve" have no difference[21] in meaning at all.

How should one train, become accustomed? Is it by thinking, application, manifestation, achievement, realization? *That speech* refers to the preceding. *Spoke* means expressed. *Son of good lineage or daughter of good lineage* is suitable to be said by nobles. The term *or* means either or both. *Those* means those who wish to practice. *Like this* [means] in the manner that appears below.

Should view means should individually analyze the various aspects. This expresses the observation by insight, which is a conceptual reflection. One should also view the observation by quiescence, which is a nonconceptual reflection with an uninterrupted and one-pointed mind. Regarding *should view correctly*, it is correct because it is not mistaken, or it is balanced because it is indivisible due to being without characteristic, or because it views in accordance with[22] viewing all phenomena in all ways. *View correctly* [272a] is a term for the observation of the limit of things made manifest[23] by quiescence and insight. This indicates the observation of the limit of things on the first stage included in the path of vision. Then, above that, there are two aspects, the limit of things and what was set forth before: on the second stage and so forth, those three observations are to be viewed. Because the dharmakāya is attained upon the completion of the tenth stage and on the stage of a tathāgata, it is the

21 Derge reads *khyad par med pa nyid*; Peking reads *khyad par ba nyid.*

22 Peking reads *mthun par par lta ba.*

23 Derge reads *mngon sum du byed*; Peking reads *mngon du byed.*

observation of the consummate purpose.[24] As the *Saṃdhinirmocana* (Explanation of the Intention) says:

> Before, in order to attain quiescence and insight, one attained the observations, which are conceptual and nonconceptual reflections. Now, in order to attain the path of vision, one attains the observation of the limit of things. When one takes to mind those three observations, thoroughly endowed thereby with the path of meditation on higher and higher [stages], in order to destroy signs and all assumptions of bad states, one finally purifies the gold-like mind on higher and higher stages until one awakens fully into unsurpassed, perfect, complete enlightenment and attains the observation of the consummate purpose.

This should be known in detail from [the sūtra] itself; here just an example has been provided.

In viewing the aggregates and so forth from the point of view of their being empty of the thing itself, and so on, it is correct because it is not mistaken, it is equal in that it has a single defining characteristic because it lacks a defining characteristic, and all phenomena are seen correctly. Why? It says *form is empty*; because of the context, [empty] of intrinsic entity should be affixed. Thus, that which appears as form and so forth is understood in two ways: there are those who say that they are real and there are those who say that they are imputations. Those who hold[25] that the appearance of form and so forth is real are the Vaibhāṣikas and the Mīmāṃsakas,[26] and so forth. Those who say that the appearance of objects is an imputation are the Sautrāntikas, who say that in fact, [things] such as blue exist externally [272b] but that with regard to experience, the aspect that is contemplated is in this consciousness. There are many ideas about the own entity of blue and so forth: that it is a whole composed of minute particles, that it is consciousness, that it is the principle (*pradhāna*), that it is pure sound. All of these nets of evil thoughts, totally different from each other, are simply destroyed through the refutation of own entity. Therefore, this is said: That very form that appears directly and clearly and that is known to everyone from cowherds and women on up is empty of intrinsic entity, like a city of the *gandharvas*. This appear-

[24] In this paragraph, Vimalamitra is employing a set of categories found in the eighth chapter of the *Saṃdhinirmocana Sūtra*. They are nonconceptual reflection (*nirvikalpakabimba*), conceptual reflection (*savikalpakabimba*), the limit of things (*vastavanta*), and the consummate purpose (*kṛtyānuṣṭhāna*). According to the sūtra, the first is quiescence (*śamatha*), the second is insight (*vipaśyanā*), and the latter two involve both quiescence and insight. For an English translation of the sūtra (with the Derge edition on facing pages), see John Powers, trans., *Wisdom of Buddha: The Saṁdhinirmocana Mahāyāna Sūtra* (Berkeley, Calif.: Dharma, 1995).

[25] Derge reads *smra*; Peking reads *snang*.

[26] Peking reads *spyod pa pa*.

ance of form is without any kind of its own entity. Therefore, this emptiness of own entity is said to be form, thereby indicating that the form asserted by the Vaibhāṣikas and the Mīmāṃsakas is empty of its own entity.

The Sautrāntikas [assert] that the appearance is of the entity of consciousness. Therefore, the appearance of blue and so forth is empty of the own entity of an [external] object. If they think that form is other than emptiness because [form is empty] only of being an external object, they are refuted by the statement *emptiness is not other than form; form is not other than emptiness.*

It might be asked how[27] one is to know that the aggregates and so forth lack their own entity, as [the sūtra] says. Here it is said that because the aggregates (skandha), sources (*āyatana*), and constituents (*dhātu*) are dependently arisen, the position that they are causeless or impermanent is dispelled. There are two analyses[28] of the position that they arise from causes: that when things are produced they are produced simultaneous with their cause or [that they are produced] at a different time. According to the first position, cause and effect and all prior and subsequent points[29] would be observed at one time, in which case cause and effect would be indivisible and an aeon would be just one year. According to the second position, since cause and effect would not come together at the same time, there would be no potency. Therefore, there would be the consequence [that things would arise] causelessly. [273a] If there is no cause, there are the consequences that [things would] be permanent or would be nonexistent because there would be nothing else on which to depend [for production]. If they were dependent, things would be occasional. There is no third possibility because [occurring] at the same time and at different times are mutually exclusive. Therefore, those that appear as forms and so forth are empty of their own entity, like the water of a mirage. Those things that are thought to arise in dependence on this and that are deceptive. Therefore, the Bhagavan said in the *Lalitavistara* (Vast Sport), "Śākyaputra, upon seeing that dependently arisen phenomena are without their own entities, one is endowed with the spacelike mind and is not distracted by seeing the demons and their hosts." The *Ratnolka[dhāraṇī]* (Precious Torch Spell) says, "[Things] are produced from conditions, not from their own entities. The body of the dharma is the body of the conquerors. Reality abides forever, like space. If it is taught, phenomena are purified." The *Sarvabuddhaviśayāvatārajñānālokālaṃkāra* (Ornament Illuminating the Knowledge for Entering the

[27] Derge reads *ga las*; Peking reads *gang las*.
[28] Derge reads *rtag* instead of *brtag*.
[29] Derge reads *phyogs*; Peking reads *tshogs*.

Sphere of All Buddhas) says: "Do not move from the nature of phenomena. By not moving from the nature of phenomena, one achieves the nature of phenomena. Attaining the nature of phenomena does not involve the slightest elaboration. Why? Because [phenomena] are produced by causes and conditions. That which is produced by causes and conditions is utterly unproduced. That which is utterly unproduced is definitely attained. That which is definitely attained, does not abide with mental activity on any phenomenon." There are such statements. Therefore, the noble Nāgārjuna says, "That which is dependently arisen is not intrinsically produced. That which is not intrinsically produced is said to be produced. The utterly unwise who impute production to very subtle things have not seen the meaning of conditional arising."

Another enumeration is that imputed form, that is, the dependent nature, permanently and constantly lacks the imaginary nature, that is, the two natures of subject and object. [273b] [This lack or] emptiness is the form of reality, the consummate nature. This[30] statement, *emptiness is form*, indicates that both the dependent and the consummate are identical because emptiness, the consummate nature, and form, the dependent nature, are determined to be identical. Therefore, it is just said that emptiness is form.

Having stated their identity from a positive standpoint, it is also stated from a negative standpoint. *Emptiness is not other than form* refutes their difference. Because it is thoroughly established as unchanging and unmistaken, it is consummate. Because it is not made by potencies upon the conjunction of causes and conditions, it is unconditioned. Duality, which is other than that, is not established. Because its continuum is not severed, it is permanent. It is the dharmakāya of the Mahāmuni [Buddha]; it exists ultimately.[31] It alone is the ultimate truth; thus it is said to be nirvāṇa, having the character of nonobscuration. There is the famous statement that if this were not so,[32] then all undertakings become meaningless.

How can those who assert that the nature of the dharmakāya as it was set forth[33] [above] understand it to exist ultimately,[34] when it is [in fact] dependent? The self and so forth that are completely imagined [to exist] by the non-Buddhists (*tīrthika*) are either permanent or momentary. If [one holds] the first position [i.e., that the self is permanent], how could there be particularities in the system of non-Buddhists such as the Vedān-

[30] Derge reads *'di* instead of *'dis*.

[31] Peking reads instead *yod pa ma yin no*, "it does not exist ultimately."

[32] Peking reads *de la ma yin* instead of *de lta ma yin*.

[33] Derge reads *ji skad bstan pa'i*; Peking reads *ji ltar bshad pa'i*.

[34] Derge reads *yod ces bya ba de*; Peking reads *yod bya pa de go*.

tins? The *Candrapradīpasamādhi* (Moon Lamp Samādhi) says, "All phenomena are always empty of their own entity. Children of the Conqueror destroy true existence. All existence is empty in all ways. The trifling emptiness of the non-Buddhists. . . ." This is to be understood to ascribe faults to the non-Buddhists. According to the second position [i.e., that the self is momentary], at a given time the prior moment is the cause of the subsequent moment. Because it has already been explained earlier that this has the fault of [the prior moment and later moment existing both at] the same time and at different times, it will not be discussed.

Such statements as "Whatever is one alone is the highest truth" [274a] is a case of indirect speech pertaining to entrance [into the teaching] (*avatāraṇābhisaṃdhi*)[35] for those who have a strong desire for nirvāṇa. In that way, all of those are dispelled by the statement in the *Akṣayamatinirdeśa*: "But if conditioned phenomena do not exist, then, what is it that when refuted makes nirvāṇa true?" It also says in the *Pañcaviṃśatisāhasrikāprajñāpāramitā* (Perfection of Wisdom in 25,000 Stanzas) and so on, "I say that even the complete and perfect Buddha is like an illusion and a dream. Nirvāṇa is also like an illusion and a dream. But if there is some phenomenon that surpasses nirvāṇa, it also is like an illusion and a dream." How undertakings become meaningful [although everything is empty] will be set forth below.

But if it is not asserted that the wisdom of the nonduality of object and subject ultimately exists, why is it not nonexistent? It is not, because it is asserted to be dependently arisen conventionally and because it has passed beyond being ultimately existent or nonexistent. Existence is overcome. The conception of nonexistence, the view that nothing exists in that way, is the extreme of annihilation; father does not exist, mother does not exist, this world does not exist, the next world does not exist, the fructifying of auspicious and faulty actions does not exist. If such deprecating characterizations of the truths, the jewels, and so forth are sinful, what is the appropriate view in the system of the exceedingly pure

[35] The four *abhisaṃdhi* and the four *abhiprāya* are listed in *Mahāyānasūtrālaṃkāra* 12.16–18. For the Sanskrit, see Swami Dwarika Das Shastri, ed., *Mahāyānasūtrālaṃkāra by Ārya Asaṅga*, Bauddha Bharati series, no. 19 (Varanasi: Bauddha Bharati, 1985), pp. 79–80. The most sophisticated work on the questions of intention and implication in Buddhist hermeneutics has been done by D. Seyfort Ruegg. See especially his "Allusiveness and Obliqueness in Buddhist Texts: *Saṃdhā, Saṃdhi, Saṃdhyā*, and *Abhisaṃdhi*," in Colette Caillat, ed., *Dialectes dan les littératures Indo-aryennes* (Paris: Collège de France, Institut de Civilisation Indienne, 1989), pp. 295–327; "Purport, Implicature, and Presupposition: Sanskrit *Abhiprāya* and Tibetan *Dgoṅs pa/dgoṅs gźi* as Hermeneutical Concepts, " *Journal of Indian Philosophy* 13 (1985): 309–25; and "An Indian Source for the Tibetan Hermeneutical Term *Dgoṅs gźi* 'Internal Ground,'" *Journal of Indian Philosophy* 16 (1988): 1–4. See also Michael Broido, "*Abhiprāya* and Intention in Tibetan Linguistics," *Journal of Indian Philosophy* 12 (1984): 1–33.

Mādhyamikas? The *Ratnāvalī* (Garland of Jewels) [1.55] says in response, "Having thought a mirage to be water and then having gone there, it would simply be stupid to hold that 'Water does not exist.'" And [1.60], "Those who rely on enlightenment have no nihilistic thought, assertion, or behavior. How can they be considered nihilists?"[36]

Objection: Because existence is refuted, is nonexistence not entailed? If nonexistence is refuted, why is existence not entailed? If those who assert that the knowledge of nonduality ultimately exists apprehend with their consciousnesses the operation of different causes, [274b] how is this nondual? Furthermore, if it is not held to be ultimately existent, how can it be omniscient? This fault of yours is similar [to the non-Buddhists'].

Answer: It is not the case. Not seeing ultimate existence is seeing reality; not seeing water in a mirage is not a case of being endowed with ignorance. As it is said, "Not seeing form is seeing form." And the *Samādhirāja* (King of Samādhis) says, "Not seeing anything is seeing all phenomena." In the same way, it is taught that the aggregates, from feeling to consciousness, like form, are, in brief, empty of their own entity. Thus, it is to be understood in this way: feeling is emptiness, emptiness is feeling. Emptiness is not other than feeling, feeling is not other than emptiness. This is to be applied in the same way to discrimination and so forth.

Having set forth that the aggregates are empty of their own entity, it is set forth also concerning the sources and constituents. It says, *It is thus, Śāriputra. . . . It is thus* means like the aggregates. *All phenomena* are the sources and constituents. "Empty of their own entity" is affixed. Having set forth that [all phenomena] are to be seen to be empty of their own entity, [the sūtra] sets forth that they are to be seen to be empty of defining characteristic. Therefore, it says, *without defining characteristic.* A defining characteristic is that which defines or that which is defined. Thus, the general defining characteristic of the form aggregate is that which is suitable as form. Therefore, it is form. The general defining characteristic of the feeling aggregate is experience. Therefore, it is feeling.

[36] The Tibetan translations of these two passages from the *Ratnāvalī* here in Vimalamitra's commentary differ markedly from the canonical Tibetan text edited by Michael Hahn. For 1.55, Vimalamitra's text reads *smig* (Derge mistakenly reads *smin*) *rgyu las ni chuo' zhes | chu yi blo yis der song nas | ci sde chu de med do zhes | 'dzin pa de ni rmongs pa nyid.* Hahn's edition reads *smig rgyu la ni 'di chu zhes | bsam de de ni song ba las | gal te chu de med do zhes | 'dzin pa de ni blun pa nyid.* (I have changed Hahn's transliterations, e.g., *źes* to *zhes*, for the sake of consistency.) For 1.60, Vimalamitra's text reads *gang la med par 'dod pa la | byang chub brten* (Peking reads *rten*) *phyir sems med cing | khas len med dang spyod med dang | de la ji ltar med par shes.* Hahn's edition reads *gang dag don gyis med nyid du | dam mi 'cha' zhing mi spyod pa | byang chub rten phyir sems med na | de dag ji ltar med par bshad.* For the edited Tibetan text and the available Sanskrit, see Michael Hahn, *Nāgārjuna's Ratnāvalī*, vol. 1, *The Basic Texts (Sanskirt, Tibetan, Chinese)* (Bonn: Indica et Tibetica Verlag, 1982), pp. 22–25.

Question: What are the particularities of this [general defining characteristic] apart from[37] [the object's] own entity?

Answer: Particularities are constituted by specific and general defining characteristics. The specific defining characteristic is [the object's] own entity; that which is the unique entity of blue, and so forth. All phenomena of the aggregates, the sources, and the constituents lack those general defining characteristics. Therefore, they are without defining characteristic. The very fact that they are without characteristic also refutes that they [have] their own entity. Therefore,[38] it is not necessary to dwell on it [further].

Question: If all phenomena [275a] are empty and without characteristic, how are they produced in accordance with their own conditions and how do they cease through the cessation of their own conditions?

Answer: They are constructed by the conditions of ignorance in that way. The branches of mundane existence, such as "consciousness," are created by the conditions of conditioned [action] and conditioned [action] is ended by putting an end to ignorance. By ending conditioned [action], the branches of mundane existence end, "consciousness ends," and so on. [The sūtra] is teaching that those [cessations] do not exist in this perfection of wisdom. Therefore, it says *unproduced, unceased.*

Question: If that is the case, then how [among] the four truths for the noble, are the thoroughly afflicted [i.e., suffering and origin] as well as the completely pure [i.e., cessation and path], [both of which] involve cause and effect, possible?

Answer: [The sūtra] says *stainless and not stainless.*[39] Because they lack an own entity that is stained by afflictions, all phenomena are *stainless*. Because they are without purity from the standpoint of the elimination of stains, they are said to be *not stainless* because all phenomena are naturally clear light.

Question: If that is the case, how do faults diminish through abiding spontaneously and signlessly so as to abandon the fault of signs on the Immovable stage [the eighth bodhisattva stage]? How is it feasible that earlier [on the path] the afflictions of the bad realms, utter obscuration, and so on were abandoned?

Answer: [The sūtra] says *undiminished*; here [diminished] is seen [to mean] "[by] faults." Similarly, on the three [pure stages], such as the ninth stage, the individual correct knowledge, the great superknowledge (*abhijñā*), and the wisdom of nonobstruction are attained in order on

[37] Derge reads *la* rather than *las*, in which case the line would read, "What particularities does an entity have?"

[38] Derge adds *ngo bos* here.

[39] Peking reads *dri ma dang bral ba* rather than *dri ma dang bral ba med pa*.

[each] stage. Therefore, [the sūtra] says *unfilled* in order to indicate that there is no increase due to good qualities. Here, "by good qualities" is to be understood[40] because this is what is said in the *Ratnakaraṇḍaka Sūtra*.

Question: Why are there only eight aspects and why are they set forth in that order?

Answer: What is explained here is the heart of the perfection of wisdom; the heart is the highest and the primary among the other parts. The primary meaning of the perfection of wisdom [275b] is the three doors of liberation, such as emptiness. These eight aspects are included in those [three]. Those aspects are ordered here in this way: emptiness and without defining characteristic are [included] in the samādhi on emptiness; the four in the middle, the refutations of production, cessation, affliction, and purity, are the samādhi of signlessness; and the last two are the samādhi of wishlessness.[41] It is wishless because it puts an end to both wishing for the abandonment of faults and the attainment of good qualities.

Now, in order to set forth the effect of viewing by means of those aspects [just] set forth, it says, *Therefore, at that time. Therefore* means to view via the aspects spoken. *At that time* means at that time. It refers to [the time at which] "In order actually to see emptiness, form is not actually seen," that is, [the time at which] to see no phenomenon is to see emptiness. *No form*, and so on teaches these refutations of the aggregates, sources, and constituents. Regarding that, from *no form* to *no consciousness* at the end refutes the aggregates. Beginning with *no eye* through *no phenomena* refutes the sources. The term *from the eye constituent* implicitly sets forth the [other] fifteen [constituents], the form constituent, the eye consciousness constituent, and so on. Because they are last, the *mental constituent* and the *mental consciousness constituent* [are mentioned explicitly]. In this way, without defining characteristic, unproduced, unceased, and so on apply to everything, no form, and so on.

Questions: But if the aggregates, sources, and constituents do not occur in emptiness, signlessness, and so forth, then how does conditioned [action] arise by the cause of ignorance and how do conditioned [actions] cease through the cessation of ignorance? In the same way, how are the twelve branches [of dependent arising] produced from their own conditions and since the conditions have ceased, how can one say they are negated?

Answer: That is true. [276a] These exist conventionally; they do not exist in emptiness, without defining characteristic, and so on. It says,

[40] Derge reads *khong nas dbyung par bya*; Peking reads *kho na sbyar bar*.

[41] Derge reads *smon pa'i ting nge 'dzin* rather than *smon pa med pa'i ting nge 'dzin*.

Ignorance does not exist. The extinction of ignorance does not exist. The term *up to* implicitly indicates conditioned [action], and so forth. Aging and death do not exist. Because they do not exist, [their] extinction does not exist.

Question: But if the branches and their extinction do not occur ultimately, then how do the noble see that suffering and so forth are just true? It is not proper that what the noble see to be true is wrong. If those are true, what is the status of the branches and their extinction?

Answer: Therefore, with respect to the emptiness of own entity, and so on, it says, *suffering*, and so on. When suffering does not exist because its own entity is not produced, how can its cause, origin, exist? Therefore, it says *cessation* and the path that serves as a method for that cessation is also utterly nonexistent. In order to abandon the fault that is the nature of signs, it sets forth that even the own entity of wisdom is not ultimately established. It says, *no wisdom*. Some editions say, *no nescience*, which means this: if wisdom does not exist because emptiness is free from the afflicted faults of signs, then one might think that nescience, whose defining characteristic is obscuration, exists. It says *no nescience* [because] how could there be [something] whose nature was the nescience of emptiness?[42] Similarly, it sets forth that if the qualities such as the correct specific knowledge, the powers, the fearlessnesses, and the nature of what attains them do not exist, then it is not correct to speak of attainment; it says, *no attainment*. Having negated the conception of attainment in that way, the conception of its opposite, nonattainment, is negated. Therefore it says, *no nonattainment*.[43] One must understand that this sets forth the profound meaning that is beyond wisdom and nescience and attainment and nonattainment and that is free from the extremes of superimposition and derogation.

Thus, because of the aspects set forth above, [276b] no qualities are attained in the perfection of wisdom in this way. Therefore, based on and completely based on being endowed thoroughly with the path of meditation, one enters and abides with special effort in the characteristic that is set forth as the so-called perfection of wisdom, that to which one aspires for the sake of enlightenment, which is strongly desired, and which is contemplated. In enlightenment no qualities whatsoever are consummated. As the *Candrapradīpasamādhi* says, "The Bhagavan sets forth enlightenment's own entity; it lacks even very subtle qualities. What is called 'very subtle' does not even exist." The *Vairocanābhisaṃbodhi*

[42] Peking reads *rang gi ngo bo stong pa nyid shes pa la 'di ga la srid.*

[43] Peking makes the same point more succinctly: *de ltar thob pa'i rnam par rtog pa dgag pa'i phyir ma thob pa med do zhes gsungs so.*

says, "Guhyapati, even very subtle qualities do not exist and are not observed. Therefore, it is called unsurpassed, perfect, complete enlightenment."

Question: But if the perfection of wisdom and unsurpassed, perfect, complete enlightenment have no qualities whatsoever, then the wisdom that comes about through eliminating qualities that have the character of fault also does not exist at all. If the attainment of the desired characteristic of good qualities does not exist, why do [bodhisattvas], beginning with [the wish for] enlightenment, depend on and abide in the perfection of wisdom? One enters into something to the extent that one has a prior hope; they all enter [the path] in order to abandon the faults they do not wish for and in order to attain the good qualities they wish for. Since anything is empty of its own entity, if all phenomena are unobservable, who is it that enters that? Why do they enter? What is the fruition of entering?

Answer: It says *because their minds are without obstruction*, and so on. Through being stopped from complete understanding of the meaning of reality, just as it is, the mind is obstructed and completely impeded. Therefore, the mind is obstructed. There are the twenty-two obscurations (*saṃmoha*), such as attachment to persons and phenomena, and eleven discordant assumptions of bad states (*dauṣṭhulya*). In order to abandon those, there are antidotes, whose purpose is destruction. They are, in order, the eleven stages, such as the Joyous. [277a] As the *Bhūmi-avatāra* [?] says: "Through collecting the eleven branches, there are eleven stages, such as the Joyous. The [twenty-] two obscurations and [ten plus] one assumptions of bad states, the discordant class, are different." Similarly, the *Saṃdhinirmocana* says:

> From that, on the first, there is the obscuration of adherence to persons and phenomena and the obscuration of the afflictions of the bad transmigrations and the discordant class of assuming their bad states. On the second, there is the obscuration of the errors that are subtle infractions and the obscuration in the various types of karmic movements and the discordant class of assuming their bad states. On the third, there is the obscuration of desire for the realm of desire and the obscuration of not fully retaining what has been heard and the discordant class of assuming their bad states. On the fourth, there is the obscuration of craving for absorption and the obscuration of craving for the doctrine and the discordant[44] class of assuming their bad states. On the fifth, there is the obscuration of directing the mind to turn away from or approach saṃsāra and the obscuration of directing the mind to turn away from or approach nirvāṇa and the discordant class of assuming their bad states. On the

[44] Peking reads *ni mthun phyogs* instead of *mi mthun phyogs*.

> sixth, there is the obscuration to making manifest[45] the arising of conditioned things and the obscuration of the arising of multiple signs and the discordant class of assuming their bad state. On the seventh, there is the obscuration of the arising of subtle signs and obscuration concerning the method of directing the mind to signlessness and the discordant class of assuming their bad states. On the eighth, there is the obscuration of fixating on signlessness and the obscuration in power over signs and the discordant class of assuming their bad states. On the ninth, there is the obscuration in the power to retain the limitless teachings of the doctrine, the limitless words and letters of the doctrine, and increasing wisdom and courage and the obscuration in power over courage [277b] and the discordant class of assuming their bad states. On the tenth, there is the obscuration to the great superknowledges and the obscuration of entering into subtle secrets and the discordant class of assuming their bad states. On the stage of a buddha, there is the obscuration that is extremely subtle attachment to all objects of knowledge and the obscuration of obstruction and the discordant class of assuming their bad states.[46]

It is taught that because those do not exist, one who abides[47] in the perfection of wisdom is without fear, that is, without fright. One who abides in that which is other than the perfection of wisdom is frightened by error; error is frightening.[48] This is taught: mental error is entry. As the *Pramāṇavarttika* (2.192cd) teaches, "In order to abandon erroneous superimpositions, the liberator makes effort, although they do not exist."

Without error, there is no entry; as it is taught in the *Daśabhūmika* (Ten Stages), "When, on the eighth stage, one attains forbearance of the nonproduction of phenomena, [it is like] when a person awakens from a dream of being carried away by water; [he understands] that his great efforts to free himself from the water were mistaken. Nirvāṇa is just like that example." Here also, to abide in the perfection of wisdom is to pass beyond error, whatever one's obscuration is; *completely gone* [means] passed beyond error. *Nirvāṇa* is the cessation of thought. *Gone to the end* [means] final. As the *Daśabhūmika* says, "Because thought that is to be abandoned by [the path of] meditation is completely abandoned, it is the completion of purity; there is no thought to be abandoned beyond that." Because nirvāṇa is the end or [because] it is the nature of the mind[49] that has gone to end, it says that [*goes to the completion of nirvāṇa*]. Therefore, because they have passed beyond sorrow as well as gone to the

45 Peking reads *byung ba mngon*; Derge reads *'byung ba mgnon sum*.

46 For another English translation, with facing Derge edition, see Powers, *Wisdom of Buddha*, pp. 229–33.

47 Peking reads *gsas* rather than *gnas*.

48 Derge reads *phyin ci log las 'jigs pa yin*.

49 Derge omits *sems*.

completion of nirvāṇa, *they have passed beyond sorrow and gone to the completion of nirvāṇa*; because they depend on and abide in the perfection of wisdom, [278a] bodhisattvas enter it. This great abandonment indicates the cause of entry for that purpose because of entering for that purpose.

The three times, and so on are indicated for the purpose of the two, the great mind, due to being supreme among all sentient beings, and great realization. The three times are the past, future, and present. All the buddhas who abide in those are buddhas because they are endowed with special awareness. Because they are both all and buddhas, it says *all buddhas.* As the *Vairocanābhisaṃbodhi* says, "Having achieved the ten stages, the aspect of power is attained. He who knows all phenomena here to be empty and like illusions and who knows all sentient beings is called a buddha."

Regarding *the perfection of wisdom*, the wisdom of the Tathāgata is the nature that is true of everything that arises; it refers to that which is called the knowledge of all aspects. Regarding *relying on the perfection of wisdom*, this is before the time of perfect, complete enlightenment. Therefore, this knowledge of all aspects is to be seen as the uninterrupted samādhi [at the end of the tenth stage]. As the *Pañcaviṃśatisāhasrikāprajñāpāramitā* and its instructions, the *Abhisamayālaṃkāra* [5.38–39] say, "Buddhahood is attained without interruption. The uninterrupted samādhi is the knowledge of all aspects. Its object is nonexistence. Mindfulness is held to be the lord. This aspect is peace;[50] its defining characteristic is the lack of defining characteristic."[51]

[The sūtra says] *unsurpassed* because there is no attainment, object, or achievement that is higher than that. *Perfect* [means] nonmistaken. It says *equal* because it is of the same defining characteristic in that it is without defining characteristic. *Enlightenment* is realization. *Manifestly* [means] direct perception. *Equally enlightened* [means] completely enlightened. [278b] As the *Pañcaviṃśatisāhasrikāprajñāpāramitā* says:

> "Bhagavan, what is unsurpassed, perfect, complete enlightenment like?" The Bhagavan said, "Subhuti, unsurpassed, perfect, complete enlightenment is just like the reality of all phenomena." Subhuti said, "Bhagavan, how is the reality of all phenomena unsurpassed, perfect, complete enlightenment?" "Subhuti, as

[50] Derge mistakenly reads *bzhi pa.*

[51] The passage as it appears here varies only slightly from that in the editon of Stcherbatsky and Obermiller, with the exception of the last line. Their edition reads: *sangs rgyas nyid kyi bar med de | bar ched med pa'i ting nge 'dzin | de ni rnam pa kun mkhyen nyid || 'di yi dmigs pa dngos med de | bdag po dran pa yin bar bzhed | rnam pa zhi nyid 'di la ni | rab tu smra rnams rgyud mar rgol.* See Th. Stcherbatsky and E. Obermiller, eds. *Abhisamayālaṅkāra-Prajñāpāramitā-Upadeśa-Śāstra* (Osnabruck: Biblio Verlag, 1970), p. 58.

> is [everything from] the reality of form to the reality of nirvāṇa, so is unsurpassed, perfect, complete enlightenment."

Regarding that, the term *unsurpassed* [implies] the greatness of mind due to being supreme among sentient beings. The rest of that is the great realization. Earlier, on the occasion of a bodhisattva, those [i.e., the three greatnesses] were taken to mind, that is, for the purpose of the three greatnesses, one entered the perfection of wisdom. Therefore, it says "for the purpose of the three." At the time of completion, the former indicates the marvelous fruitional state of abandonment, and the latter two indicate the marvelous fruitional realization. Just as a king makes gifts in order to procure land and in the end, the effect is that he receives the land, so one relies on the perfection of wisdom in order to be free from error and in order to attain realization.

In order to indicate that the perfection of wisdom itself is a mantra, it says, *Therefore, Śāriputra*, and so on. The definition of the perfection of wisdom has already been set forth. A secret mantra [is so-called] because of being a mind [manas] and because of being a protector [*traya*]. Those[52] two meanings will be clarified by subsequent words. It is great because of being pervasive. Pervasion [means] pervasion of time and pervasion of place; in this way, it [means] the unmistaken entry into all phenomena and all times. This indicates specifically that this is other [i.e., superior to] mantras that are used for Īśvara, and so on. As the *Vairocanābhisaṃbodhi* says [279a]:

> The state of dependent arising is far beyond the three times. The seen and unseen[53] fruition exists in the body, speech, and mind. It is explained by the world that fruition is calculated [to occur] in one aeon. It is explained by the complete Buddha that the fruition of secret mantra is beyond aeons. The samādhi of the buddhas, the great sages, and the conquerors' children has abandoned signs and is pure. Those of the world have signs. The fruit ripens here; they attain the effect through karma. When they attain siddhis karma is overturned because the mind lacks its own entity and because they abandon causes[54] and effects. Free from birth due to karma,[55] birth is like the sky.

Because they know and understand this, or they achieve the desired feat, [the sūtra says] *knowledge*. Because it is both knowledge and also great, it is *great knowledge*. Because the great knowledge itself is a secret mantra, [it says] *the secret mantra of great knowledge*. Therefore, because

[52] Derge reads *de gnyis*; Peking reads *de nyid*.

[53] Peking reads *mthong dang ma mthong*; Derge reads *mthong nas ma mthong*.

[54] Peking reads *rgyun*.

[55] Peking reads *las kyi skye ba rnams las thar*; Derge reads *las kyi skye ba rnams las kyang*.

there is nothing that is superior to this, it is the *unsurpassed secret mantra*. Because there is nothing that is equal or similar to it, the *unequaled* is the sky. Because it is equal to that, it is *equal to the unequaled*. In the *Bodhisattvapiṭaka*, the Bhagavan himself uses the words "equal to the unequaled." Also, it is taught in the *Tathāgatācintyaguhya* (Inconceivable Secret of the Tathāgata): "How does one exemplify the Buddha and the teaching? The Conqueror declared that nothing approximates the Buddha; there is one example of what is equal to the Buddha's teaching. He taught that it is the measureless realm of the sky." Because it is equal to the sky, it is to be seen as pervasive, unobstructed, and uninterrupted. These set forth the meaning of mind [279b] [and] the meaning of protection [in the term *mantra*]. It says, *all suffering*. It thoroughly pacifies, that is, severs the continuum of all suffering, which has the character of the suffering of conditioning, of change, and of suffering; it is the secret *mantra that pacifies all suffering*. Having set forth the meaning of the etymology of secret mantra, the meaning of the etymology of that which is expressed secretly is set forth. Therefore, it says, *it is true because it is not mistaken*. That which is true is suchness, perfect exactly as it is. That which is perfect exactly as it is is not mistaken. Therefore, it is correct for it to be the mantra of the perfection of wisdom.

To set forth this statement: Persons of dull faculties to whom anything [tantric] is taught are not able to see it. For them, it is as if it were taught secretly. They take the perfection of wisdom to be like a secret mantra. The etymology of secret mantra is "that which is explained secretly." This is the context of this statement. Or, because it is the protector of that which abides in the mind, it is a secret mantra. By the power[56] of the perfection of wisdom, it is taken to mind uninterruptedly. Because it is suitable, it is correct. Because it is suitable, it is to be known; it is to be retained.

Like that [means] that it is to be trained in in the manner in which it was set forth. *Then* [means] at that time without interruption. *Samādhi* was explained earlier. *Having risen* [means] having mentally relinquished. Saying *well done* is a gift to the expositor and [indicates] agreement with the explanation. The nature of the gift of saying *well done* is *child of good lineage, well done, well done*. It is repeated twice in order to [indicate] joy or great joy. *It is like that* indicates agreement with the explanation. It is like that, it is not otherwise. [280a] Why? It says, *one should train in the perfection of wisdom*. What is it like? It says, *it is just as you have taught it*. The words are, "one should train in what does not contradict your teaching." The Bhagavan, having indicated his own agreement with the teaching of the noble Avalokiteśvara in that way,

[56] Derge reads *gus pa* rather than *nus pa*.

indicates that "Even the other tathāgatas rejoice in what you have taught." Therefore, it says, *Even the tathāgatas admire this. Admire* [means] that it is not to be doubted and that the meaning of its purpose is to be determined. The tathāgatas' admiration of such an explanation makes it undoubtable. The agreement and the admiration indicate that it is proper that the tathāgatas rejoice in the explanation of this.

Therefore, it says, *the Bhagavan having spoken that speech. That speech* is [everything] from Śāriputra's question to *even the tathāgatas admire this. Having spoken* [means] having been spoken by the Tathāgata. The noble Avalokiteśvara explained this. However, it is the word of the Tathāgata; it was blessed by the Tathāgata in this way. If everything that is explained [in other sūtras] even by śrāvakas is the word of the Tathāgata, what need is there to consider what was explained by the likes of the noble Avalokiteśvara, Samantabhadra, and Mañjuśrī, who abide perfectly in buddhahood? I have already explained the meaning of this earlier.

Admiration is stated with reference to the admiration and joy in properly hearing and explaining the meaning of what the *Heart of the Perfection of Wisdom* is specifically like, [that meaning being] excellent because it is the foremost among the meanings that are set forth in the *Śatasāhasrikāprajñāpāramitā.* [280b] It refers to Śāriputra, the noble Avalokiteśvara, and so on. According to some, it refers also to the Bhagavan; at that time, it caused joy[57] [in the Buddha to see] the disciples apprehending the primary meaning of the perfection of wisdom exactly as it is.

Everyone gathered refers to those gathered in admiration and praise. Because all the bodhisattvas, monks, laymen, and laywomen were sitting there, it says, *all those surrounding*. The *gods* are the four royal lineages, and so on. *Humans* are well known. *Demigods* are so-called because they gave up the beer that arose when the ocean of milk was churned. They are also [called] *daitya*s and *danava*s. The *gandharva*s[58] are the divine musicians and protectors of the country, and so forth. The *world* is the gods, humans, demigods, and *gandharva*s who are seated with the gods and so forth. Because they [the gods] are foremost, they are named first. Because it disintegrates, it is the *world*; its nature is the five aggregates. *The word of the Buddha* is the entity of the explanation itself. *Praised* means that they had manifest joy and were grasped by joy.

Through the merit I have attained by opening the heart of the perfection of wisdom, may the world definitely possess the perfection of wisdom.

[57] Derge reads *rgyud* rather than *rgyu*.

[58] Derge mistakenly reads *dri ba* rather than *dri za*.

The extensive explanation of the *Heart of the Perfection of Wisdom* was made by Vimala in the presence of the assembly of monks at the temple of Tshang pa'i 'byung gnas.

This completes the extensive explanation of the noble *Heart of the Perfection of Wisdom* by the Indian abbot Vimalamitra. It was translated and revised by the Indian abbot Vimalamitra himself and by great Tibetan redactors and translators, such as the monks Nam mkha' and Ye shes snying po.

Atiśa's[59] Explanation of the *Heart Sūtra*

Homage to the Perfection of Wisdom

When all of the topics of the second wheel of doctrine [which comprises the Perfection of Wisdom sūtras] spoken by the Sugata are summarized, there are two: the topic of realizations and the topic of the essence. The three extensive and intermediate [length] sūtras[60] primarily set forth the realizations in terms of three persons [those with interest in extensive, intermediate, and brief expositions]. Such sūtras as the *Saptaśatikā* (Perfection of Wisdom in 700 Stanzas) primarily teach the topic of the essence. [In the sūtras of the second wheel] the realizations on the path [and] the objects of wisdom are primarily set forth. The three extensive and intermediate primarily set forth the realizations and set forth the essence implicitly. Sūtras such as the *Saptaśatikā* primarily set forth the topic of the essence and ancillarily set forth the realizations. Here [in the *Heart Sūtra*], the topic of the essence is set forth.

According to Vimalamitra, the entire meaning of this sūtra is set forth through eight topics. He sets forth the body [of the text] with statements such as, "eight topics: the opening. . . ." Such masters as Dignāga [313b] explain the meaning of the sūtra differently: there is the cause from which the sūtra arises and the actual sūtra. The first has two parts: the opening and the setting. The difference between the two is that [one] is the condition for the arising of the words and [the other] is the cause for the arising of the sūtra. The beginning and the end are the opening. The setting has

[59] *Jo bo rjes mdzad ba* is absent in the Derge.

[60] The three extensive sūtras are presumably the Perfection of Wisdom in 100,000, 25,000, and 18,000 stanzas (the *Śatasāhasrikāprajñāpāramitā*, the *Pañcaviṃśatisāhasrikāprajñāpāramitā*, and the *Aṣṭadaśasāhasrikāprajñāpāramitā*). The three intermediate sūtras are the Perfection of Wisdom in 10,000 Stanzas (*Daśasāhasrikāprajñāpāramitā*), the Perfection of Wisdom in 8,000 Stanzas (*Aṣṭasāhasrikāprajñāpāramitā*), and the Condensed Verses (*Ratnaguṇasaṃcayagāthā*).

two parts: the common and special setting. What distinguishes these two is that [the first] is common to all sūtras and [the latter] exists in this sūtra and not in others. The common setting has four components: the time, the teacher, the location, and the audience. The special setting has two parts: the primary one [the Buddha] and the audience entering into samādhi. That is the summary. The meaning of the purpose[61] (*prayojana*) [of saying, "Thus did I hear at one time"] is to make the compiler himself into a reliable person. If he says, "Just at that time, I heard this teacher [teach] this audience in this place" with witnesses [i.e., the monks and bodhisattvas] and with understanding of the meaning, then the compiler will be believed and [people] will say, "Well, this explanation of his is true." It is thus: even in the world what someone says is understood to be true through a careful examination of the witness and the meaning. As the master Dignāga says, "In order to establish his validity, the compiler indicates the teacher, the audience, the witness, the time, and the place as factors [causing] the faithful to enter [the teaching], just as in the world, if someone has a witness indicating the place and the time, he is a reliable person." The meaning of these words and their relevance are clear. Therefore, it is taught in Dignaga's *Aṣṭasāhasrikāpīṇḍārtha* that all sūtras are to be so explained. The rest is agreed upon.

Here, Vimalamitra refutes that. In order to clarify [our] position, first [I will set forth his] refutation [of Dignāga]. There are two faults, that of inability and that of not being a witness. Inability is said to be the inability to establish the purpose. One says that ["Thus did I hear."] to establish oneself as a reliable person as a condition for the entry of followers of faith [to accept the sūtra] now. The purpose of having a witness is that if they develop doubts later, they meet with him. In that case, those who have attained magical powers and [314a] the superknowledges cannot determine the meaning of the sūtra [because they were not physically present]. Also, some of the witnesses have passed into nirvāṇa [i.e., died] and some abide elsewhere: "Those who desire to hear the jewel of the profound and limitless sūtras go everywhere for the welfare of all the worldly realms." Some are here but we do not have the fortune to see them, like Mahākaśyapa [who is said to be still living inside a mountain].

The second fault is that even though one is able to fulfill the purpose, there may be no witness. Regarding having a witness, if one asserts that having a witness means indicating the names of the audience, "so and so," then having a witness depends on indicating actual names such as

[61] For a discussion of this term, see F. Th. Stcherbatsky, *Buddhist Logic*, vol. 2 (New York: Dover, 1962), pp. 1–2; and Michael M. Broido, "A Note on Dgos-'brel," *Journal of the Tibet Society* 3 (1983): 5–19.

Subhūti. If that is the case, then how, says [Vimalamitra], can there be a witness [in a sūtra] in which there are no names of the audience, as in this sūtra?

Therefore, it is explained in this way [by Vimalamitra]. The statement, "Thus did I hear," serves as an opening prior to the explanation of the sūtra together with the setting of what occurred before. This indicates that it was heard correctly without addition or ellision so that the audience will direct their ears well to the compiler, knowing that he set it forth without error.

Now we turn to the situation that serves as the context on which the arising of the sūtra depends [i.e., the setting]. That begins with *At one time the Bhagavan*. One might wonder about what kind of persons gathered to be included in the teaching of a sūtra that arose under such circumstances. Thus, [it says] *a great assembly of monks*, and so on; the congregation of those who have the good fortune to hear the teaching are called "those gathered to be included in the teaching."

What is the special setting? *At that time . . .* indicates the entry into samādhi of both the primary one and the audience. Then what is the sūtra that begins with those two settings serving as the cause? The teaching of both the question and answer, indicated by *Then . . . should practice*. [314b] In order to overcome the wrong ideas of the audience, who wonder whether it is correct that this is explained by Avalokiteśvara and is not spoken by the Tathāgata, Śākyamuni himself agrees with it [at the end]. Someone might wonder, "Because [Śākyamuni] became enlightened at the time of the increase of the five degenerations, his light and so forth is less than that of other buddhas. Therefore, is he correct [when he admires Avalokiteśvara's teaching]? [In answer, the sūtra] says *Even the tathāgatas admire this*, thereby implying that they think it is exactly like that. These two [the Buddha and the tathāgatas] are in agreement. Furthermore, because it says *Even the tathāgatas*, [this agreement] also pertains to the admiration. Thus, it says *Then, the Bhagavan*, and so on regarding his admiration, having derived joy from the explanation of the precious sūtra. That is just an abbreviation of the general meaning.

The question is *Then [by the power of the Buddha, the venerable Śāriputra]. . . .* With respect to the meaning of this, the basis, the person is whoever wishes [to practice], that is, a bodhisattva who has generated the aspiration [to buddhahood], without [further] specification.[62] *How one should practice* is the path of accumulation, the path of preparation, the path of vision, the path of meditation, and the path of no more learning. The nature of these five are known as thought, preparation, actualization, achievement, and realization. The instruction on that is this: how

[62] Derge reads *bye brag sgrub pa* rather than *bye brag med pa*.

should a person with the [Mahāyāna] lineage who has created the aspiration to enlightenment practice the five paths? This is the meaning of the question.

The answer is in eleven parts by way of a teaching that divides the path into five parts. [The eleven are divided into] two in terms of those of dull faculties and those of sharp faculties. When those of dull faculties train in the five paths, it is from the perspective of fully teaching them all of the characteristics in terms of each of the five paths. When the method for training them in the five paths is divided from that point of view, there are ten. Those of sharp faculties understand with the first indication; for their sake the earlier teaching of the tenfold topic is condensed and taught as the topic of the mantra. Thus, the answer has eleven parts.

In general, both are disciples of sharp faculties, but because there is a difference, they are divided into two. [315a] Here, the teaching for those of dull faculties becomes a secret mantra for others of dull faculties because, although it is not secret, it is as if it were taught secretly. Furthermore, whether something is secret or not secret is a matter of awareness; in fact, there is no difference in what is taught. The Teacher does not have a closed fist. Therefore, here also the explanation of the meaning of the secret mantra itself operates like a secret teaching for the former [i.e., those of dull faculties in the context of the sūtra]. Thus, it fulfills the etymology of secret mantra.

First, with regard to the sūtra, a person who, on the basis of being endowed with the lineage, has created the intention to achieve supreme enlightenment is the person who is the basis for the generation of the path. That is explained by *Śāriputra . . . a son or daughter of good lineage*. This sets forth the person endowed with lineage. *Profound perfection of wisdom* and *who wishes to practice* explain in sequence [1] the object of observation and [2] the creation of the aspirational intention.[63] This is the general teaching that is not differentiated for those of sharp and dull faculties.

The ten answers in terms of those of dull faculties can be aligned implicitly by explaining the four types of objects of observation from the *Saṃdhinirmocana* (Explanation of the Intention): the observation that is insight (*vipaśyanā*), which is a conceptual reflection; the observation that is quiescence (*śamatha*), which is a nonconceptual reflection; the observation of the limit of things; and the observation of the consummate pur-

[63] The intention to achieve enlightenment for the sake of others (*bodhicitta*) has two forms: the aspirational intention (*bodhipraṇidhicitta*), which is the wish to achieve enlightenment, and the practical intention (*bodhiprasthānacitta*), which is actually embarking on the practice of the six perfections in order to fulfill that wish. The distinction is made (among other places) by Śāntideva at *Bodhicaryāvatāra* 1.15–19, where they are compared to the wish to go someplace and actually setting out on the journey.

pose.[64] It should be understood that these four set forth the path of accumulation, the path of preparation, the path of vision, and the path of no more learning, respectively. Here, the path of meditation is not set forth separately because it has no object of observation beyond what is observed in the first three observations. As Maitreyanātha says [at *Abhisamayālaṃkāra* 4.53]: "The path of meditation is the repeated contemplation, comprehension, and ascertainment of [what was seen] on the branches of discernment [i.e., the path of preparation], the path of vision, and the path of meditation."

The observation that is insight, a conceptual reflection, [315b] is indicated by *should view things in this way.* This indicates the wisdom that specifically analyzes the reality that exists on the occasion of the path of accumulation. On the path of vision, all objects of observation are understood to be equal. Therefore, there is no viewing of different types of objects of observation. Here [on the path of accumulation], a variety of aspects, such as emptiness, are adhered to and conceived to be realities. Thought conceives of [objects] as different or various. Thus, because the conceptual wisdom lacks samādhi, it is of the nature of mere insight; it is a mere reflection of the nonconceptual state produced on the path of vision. Therefore, it is called the observation that is insight, a conceptual reflection. Therefore, *should view in that way* indicates that one should individually analyze a variety of aspects. It is explained in the context of the question. With respect to generating the path of accumulation in that way, the discernments (*nirvedhāṅga*), such as heat (*uṣmagata*) [the first of the four levels of the path of preparation], are produced without being interrupted by other consciousnesses. Therefore, the words of the sūtra explain the observation that is quiescence, a nonconceptual reflection, with the very [same phrase]. Regarding the nonconceptual, the consciousnesses of hearing and thinking set forth above were directed outward. Then, the conception of a variety of objects of observation does not conceive [objects] in that way and thought is gathered in one-pointedly. That also lacks the kind of insight produced on the path of vision, which realizes the equality of all phenomena. However, since it has the nature of quiescence, it is the observation that is quiescence, a nonconceptual reflection, as before.

Having explained the two observations in that way, now the third, the observation of the limit of things, is set forth. Things are form, and so forth. Their limit is their nature or reality. The observation of that is the observation of the limit of things. This is the path of vision. It has three parts: the object, the aspect that engages that object, and the fruition seen

[64] See n. 24.

by that aspect. *Those five aggregates also are to be viewed correctly as empty of intrinsic entity*[65] [316a] sets forth the three things: the things, the limit, and the observation of that, as was set forth above. Therefore, the observation on the path of vision is set forth. The meaning of the terms is clear from [Vimalamitra's] commentary. Regarding that observation, if it is asked how one views correctly when one enters into non-mistaken viewing, [the sūtra says] *Form is empty. . . .*

This has three parts: the character of the individual aspects, the determination of the number, and the determination of the order. The determination of the number is the explanation of the meaning of essence [as mentioned at the beginning of the commentary] here. The primary meaning of the essence is the three doors of liberation.[66] The three doors of liberation are in turn included in the eight profound meanings. The emptiness of intrinsic entity of phenomena is the door of liberation emptiness. *Emptiness and without defining characteristic* explain [that phenomena] lack a specific entity and a general entity [respectively]. Because all meanings of emptiness are included in those two perspectives, [the classification of emptiness and without characteristic under the door emptiness] is explained. Signlessness is the lack of causes, and causes are posited as causes in terms of effects. *Unproduced, unceased, stainless, not stainless* [are classified under the door of liberation signlessness] because they include the cause and effect of the thoroughly afflicted and the cause and effect of the completely pure, respectively. Regarding wishlessness, there are two effects that are wished for: the wish to be separated from faults and the wish to be endowed with good qualities. Freedom from these two [wishes] [indicated in the sūtra by *undiminished, unfilled*] is wishlessness. Therefore, the nature of the three doors of liberation is determined to be only the eight negations of the eight objects of negation. That is the determination of the number.

With respect to the determination of the order, in all sūtras the Sugata teaches the door of liberation emptiness first, then signlessness, and finally wishlessness. Here, [the order] is determined in just that [way]. In order to produce the view, deeds, and fruition of a buddha in sequence, the three antidotes to attachment to those three are set forth in sequence. The determination of the number also determines the order. Therefore, the primary subject matter of this sūtra is this eightfold meaning of the profound. [316b] This is explained by Vimalamitra.

Now, with respect to that observation, in order to set forth how the

[65] The text reads *phung po lnga po de dag la yang ngo bo nyid kyis stong par yang yang dag par rjes su bltao'*.

[66] See my *The Heart Sūtra Explained*, pp. 89–93.

subjective appearance—the effect of viewing things from the perspective of these eight aspects—is produced, [it says], *Therefore, Śāriputra, at that time, in emptiness. . . .*[67] *Therefore*: when one views that object of observation via the [eight] aspects stated. *At that time*: at that time of viewing. How does the effect arise? *In emptiness, there is no form*, and so on, that is, in the vision of emptiness, a consciousness is produced that does not observe form, and so on to be real. Therefore, with regard to the object of observation it is indicating that the fruition of the path of vision is the generation of such a consciousness that perceives the emptiness to which it has become accustomed through these eight aspects.

The path of vision having been produced in that way, the path of meditation is produced. Thus, the sūtra teaches, *Therefore, Śāriputra*. This is clear from the commentary [of Vimalamitra]. One might assert that right after that, apart from the *vajra*-like samādhi, the uninterrupted path (*ānantaryamārga*), [the rest of the path of meditation] is not set forth and that the teaching of the great abandonment of the stage of a buddha is the great abandonment of the two obstructions on the path of meditation. In order to make known the connection of that [great abandonment] and the path of meditation, it is set forth after the path of meditation. The abandonment here is a single path [i.e., the path of meditation]. Regarding that, *Their minds are without obstruction and without fear* is easy to understand. In order to set forth the uninterrupted path [the sūtra says] *in dependence on [the perfection of wisdom, all the buddhas] of the three times. All the buddhas* here are buddhas, but they are not perfect, complete buddhas; they are bodhisattvas abiding on the path that is a special tenth stage. It is clearly explained in the commentary that their path is the *vajra*-like samādhi.

Here, the greatness of realization and the greatness of mind are primarily taught in the sūtra; the fact that this causes the uninterrupted [abandonment of obstructions] is taught ancillarily. Having taught the nature of abandonment in that way, in order to indicate the twofold nature of realization, it says *unsurpassed*, and so forth. [317a] There are two: the knowledge of the varieties [of phenomena] and the knowledge of the modes [of being, i.e., emptiness]. They are the greatness of mind and the greatness of realization, therefore, it is put twice [i.e., the sūtra says, literally *fully enlightened into unsurpassed, complete, perfect enlightenment*]. Regarding that, *unsurpassed* indicates the wisdom that is the knowledge of the varieties through the three: object of observation, the cause for the subsequent achievement of that, and unsurpassed attainment of the fruition. By being endowed with these three, one knows all things that are

[67] *Shā ri'i bu de lta bas na de'i tshe stong pa nyid la.* Atiśa seems to add *de'i tshe* to the sūtra.

knowable, like an olive placed in the palm of the hand. *Fully awakened into perfectly equal*[68] *enlightenment* indicates the wisdom that is knowledge of the modes; this is clearly set forth in the commentary.

Thus, for those of dull faculties the mode of training in the five paths is explained well with ten answers: individual answers for the path of accumulation and the path of preparation, three for the path of vision, one for the path of meditation, one for the uninterrupted path [i.e., *vajra*-like samādhi], and three for the stage of buddhahood.

Now, regarding the explanation of the meaning of the mantra, through abbreviating the meaning of the perfection of wisdom for those of sharp faculties [the sūtra says], *Therefore, Śāriputra* . . . ; the meaning of the knowledge of the five paths, the meaning of protection, the benefit of these two, and the explanation of the mantra itself are one answer.

Now, at the time of the question, it said, *How should one practice?* In order to indicate that the answer is complete, it says, *One should practice in that way.*

> This is a good explanation requested by the monk Legs pa shes rab [from] Dīpaṃkaraśrījñāna [Atiśa]. I have written the meaning in a text. Today in this kingdom of Tibet because [people] are attached to the evil system of the past, they still do not understand that excellent instructions are well spoken. Nonetheless, I have written this with munificence and compassion in mind for those endowed with wisdom. May they know the mother of conquerors well and not speak with hatred.

This was translated and revised by the Indian abbot Dīpaṃkaraśrījñāna and the Tibetan translator Tshul khrims rgyal ba.

[68] The text reads *mnyam pa* rather than *rdzogs pa*.

Three

The *Heart Sūtra* as Tantra

> Once the indigenous conception has been isolated, it must be reduced by an objective critique so as to reach the underlying reality. We have very little chance of finding that reality in conscious formulations; a better chance, in unconscious mental structures to which institutions give us access, but a better chance yet, in language.
> —Lévi-Strauss, *Introduction to the Work of Marcel Mauss*

> But if someone wished to say: "There is something common to all these constructions—namely the disjunction of all their common properties"—I should reply: Now you are only playing with words. One might say: "Something runs through the whole thread—namely the continuous overlapping of those fibres."
> —Wittgenstein, *Philosophical Investigations*

In the Sunday crossword puzzle published by the Los Angeles Times Syndicate on October 6, 1991, the clue for a six-letter word at 88 Across read, "Buddhist treatise." The obvious answer, "sūtra," had only five letters. The next choice, "śāstra," required that the term be rendered not as it would probably be in a crossword puzzle, as "shastra" but rather as "sastra," eliding the diacritic. It was only through filling in the letters in the "Down" columns that a professional scholar of Buddhism who had written his master's thesis on the topic was able to discern that 88 Across, "Buddhist treatise," was "tantra." The failure to know the answer may be attributed to the scholar having long ago given up any hope of finding so simple a description of the term as "a Buddhist treatise" which, of course, "tantra" also is.

That the question of the meaning of "tantra" is germane to the study of the *Heart Sūtra* is evident from the fact that in the Peking edition of the Tibetan canon, the *Heart Sūtra* appears in the tantra section, while in the

Derge edition, it appears in both the *prajñāpāramitā* section and the tantra section. It is a sūtra that gives prominence within its short extent to a mantra, a mantra that (at least in the longer version of the sūtra) seems more than a mere appendage, as are the dhāraṇīs at the end of other sūtras. Furthermore, among the Indian commentaries to the *Heart Sūtra*, we find two (whose translation appears in Chapter 4), which offer conflicting renditions of the meaning of the sūtra, settling on opposite sides of the apparent sūtra–tantra divide. The authors of the texts are two of the key figures in the first dissemination of Buddhism in Tibet: the Indian master Kamalaśīla and Tibetan translator and tantric adept Vairocana. Kamalaśīla sees the *Heart Sūtra* as a *prajñāpāramitā* text and seeks to extract as many of the terms and categories of the *Abhisamayālaṃkāra* from it as he can. Vairocana attributes his commentary to his teacher, the tantric adept Śrīsiṃha, and declares at the outset that his purpose is to explain the sūtra as mantra (*sngags su 'grel pa*), that is, tantrically.

Let us consider these two commentaries in turn. Unlike the seven other extant commentaries to the *Heart Sūtra*, Kamalaśīla's study makes no attempt to provide a methodical exegesis of the exposition of the doctrine of emptiness for which the sūtra is so famous. Rather, his commentary is devoted exclusively to demonstrating that the *Heart Sūtra*, which contains no direct reference to the bodhisattva path, indeed sets forth the five paths to buddhahood. After the expression of worship to the perfection of wisdom, the mother of all buddhas, Kamalaśīla states, "When the Bhagavan set forth the sublime perfection of wisdom, he set forth eight topics, beginning with the knowledge of all aspects (*sarvākārajñāna*) [and ending with] the dharmakāya." The eight topics are those of eight chapters of the *Abhisamayālaṃkāra*. He then describes the five paths, aligning the first four with the thirty-seven categories of enlightenment (*bodhipakṣa*); the path of accumulation (*saṃbhāramārga*) encompasses the four establishments of mindfulness (*smṛtyupasthāna*) and the four legs of manifestation (*ṛddhipāda*). The path of preparation (*prayogamārga*) includes the five powers (*indriya*) and the five forces (*bala*). On the third path, that of vision (*darśanamārga*), the seven branches of enlightenment (*bodhyaṅga*) are attained. The eightfold path, the last division of the thirty-seven categories, is achieved with the path of meditation (*bhāvanāmārga*). The fifth path, the path of no further learning (*aśaikṣamārga*), is synonymous with enlightenment, and brings with it the three bodies, the ten powers, and the other qualities of a buddha. The content and possible accuracy of this elaborate process of matching are perhaps less immediately noteworthy than the simple fact that none of these terms occurs anywhere in the *Heart Sūtra*, perhaps lending credence to the traditional claim that the structure of the path is the hidden teaching of the Perfection of Wisdom sūtras.

Kamalaśīla explains that bodhisattvas of sharp faculties understand the perfection of wisdom simply by hearing the teaching of the twenty-two similes of the creation of the aspiration to enlightenment (*bodhicittotpāda*), the first of the eleven topics illustrating the knowledge of all aspects. Bodhisattvas of intermediate and inferior faculties require the exposition of the remaining ten topics, from precepts (*avavāda*) through the activity of emergence (*niryanapratipatti*). The remaining seven categories are taught to various types of gods.

Moving finally to the *Heart Sūtra* in the second third of the commentary, Kamalaśīla notes that all of these topics are set forth in the *100,000 Stanza* and the *25,000 Stanza* Perfection of Wisdom sūtras. In the briefest of the three major sūtras, the *8,000*, some of the topics, such as the twenty-two similes, are absent. The *Heart Sūtra* is the condensation of these three; it does not set forth the eight categories, but rather the five paths, which are the meaning of the eight categories of the *Abhisamayālaṃkāra*. The first term in the sūtra with which Kamalaśīla deals is "perception of the profound," the name of the Buddha's samādhi mentioned in the setting of the sūtra. Kamalaśīla states, without explanation, that this term suggests the connection between merit and wisdom. He then goes on to specify the meditative state from which the noble Avalokiteśvara saw that the five aggregates are empty of any intrinsic nature, explaining that "he viewed the categories of phenomena with the supramundane wisdom of subsequent attainment (*lokottarapṛṣṭhalabdhajñāna*)," the state that occurs on the paths of vision and meditation when the bodhisattva rises from samādhi on emptiness to again view the world.

Kamalaśīla's commentary says almost nothing about the explicit content of the sūtra, making no attempt to explicate the doctrine of emptiness. He lets the most famous passages of the sūtra pass without comment; he is unique among the commentators in ignoring the "form is empty, emptiness is form" line. The only section of the sūtra that he treats in any detail is Avalokiteśvara's short answer, that children of good lineage should practice the perfection of wisdom by seeing that all phenomena are empty. Here, he does not pause to consider what emptiness means or what the perfection of wisdom is in this context, but rather focuses only on what it means to see. He is emphatic that this seeing is an inferential understanding, gained through the process of reasoning. Direct perception is gained by yogins only after the cultivation of inferential understanding.

How might we account for Kamalaśīla's creative exegesis of the *Heart Sūtra*? One avenue of investigation would be to speculate about the context of Kamalaśīla's commentary. By context, I mean nothing more specific than the land in which the text was written: did he compose his *Prajñāpāramitā-hṛdaya-nāma-ṭīkā* in India or Tibet?

If the text was written in India, it would appear to be little more than an exercise in exegesis, demonstrating the "hidden meaning of the perfection of wisdom" by excavating the Perfection of Wisdom sūtras to unearth the structure of the path. That such an exercise was popular in the time of the Yogācāra-Mādhyamika synthesis seems evident from the fact that we have extant twenty-one commentaries to the *Abhisamayālaṃkāra* from this general period. Admittedly, these twenty-one commentaries sought to find the eight categories and seventy topics of the *Abhisamayālaṃkāra* in the longer sūtras, usually the *25,000* and the *8,000* as Haribhadra (a disciple of Śāntarakṣita and possibly a fellow student of Kamalaśīla) did. But it is not inconceivable that Kamalaśīla would have sought to do these commentators one better by finding the structure of the path revealed even in the briefest expositions of the perfection of wisdom, the sūtra that is its heart or essence. (By this reasoning, the ultimate achievement would have been to find the seventy topics in the *Perfection of Wisdom in One Letter, Ekākṣarīprajñāpāramitā.*)

Kamalaśīla's major works (his commentary on the *Tattvasaṃgraha*, his *Madhyamakāloka*, and the three *Bhāvanākrama*) are marked by a methodical style, logical structure, clarity of expression, and the presence of supporting citations from a wide range of sūtras and śāstras. His *Heart Sūtra* commentary displays none of these characteristics. It has the tone of a work hurriedly written, or dictated, or even reconstructed from the memory of a student. And his almost strident emphasis on the importance of inference suggests that his commentary is somehow more programmatic than a mechanical exercise in exegesis. His focus is clearly on the gradual path and he is at pains to demonstrate its presence in a work in which it is overtly absent. If this sense of the work is accurate, suggesting that the commentary was written in Tibet rather than India, it is necessary next to determine what status the *Heart Sūtra* enjoyed among the various factions in Tibet at the end of the eighth century, factions with whose views Kamalaśīla would have found himself at odds.[1]

[1] The fact that the *Heart Sūtra* was known in Tibet during Kamalaśīla's tenure is not enough to establish Tibet as the site of the work's composition. Weighing against the thesis that the work was composed in Tibet is the fact that Kamalaśīla was commenting on the longer version of the sūtra, which may not have been translated into Tibetan before his death; the translation preserved in the Tibetan canons is that by Vimalamitra, who, according to some accounts, did not arrive in Tibet until after the death of Khri srong lde btsan in 797. According to the colophon appended to some Tibetan translations of the sūtra, the *Heart Sūtra* was also written "on wall of the dGe rgyas bye ma gling [temple] of the glorious spontaneously established bSam yas monastery." The title of the sūtra does appear in the lDan dkar ma catalogue, said to represent those works available in Tibetan translation during the reign of Khri srong lde btsan. It is number 14 of the works "included in the prajñāpāramitā category of the Mahāyāna sūtras." See Marcelle Lalou, "Les Textes Bouddhiques au temps du roi Khri-sroṅ-lde-bcan," *Journal Asiatique* 241 (1953): 319.

There is also some question whether the technical vocabulary of the *Abhi-*

The first faction to consider is, of course, the Chan. The *Heart Sūtra* was translated into Chinese by Hsuan-tsang in 649. In the next century, a number of Chan commentaries were composed, including those of Huijing and Zhishen, which were preserved at Dunhuang. We know that scores of manuscripts of the *Heart Sūtra* in Chinese and Tibetan have been unearthed at Dunhuang and that some of the Tibetan translations (one edited by Ueyama) were rendered into Tibetan from Chinese rather than Sanskrit, apparently prior to the standardization of terminology set in the *Mahāvyutpatti*, composed at the order of King Ral pa can (ascended 815).[2] Thus, it seems very plausible that the *Heart Sūtra* was current in Tibet at the time of Kamalaśīla's residence and that it was also known to the Chan faction. It is also easy to imagine that the Northern Chan monk and leader of the Chinese faction, Mo-ho-yen, could make good use of a sūtra that states, "there is no suffering, no origin, no cessation, no path, no wisdom, no attainment, no non-attainment. Therefore, Śāriputra, because bodhisattvas have no attainment, they depend on and abide in the perfection of wisdom."

But the *Heart Sūtra* seems to have been important to another faction in Tibet at the end of the eighth century, that of the *māntrikas*, which brings us to Vairocana. Vairocana was among the group of six or seven or nine Tibetans ordained by Śāntarakṣita at bSam yas around 779. Although he initially remained loyal to the teachings of the abbot against the teachings of Mo-ho-yen, Vairocana, who was also a student of Padmasambhava, seems eventually to have fallen away, and may have been absent during the so-called Council of bSam yas, in which the Indian and Chinese factions are said to have debated the question of sudden versus gradual enlightenment, with the Tibetan king serving as judge. He was summoned back by the king but was exiled to eastern Tibet shortly thereafter, apparently for slandering the Indians. Upon his return he was censured by the Indians, who regarded him as a traitor, someone who had traveled to India, had been ordained by Śāntarakṣita himself, and yet came to hold heretical views. But according to his hagiography, Vairocana had studied mundane philosophy in India only during the day, having been tutored at night in the eighteen "Instructions on the Mind" (*man ngag sde*) by Śrīsiṃha.[3]

---

samayālaṃkāra that he employs would have been comprehensible to the Tibetan audience of his day; the *Abhisamayālaṃkāra* was first translated into Tibetan by Ka pa dpal brtsegs in the ninth century.

[2] For example, *rūpa* is rendered as *kha dog*, *samudaya* as *'dus pa*.

[3] On Vairocana, see Dudjom Rinpoche, *The Nyingma School of Buddhism: Its Fundamentals and History*, vol. 1, trans. and ed. Gyurme Dorje (Boston: Wisdom, 1991), pp. 538–40 et passim (see index) and especially Samten G. Karmay, *The Great Perfection: A Philosophical and Meditative Teaching of Tibetan Buddhism* (Leiden: E. J. Brill, 1988),

That Vairocana's view on the *Heart Sūtra* did indeed differ from that of Kamalaśīla is evident from a work entitled *Mantric Commentary on the Heart Sūtra* (*Sher snying 'grel pa sngags su 'grel pa*, Toh. 4353), ascribed to Vairocana. However, according to the colophon, the commentary was written by Śrīsiṃha and presented by Vairocana to King Khri srong lde btsan and his son. This work explains the words of the sūtra according to the standard triad of the outer, inner, and secret. In most cases, the secret meaning is awareness (*rig pa*). For example, the outer meaning of Vulture Peak is a mountain near Rājagṛha, the inner meaning is the pure land of Akaniṣṭha, the secret meaning is awareness. That this interpretation is one which Vairocana deemed superior to that of Kamalaśīla and his followers is suggested by the statement that this explanation of the meaning of the sūtra is not to be taught to *rtog ge ba*, that is, logicians (*tārkika*). This commentary is not grouped with the seven others in the Tibetan canons, which are placed together in the "Perfection of Wisdom" (*shes phyin*) section. Śrīsiṃha's is found separately, in the "Miscellaneous" (*sna tshogs*) section among works attributed to Tibetan authors.

With such opposing valuations of the sūtra, as *prajñāpāramitā* and as tantra, it would perhaps be useful to pause to consider what the term "tantra" might mean. The difficulty of delimiting the wide range of connotations and denotations encompassed by the term "tantra" in Indian literature, both Hindu and Buddhist, is suggested immediately by the strange exfoliation of adjectives and abstract nouns that have sprung from its root: tantric, tantrism, tantricism, tantristic, tantricistic, and so on. We furthermore have the testimony of one of the leading contemporary scholars of tantrism, André Padoux: "An objective and scientific assessment of Tantrism is not easy, for the subject is controversial and perplexing. Not only do authorities give different definitions of Tantrism, but its very existence has sometimes been denied. (These uncertainties apply more to Hindu Tantrism than to Buddhist Tantrism)."[4] Yet Louis

---

pp. 17–37 et passim. See also Eva Dargyay, *The Rise of Esoteric Buddhism in Tibet* (Delhi: Motilal Banarsidass, 1977), pp. 44ff.; and Giuseppe Tucci, *Minor Buddhist Texts*, pts. 1–2 (Delhi: Motilal Banarsidass, 1986), pp. 352–53 (or pt. 2, pp. 42–43). Tucci provides a summary of Vairocana's rendition of Śrīsiṃha's commentary on the *Heart Sūtra* on pp. 436–38 (pt. 2, pp. 126–28). Karmay's work on Vairocana's biography supersedes that found in the doctoral dissertation of A. W. Hanson-Barber, *The Life and Teachings of Vairocana* (University of Wisconsin, 1984). Hanson-Barber's dissertation contains a translation of Śrīsiṃha's *Heart Sūtra* commentary with numerous errors.

[4] André Padoux, "Tantrism," in Mircea Eliade, ed., *The Encyclopedia of Religion*, vol. 14 (New York: Macmillan, 1987), p. 272. In the following entry in the encyclopedia, "Hindu Tantrism," Padoux makes the startling declaration that "Tantrism is fundamentally a Hindu phenomenon (p. 274)." In the same entry, he states that "Tantrism may be briefly characterized as a practical way to attain supernatural powers and liberation in this life through the use of specific and complex techniques based on a particular ideology, that

de la Vallée Poussin had written in 1922 that "Buddhists were not quite clear as to the specific meaning of the word *tantra*, 'book.'"[5]

As fruitful as the enterprise may be, we are not able here to survey the history of attempts to define the term "tantra" and its various derivatives, apart from noting some examples. David Snellgrove, in the glossary to his study of the *Hevajra Tantra*, confines himself to the most limited sense of tantra to state confidently that "the term tantra refers to a clearly definable type of ritual text common to both Hindu and Buddhist tradition, concerned with the evoking of deities and the gaining of various kinds of *siddhi* by means of various kinds of *mantra*, *dhyāna*, *mudrā*, and *maṇḍala*."[6] Snellgrove sails the safer course of delimiting the term to its specific textual use, rather than its broader use as a system of religious praxis. He could have simply said that a tantra is a text with the term "tantra" in its title. But even such an apparently solipsistic definition has its counterexamples, such as the *Uttaratantra*, one of the five works of Maitreya. Hence, Snellgrove provides a list of terms that must also appear in a text called tantra in order for it to be a tantra, terms such as "mantra," "mudrā," and "maṇḍala." This approach has a long history, appearing perhaps for the first time in Alexander Csoma de Kőrös's 1839 essay on the contents of the Tibetan bKa' 'gyur, where he explains: "These volumes, in general, contain mystical theology. There are descriptions of several gods and goddesses. Instructions for preparing the *mandalas*, or circles, for the reception of those divinities. Offerings or sacrifices presented to them for obtaining their favour. Prayers, hymns, charms, &c. &c. addressed to them. There are also some works on astronomy, astrology, chronology, medicine, and natural philosophy."[7]

---

of a cosmic reintegration by means of which the adept is established in a position of power, freed from worldly fetters, while remaining in this world and dominating it by union with (or proximity to) a godhead who is the supreme power itself." In addition to other problems, it is difficult to see why this characterization would not apply equally to bhakti. For a useful discussion of the relations between tantra and bhakti, see Madeleine Biardeau, *Hinduism: The Anthropology of a Civilization*, trans. Richard Nice (Delhi: Oxford University Press, 1989), pp. 148ff.

[5] Louis de la Vallée Poussin, "Tāntrism (Buddhist)," in James Hastings, ed., *Encyclopedia of Religion and Ethics*, vol. 12 (New York: Charles Scribner's Sons, 1922), p. 193.

[6] David L. Snellgrove, *The Hevajra Tantra: A Critical Study*, pt. 1 (London: Oxford University Press, 1959), p. 138.

[7] Alexander Csoma de Kőrös, "Analysis of the Sher-chin-p'hal-ch'hen-dkon-séks-do-dé-nyáng-dás and Gyut: being the 2nd, 3rd, 4th, 5th, 6th, and 7th divisions of the Tibetan Work, entitled the Kah-Gyur," *Journal of the Asiatic Society of Bengal* 20, pt. 2 (1839): 487. Reprinted in Alexander Csoma de Kőrös, *Tibetan Studies*, in J. Terjék, ed., *Collected Works of Alexander Csoma de Kőrös*, vol. 4 (Budapest: Akadémiai Kiadó, 1984), p. 359. This volume is itself a reprint of E. Denison Ross's edition, also entitled *Tibetan Studies* (Calcutta: Baptist Mission, 1912).

The problems of definition multiply exponentially when the term "tantra" is excised from its place in the colophon of a Sanskrit manuscript and allowed to float free as an abstract noun. John Newman, in his dissertation on the *Kālacakra*, defines tantra in terms drawn from medieval scholasticism, as "theurgy utilized as a path of soteriological apotheosis."[8] Richard Gombrich provides this glossary entry: "*tantra* (S) form of Buddhism, and of other religions indigenous to India, in which the means to both salvation and magical power is to link meditation with an elaborate ritual. The teachings are transmitted esoterically. In a religious context the word basically designates a type of scripture. The Sanskrit adjective is *tāntrika*, whence English tantric."[9] But rather than listing attempts to define tantra and pointing out counterexamples, it is perhaps more prudent to conclude, following Teun Goudriaan, that "The extremely varied and complicated nature of Tantrism, one of the main currents in the Indian religious tradition of the last fifteen hundred years, renders the manipulation of a single definition almost impossible. There is, accordingly, a general uncertainty about the exact scope of the word."[10] Despite this uncertainty, however, it would seem useful to consider some of the ways in which the term has been used, by both modern scholars and traditional commentators, thereby gaining, if not a better definition of tantra, at least a clearer idea of the kinds of discursive purposes definitions of tantra are intended to serve.

One apparent route around the roadblock of defining tantra is to eschew definition altogether, regarding tantra instead as the undifferentiated substratum of Indian culture, subconsciously underlying all forms of Indian religiosity and manifesting itself overtly at certain key junctures in the development of the Hindu and Buddhist traditions—tantra as "a name for a polymorphous reservoir of ritual possibilities, continuously flirted with by orthodoxies yet also the basis of countering them."[11] But when we attempt to identify tantra in the history of Indian religion we are almost immediately daunted, unable to find its starting point, watching its putative features proliferate backward to the very beginnings, to the ithyphallic horned figure of the Harappan seals. Tantra appears as the late development of what was always there. And we use language of

[8] John Ronald Newman, *The Outer Wheel of Time: Vajrayāna Buddhist Cosmology in the Kālacakra Tantra* (Ph.D. diss., University of Wisconsin, 1987), p. 5.

[9] In Heinz Bechert and Richard Gombrich, eds., *The World of Buddhism* (London: Thames and Hudson, 1984), p. 292.

[10] Sanjukta Gupta, Dirk Jan Hoens, and Teun Goudriaan, *Hindu Tantrism,* (Leiden: E. J. Brill, 1979), p. 5.

[11] See James A. Boon, *Affinities and Extremes: Crisscrossing the Bittersweet Ethnology of East Indies History, Hindu-Balinese Culture, and Indo-European Allure* (Chicago: University of Chicago Press, 1990), p. 165.

descent and ascent, that like Kṛṣṇa, tantra descends into the history of Indian religion in age after age (*sambhavāmi yuge yuge*) when there are discrepancies in the dharma—inspiring the śramaṇas to leave the village for the forest, inspiring the *ṛṣis* of the *Upaniṣads* against the corruption of the sacerdotal brahmans, inspiring bhakti in the Dark Lord and the snake-garlanded Lord of Beasts, inspiring Buddhists to return to the immediacy of experience from the arid scholasticism of the Ābhidharmikas, both Hīnayāna and Mahāyāna. In this reading, tantra is the substratum of authentic Indian religiosity, rendering the "great tradition" epiphenomenal, the substratum that erupts into history at key moments, the corrective. It is the subversive origin that can only be temporarily repressed, the forever primitive.[12]

Another approach would be to employ the notion of polythetic classification. In monothetic classification, the composition of a conceptual class is determined by the invariable presence of certain common properties found in each and every member of that class. In a polythetic classification, however, no single feature is deemed necessary or sufficient for inclusion in the class. The members of the class do not share a single feature in common, but are grouped together based on the greatest number of features in common, with no a priori decision as to the relative importance of these multiple features.[13] Under a polythetic classification, tantra, instead of being reduced to some essence, would constitute the intersection of certain of a larger number of family resemblances. The features constituting this family serve as descriptions rather than criteria. Among these features, one would immediately include elements such as those listed by Gombrich in his definition above, that is, elements that commonly occur in texts called tantras, such as mantras, mudrās, and maṇḍalas. To these one could quickly add the importance of the guru, abhiṣekha (empowerment), *vajra* (diamond or thunderbolt), *sukha* (bliss), *sahaja* ("together-born"), and siddhis (powers). From here, one could move to traditional characterizations of tantra as a form of practice that is secret, easy, and rapid in its effect, based upon the premise that reality resides in the mundane. In modern studies, tantric texts are described as highly ritualistic, antinomian, and nonspeculative, evincing nonduality and often setting forth an elaborate esoteric physiology of cakras and *nāḍīs* that give special importance to the genitals.

The delineation and the delimitation of the constellation of factors connoted by the term "tantra" into a history of Indian religions and In-

12 For a circumspect discussion of some of the fallacies entailed by such a substratum theory, see Jan Gonda, "Introduction: Some Critical Remarks apropos of Substratum Theories," in *Change and Continuity in Indian Religion* (London, 1965), pp. 7–37.

13 See Rodney Needham, "Polythetic Classification," *Man*, n.s., 10, no. 3 (1975): 349–69.

dian Buddhism in particular is a vexing task. The factors are many and diffuse; one need only read down the section headings of the table of contents in perhaps the most comprehensive study of Buddhist tantra produced in the West, David Snellgrove's 1987 *Indo-Tibetan Buddhism*: "the Vajrayāna as a new and distinct way," "Vajrapāṇi (alias Vajradhara)," "magical formulas," "the votaries of Tantra," "Tantric feasts," "the argument for implicit interpretations," "the importance of one's chosen teacher," "Buddha-families," "the maṇḍala," "initiations and consecrations," "wisdom and means," "the cult of the human body." There seem almost unlimited possibilities for expanding the list of elements that might constitute the family from which to derive the resemblance called tantra.[14]

When popular representations are taken into account, the tantric family rapidly grows to encompass associations dizzying in their geographical and historical sweep. An advertisement for *Tantra: The Magazine*

[14] One such list has recently been provided by Stephen Hodge:

> **1.** Tantric Buddhism offers an alternative path to Enlightenment in addition to the standard Mahāyāna one.
>
> **2.** Its teachings are aimed at lay practitioners in particular, rather than monks and nuns.
>
> **3.** As a consequence of this, it recognizes mundane aims and attainments, and often deals with practices which are more magical in character than spiritual.
>
> **4.** It teaches special types of meditation (*sādhana*) as the path to realization, aimed at transforming the individual into an embodiment of the divine in this lifetime or after a short span of time.
>
> **5.** Such kinds of meditation make extensive use of various kinds of *maṇḍalas*, *mudrās*, *mantras*, and *dhāraṇīs* as concrete expressions of the nature of reality.
>
> **6.** The formation of images of the various deities during meditation by means of creative imagination plays a key role in the process of realization. These images may be viewed as being present externally or internally.
>
> **7.** There is an exuberant proliferation in the number and types of Buddhas and other deities.
>
> **8.** Great stress is laid upon the importance of the guru and the necessity of receiving the instructions and appropriate initiations for the *sādhanas* from him.
>
> **9.** Speculations on the nature and power of speech are prominent, especially with regard to the letters of the Sanskrit alphabet.
>
> **10.** Various customs and rituals, often of non-Buddhist origins, such as the homa rituals, are incorporated and adapted to Buddhist ends.
>
> **11.** A spiritual physiology is taught as part of the process of transformation.
>
> **12.** It stresses the importance of the feminine and utilizes various forms of sexual yoga.

See Stephen Hodge, "Considerations on the Dating and Geographical Origins of the *Mahāvairocanābhisaṃbodhi-sūtra*," in Tadeusz Skorupski and Ulrich Pagel, eds., *The Buddhist Forum III* (London: School of Oriental and African Studies, University of London, 1994), p. 59.

states that "Tantra has been embraced by the mystical aspects of all religions at various stages of human history," religions such as the Egyptian, "East Indian," Tibetan, Daoist, Sufi, Native American, Cabalist, and Christian. The advertisement goes on to explain that "Tantra is a synthesis of art and science that acknowledges the physical and metaphysical experience of being human. Tantra practice offers the individual an opportunity to come into balance and harmony within daily life." Finally, "Tantra evokes the sensitive exploration of the relationships between man, woman, and the Divine."[15] It seems, then, that when such popular resemblances of the term are admitted into the tantric family, the term becomes overdetermined toward the point of meaninglessness.

It might prove more fruitful, therefore, to consider "tantra" by considering what it is not, by opposing it with another term. The ancients, both Vedic and Buddhist, tended to understand tantra as the member (usually the second member) of a dyad. For example, the Vedic ritualists distinguished between the primary part of the sacrifice, the *pradhāna*, which was made up of the main offerings and which varied according to deity and oblational material, and the tantra, the auxiliary acts that remained largely interchangeable among different sacrifices.[16] Buddhist writers sought to distinguish sūtra and tantra (or, more commonly in their vocabulary, *pāramitāyāna* and *vajrayāna*). In these efforts, they appear to have had two separate, although not unrelated, motives: the establishment of the superiority of the tantric path and the integration of later tradition with the former. The features that elevate the *mantrayāna* above the exoteric path are nearly as numerous as those that latter-day scholars enumerate to characterize tantra. In his *Sarvasamayasaṃgraha* (Summary of All Vows), Atiśa reports that the master Indrabhūti contended that the Mantra Vehicle is superior to the Perfection Vehicle for seven reasons: the guru, the vessel (*snod*) [i.e., the disciple], the rite (*cho ka*), the activity (*las*), the pledge (*dam tshig*), the view (*lta ba*), and the practice (*spyod pa*); the master Buddhajñānapāda enumerated three unique features of the *mantrayāna*: the practitioner (*sgrub pa po*), the path (*lam*), and the fruition (*'bras bu*).[17] Ratnākaraśānti says in his *Triyānavyavasthāna* (Presentation of the Three Vehicles):

> Therefore, there is no second ultimate truth different from the ultimate truth set forth by the Bhagavan, Nāgārjuna, and so forth. What is discussed here as being "vaster" is from the point of view of merely the conventional:

[15] The quotations are taken from a mailing soliciting subscriptions to *Tantra: The Magazine*, P.O. Box 79, Torreon, NM.

[16] See J. C. Heesterman, *The Broken World of Sacrifice: An Essay in Ancient Indian Ritual* (Chicago: University of Chicago Press, 1993), p. 61.

[17] Toh. 3725, rgyud tshu, 44a6–7.

> Because of a very pure object, the power of assistance, and deeds,
> The vehicle of the intelligent is known as the great of the great.

> This means that the objects that appear are understood to be of the nature of a pure deity. Therefore, the object is vaster. The vows that are supported by the conquerors in the three times are maintained according to one's wish. The special blessings created thereby are the vaster "assistance." The way that buddhas and lords [bodhisattvas] of the tenth stage act for the welfare of transmigrators and the way that they are reborn in pure lands through their blessing are vaster deeds.[18]

According to Atiśa, Vajragandha has four reasons: the person who is the basis of the practice (*rten gyi gang zag*), the path, the final fruition, and renunciation (*mngon par 'byung ba*). Ḍombhiheruka has five reasons: the purity of the vessel (*snod gyi byang ba*), the rites that make [persons] into vessels (*snod du byed pa'i cho ga*), the texts (*gzhung*), the path, and the fruition. Atiśa's own teacher, Samayavajra, has five different reasons: the guru, the initiation (*dbang bskur*), the pledges, the instructions (*man ngag*), and the effort (*btson 'grus*).[19]

The most influential declaration of the superiority of tantra for the Tibetan tradition was that of Tripiṭakamāla in his *Nayatrayapradīpa* (Lamp for the Three Modes): "Even if the aim is the same, the Mantra Vehicle is superior due to nonobscuration, many skillful methods, nondifficulty, and being designed for those of sharp faculties." Tripiṭakamāla explains that followers of the Perfection Vehicle are not entirely deluded with regard to method (*upāya*) because they practice the six perfections, but are nonetheless somewhat deluded because they do such things as give away their body parts, notably their heads. This, he argues, is not the way that the perfection of giving is fulfilled. Followers of the Mantrayāna look down upon such practices and fulfill all six perfections in a samādhi that unites method and wisdom. Tripiṭakamāla argues furthermore that the Mantrayāna has more methods than the exclusively peaceful practices of asceticism and vow-keeping found in the Perfection Vehicle; practitioners of mantra have techniques for transmuting the five poisons into the five buddha lineages. The Mantrayāna is also easier than the Pāramitāyāna because in the former one uses the bliss of desire to achieve the bliss of enlightenment. He sets forth a hierarchy of tantric practitioners, the lowest of whom achieve enlightenment through the bliss achieved in union with an actual consort, called either a *samayamudrā* or a *karmamudrā*. The practitioners of an intermediate level consort with an imagined woman, called a *jñānamudrā*, and the best, already free from

[18] Toh. 3712, rgyud tsu, 101b3–6.
[19] Toh. 3725, rgyud tshu, 44b1–5.

desire, have no consort and know the *mahāmudrā*, the wisdom of nonduality. Finally, Tripiṭakamāla argues that followers of the Mantrayāna have greater intelligence than others. Followers of the Hīnayāna are confused about the nature of reality. Followers of the exoteric Mahāyāna understand emptiness but are confused about method, whereas the followers of the Mantrayāna are not confused about anything and can perform deeds that would cause others to fall into an unfortunate realm of rebirth.[20]

Thus, in the Indian literature from this period, surveyed by Atiśa, we find the term "tantra" being defined relationally, specifically in contradistinction to the term "sūtra." These authors distinguish tantra by enumerating the various ways in which it is superior to sūtra practices, designated generally as the Pāramitāyāna. But no two authors can seem to agree on the set of characteristics that distinguishes tantra. Furthermore, these characteristics appear invariably vague. Nonetheless, to consider tantra not as a free-floating category, but relationally, especially in relation to the term "sūtra," may represent an advance. For sūtra, like tantra, is another name for a kind of text, a name which, again like tantra, is sometimes traditionally taken to mean, by extension, the doctrines and practices set forth in those texts. Both sūtra and tantra are derived from verbs for sewing (hence the epigraph from Wittgenstein). Sūtra comes from the root *siv*, "to sew" and means most basically a thread that runs through, providing continuity and connection.[21] Tantra is the woof or

[20] Toh. 3707, rgyud tsu, 16b3ff. The verse from Tripiṭakamāla above is widely cited in Tibetan discussions about the difference between sūtra and tantra, often without comment. However, certain authors, most notably Tsong kha pa, reject this characterization by arguing that the special features that Tripiṭakamāla claims for tantra are either found also in sūtras or are exclusive to Anuttarayogatantra and hence inapplicable to the three other tantric divisions: Yoga, Caryā, and Kriyā. For Tsong kha pa, who has his own Indian works for support, the distinguishing feature of tantric practice is "deity yoga" (*lha'i rnal 'byor*), in which the mind understanding emptiness is made to appear in the form of a buddha. He goes to considerable exegetical lengths to find this practice in tantric texts where it is ostensibly absent. For English translations of these arguments, see H. H. the Dalai Lama, Tsong-ka-pa [sic], and Jeffrey Hopkins, *Tantra in Tibet* (Ithaca: Snow Lion, 1987), pp. 105–28 and H. H. the Dalai Lama, Tsong-ka-pa [sic], and Jeffrey Hopkins, *Deity Yoga* (Ithaca: Snow Lion, 1987), pp. 47–62. The latter work was originally published as *The Yoga of Tibet* (London: Allen and Unwin, 1981).

Much more extensive critiques of Tripiṭakamāla are to be found in Bo dong Phyogs las rnam rgyal's *rGyud sde spyi'i rnam bshad*, *Encyclopedia Tibetica*, vol. 24 (New Delhi: Tibet House, 1971) and the first Pan chen Lama bLo bzang chos kyi rgyal mtshan's *bsTan pa spyi dang rgyud sde bzhi'i rnam par gzhag pa'i zin bris*, *Collected Works*, vol. 4 (New Delhi: Guru Deva, 1973).

[21] In Tibetan, sūtra is translated as *mdo*, "condensation," and in Indian literature sūtras are generally aphorisms—pithy, memorable statements. Richard Gombrich, however, makes the important point that a Buddhist sūtra is rarely particularly brief or laconic. This

crossing thread in a fabric, providing the texture; *tantrin* is that which is made of threads; *tanoti* means to stretch out or weave, and is used by extension for the performance of a sacrifice. Perhaps, then, we should not seek the meaning of tantra "in an order of realities different from the relationships it helps to construct."[22]

As we have seen, the most obvious of those relationships is in the sūtra–tantra dyad, a traditional pairing that has generally received opposing valuations by Buddhists and by Buddhologists (especially of the previous generations). Indian tantric exegetes (and their Tibetan descendants) employed a number of strategies to legitimate the tantras as authentic and authoritative teachings, strategies in many cases already familiar from the Mahāyāna sūtras. Hence, as with certain Mahāyāna sūtras, such as the *Pratyutpanna-buddha-saṃmukhāvasthita-samādhi-sūtra*, the late appearance of the tantras is explained by the fact that they were hidden at the time of the Buddha to be discovered and revealed at a more appropriate time. Or, as with the claim of the *Lotus* that all arhats will eventually enter the bodhisattva path and become buddhas, so in certain exegetical systems of *anuttarayogatantra* do we find the claim that only through its path has buddhahood ever been attained. As is noted in the quotation from Ratnākaraśānti's *Triyānavyavasthāna* above, the superiority of tantra (at times portrayed as its indispensability) lay not in the first member of another central dyad of Indian Buddhism, that of *prajñā*; it was often said by the tantric exegetes that there was no reality more profound than that set forth in the *prajñāpāramitā* sūtras and explicated by Nāgārjuna. Instead, the superiority of tantra was to be found in *upāya*, in its superior methods for achieving buddhahood. In this scheme, the tantric path is seen as the necessary extension of the bodhisattva's path as set forth in the Mahāyāna sūtras, just as the *Lotus* portrayed the bodhisattva's path as the necessary extension of the arhat's path set forth in the Nikāyas.

The tantric path thus is represented as the supplement to the sūtra path, providing what is essential for the goal of the sūtra path, buddhahood, to be fulfilled. As Tsong kha pa writes at the conclusion of his *Lam rim chen mo*, "After training in the paths common to both sūtra and mantra in that way, you must undoubtedly enter Secret Mantra because that path is very much rarer than any other doctrine and because it quickly brings the two collections [of merit and wisdom] to comple-

---

leads him to speculate that the Pāli *sutta* derives not from *sūtra* but from *sūkta*, "well spoken." See Richard F. Gombrich, "How the Mahāyāna Began," in Tadeusz Skorupski, ed., *The Buddhist Forum*, vol. 1 (London: School of Oriental and African Studies, 1990), p. 23.

22 Claude Levi-Strauss, *Introduction to the Work of Marcel Mauss*, trans. Felicity Baker (London: Routledge and Kegan Paul, 1987), p. 56.

tion."[23] The tantric path, then, is seen to provide the necessary addendum to bring the bodhisattva to buddhahood; without it he cannot pass beyond the tenth *bhūmi*. Even Śākyamuni, in his last lifetime before buddhahood, became fully enlightened through the practice of sexual yoga with Devī Tilottamā in Akaniṣṭha.[24]

In the *Lotus*, the nirvāṇa of the arhat is portrayed not merely as a lesser attainment but as an illusion, a city conjured by a magician as a rest for weary travelers. The only true path is the bodhisattva path, and those who insist on following the path of the śrāvaka only prolong their time in saṃsāra.[25] The Mahāyāna is thus not only the completion of the Hīnayāna but is at once its necessary precursor and eventual substitute; that which is later is portrayed as actually prior. The Buddha declares in the *Lotus* that by practicing the teachings of the very sūtra he was at that moment expounding, he had been enlightened aeons before his birth as the Gotamid prince. What the arhats had perceived as the true teaching, original and natural, was in fact secondary and contrived. The tantric path, the Vajrayāna, is similarly portrayed, as providing what is essential to the completion of the bodhisattva path; the *upāya* set forth in sūtras like the *Lotus* are in themselves inadequate to provide the means to buddhahood. Those who remain on the sūtra path only prolong their time in saṃsāra, which can be reduced from three periods of countless aeons (calculated by Har Dayal at 384×10^{58} years) to three years and three months by the practice of *anuttarayogatantra*, the very path that Śākyamuni himself eventually entered. Indeed, it was his practice of the tantric path that provided Śākyamuni with the means to become a buddha and to then set forth the sūtra path for those unsuited for tantra.

Tantra thus both adds to and displaces sūtra, sometimes with an appeal to its superiority, sometimes with an appeal to its timeliness, the possibility of enlightenment by the previous paths always deferred by a claim to the priority of tantra as the vehicle of the Buddha's enlightenment in the incalculable past. With the addition of the Mahāyāna to the Hīnayāna and the Vajrayāna to the Pāramitāyāna, it is as if a unity has been restored to that which was not heretofore perceived as incomplete; the fulfillment can only perform its function through the identification of

[23] Tsong kha pa, *Mnyam med tsong kha pa chen pos mdzad pa'i byang chub lam rim che pa* (mTsho sngon mi rigs dbe skrun khang, 1985), p. 808.

[24] See Ferdinand D. Lessing and Alex Wayman, *Introduction to the Buddhist Tantrica Systems* (Delhi: Motilal Banarsidass, 1978), pp. 36–39.

[25] For various Indian exegetical portrayals of the Hīnayāna nirvāṇa, see my "Paths Terminable and Interminable," in Robert E. Buswell, Jr. and Robert M. Gimello, eds., *Paths to Liberation: The Mārga and Its Transformations in Buddhist Thought*, Kuroda Institute Studies in East Asian Buddhism, no. 7 (Honolulu: University of Hawaii Press, 1992), pp. 158–70.

an essential, originary absence in what was once seen as essential, original, even natural. In the process, the original, whether it be the nirvāṇa of the arhat or the buddhahood of the *Lotus Sūtra*, is denatured, declared to be derivative, a mere expedient, a concession for those who cannot truly see. Tantra is thus represented as a supplement to the sūtras, to the common, exoteric teachings, providing those elements that the sūtras are said to lack through a process of fulfillment that becomes in the end a substitution. The *Guhyasamāja* begins, "Thus did I hear. At one time the Bhagavan was abiding in the vaginas of the vajra-maidens, the essence of the body, speech, and mind of all the buddhas."[26]

In European studies of tantra in the nineteenth century, the tantras held a very different relation to the sūtras. Space does not permit a full treatment of the history of the excoriation of the tantras by European scholars and their Asian students. We can cite as an example the following description of the *Guhyasamāja* (regarded by the Tibetans as "the king of tantras") by Rajendralala Mitra in 1882:

> As a Tántric composition of the esoteric kind, it has all the characteristics of the worst specimens of Śákta works of that type. The professed object, in either case, is devotion of the highest kind—absolute and unconditional—at the sacrifice of all worldly attachments, wishes and aspirations; but in working it out theories are indulged in and practices enjoined which are at once the most revolting and horrible that human depravity could think of, and compared to which the worst specimens of Holiwell Street literature of the last century would appear absolutely pure. A shroud of mystery alone serves to prevent their true characters being seen, but divested of it works of the description would deserve to be burnt by the common hangman. Looking at them philosophically the great wonder is that even a system of religion so pure and so lofty in its aspirations as Buddhism could be made to ally itself with such pestilent dogmas and practices. . . . Such injunctions would, doubtless, be best treated as the ravings of madmen. Seeing, however, that the work in which they occur is reckoned to be the sacred scripture of millions of intelligent human beings, and their counterparts exist in almost the same words in Tantras which are held equally sacred by men who are by no means wanting in intellectual faculties of a high order, we can only deplore the weakness of human understanding which yields to such delusion in the name of religion, and the villainy of the priesthood which so successfully inculcates them.[27]

And in 1931, Benoytosh Bhattacharyya wrote in the preface to his *Introduction to Buddhist Esotericism*:

[26] S. Bagchi, ed., *The Guhyasamāja Tantra* (Darbhanga: The Mithila Institute, 1965), p. 1.

[27] Rajendralala Mitra, *The Sanskrit Buddhist Literature of Nepal* (New Delhi: Cosmo, 1981), pp. 261, 264 (reprint of 1882 edition).

> If at any time in the history of India the mind of the nation as a whole has been diseased, it was in the Tāntric Age, or the period immediately preceding the Muhammedan conquest of India. The story related in the pages of numerous Tāntric works is supposed to be so repugnant that, excepting a few, all respectable scholars have condemned them wholesale and left the field of Tantras severely alone. But in spite of what the great historians of Sanskrit literature have said against Tāntrism and the Tāntric literature, no one should forget that the Hindu population of India as a whole is even today in the grip of this very Tantra in its daily life, customs and usages, and is suffering from the same disease which originated 1,300 years ago and consumed the vitality slowly but surely during the long centuries. Someone should therefore take up the study comprising the diagnosis, aetiology, pathology and prognosis of the disease, so that more capable men may take up its treatment and eradication in the future.[28]

We cannot pause to consider here the still nebulous network of relations between what is called Hindu tantra and Buddhist tantra, other than to note that the common European narrative of "medieval" Hindu practices attaching themselves to Buddhism to produce Buddhist tantra must be read within a larger colonial history that has as one of its products the Victorian creation of a simple ethical creed called "primitive Buddhism," long extinct in India, remaining only as a relic best preserved by the European scholar.[29]

We find this particular etiology of tantra as early as Eugène Burnouf's 1844 *Introduction a l'histoire du Buddhisme indien*. There he describes the tantras as treatises of a very special character, in which a cult of bizarre gods and goddesses is mixed with the monotheistic system of northern Buddhism, with its theory of a supreme buddha and superhuman bodhisattvas. He notes that the tantras were not among the first of the Sanskrit manuscripts given to Brian Hodgson (the British Resident at the Court of Nepal and Burnouf's supplier of Buddhist texts) by his Nepalese informant; they were only provided to him after he had obtained many other works of a different kind. The tantras, however, represent an impure and vulgar cult of personification of the female principle, as found among the Śaivas. "One understands," Burnouf concludes, "that an honest Buddhist would hesitate to turn over to a stranger the proofs of an alliance so monstrous" so contrary is it to the simplicity of primitive Buddhism.[30] A study of the tantras, he concedes nonetheless, is impor-

[28] Benoytosh Bhattacharyya, *An Introduction to Buddhist Esotericism* (Delhi: Motilal Banarsidass, 1980), p. vii.

[29] See Donald S. Lopez, Jr., ed., *Curators of the Buddha: The Study of Buddhism under Colonialism* (Chicago: University of Chicago Press, 1995).

[30] Eugène Burnouf, *Introduction a l'histoire du Buddhisme indien* (Paris: Imprimerie Royale, 1844), p. 523.

tant for the history of human superstition. Furthermore, "it is certainly not without interest to see Buddhism, which in its first form had so little of what constitutes a religion, end in practices so puerile and superstitions so exaggerated. But this deplorable spectacle very quickly wearies the curiosity and insults the intelligence."[31]

Burnouf is therefore somewhat vexed to find that the Transylvanian scholar Alexander Csoma de Kőrös had praised certain tantras in his 1839 survey of the Tibetan canon. For example, he wrote of the *Guhyasamāja* (the very work scorned by Mitra above), "This and the preceding work [the *Śrīcaṇḍamahāroṣaṇa*, which he calls "an excellent *tantra*, and in a good and easy translation"] are well worthy of being read and studied, as they will give an idea of what the ancients thought of the human soul and of God."[32] Another tantra has "several passages containing excellent ideas of the Supreme being."[33] The *Mañjuśrīmūlatantra* "is a very learned and interesting treatise and is frequently cited by Tibetan writers."[34] Burnouf expresses his surprise that this distinguished scholar "would find only words of admiration and enthusiasm for books that seem to me the miserable product of ignorance and the most coarse credulity. But the Tantras, in replacing the simple cult of Śākyamuni with adoration for a throng of fantastic divinities, have evidently transformed Buddhism and thereby given birth to a particular literary development that can be seen to have an appealing side. I only regret not having seen it, or perhaps having lost the requisite courage to seek it."[35]

For Burnouf, the source of the superstitions and debased practices is Śaivism, which, through a process of unnatural association, eventually (and quite late) came to pollute Buddhism, resulting in the composition of the Buddhist tantras. With the exception of the individual practice of asceticism, "one seeks vainly elsewhere for evidence of harmony between the two doctrines, and it is necessary to descend as far as the Tantras to see them combined in a way that is [both] monstrous and unknown to all the schools of Buddhism, except that of the north."[36] This alliance with Śaivism, then, unknown to primitive Buddhism because it is contrary to

[31] Ibid., p. 527.

[32] Csoma de Kőrös, *Tibetan Studies*, p. 497; reprint p. 369.

[33] Ibid., p. 492; reprint p. 364.

[34] Ibid., p. 513; reprint p. 385.

[35] Burnouf, *Introduction*, p. 528. He goes on to challenge Csoma politely in a note on the same page: "But would it not be necessary to establish beforehand that these Tantras were in effect ancient productions, and is it not useful to remark that nothing that they teach is found in either the Vinaya or the Sūtras, which are, on the contrary, almost completely filled with the history of Śākyamuni or his disciples, the relatively early date of which is not questioned by anyone?"

[36] Ibid., p. 554.

its spirit, is the result of later borrowing. There was never a complete fusion of Buddhism and Śaivism. Rather, "there is only a practice of various ceremonies and an adoration of various Śivaist divinities by the Buddhists, who seem little concerned by the discordance that exists between their ancient path and these new superstitions." Burnouf speculates, then, that the responsibility lies with Buddhists, "who in guarding their beliefs and their philosophy from them [the Śaivites], were willing to practice certain Śivaist rites which promised them well-being in this world, and carried their origin back to Śakyamuni in order to further legitimate them."[37]

The next European scholar to investigate Buddhist tantra was Louis de la Vallée Poussin (1869–1937), whose early research (1894–98) centered on the *Pañcakrama*, a commentary on the *Guhyasamāja* attributed to Nāgārjuna.[38] Although he largely turned away from tantric studies (perhaps in part because of the opprobrium with which tantra was regarded at that time), he was invited to write the article on Buddhist tantrism for the 1922 *Encyclopedia of Religion and Ethics*. Although he repeats the view current from the time of Burnouf, that "Buddhist tāntrism is practically Buddhist Hinduism, Hinduism or Śaivism in Buddhist garb,"[39] he acknowledges, as Burnouf did not, that tantric elements were present in primitive Buddhism: "The Old Buddhism, as preserved in the Pāli canon and in the Sanskrit Hīnayāna literature, has a number of features which are not specifically Buddhist, which are alien to the noble eightfold path, which, to put it otherwise, are more or less Tāntrik or open the way to Tantrism properly so called."[40] These include: (1) the belief in the power of "statements of truth" (*satyavacana*), which he describes as "half-magical 'formulas of protection'"; (2) respect paid to powerful and unfriendly deities; (3) the worship of relics, the construction of stūpas, the practice of pilgrimage, and "idolatry"; and (4) what he calls "the machinery of meditation," by which he means the various techniques for attaining the dhyānas (concentrations) and *samāpatti*s (absorptions),

[37] Ibid., p. 549.

[38] De la Vallée Poussin's publications during this period include "Note sur le Pañcakrama," *Actes du Xe Congrès international des Orientalistes* 1 (1894): 137–46; *Études et textes tantriques, I. Pañcakrama*, Recueil de travaux publ. par la Faculté de Philosophie et Lettres, Universite de Gand, fasc. 16 (1896); "Une practique des Tantras," *Actes du XIe Congrès international des Orientalistes* 1 (1897): 241–44; and chap. 5 of his *Bouddhisme: Études et Matériaux. Ādikarmapradīpa, Bodhicaryāvatāraṭīkā* (London: Luzac, 1898).

[39] Louis de la Vallée Poussin, "Tāntrism (Buddhist)," in James Hastings, ed., *Encyclopedia of Religion and Ethics*, vol. 12 (New York: Charles Scribner's Sons, 1922), p. 193. He discusses tantrism at length earlier in *Bouddhisme: Opinions sur l'histoire de la dogmatique* (Paris: Gabriel Beauchesne et Cie., 1908), pp. 342–412, and *Bouddhisme: Études et Matériaux*, pp. 72–81, 118–76.

[40] De la Vallée Poussin, "Tāntrism (Buddhist)," p. 194.

prerequisites for gaining the salvific knowledge of nirvāṇa. All of these states of absorption and the methods for attaining them "have been borrowed by Buddhism from Hindu *yoga*."[41]

Throughout his wide-ranging Buddhist studies, de la Vallée Poussin appears as the most anti-essentialist of the major Buddhologists of the late nineteenth and early twentieth centuries. He argued at the beginning of his career that in his opinion Buddhism was not simply the doctrine preached by Śākyamuni but rather "the general state of beliefs that has condensed around the name of the Buddha."[42] And at the end of his career, after scores of detailed studies of a wide variety of Indian Buddhist texts, he concluded that "Buddhism is not wholly original; it appears during the centuries, as a 'buddhification' of institutions, ideas, or feelings which were simply Indian. . . . In short, Buddhism is only the 'buddhized' aspect of contemporaneous Hinduism."[43] He writes with a certain bemusement of the "indiscreet zeal" that Buddhism has generated, especially in America, England, and Germany, where "one finds some strange ideas about Buddhism. Many writers assert that by a privilege unique in the history of religions it possesses a purely rationalist philosophy, an ideal compatible with modern science, and a morality without a god and without a soul."[44] Buddhism, for de la Vallée Poussin, was instead a branch of yoga, by which he meant "An ensemble of practices honored since the most ancient times of Aryan or autochthonous India: practices of sorcerers and thaumaturges of which the dominant motif appears to be inquiry into hypnotic states. . . . In itself it is a technique foreign to all morality, as it is to any religious or philosophical view. But from this technique could emerge, to this technique could be added morality, theology, devotion, and—it is said—theosophy."[45] What was added to this yoga to make it Buddhist was little more than a devotion to the cult of the Buddha. The earliest Buddhism had nothing that could strictly be termed philosophy or metaphysics. All of that was added later. "Buddhism ends in an act of faith. Śākyamuni will lead us to salvation provided we close our eyes and follow blindly his ordinance."[46]

De la Vallée Poussin, then, unlike many of his British contemporaries,

[41] Ibid.

[42] This statement occurs in the *Journal of the Royal Asiatic Society* (1899): 142 in his brief response to E. J. Rapson's review of his *Bouddhisme: Études et Matériaux. Ādikarmapradīpa, Bodhicāryāvatara*.

[43] Louis de la Vallée Poussin, "Buddhism," in Geoffrey. T. Garratt, ed., *The Legacy of India* (Oxford: Clarendon, 1937), p. 162.

[44] Louis de la Vallée Poussin, *Bouddhisme*: *Opinions*, pp. 1–2.

[45] Louis de la Vallée Poussin, *Nirvāṇa* (Paris: Gabriel Beauchesne, 1925), p. 12.

[46] Louis de la Vallée Poussin, *The Way to Nirvāṇa: Six Lectures on Ancient Buddhism as a Discipline of Salvation* (Cambridge: The University Press, 1917), p. 138.

rejected the notion of what he termed in 1898 "l'antériorité du Bouddhisme atheé et philosophique,"[47] an original or primitive Buddhism that only eventually had succumbed to popular accretions. These elements have most certainly been mixed into Buddhism, but unlike his predecessors and contemporaries, de la Vallée Poussin finds these alien elements present from the beginning; as he says, "Old Buddhism . . . has a number of features which are not specifically Buddhist." He generally resists speculation about what it might be, then, that is specifically Buddhist, renouncing the reification of Buddhism as something unique or even particularly distinctive within what he perceives as the main currents of Indian religiosity. He seems to prefer instead simply to hold that Buddhism is the various beliefs and practices of people who have historically called themselves Buddhists.

It is therefore noteworthy that despite eschewing a prior Buddhism, de la Vallée Poussin still wants to see tantra as somehow "alien." As noted earlier, in his article on tantra in the *Encyclopedia of Religion and Ethics* he discerns in the Old Buddhism "a number of features which are not specifically Buddhist, which are alien to the noble eightfold path, which, to put it otherwise, are more or less Tāntrik or open the way to Tantrism properly so called."[48] What is specifically Buddhist seems here to be the eightfold path, despite the fact that dhyāna (what he calls "trance") is at once both the fourth of the alien elements (as listed above) as well as the eighth constituent of the eightfold path. These alien elements only increase in the Mahāyāna, where formulas are mechanically recited and offerings are symbolically made with the promise of wonderful, but mundane, advantages. This leads eventually to "Tantrism proper," which, for de la Vallée Poussin has two distinct elements. On the one hand, there are "the vulgar magical rites" that had been present for many centuries in the religions of India, including Buddhism. On the other hand, however, there is the Vajrayāna, a highly developed mysticism, a "theurgy" that is "an innovation in Buddhism."[49] He does not elaborate on what is particularly "Buddhist" about this innovation, since theurgy, a technique for compelling a god to act, would seem to have been present in India since the early performance of Vedic sacrifice.

There appears, then, to be something about tantra that attracts to itself, even for such an anti-essentialist as de la Vallée Poussin, notions of admixture and decline. The moment he posits something that is "specifically Buddhist" to which alien elements become added, the mixing bowl spins out of control. If the specifically Buddhist is the eightfold path, then

[47] Louis de la Vallée Poussin, *Bouddhisme: Études et Matériaux*, p. 43.

[48] Louis de la Vallée Poussin, "Tāntrism (Buddhist)," p. 194.

[49] Ibid., p. 195.

the very yogic practices that he characterizes as "tantric" are implicated in the final constituent of the list, dhyāna. The process of incorporation of the alien continues until it is possible to discern something called "tantrism proper" where he sees an "innovation of Buddhism" in the theurgy of the Vajrayāna, perhaps one of the most archaic (and certainly pre-Buddhist) of Indian ritual forms. Elsewhere, as noted above, de la Vallée Poussin had pointed to devotion to the Buddha as what set Buddhism apart. Yet in his article on tantra he asserts that "Worship, with the whole of the religious practices, is a Tāntrik topic."[50] Does it follow, then, that what is specifically Buddhist is specifically tantric?

This is the logic of the supplement, the inessential entity added to compensate for a lack in that which is apparently complete in itself, only to take the place of the supplemented. "The supplement adds itself, it is a surplus, a plenitude enriching another plenitude, the fullest measure of presence."[51] Yet the supplement also "adds only to replace. It intervenes or insinuates itself in-the-place-of; if it fills, it is as if one fills a void."[52] Tantra functions as a lamented supplement in the European construction of an original Buddhism. As Monier Williams described Buddhism in his 1888 Duff Lectures, "It had no hierarchy in the proper sense of that term—no church, no priests, no true form of prayer, no religious rites, no ceremonial observances."[53] In order for this pure Buddhism to be posited, it must eventually be made impure, and in the nineteenth century, the alien element added was generally named "tantra." The process of admixture was portrayed as a graft gone wrong. Whereas the Indian and Tibetan exegetes tended to portray tantra as the addition of what was essential to bring forth the fruit of enlightenment, Victorian scholars viewed tantra as a parasite that destroyed its host. "And this Yoga parasite, containing within itself the germs of Tantrism, seized strong hold of its host and soon developed its monster outgrowths, which crushed and cankered most of the little life of purely Buddhist stock yet left in the Mahāyāna."[54] The result in Tibet was a degenerate form so alien to the original that it no longer could be called Buddhism; it was more accurately termed "Lamaism."[55]

[50] Ibid., p. 194.

[51] Jacques Derrida, *Of Grammatology*, trans. Gayatri Chakravorty Spivak (Baltimore: Johns Hopkins University Press, 1976), p. 144.

[52] Ibid., p. 145.

[53] Sir Monier Monier-Williams, *Buddhism, In Its Connexion with Brāhmanism and Hindūism, and In Its Contrast with Christianity* (Varanasi: Cowkhamba Sanskrit Series Office, 1964), p. 253.

[54] Ibid., p. 14.

[55] See Donald S. Lopez, Jr., "'Lamaism' and the Disappearance of Tibet," *Comparative Studies in Society and History*, 38, no. 1 (January 1996).

In this scheme, tantra is emblematic of the category of the other in Indian religion, that factor in contradistinction from which an orthodoxy is defined by the Western scholar. Tantra, so generally excoriated as non-Buddhist, as popular, as degenerate, as a late development, proves to be the condition for the very possibility of representing an original Buddhism. In the binary hierarchy, whether it be the Buddhist's sūtra/tantra or the Buddhologist's primitive Buddhism/tantric Buddhism, the second term comes to replace the first, serving as a substitute for it. For the Indian exegetes *sūtrayāna* comes to be known (sometimes dismissively) as the "definition vehicle" (*lakṣanayāna*). For the Western exegete, the replacement of primitive Buddhism by tantric Buddhism is portrayed as a lamentable historical eventuality, but as our reading of de la Vallée Poussin suggests, it was an eventuality fully present from the beginning; it was what was most Buddhist about old Buddhism. The term "tantra" is a point of condensation, an element of opposition that serves also to subvert the opposition. Its identification, therefore, continues to remain elusive. As Derrida writes, "It is the strange essence of the supplement not to have essentiality: it may always not have taken place. Moreover, literally, it has never taken place: it is never present, here and now. If it were, it would not be what it is, a supplement, taking and keeping the place of the other."[56]

All of this may lead to the conclusion that tantra is a term that somehow resists definition. Wayne Proudfoot has identified certain terms, especially those connected with certain "mystical" traditions, as "placeholders." For example, the opening passage of the *Dao de jing* says that the *dao* that can be spoken of is not the *dao*. From that point on in the text, Proudfoot argues, the term *dao* excludes all predicates, descriptions, and ordinary connotations that might serve to differentiate it while at the same time creating a sense of mystery.[57] Placeholders repel all attributions, their very opacity lending them a quality of ineffability and transcendence. But despite tantra's apparent resistance to definition, it seems also to resist characterization as a placeholder. For as we have seen, far from repelling attributions and connotations, it seems to attract them like a magnet. And though it seems thus far to remain ineffable, its inef-

[56] Derrida, *Of Grammatology*, p. 314.

[57] Wayne Proudfoot, *Religious Experience* (Berkeley: University of California Press, 1985), pp. 127–28. He gives as other examples *neti neti* of the *Chandogya Upaniṣad* and *śunyātā* [sic], because Nāgārjuna says that *śūnyatā* is also empty. Proudfoot does not pursue the question of what it is of which emptiness is empty. Had he done so, it is unlikely that he would have called it a "placeholder" despite the apparent links between *śūnya* and zero (which he does not consider). Furthermore, although some persist in characterizing the *Dao de jing* and *Upaniṣads* with the problematic term "mystical," there would seem to be few who would so characterize the *Madhyamakaśāstra*.

fability is of a distinctively quotidian rather than transcendent quality. But Proudfoot distinguishes a second category of "placeholder." In addition to those terms that systematically preclude determinate attributions within a particular tradition are those extracted from their traditional linguistic context, emptied of their original meaning, and employed by scholars to designate a universal religious essence, terms such as *numinous*, *mana*, and *tabu*, whose ineffability is enhanced by remaining untranslated.[58] Tantra would seem better suited as this type of placeholder, especially in such terms as "Native American tantra." But before reaching such a conclusion, there is perhaps some value in considering the case of *mana* at greater length.

In his *Theories of Primitive Religion*, Evans-Pritchard described *mana* as "a Melanesian word anthropologists had adopted into their vocabulary with, I believe, disastrous results."[59] One of the anthropologists that Evans-Pritchard names is Marcel Mauss, whose 1902 *A General Theory of Magic* makes substantial use of the notion of *mana*. Mauss writes:

> It is not enough to say that the quality of *mana* is attributed to certain things because of the relative position they hold in society. We must add that the idea of *mana* is none other than the idea of these relative values and the idea of these differences in potential. . . . It goes without saying that ideas like this have no *raison d'être* outside society, that they are absurd as far as pure reason is concerned and that they derive purely and simply from the functioning of collective life.
>
> . . . They are the expression of social sentiments which are formed—sometimes inexorably and universally, sometimes fortuitously—with regard to certain things, chosen for the most part in an arbitrary fashion.[60]

Levi-Strauss, in his discussion of the role of *mana* in Mauss, has no particular problem with the fact that *mana* has been taken out of its Melanesian context. He even argues that "conceptions of the *mana* type are so frequent and so widespread that it is appropriate to wonder whether we are not dealing with a universal and permanent form of thought, which . . . might be a function of a certain way that the mind situates itself in the presence of things, which must therefore make an appearance whenever that mental situation is given."[61] For Levi-Strauss, unlike Proudfoot, such conceptions do not merely repel signification; they repre-

[58] Ibid., pp. 131–32. Proudfoot seems to rely heavily on Evans-Pritchard here. See his *Theories of Primitive Religion* (Oxford: Clarendon, 1965), pp. 11–12.

[59] Evans-Pritchard, *Theories*, p. 33.

[60] Marcel Mauss, *A General Theory of Magic*, trans. Robert Brain (New York: W. W. Norton, 1972), p. 121.

[61] Claude Levi-Strauss, *Introduction to the Work of Marcel Mauss*, trans. Felicity Baker (London: Routledge and Kegan Paul, 1987), p. 53.

sent "an indeterminate value of signification, in itself devoid of meaning and thus susceptible of receiving any meaning at all." He seems here to be referring to nothing more than the tendency to use a particular term to designate that which is difficult to articulate, what we might call "that certain something." Such terms, which occur in all societies, provide a means for assimilating that which is of indeterminate value. In industrial societies, however, their use is more fluid and spontaneous, whereas in primitive societies "they serve as the ground of considered, official interpretive systems."[62]

Levi-Strauss argues that the function of terms like *mana* is to signal "a relationship of nonequivalence" between the signifier and signified.[63] The nonequivalence or "inadequation" derives from an imbalance between what Saussure calls the "two amorphous masses" of acoustical images and ideational material. Specifically, there is a surplus of signifiers relative to the signifieds to which they can be allocated. This is not, then, a case of a deficiency of signifiers, an inability of language to adequately describe reality (a notion familiar to us from various Western mystical traditions and from Buddhist texts such as the *Heart Sūtra*). The problem is an excess of signifiers. Since in Saussure's system there cannot in general be a signifier without a signified, it is necessary, as he says, "to maintain the parallelism between the two orders of difference."[64] Therefore, this overspill of signification must be soaked up so that "the available signifier and the mapped-out signified may remain in the relationship of complementarity which is the very condition of the exercise of symbolic thinking."[65] Terms like *mana*, which Levi-Strauss calls "floating signifiers," sit atop this overflow of signifiers so as to channel and contain it. In the performance of that function, such notions gather to themselves a range of contradictory qualities. It is possible for the floating signifier to be all of those things because it is none of them and thus able to assume any symbolic content. "In the system of symbols which makes up any cosmology, it would just be a zero symbolic value, that is, a sign marking the necessity of a supplementary symbolic content over and above that which the signified already contains, which can be any value at all, provided it is still part of the available reserve, and is not already, as the phonologists say, a term in a set."[66]

[62] Ibid., p. 55.

[63] Ibid., pp. 55–56.

[64] Ferdinand de Saussure, *Course in General Linguistics*, trans. Wade Baskin (New York: McGraw-Hill, 1966), p. 121.

[65] Levi-Strauss, *Introduction*, p. 63.

[66] Ibid., p. 64. For discussions of this passage by Derrida, see "Structure, Sign, and Play in the Discourse of the Human Sciences," in Jacques Derrida, *Writing and Difference*, trans. Alan Bass (Chicago: University of Chicago Press, 1978), pp. 288–90; and, more recently,

Levi-Strauss's criticism of Mauss is not that he used the term *mana* in a general theory outside of a specific social-historical context, but how he used it, imputing properties to *mana* in order to resolve contradictions that were evident only to him and that did not occur in Melanesia; "one wonders whether their [Durkheim and Mauss's] theory of *mana* is anything other than a device for imputing properties to indigenous thought which are implied by the very peculiar place that the idea of *mana* is called on to occupy in their own thinking."[67] Levi-Strauss thus seems on the one hand to posit the existence of "floating signifiers" in all societies; in our society such notions are of a "spontaneous character" whereas in primitive societies they provide the foundation for systems of interpretation, a role we give to science. On the other hand, Levi-Strauss condemns Mauss for seeking the origin of *mana* in this very same fluid realm of feelings and beliefs, "in an order of realities different from the relationships that it helps to construct. . . . But the notions of sentiment, fated inexorability, the fortuitous and the arbitrary are not scientific notions."[68] Mauss, it seems, is guilty of taking *mana*, which is a floating signifier for Melanesians, and using it as a floating signifier in a larger system, using it to soak up contradictions. In doing so, Mauss eschews science in favor of the epiphenomenal and mysterious.

The purpose of this excursus on *mana* is, of course, to raise the question of the value of replacing *mana* with the term "tantra" in the discussion above. Are modern scholars of Asian religion guilty, as Levi-Strauss judges Mauss to be, of using the term "tantra" to resolve contradictions that are ours alone, that is, which do not arise within "the tradition"? Herbert Guenther remarked in his study of Nāropa that tantrism is "probably one of the haziest notions and misconceptions the Western mind has evolved."[69] That the notion is hazy is certainly unobjectionable. The more interesting question is whether tantrism is somehow a product of the Western mind. We have noted briefly several of the disparate uses to which the term "tantra" (and its traditional synonyms) is put in Sanskrit and Tibetan Buddhist texts, raising the possibility that tantra is also a floating signifier in India and Tibet, gathering to itself over many centuries a range of contradictory qualities, "a zero symbolic value, that is, a sign marking the necessity of a supplementary symbolic content over and above that which the signified already contains." It is

---

Jacques Derrida, *Given Time: I. Counterfeit Money*, trans. Peggy Kamuf (Chicago: University of Chicago Press, 1992), pp. 77–78.

[67] Levi-Strauss, *Introduction*, p. 57.

[68] Ibid., p. 56.

[69] Herbert Guenther, *Life and Teachings of Nāropa*, (London: Oxford University Press, 1963), p. 112.

this supplementary content that would seem to be the key, suggesting that the various dyadic relations in which tantra holds the second position (*pradhāna*/tantra in Vedic sacrifice, sūtra/tantra in Buddhist scholasticism, original Buddhism/tantric Buddhism in Victorian Buddhology) is not merely a case of binary opposition. It may be, as Saussure notes, that "its value clearly depends on what is outside and around it."[70]

[70] Saussure, *General Linguistics*, p. 116.

Four

The Commentaries of Kamalaśīla and Śrīsiṃha

Commentary on the "Heart of the Perfection of Wisdom"

Prajñāpāramitāhṛdayanāmaṭīkā

KAMALAŚĪLA

Homage to the Noble Bhagavatī Perfection of Wisdom

Bowing to the Perfection of Wisdom, sole mother of all the buddhas, I write this commentary on its heart so that those who seek may understand.

When the Bhagavan set forth the noble perfection of wisdom, he set forth eight topics, beginning with the knowledge of all aspects (*sarvākārajñatā*) and concluding with the (dharmakāya), which explains the three bodies (trikāya).[1] [The perfection of wisdom was taught] to an audience composed of those of superior, intermediate, and inferior faculties: [331a] monks, bodhisattvas, and gods—the twenty thousand [gods] such as the king of gods, Śakra [Indra], who dwell in the realm of desire (*kāmadhātu*) and the realm of form (*rūpadhātu)*, as well as the [gods], such as Śakra, who abide in the three billion buddha lands. The five paths are those of accumulation (*saṃbhāra*), preparation (*prayoga*), vision (*darśana*), meditation (*bhāvanā*), and no more learning (*aśaikṣa*). With regard to these, the first comprises the establishments of mindfulness (*smṛtyupasthāna*)[2] through the final limb of emanation (*ṛddhipāda*).[3] The

[1] The eight topics of the Perfection of Wisdom sūtras are: the knowledge of all aspects (*sarvākārajñatā*), the knowledge of paths (*mārgajñatā*), the knowledge of the basis (*vastujñāna*), complete realization of all aspects (*sarvākārābhisaṃbodha*), peak realization (*mūrdhābhisamaya*), final realization (*anupūrvābhisamaya*), realization in one moment (*ekakṣanābhisaṃbodha*), and the dharmakāya.

[2] The four establishments of mindfulness are forms of meditation concentrating on the body, feelings, thoughts, and phenomena.

[3] The four limbs of emanation are aspiration (*chanda*), effort (*vīrya*), thought (*citta*), and analysis (*mīmāṃsā*). When Kamalaśīla says, "the establishments of mindfulness through the final limb of emanation," he is implying an intervening category, that of the four abandonments (*prahāṇa*): the wish to abandon afflictions (or nonvirtues) that have already been produced, the wish not to produce afflictions yet unproduced, the wish to

second [includes] the faculties (*indriya*) and powers (*bala*);[4] the third, the limbs of enlightenment (*bodhyaṅga*);[5] the fourth, the [eight]fold path of nobles (ārya); and the fifth, the so-called [bodies] of truth (dharmakāya), enjoyment (saṃbhogakāya), and emanation (nirmāṇakāya), the ten powers (*bala*), and so on.[6]

The assembly of bodhisattvas of superior faculties understands the perfection of wisdom, which is expressed by the five paths, through a single transmission that simply sets forth the twenty-two creations of the [altruistic] aspiration (*cittotpāda*) of [the category] of the knowledge of all aspects (*sarvākārajñatā*).[7] Precepts (*avavāda*) through collection (*saṃbhārapratipatti*) together with certain emergence (*niryāṇapratipatti*) at the end are taught for those of intermediate and inferior faculties.[8] Thus, the ten aspects [of *sarvākārajñatā*] are taught in order that the knowledge of all aspects be the object of bodhisattvas of superior, intermediate, and inferior faculties. Again, the knowledge of paths (*mārgajñatā*) and the knowledge of bases (*vastujñāna*) are taught to the audience of gods of the form and formless realms. The [realization of the] completion of all aspects (*sarvākārābhisaṃbodha*) to the [topic of] the dharmakāya are taught to the gods who abide in the three billion buddha lands. [331b]

In the very extensive teaching, the *Śatasāhasrikā* (Perfection of Wisdom in 100,000 Stanzas) all of the topics, such as the twenty-two creations of the [altruistic] mind, are explained to the best of the bodhisat-

---

increase pure phenomena (or virtues) already produced, and the wish to produce pure phenomena yet unproduced.

[4] The faculties and powers are faith (śraddhā), effort (*vīrya*), mindfulness (*smṛti*), samādhi, and wisdom (prajñā), with the faculties being attained on the heat and peak levels of the path of preparation and the powers being attained on the forbearance and supreme mundane quality levels of the path of preparation.

[5] The seven limbs of enlightenment are: mindfulness (*smṛti*), analysis of phenomena (*dharmapravicaya*), effort (*vīrya*), joy (*prīti*), pliancy (*praśrabdhi*), samādhi, and equanimity (*upekṣā*).

[6] For a description of the ten powers of a buddha, see Jeffrey Hopkins, *Meditation on Emptiness* (London: Wisdom, 1983), pp. 208–10. "And so on" presumably refers to other qualities of a buddha, such as the four fearlessnesses (*vaiśāradya*) and the eighteen unique attributes (*āveṇikadharma*).

[7] The first of the ten topics that illustrate the knowledge of all aspects (the first of the eight categories of the Perfection of Wisdom sūtras) is the creation of the aspiration to enlightenment (*cittotpāda*). *Abhisamayālaṃkāra* 1.19–20 lists twenty-two metaphoric types of the bodhisattva's aspiration: earth, gold, moon, fire, treasure, jewel-mine, ocean, fire, *vajra*, mountain, medicine, virtuous friend, wish-granting gem, sun, song, king, treasury, highway, vehicle, fountain, euphonous sound, river, and cloud. For Haribhadra's description of how each derives its name, see E. Obermiller, *Analysis of the Abhisamayālaṃkāra*, Calcutta Oriental series, no. 27 (London: Luzac, 1933), pp. 22–32.

[8] Precepts (*avavāda*) is the second of ten topics illustrating the knowledge of all aspects. Collection (*saṃbhāra*) and certain emergence (*niryāṇa*) are the ninth and tenth.

tvas of superior faculties, such as Bhadrapāla and Ratnasambhava, and are [also] explained in the *Pañcaviṃśati* (Perfection of Wisdom in 25,000 Stanzas), the explanation of intermediate length. In the condensed version, the *Aṣṭasāhasrikā* (Perfection of Wisdom in 8,000 Stanzas), they are absent. However, the commentators assert that the fault of the rapporteur [not mentioning bodhisattvas] is eliminated because the twenty-two creations of the [altruistic] aspiration are explained by these words of the bodhisattva, "Subhūti, bodhisattva *mahāsattvas* begin from the perfection of wisdom. As bodhisattva *mahāsattvas* emerge into the perfection of wisdom, so should you be courageous."

Here, in the text that condenses the three perfections of wisdom [the extensive, intermediate, and condensed], the fivefold nature is said to be the meaning of the eight aspects. Regarding that, at the beginning, the connection is set forth through the statement of the setting, which has five marvels: the time of the teaching, the teacher, the place, the audience, and the doctrine. The relation between merit and wisdom is indicated by the words *perception of the profound* because, since [phenomena] are by nature like illusions, they appear from the nonexistent. Here, the bhagavan, the noble Avalokiteśvara, views the categories of phenomena with the supramundane wisdom of subsequent attainment (*pṛṣṭalabdhajñāna*). Right after that, Śāriputra, in order that the threefold audience [332a] might understand, says, through the blessing of the Buddha, to Avalokiteśvara, an emanation of the Buddha, *How should one train?* The assumption of the question is that one must make effort at training; making effort is certain. Moreover, [one must do so] with valid knowledge (*pramāṇa*). Valid knowledge is of two types. Because the direct perception of those who look nearby [i.e., the unenlightened] observes the real and the unreal, they are lost; they completely misunderstand the way things are. And that [is also the case] with [their] inference, because it is preceded [by such direct perception]. Furthermore, because they lack valid knowledge, they come to have doubt. And Śāradvatīputra [i.e., Śāriputra] asks the noble Avalokiteśvara. And the noble Avalokiteśvara, having been blessed by the perfect and complete Buddha, relies on the illusion-like nature that is empty of existence and nonexistence. This is the asking of the question and the giving of the answer.

Because it teaches the five paths, it is like this, beginning from, *Those five aggregates are empty of intrinsic entity* to *they are completely awakened into unsurpassed, perfect, complete enlightenment.* The meaning of his answer is, "Śāradvatīputra, the three audiences of bodhisattvas should train by inferentially understanding the object, the ultimate truth. It is not to be done with direct perception because it is not an object of the direct perception of those who look nearby, because they have no valid knowledge of the object [the ultimate truth], and because they lack the capacity. Yogins [see emptiness with] direct perception because they have already trained in [inferential understanding] and because they have no need to train in it [further]. One should train in the ultimate with inferential consciousness." [332b] Here, it is the inferential consciousness that will ascertain the perfection of wisdom, which is the illusion-like emptiness.

The assembly of monks, the bodhisattvas, and the gathering of gods analyze how the aggregates, which are spoken of as objects of knowledge and consciousnesses, have an entity of causes or a nature of effects [and see] indeed that that which is ultimate is not produced through connection with a cause because [production] by what is the same, different, both, or neither is not feasible. It is also not correct that effects [are produced] from the existent or the nonexistent.

With respect to that, beginning with *Thus, even those five aggregates are empty of intrinsic existence* through *consciousness is empty* sets forth the paths of accumulation and preparation. The eight terms from *Śāriputra, it is thus* through *unfilled*, set forth the path of vision, which has a nature of the uninterrupted path and the path of liberation. From *Śāriputra, it is thus* through *no attainment* sets forth the path of meditation. From *Śāriputra, it is thus* through *relying on* indicates one [thing], the first path that is a preparation for the path of no more learning, the *vajra*-like samādhi. *Because their minds are without observation*[9] they pass completely beyond error is the second characteristic which is the actual [attainment of the path of no more learning]. *They go to the completion of nirvāṇa* to *they are awakened into unsurpassed, complete, perfect enlightenment* [indicates] the third characteristic, the bodies of enjoyment and emanation [achieved] through subsequent attainment (*pṛṣṭhalabdhajñāna*). *Therefore, it should be known* [333a] sets forth the five paths from the standpoint of the benefits [provided] by the five words of the mantra. Those five paths are the meaning of the perfection of wisdom.

Also, the statement of Asaṅga is thus: Regarding armor (*saṃnāha*), the nature of the six perfections is the path of accumulation. Regarding entry (*pravṛtti*), heat (*ūṣma*), peak (*mūrdha*), and forbearance (*kṣānti*) are the nature of the path of preparation. Fifteen of the seventeen accumulations[10] are included in supreme mundane qualities (*laukika-agradharma*) that are contained in the path of preparation. The collection of the stages (*bhūmisaṃbhāra*),[11] the collection of the antidotes (*pratipakṣa*-

[9] The text reads *sems la dmigs pa med pa 'dis* instead of *sems la sgrib pa med pas.*

[10] For a description of the seventeen accumulations, see Obermiller, *Analysis of the Abhisamyālaṃkāra*, pp. 119–84

[11] See ibid., pp. 144–79.

saṃbhāra),[12] the path of vision, the path of meditation, and the eight emergences (*niryāṇa*)[13] are the *vajra*-like samādhi. The actualization of enlightenment in one moment (*ekakṣanābhisaṃbodha*) is the path of no more learning.[14] *Those monks*[15] to *all surrounding* indicates the coming together at the end.

This completes the commentary on the heart of the perfection of wisdom by the master Kamalaśīla. It was translated and revised by the Indian master Kumāraśrībhadra and the Tibetan translator 'Phags pa shes rab.

Commentary on the Heart Sūtra as Mantra

ŚRĪSIṂHA

I bow down and go for refuge to the Bhagavan Vairocana, and so on, [206a] the two mothers, and the saṃgha—the supreme of assemblies.

I will set forth this elucidation of the sūtra as mantra to supreme beings in order that all the *bodhicitta* and compassion-observing sentient beings not be separated from the sūtra itself, endowed with the three words (*evaṃ mayā śrutam*). I do not set this forth for logicians. *Thus did I hear at one time* specifies the time as this and not another time. Furthermore, it is not one's own [i.e., the rapporteur's] understanding; it is the time of hearing this speech from another. In addition, it means that the rapporteur himself is a great listener. The time is the time of the assembly of the primary audience. *At one time* [means] that it is not as if they asked many times or repeatedly; the primary audience gathered at one time.

Bhagavan indicates the nature of the teacher. The ordinary [meaning] is that he destroyed the four *māra*s, was endowed with the six perfections, and passed beyond wrong consciousness. The special [meaning] is that he destroyed the realm of appearance, such as the five aggregates, [and transformed them] into the nature of deities [i.e., buddhas], he was endowed with the meaning of reality, and he passed beyond the conception of objects. The special unsurpassed destruction is the destruction that is free from exertion, within the state of the essence of the phenomena of saṃsāra and nirvāṇa, whereby one is endowed with the great wis-

[12] See ibid., pp. 179–84.

[13] See ibid., pp. 185–91.

[14] See E. Obermiller, *Prajñāpāramitā in Tibetan Buddhism*, ed. Harcharan Singh Sobti (Delhi: Motilal Banarsidass, 1988), p. 77, n. 7.

[15] This phrase (*dge slong de dag*) does not appear in the sūtra.

dom of self-awareness. One passes beyond the words or extremes of the dualistic appearances of saṃsāra and nirvāṇa because nothing is established as an entity.

Vulture Peak in Rājagṛha indicates the specific place. The external place is the mountain that is [shaped] like a pile of jewels or like a round stūpa in the eastern part of the land of Magadha, the abode of King Bimbisāra, where the buddhas abide, the special place among all mountains. The internal place is the [pure land of] Akaniṣṭha, where one does not go to the depths of form, signs, or apprehension. The secret place is the awareness [and] *bodhicitta* that abide throughout saṃsāra and nirvāṇa.

Was abiding with a great assembly of monks [206b] *and a great assembly of bodhisattvas* indicates the audience. The outer audience are monks because they are aspirants on the stage of belief and abide in virtue. Those who are heroic in practice and in the intention to meditate on the view are the great assembly; those who are able [to bring about] the welfare of others is the assembly of bodhisattvas. An audience of such [persons] abides together. The inner audience is the audience of saṃbhogakāyas such as the buddhas of the five lineages. The secret audience is the indivisible essence of the wisdom of self-awareness. The dharma was set forth at that time. The outer dharma is dharma for training, such as the ten virtues. The inner dharma is the dharma of the Mahāyāna. The secret dharma is the wisdom that is awareness.

At that time, the Bhagavan was absorbed in a samādhi on the enumerations of phenomena called "perception of the profound" [means] when the five marvels were present. At the time of the maturation of the audience, the Bhagavan abided in absorption without observation in such a samādhi on the enumerations of phenomena—the outer, inner, and secret phenomena—on the profundity of emptiness, that is, on the meaning of the profound, the nonexistence of real phenomena. Furthermore, the outer samādhi abides on the real phenomena; the inner samādhi, on the nonexistence of the real; the secret, on the meaning of not making a division into those.

Also at that time, the bodhisattva, the mahāsattva, the noble Avalokiteśvara beheld the practice of the profound perfection of wisdom and saw that those five aggregates also are empty of intrinsic nature. While the teacher abided in the solitary state of reality, the primary member of the audience [Avalokiteśvara] remained naturally. Regarding *bodhisattva*, the outer [meaning] is one who abides on the level of training. The inner [meaning] is to master the ten stages and above. The secret [meaning] is the essential meaning itself. Also, bodhisattva [means] achieving one's own welfare; *mahāsattva* [means] achieving the welfare of others. [207a] The ordinary [meaning] of *noble* (ārya) is [one] who is far above the afflictions or saṃsāra. The special [meaning] is the retinue of a saṃbhogakāya. The unsurpassed [meaning] is the essential meaning of awareness, the dharmakāya. For his own welfare, he looks down, that is, he understands the meaning himself. For the welfare of others he looks, that is, he is able to teach disciples of whatever inclination. Therefore, he is the lord of self and other or of saṃsāra and nirvāṇa. That is the meaning [of his name].

With the wisdom of scripture, one is able to set forth saṃsāra and nirvāṇa. With the wisdom of awareness, one arrives at the meaning. With the unobservable wisdom, nothing is divided. Therefore, one goes beyond saṃsāra, one goes beyond the nirvāṇa that is the absence of suffering, and compassion comes forth. Regarding *profound*, it is profound because its entity does not appear as a thing; it is profound because it is difficult to explain; it is profound because it is beyond cause and effect. *Practice* is one's comprehension of such a meaning. Therefore, it is viewing reality again and again without observation. The object that is viewed is the *aggregates*. *Five* is their number. Regarding the five aggregates, the common five are the five such as form. The special five are the buddhas of the five lineages. The qualities of the five aggregates are the five unsurpassed wisdoms. Those entities of the aggregates are pure. One who is endowed with purity through contemplation is one on the stages and the paths, a person of belief. Seeing [things] to be free of intrinsic nature is the realization of the meaning. The very meaning of reality is empty. The [meaning of empty] in seeing [things as] empty is not like the nonexistence of one thing in another. The emptiness of nonexistence is the entity of awareness, and so on; the emptiness of something that has been destroyed is made up of particles. The thing or the object of observation that is the emptiness of intrinsic nature is the essential meaning. The wisdom that lacks observation in that way is the meaning of see.

Then, by the power of the Buddha, the venerable Śāriputra said this to the bodhisattva, the mahāsattva, the noble Avalokiteśvara. [207b] *How should sons of good lineage who wish to practice the profound perfection of wisdom train?* This is Śāriputra's question to Avalokiteśvara. Avalokiteśvara was liberated by the power of Śākyamuni Buddha. Śāriputra was able to have the capacity of the question due to his power. Therefore, [the sūtra says] *by the power of the Buddha*. Because he is free from birth and death, he has a deathless life [and is therefore *venerable*]. He has completely abandoned mothers of other lineages; his mother is the Śākya lineage. He asked the question considering the welfare of others. He asks, "What method of training, other than Avalokiteśvara's practice, should those children of the lineage of belief in the Mahāyāna train in if they desire to practice the meaning of the profound perfection of wisdom of the unobservable?"

The bodhisattva, the mahāsattva, the noble Avalokita said this to the venerable Śāradvatīputra. This indicates the answer. *Śāriputra, a son of good lineage or a daughter of good lineage who wishes to practice the profound perfection of wisdom, should train in this way.* This is the spoken statement. It means, "If you, a male or female of the lineage of belief in the Mahāyāna, wish now to practice the meaning of the practice of the wisdom of nonobservation, train like this." *View those five aggregates also as empty of intrinsic nature.* Such things as those ordinary aggregates are primordially empty. Therefore, see them as I do, as empty of intrinsic nature. [He said that] so that they would believe. *Form is empty* [means that] the entity of form is the nature of emptiness. *Emptiness is form* [means that] because emptiness does not negate object and awareness it appears as form. *Form is not other than emptiness* [means that] the phenomena of saṃsāra and nirvāṇa do not appear apart from emptiness; [208a] there is no other appearance of form apart from nonnegation of the qualities of emptiness. Just as form abides, feeling, discrimination, conditioning factors, and so on abide in that in the same way. That is the meaning of abiding like form.

In the same way Śāriputra, all phenomena are emptiness. Śāriputra, the things of saṃsāra such as form [are] emptiness, without reality. Therefore, all the phenomena of nirvāṇa are the emptiness of intrinsic nature. Regarding the meaning of *emptiness*, the very meaning of emptiness is like this: form or emptiness are utterly *without characteristic*; it is *not produced* by causes and conditions; the qualities of its entity are ever *not destroyed*; the *stains* of things *do not exist* in any way; because it has never, from the beginning, fallen to the position of subject or object, it also is *not stainless*; the essential meaning is *undiminished* by conditions; having been produced by other causes, there is no cause for it to be filled with qualities, [therefore it is *unfilled*].

Therefore, Śāriputra [indicates] that apart from emptiness, which is the object of observation, there is nothing to be practiced and nothing to be established because form is emptiness. Therefore, feeling, and so on are also without duality. Nothing, the five doors of the senses, such as the *eye*, the five [sense] activities, or the five phenomena, exist as objects of observation. Their constituents, such as the eye, are also indivisible. Thus, the essential meaning is that ignorance does not exist and the cause of its *extinction does not exist*. In the meaning of emptiness itself, *aging and death do not exist*. Therefore, *the extinction* of the dependent arising *of* birth, *aging*, sickness, *and death do not exist*. Thus, in the meaning itself *suffering*, that is, what is established through the five poisons, *does not exist*; the afflictions that are their *origin do not exist*. Because of that, the establishment of the miserable in happiness [i.e., *cessation*] also *does not exist*. Because of that, if there are no things to be practiced in saṃsāra, there is *no* cause for attaining the *path* that brings about nirvāṇa; the paths and stages do not exist for practice or progress. [208b] That even the five common wisdoms do not exist means that apart from the essential meaning, there is *no attainment*. Because the meaning of their own substance is self-arisen from the beginning, there is also *no* cause of *nonattainment*.

Therefore, Śāriputra, because bodhisattvas have no attainment, they rely on and abide in the perfection of wisdom. Śāriputra, there is no cause of attainment other than the path. Therefore, there is no attainment other than fruition. Thus, because it is without observation, the perfection of wisdom is called the complete essential teaching. [The sūtra] says [that bodhisattvas] rely and abide in that fruition. *Because their minds are without obstructions, they are without fear. Having completely passed beyond all error, they go to the completion of nirvāṇa*. Because the meaning of the fruition abides as self-arisen, there is nothing other than that. Hence, there are no obstructive factors in their minds. Because there is nothing to be attained elsewhere, there is also no fear of doubt. They have completely passed beyond all wrong consciousness, that is, they have no consciousness that observes saṃsāra. They have gone to completion in nirvāṇa, that is, to the stage of buddhahood.

All the buddhas who abide in the three times have been fully awakened into unsurpassed, perfect, complete enlightenment through relying on the perfection of wisdom. Thus, having established the sole cause of the effect, it is not that there is no cause of attainment. Relying on the meaning of nonobservation, the buddhas of the past, future, and present have no object other than the unsurpassed [state] of all the buddhas; they have fulfilled the teaching and so forth perfectly; are purified of the obstructions to omniscience; have perfected the essential meaning, the welfare of oneself and others; and have themselves been fully awakened to all good qualities as self-arisen.

Therefore, Śāriputra, the mantra of the perfection of wisdom. There is no cause for nonattainment coming from anything other than the object to be observed in that way, the method of practice, and the final fruition. Therefore, this means that the supreme consciousness [209a] has gone beyond saṃsāra. The meaning of that is called "mantra"; it possesses five qualities. It is called a mantra because it abides in itself and does not rely on the meaning of another. Regarding its qualities, because it knows itself by itself, it is the *mantra of great knowledge*; because it is not recited to others, it is *unsurpassed*; because it is not established as a thing, it is *not equal* with signs. Because the sign itself is its quality, it is *equal* to the indivisible essential meaning. Upon understanding the essential meaning it supremely *pacifies the suffering* of error. Because the meaning of the mantra that abides in the clarity of nonobservation *is not false*, the essential meaning *is known to be true*. Therefore, the mantra of all the perfections of wisdom is stated by Avalokita. *Tadyathā* means that it is thus, that the meaning of saṃsāra and nirvāṇa is thus identical in essence; it is thus that their identity in being unobservable and identity in being indivisible is the meaning of unchanging nature. Regarding *oṃ*, that which appears as the five poisons at the time of saṃsāra, appears as the five fathers of the five [buddha] lineages at the time of the fruition; that which appears to a wrong consciousness is not observed in reality. Understand that wisdom does not abide elsewhere. *Gate* [gone] beyond to the fruition is gone for one's own welfare. The [second] *gate* means gone also for the welfare of others. *Pāragate* [means] that one has gone to the supreme state of one's own welfare and there is nothing to hope for elsewhere. *Pārasaṃgate* [means] that one has [gone] to the supreme state or perfected the welfare of others and the compassion observing disciples arises; the appearance to disciples of pure karma is a nirmāṇakāya, the appearance to [disciples] of pure nature is a saṃbhogakāya. *Bodhi* is uninterrupted compassion arising as the meaning of the perfection of wisdom for disciples. *Svāhā* means the self-liberation of the minds [of disciples]; this is the meaning of liberation of itself by itself. The essential meaning never relies on anything else.

Śāriputra, [they] should train in the profound meaning in that way. Then the Bhagavan rose from samādhi [209b] *and said to the bodhisattva, the mahāsattva, the noble Avaloitesvara, "Well done."* Then after, Avalokita's teaching to Śāriputra, without interruption by another time, the Bhagavan arose from the samādhi that ripened the audience, [and said] to the noble Avalokita, "You have taught well, teaching the excellent dharma without error, as I teach. Thus, the teaching is good, child of good lineage, one's own welfare is like that; the welfare of others [is like that]. My teaching that the basis, path, and fruition are self-arisen is like that. Just as you, noble Avalokita, have taught Śāriputra, so should disciples train, because the perfection of wisdom exists as the self-arisen knowledge." These are the actual words spoken by the Bhagavan. *Even the tathāgatas admire this* [means that] because the actual words spoken by the Bhagavan and the blessed words of Avalokita are in harmony, all the lineages of tathāgatas admire the meaning of the harmonious words. *The Bhagavan having so spoken . . .* [means] that they rejoiced in the meaning of the harmonious words and the teacher taught the dharma to the audience and Avalokita. It was praised by the fourfold audience, and so on: the king of gods, the excellent Śakra or Agratāṃ Prāpta; the king of demigods, Vemacitra; the king of *gandharvas*, such as Pañcatīra.

The commentary composed by Śrīsiṃha elucidating the sūtra as mantra for the welfare of Vairocana, a clear lamp of few words and great meaning, is complete. This commentary was given by the master Vairocana to the king Khri srong lde btsan and his son when he was proud of his practice of the dharma of signs.[16]

[16] The term *mtshan ma'i chos spyod pa* may be translated as "practice of the dharma of signs," a disparaging term for exoteric teachings, or it can be read as "the practice of night doctrines," a possible reference to the Vairocana's giving the king esoteric teachings at night. I am grateful to David Germano and Mkhan po Bsod nams stob rgyal for the latter reading.

Five

The *Heart Sūtra* as Sādhana

> What! You still need the theatre! Are you still so young? Grow wise, and seek for tragedy and comedy where they are better acted! Where things are more interesting and interested! It is not altogether easy, I know, to remain a mere spectator in these cases—but learn it! And then, in almost every situation you find hard and painful you will have a little portal to joy and a refuge even when your own passions assail you. Open your theatre-eye, the great third eye which looks out into the world through the other two!
> —Nietzsche, *Daybreak*

SHOULD WE BE FORCED to characterize tantric practice, we might suggest that tantra entails enactment. This certainly is not enough, for it would be to conclude from the preponderance of the instrumental and the architectonic elements of many texts called tantras that tantra is ritual, to see tantrism, with Jean Filliozat, as "only the ritualistic technical aspect of religion, be it Śaiva, Vaiṣṇava, Buddhist, or Jain."[1] This would be to do nothing more than equate two impossibly elusive terms. Yet much of the practice described in tantric sādhanas involves the embodiment and enactment of a world, the fantastic jewel-encrusted world of the Mahāyāna sūtras (or the horrific world of the charnel ground). In the sūtras, these worlds appear before the audience of the sūtra at the command of the Buddha, as in the *Lotus* (with the apparition of the stūpa) or in the opening chapter of the *Vimalakīrti*, or are described by him, as in the *Sukhāvatīvyūha*. In the tantras, it is the practitioner who manifests that world through visualization, through a process of invitation, descent, and identification. In the sādhana, it is the practitioner who manifests the world that the sūtras declare to be immanent, yet only describe. The tantric sādhana is, in this sense, the making of the world of the Mahāyāna sūtras.

[1] Jean Filliozat in a book review of Alice Boner and Sadāśiva Rath Śarmā, "*Śilaprakāśa*: Mediaeval Orissan Sanskrit Text on Temple Architecture by Rāmacandra Kaulcāra," *Journal asiatique* 256 (1968): 267.

We have already encountered some of the vicissitudes of the term "tantra" in exploring the apparent confusion in the canonical categorization of the *Heart Sūtra*. Is it a sūtra, a tantra, or both? The complication is compounded by the consecutive presence in the tantra section of the Tibetan canons of two sādhanas that make mention of the *Heart Sūtra*: the *Prajñāpāramitāsādhana*,[2] ascribed to one Nāgārjunagarbha (kLu sgrub snying po); and the *Prajñāpāramitāsādhananāma*,[3] ascribed to Dārikapa, one of the eighty-four siddhas, known for his association with prostitutes.

If one of the factors that distinguishes tantra is instrumentality, that instrumentality is made evident in the genre of tantric literature called the sādhana, the "means of success" or (as translated by the Tibetan *sgrub thabs*) "means of achievement." Sādhanas are works, usually connected with a particular tantric cycle, which set forth often quite elaborate rites whereby the various powers, mundane and supramundane, promised by the tantras can be acquired. In many cases they serve as detailed instructions for daily practice employing the deities and mantras that appear less systematically in a given tantra.

Although there are many exceptions, tantric sādhanas tend to follow a fairly set sequence, whether they are simple and brief, such as the two *Heart Sūtra* sādhanas, or more detailed and prolix, such as some of the sādhanas connected with the *Guhyasamāja* and *Kālacakra* tantras. Dārikapa's sādhana on the *Heart Sūtra* is quite simple, whereas more elaborate sādhanas may include the recitation of a lineage of gurus; the creation of a protection wheel guarded by wrathful deities to subjugate enemies; the creation of a body maṇḍala, in which a pantheon of deities take residence at various parts of the meditator's body, and so on.[4] Furthermore, the maṇḍala of Dārikapa's sādhana is quite spare. It consists of an undescribed palace with only five deities. The Guhyasamāja maṇḍala, in contrast, is articulated in great detail, with five layers of walls of white, yellow, red, green, and blue. It has a jewelled molding, archways, a quadruple colonnade; it is festooned with jewels and pendants; and it is populated by thirty-two deities, each on its own throne, arrayed on two levels.[5]

2 P 3464, vol. 77, 295.1–30.4.8. Toh. 2640, ju 243b4-245b2.

3 P 3465, vol. 77, 30.4.8–31.2.4. Toh. 2641, ju 245b3-246b2.

4 See, for example, the commonly recited *'Dus pa phags lugs kyi sgrub thabs mdor bsdus mchog gi dga' ston* found in the handbook of commonly recited sādhanas and prayers *bLa ma'i rnal 'byor dang yi dam khag gi bdag bskyed sogs zhal 'don gces btus* (Dharamsala, India: Tibetan Cultural Printing Press, 1977), pp. 187–262.

5 Ibid., 212–14. For a detailed description of a maṇḍala in English, see Tenzin Gyatso, *The Kālachakra Tantra: Rite of Initiation for the Stage of Generation*, trans. and ed. Jeffrey Hopkins (London: Wisdom, 1975), pp. 75–91.

Dārikapa's *Heart Sūtra* sādhana, to be considered in some detail in this chapter, is much shorter and much less elaborate. Before proceeding further, it is perhaps useful at this point to provide a full translation of the work, interspersing occasional explanatory comments.[6]

> Paying homage to the Mother of the Conquerors, who, through acting in the past, [achieved] peace and omniscience, I will call to mind the rite of the sādhana.
>
> In a place remote and pleasing, sitting on a comfortable cushion, [imagine that] on a sun in the center of a lotus at the heart there is a *maṃ* radiating light,
>
> Inviting the Conquerors with their children from the ten directions. Imagine that they abide in the direction of the space [in front]. Make offerings and confess faults, admire [their virtues], and entreat [them to remain in the world].
>
> Go for refuge and create the aspiration [to buddhahood] and dedicate [all this] to great enlightenment. Cultivate the abodes of purity: love, compassion, joy, and equanimity.
>
> Recite fully this secret mantra: *oṃ svabhāvaśuddhāḥ sarvadharmāḥ svabhāvaśuddho 'haṃ*. Be mindful that everything, the moving and unmoving, is naturally empty primordially.

After paying homage to the goddess Prajñāpāramitā, the mother of all the buddhas, the meditator imagines a lotus at his (or her) heart upon which lies a horizontal sun disc. Standing upright on the sun disc is the letter *maṃ* from which light radiates, inviting buddhas and bodhisattvas from throughout the universe. Visualizing them arrayed in the space before him, the meditator then performs a series of standard preliminary practices derived from the twelve opening stanzas of the *Bhadracaryāpraṇidhāna* (Prayer for the Deeds of Samantabhadra) of the *Avataṃsaka Sūtra*. He begins by presenting offerings (it is unclear whether these offerings are real or imagined). Next comes a highly abbreviated version of the basic Mahāyāna ritual known as "the threefold service" (*triskandhaka*), consisting of confessing one's faults to the assembled buddhas and bodhisattvas, admiring and rejoicing in one's own and others' virtue, and entreating the buddhas to remain in the world to teach

[6] The other sādhana, ascribed to Nāgārjuna or Nāgārjunagarbha, is devoted largely to the performance of obeisance, offering, confession, and so on. It describes a maṇḍala in which Śākyamuni occupies the central position, with the goddess Prajñāpāramitā in the east, Vajrapāṇi in the south, Śāriputra in the west, and Avalokiteśvara in the north. Apart from these references to three of its principals, the only connection to the *Heart Sūtra* is the statement near the end of the sādhana, "If you are tired, recite the mantra of truth, saying *gate gate pāragate pārasaṃgate bodhi svāhā*, adding *tadyathā* and *oṃ*." See P 3464, vol. 77, 30.4.1–2.

the doctrine and not pass into nirvāṇa. The meditator then goes for refuge to the three jewels, creates the aspiration to enlightenment (*bodhicittotpāda*), and dedicates the merit from the foregoing and subsequent practices toward that end.[7] The meditator next cultivates the four pure abodes (*brahmavihāra*) of love, compassion, joy, and equanimity, before meditating on emptiness and reciting the purificatory mantra, *oṃ svabhāvaśuddhāḥ sarvadharmāḥ svabhāvaśuddho 'haṃ*, "Oṃ, naturally pure are all phenomena, naturally pure am I," understanding that emptiness is the primordial nature of everything, the unmoving world and the beings who move upon it. Out of this emptiness, the meditator next creates the maṇḍala.

> After that, from the nature of emptiness imagine the four elements as *yaṃ raṃ baṃ laṃ*. From *suṃ* arises Mount Meru. On it, from *bhruṃ*, a beautiful palace, expansive and ornamented.
>
> In its center is a lion throne where, seated on lotus and sun, is the orange Mother of the Conquerors; her body glistening, full-bodied, with one face and four arms.
>
> Imagine that her two right hands hold a *vajra* and bestow protection, her two left hands hold a text and teach the doctrine.[8] She is endowed with the ornaments of a saṃbhogakāya.
>
> In the east, on a moon on a lion [throne] is a *sa*, from which the Conqueror Śākyamuni is created. He is a nirmāṇakāya, the color of refined gold, and has a crown protrusion.
>
> Imagine that in the west, on a lotus and moon, is a *hrīḥ*, from which Lokeśvara [arises], very white and beautifully adorned; he sits in the cross-legged posture of a [bodhi]sattva.

[7] The preliminary practices are normally listed as seven: (1) obeisance (*vandana*), (2) offering (*pūjanā*), (3) confession of sins (*pāpadeśana*), (4) admiration (*anumodana*), (5) entreaty (*adhyeṣaṇā*), (6) supplication (*yācana*), and (7) dedication (*pariṇamanā*). The sevenfold rite and various ways of extracting it from the *Bhadracaryāpraṇidhāna* are discussed by Atiśa in his *Bodhimārgapradīpapañjikā* (P 5344, vol. 103, 280a–284a). An expanded version of the seven practices is provided by Śāntideva in his *Bodhicaryāvatāra*, 1.26–3.7. For the Sanskrit, see P. L. Vaidya, ed., *Bodhicaryāvatāra of Śāntideva*, Buddhist Sanskrit Texts, no. 12 (Darbhanga: The Mithila Institute, 1960), pp. 20–39. On the *triskandhaka*, see also Śāntideva's *Śikṣasamuccaya*. In Dārikapa's sādhana, the order of the practices is obeisance, offering, confession, and admiration. The next two components, entreaty and supplication, are conflated. These are followed by two other standard preliminary steps not included in the seven, going for refuge and creating the aspiration to enlightenment, before the seventh step of the dedication of merit.

[8] This particular four-armed form corresponds to none of the eight versions described by Edward Conze in his "Iconography of Prajñāpāramitā," in his *Thirty Years of Buddhist Studies* (Oxford: Bruno Cassirer, 1967), pp. 248–49, 262.

Imagine that in the south, from a *maṃ*, is Śāriputra. He is dressed as an ascetic; his body is light red. He is kneeling and the palms of his hands are joined. His body is very beautiful.

In the north, create Ānanda, born from *da*. He is red, [seated] on a lotus, in the mode of respecting the Conqueror.

Having thus completed the creation, light radiates from the *maṃ* at one's own heart, drawing forth the wisdom-beings. Make offerings. Through *jaḥ hūṃ baṃ hoḥ* they enter [the residents of the maṇḍala].

The conquerors confer initiation on them. They are marked [with the seals] of Vairocana, Akṣobhya, Ratnasambhava, and Anantajịnatva and blessed with the three syllables.

The meditator here creates an imaginary universe out of emptiness. The foundation is provided by the four elements (wind, fire, water, and earth, represented by the letters *yaṃ*, *raṃ*, *baṃ*, and *laṃ*, respectively). On top of these, a *suṃ* appears from which the cosmic mountain Meru arises and atop the mountain, a palace appears from the syllable *bhruṃ*. In the center of the palace is a throne supported on the backs of lions where, on cushions of lotus and sun disc, sits the goddess Prajñāpāramitā, the embodiment of the knowledge of emptiness. She has four arms; one holds a *vajra*, another holds a text, another is in the gesture of bestowing protection (*abhayamudrā*), another makes the gesture of teaching the doctrine (*vitarkamudrā*). She is surrounded on thrones in the four cardinal directions by the dramatis personae of the *Heart Sūtra*, each of whom arises from a seed syllable: Śākyamuni Buddha, Avalokiteśvara, Śāriputra, and Ānanda, the unidentified rapporteur (*saṃgītikartṛ*) of the sūtra. (We should note in passing how rare it is for Śākyamuni to appear in a maṇḍala in his "historical" nirmāṇakāya form. It is also highly unusual for Hīnayāna śrāvakas such as Śāriputra and Ānanda to be seen frequenting such an esoteric domain.) These five beings created through the efforts of the meditator in one-pointed samādhi are called "pledge-beings" (*samayasattva*)[9] and are images or reflections of the actual Prajñāpāramitā, Śākyamuni, Avalokiteśvara, Śāriputra, and Ānanda.

[9] The Sanskrit *samayasattva* is translated into Tibetan as *dam tshig sems dpa'*, "pledge-being." This sense of the term seems to be related to a statement from Buddhaguhya that the person who imagines the deity is one who keeps the tantric pledges (*dam tshig can*). See Ferdinand Lessing and Alex Wayman, *Introduction to the Tantrica Systems* (Delhi: Motilal Banarsidass, 1978), p. 234, n. 30. Thus, when the meditator imagines himself as a deity, he is the pledge-being because he maintains the tantric pledges. In the case of a sādhana like Dārikapa's in which the meditator creates a maṇḍala that he does not enter, the residents of the maṇḍala that he creates are called pledge-beings because they are created by someone who keeps the tantric pledges. According to Tsong kha pa, the term *samayasattva* is related to the Sanskrit *sameta* ("united") and *milat* ("joining"), suggesting the fusion of *samayasat-*

Having created this scene, the meditator now animates the residents of the maṇḍala by causing the actual Prajñāpāramitā, Śākyamuni, Avalokiteśvara, Śāriputra, and Ānanda, referred to as "wisdom-beings" (*jñānasattva*), to descend and merge with their imagined doubles, the "pledge-beings." Light radiates from the *maṃ* at the meditator's heart, drawing the wisdom-beings to the maṇḍala where, through offerings and the recitation of the mantra *jaḥ hūṃ baṃ hoḥ* ("Be summoned, enter, become fused with, be pleased"),[10] they are caused to enter the residents of the maṇḍala. Next, the union of the wisdom-beings with the pledge-beings is marked with four seals (*mudrā*) for each of the four buddha lineages: Vairocana, Akṣobhya, Ratnasambahava, Anantajinatva (Amitābha).[11] The residents are then blessed with the three syllables: a white *oṃ* at the crown of the head, a red *āḥ* at the throat, and a blue *hūṃ* at the heart.

> Imagine that the Conqueror [Śākyamuni] is drawn to the heart of the Mother and enters into samādhi. [Avalokiteśvara] gives answers to [Śāriputra's] question about the meaning of emptiness for all those surrounding.

With the preliminary visualization now complete, the stage is set for the central meditation of the sādhana. It begins with the *Heart Sūtra* being inserted, in effect, into the tantric rite as Śākyamuni enters into samādhi,

---

tva and the *jñānasattva*. See his *Ngags rim chen mo*, in *The Collected Works (gSung 'Bum) of the Incomparable Lord Tsoṅ-kha-pa bLo-bzaṅ-grags-pa*, vol. 3 (New Delhi: Mongolian Lama Guru Deva, 1978), 364b3.

[10] According to the *Sādhanamālā*, this mantra is a condensation of a longer mantra by which the wisdom-beings are forcibly summoned, caused to enter the maṇḍala, bound to the maṇḍala, and subdued. See Lessing and Wayman, *Tantrica Systems*, p. 236, n. 32. This apparent violence is mollified by an interpretation provided by Padmavajra in his *Tantrārthāvatāravyākhyāna*, where summoning means making offerings and inviting the wisdom-beings, entering means that the wisdom-being enters the pledge-being and the two become one, binding means that there is no difference between the practitioner and the goal (*sgrub pa dang bsgrub bya*), and subduing means pleasing the wisdom-being. See Lessing and Wayman, *Tantrica Systems*, p. 236, nn. 33–36.

[11] The exact meaning of the text is not clear here. It reads: *rgyal bas dbang bskur so so la | rnam snang mi bskyod rin 'byung dang | mtha' yas rgyal ba nyid kyi sems | yi ge gsum gyis byin gyis brlab*. It seems fairly clear that Anantajinatva is Amitābha. The fact that only four of the buddhas are mentioned (Amogasiddha is absent) suggests that this sādhana is associated with the yoga tantra class, for in the *Tattvasaṃgraha*, only four of the five buddhas are mentioned. (See *Ngags rim chen mo*, 85b2–5). In mKhas sgrub rje's *rGyud sde spyi'i rnam* there is a long section on how the four seals are applied for each of the four buddha lineages in order to make the body, speech, mind, and activities of the wisdom-being indivisible from the body, speech, mind, and activities of the pledge-being; see Lessing and Wayman, *Tantrica Systems*, p. 234. In n. 21, p. 228, it is reported that Padmavajra lists *nimitta* (*mtshan ma*) as a synonym for *mudrā* (*phyag rgya*); *mtshan* is the term translated as "marked" in the sādhana.

just as it occurs in the prologue to the sūtra, "At that time, the Bhagavan was absorbed in a samādhi on the enumerations of phenomena called 'perception of the profound.'" Unlike the sūtra, however, he here is drawn to the heart of the goddess at the center of the maṇḍala. Avalokiteśvara then gives "answers to [Śāriputra's] question about the meaning of emptiness," as in the sūtra. Presumably the meditator would also listen, contemplating emptiness.

> In this way, all of the retinue, who are elaborated out of the pacification of all phenomena, are drawn into the Mother. Observe the letter [*maṃ*] in the samādhi with signs clearly and without conception.
>
> All phenomena, originally quiescent, appear mistakenly through the power of conditions. When reality [is realized], they are pacified, when they are pacified, they appear like illusions.
>
> Do not be devoid of not conceiving of the four extremes.[12] The basic mind, without abiding in laxity or excitement, is clear light, not meditating on anything. This is the perfection of the signless yoga.
>
> Because the Conqueror said that [all phenomena] are peaceful and because of the lack of being one or many, and so on, elaborations cease and the nonconceptual is known, fully and perfectly.

Through Avalokiteśvara's teaching of emptiness, all the residents of the maṇḍala and the surrounding buddhas and bodhisattvas are drawn into the heart of the central figure, Prajñāpāramitā. The meditator then turns to the practice of the signed and signless samādhis.[13] The meditator concentrates on the letter *maṃ* at his heart in order to induce mental stability. Next the meditator understands that all phenomena are originally peaceful, only appearing to be real through the influence of adventitious conditions. With this understanding, he then passes on to a more direct meditation on emptiness. By not conceiving of the four extremes (*catuṣkoti*, that things exist, do not exist, both exist and not exist, neither exist nor not exist), the basic mind, whose nature is clear light, is found to be free of laxity (*laya*) and excitement (*auddhatya*), the chief impediments to the state of mental clarity and quiescence called *śamatha*.[14] The mind

[12] The Tibetan construction is as convoluted as my translation. It reads *mtha' bzhir mi rtog bral bar min.*

[13] "Samādhi with signs" (*nimittasamādhi*) and "samādhi without signs" (*animittasamādhi*), more commonly referred to as yoga with signs (*nimittayoga*) and yoga without signs (*animittayoga*), are a major category in the *kriyā*, *caryā*, and yoga tantras, although exactly how they are to be differentiated is somewhat problematic. For a discussion of this issue, see Donald S. Lopez, Jr., "Dārikapa's Tantric Sādhana on the *Heart Sūtra*," *Wiener Zeitschrift für die Kunde Südasiens* 34 (1990): 218–22.

[14] Laxity and excitement together constitute one of the five faults that prevents the

does not meditate on anything, abiding in emptiness. The sādhana alludes to the proof of emptiness by scripture (*āgama*), such as the numerous occasions in the Prajñāpāramitā sūtras where all phenomena are declared to be peaceful, and the proof by reasoning (*yukti*) that phenomena do not intrinsically exist because of being neither truly one nor many, an argument developed at length by Śāntarakṣita in his *Madhayamakālaṃkāra*. The elaborations of intrinsic existence spawned by ignorance cease and a state beyond conception is attained.

> When you are tired, repeat, *tadyathā oṃ gate gate pāragate pārasaṃgate bodhi svāhā*.

The final reference to the *Heart Sūtra* occurs here, although the mantra holds a somewhat less exalted place than it does in the sūtra. No comment is made about its significance. Rather, it is to be recited near the end of the meditative session, when the main visualization and the contemplation of emptiness have concluded. The recitation of mantra as a means of resting at the end of a session is a common feature of sādhanas.[15]

> Lights rays of [the letters of] the mantra surrounding [*maṃ*] around the center [of the lotus at one's heart] are emitted and withdrawn, performing the two purposes. Make offerings to the wisdom-beings and [invite them to] depart.

> Speak the eighteen kinds of emptiness; all the pledge-beings and palace become unobservable.

The meditator visualizes the letters of the *Heart Sūtra* mantra standing upright in a circle around the *maṃ* in the center of the lotus at his heart. Rays of light shine forth from the letters, performing the two purposes of making offerings to the buddhas and bodhisattvas and alleviating the suffering of the beings of saṃsāra.[16] The light then returns to the letters and the meditator makes mental offerings to the assembly before inviting them to leave. The meditator goes on to recite the eighteen emptinesses,[17]

---

achievement of *śamatha*, according to the *Madhyāntavibhāga* 4.4. See Ramchandra Pandeya, ed., *Madhyānta-Vibhāga-Śāstra* (Delhi: Motilal Banarsidass, 1971), p. 130. Laxity and excitement are discussed at length, with citation of Indian sources in the *śamatha* (*zhi gnas*) section of Tsong kha pa's *Lam rim chen mo* and in 'Jam dbyangs bzhad pa's *bSam gzugs kyi snyoms 'jug kyi rnams par bzhag pa*. For a discussion in English, see Gedun Lodro, *Walking through Walls* (Ithaca: Snow Lion, 1992).

[15] See, for example, the comments of the current Dalai Lama in Tsong kha pa, *Yoga of Tibet* (London: Allen and Unwin, 1981), pp. 26–27.

[16] An alternative interpretation of the two purposes is offered by Lessing and Wayman, *Tantrica Systems*, p. 215, n. 3.

[17] The more common listing is of sixteen emptinesses, found in a number of śāstras, including Candrakīrti's *Madhyamakāvatāra* 6.180–218. See Louis de la Vallée Poussin, ed., *Madhyamakāvatāra par Candrakīrti* (Osnabrück: Biblio Verlag, 1970), pp. 302–38. Can-

at which point the entire visualization, the palace and its residents, dissolve into emptiness.

> [I] have written this excellent rite, a supreme technique, based on the words of the Conqueror and the statements of Nāgārjuna, for the sake of those with interest and to discipline myself. May scholars be tolerant of the stains of my mind. By the roots of virtue of my work here may transmigrators understand the meaning of the pure heart and fully attain the state of a conqueror; may transmigrators be set on the path of peace.

The sādhana ends with a traditional statement of the sources for the work, an apology for any mistakes, and a dedication of the merit accrued from the composition to the welfare of all beings.

Dārikapa's sādhana on the *Heart Sūtra* is one of hundreds of such texts that fill volumes of the "tantric commentary" (*rgyud 'grel*) section of the various Tibetan canons. The text is not widely known among Tibetan authors, nor do we find reference to its practice, in either India or Tibet. It is therefore difficult to argue for its historical importance. In fact, the importance of the sādhana for Tibetan scholars has been as an item of evidence to be either accepted or rejected in seeking to solve the exegetical quandary with which we have already been engaged: Is the *Heart Sūtra* a sūtra or a tantra? Or, to put the question more precisely, Does the presence of a mantra in the sūtra make the sūtra a tantra? As discussed in chapter 3, this was a problem that clearly vexed compilers of the various Tibetan canons. In the Peking edition, the *Heart Sūtra* appears in the tantra section. In the Derge edition, it appears in both the *prajñāpāramitā* and the tantra section. This is the context in which we find mention of Dārikapa's work. The great scholar Bu ston (1290–1364), generally credited with establishing the contents of the *bKa' 'gyur* and *bsTan 'gyur*, noted in his catalogue: "The *Heart Sūtra* (*Sher snying*) and the *Nayaśatapañcāsatikā* are also [*prajñāpāramitā* sūtras]. However, because the *Heart Sūtra* appears to have a sādhana composed by Nāgārjuna and because there is a commentary that explains the *Nayaśatapañcāsatikā* as a mantra, it is not contradictory [to classify them] in the mantra [section] as well."[18] Five centuries later, the issue seems still not to have been

drakīrti also adds a second list of four emptinesses (6.219–233), two of which, the emptiness of things (*bhāva*) and the emptiness of non-things (*abhāva*), are added to make a list of eighteen. The list appears in *Mahāvyutpatti* 37.1–18. An extensive exposition of the eighteen emptinesses occurs in Étienne Lamotte, *Le Traité de la grande vertu de sagesse de Nāgārjuna*, tome 4 (Louvain: Institut Orientaliste, 1976), pp. 2027–2151.

18 See Nishioka Soshū, "Putun Bukkyōshi' Mokurokubu Sakuin III," *Tōkyō Daigaku Bungakubu Bunka Kōryū Kenkyū Shisetsu Kenkyū Kiyō* 6 (1983): 65. See also Helmut Eimer, *Der Tantra-Katalog des Bu ston im Vergleich mit der Abteilung Tantra des tibetischen Kanjur*, Indica et Tibetica, no. 17 (Bonn: Indica et Tibetica Verlag, 1989), p. 89. I am grateful to Jonathan Silk for these references.

resolved. The dGe lugs pa scholar bsTan dar lha ram pa says in his 1839 commentary on the *Heart Sūtra*:

> Some scholars say that this mantra [of the *Heart Sūtra*] is not included in the tantras, understanding it to belong primarily to the sūtra system, but because the sādhanas of Nāgārjuna and Dārikapa are clearly in the mantra system, there must be a context for including this mantra in the tantras. However, mKhas grub rje [1385–1438] said that the sādhanas of Nāgārjuna and Dārikapa are spurious, but some scholars say they are authentic. Also, there is a commentary on the *Heart Sūtra* in a mantric way by one "Śrīsiṃha." It therefore seems difficult to analyze.[19]

Beyond this question, the ostensible interest of this text lies in the fact that it makes reference to one of the most famous Buddhist sūtras, but even that fact is not evident from its title, which is simply *Prajñāpāramitāsādhananāma*. In short, the text would not have drawn our attention had not the vexing "sūtra or tantra" issue been raised by Tibetan exegetes, in the process of which one of their most esteemed members (mKhas grub rje, one of the chief disciples of Tsong kha pa and a renowned tantric scholar) declared the text to be spurious.

Nonetheless, having been thereby caused to read the text, it would seem to bear our interest beyond the boundaries of the sūtra or tantra quandary. In order to compound this interest, we can begin by reviewing the sequence of the sādhana:

> 1. The meditator imagines a seed syllable at his heart from which light rays are emitted, inviting the buddhas and bodhisattvas into his presence.
> 2. The meditator, with the buddhas and bodhisattvas appearing in space before him, performs a fairly standard Mahāyāna rite of obeisance (offering, confession of faults, admiration of virtue, entreaty, supplication, going for refuge, creating the aspiration to enlightenment, and dedication of merit).
> 3. The meditator recites a purificatory mantra and contemplates emptiness.
> 4. Upon emptiness the meditator creates a maṇḍala in the space before him in the form of a palace. Within it he creates images (called "pledge-beings") of the goddess Prajñāpāramitā (in the center) with Śākyamuni, Avalokiteśvara, Śāriputra, and Ānanda seated in the four cardinal directions. Through the recitation of another mantra, the actual Prajñāpāramitā, Śākyamuni, Avalokiteśvara, Śāriputra, and Ānanda (called "wisdom-beings") fuse with their surrogates.

[19] bsTan dar lha ram pa, *Shes rab snying po'i 'grel pa don gsal nor bu'i 'od*, in *Collected Works of Bstan-dar Lha-ram of A-lag-śa*, vol. 1 (New Delhi: Lama Guru Deva, 1971), 320.2–4. mKhas grub's statement occurs in his *sGyud sde spyi'i rnam*. See Lessing and Wayman, *Tantrica Systems*, p. 108.

5. While visualizing the maṇḍala, the meditator imagines that Śākyamuni is drawn to the heart of Prajñāpāramitā and that Avalokiteśvara recites the sūtra, after which the three other figures are drawn into Prajñāpāramitā.

6. The meditator contemplates emptiness while concentrating on a seed syllable.

7. The meditator recites the *Heart Sūtra*'s mantra, visualizing its letters standing upright around the sun disc at his heart, the letters emitting rays of light that relieve the sufferings of the universe.

8. The meditator offers parting gifts to the residents of the maṇḍala and then invites them to depart from their images.

9. The remaining maṇḍala with its images of Prajñāpāramitā, Śākyamuni, Avalokiteśvara, Śāriputra, and Ānanda dissolves into emptiness.

10. The meditator dedicates the merit accrued during the session.

There are obviously a great many issues that could be explored here. One that might prove particularly fruitful is that of structural continuities between Vedic sacrifice and tantric sādhana. In both, the host beckons deities, through a combination of invitation and coercion, to come to a carefully prepared place of offering to receive gifts. In both, we observe the pattern of entry and exit discussed by Hubert and Mauss in 1898.[20] In the sādhana, it is the meditator who must serve as both patron and officiant. Nevertheless, as in Vedic sacrifice, there is a parallelism in the structure of the sādhana, with offering of gifts to the buddhas and bodhisattvas at both the beginning (like the Vedic *prāyaṇīyeṣṭi*) and the end (like the Vedic *udanīyeṣṭi*); an invitation to them to enter into the maṇḍala at the beginning (like the Vedic *adhyavasāna*); and an invitation to depart at the end (like the Vedic *udavasāna*). There is purification at the beginning and at the end, like the Vedic consecration (*dikṣa*) at the beginning and final bath (*avabhṛtha*) at the end. However, unlike the Vedic purificatory rites, lustration is provided not by water but by emptiness. The sādhana thus has something of the symmetry of a Vedic sacrifice, with the enactment of the *Heart Sūtra* standing at the center, flanked by contemplations of emptiness, the creation and dissolution of the maṇ-

[20] See Henri Hubert and Marcel Mauss, *Sacrifice: Its Nature and Function*, trans. W. D. Hall (Chicago: University of Chicago Press, 1964), especially chap. 2. For far more thorough studies, see Madeline Biardeau and Charles Malamoud, eds., *Le sacrifice dans l'Inde ancienne* (Paris: Presses universitaires de France, 1976); Frits Staal, *AGNI: The Vedic Ritual of the Fire Altar*, 2 vols. (Berkeley: Asian Humanities Press, 1983); Frits Staal, *Rules without Meaning: Ritual, Mantras and the Human Sciences* (New York: Peter Lang, 1993), pp. 61–190; and Jan Gonda, *Vedic Ritual: The Non-Solemn Rites* (Leiden: E. J. Brill, 1980). It might prove useful to explore in particular parallels between the sādhana and the *prāṇāgnihotra*, the "internal" sacrifice in the fire of the breath. See H. W. Bodewitz, *Jaiminīya Brāhmaṇa 1.1–65, with a Study of the Agnihotra and Prāṇāgnihotra* (Leiden: E. J. Brill, 1973).

ḍala, the invitation and departure of the deities, offerings to the residents of the maṇḍala before and after, and the recitation of mantra. The question of what constitutes the sacrificial victim in the sādhana remains problematic, although the absorption of Śākyamuni into the mother Prajñāpāramitā provides perhaps a better possibility than the more predictable sacrifice of the meditator's "ego." Finally, the sādhana ends, like so many Mahāyāna Buddhist rituals, whether it be the act of meditation, a rite of initiation, or the composition of a text, with a dedication of merit. In Vedic rituals, at the end of each act of oblation, the officiating priest recites the *tyāgā* (renunciation, abandonment) formula, for example, "This is for Agni, not for me" (*agnaye idaṃ na mama*). In the sādhana, the dedication occurs only at the end and what is consigned is merit, not to the gods, but to all sentient beings.[21]

As fruitful as it might be to pursue these parallels in a more sustained manner, in the remainder of this chapter I will consider another of the many questions raised by this sādhana, the question of visualization. Structured visualization has a long history in Buddhism. Extensive instructions appear in the Pāli Nikāyas, largely centered around practices for the development of concentration (*jhāna*). A certain level of concentration is necessary in order for the understanding of nibbāna (nirvāṇa) to be salvific, that is, for the understanding of nibbāna to destroy the seeds of future rebirth, resulting in attainment of the state of an arahant and passage into nibbāna at death. Hence, in his long catalogue of the benefits of samādhi, the state of one-pointed focus on a single object that leads to *jhāna*, Buddhaghosa begins by saying that for persons who have not yet been liberated from future rebirth, the benefit of samādhi is that it is the prerequisite for insight into reality.[22] But samādhi also brings other benefits prior to the ultimate passage into nibbāna. These include not only rebirth in the heaven of Brahmā, but a wealth of supernormal abilities coextensive with what in tantric literature are called mundane powers (*laukikasiddhi*). Thus, because of his attainment of *jhāna*, Sāriputta survives a blow on the head, "the noise of which was like a thunder clap." Another monk survives immolation unburned, another is protected from robbers, a laywoman is unhurt by boiling oil, a queen repels a poison arrow.[23] Describing the monk who has directed his concentration to the attainment of power (*iddhi*), the *Dīghanikāya* (1. 77) says: "Having become one, he becomes many; having been many, he be-

[21] See Staal, *Rules without Meaning*, p. 121. On p. 133, Staal mentions parallels between *tyāgā* and the Gītā's karma yoga, as well as with *wu wei* and Kant's categorical imperative, as evidence of the fact that ritual is performed for its own sake.

[22] See Buddhaghosa, *The Path of Purification (Visuddhimagga)*, 2nd ed., trans. Bhikkhu N̄yāṇamoli [sic] (Colombo, Ceylon: A. Semage, 1964), p. 407.

[23] Ibid., pp. 416–17.

comes one. He appears and vanishes. He goes unhindered through walls, through enclosures, through mountains, as though in open space. He dives in and out of the earth as though in water. He goes unbroken in water as though on earth. Sitting cross-legged he travels in space like a winged bird. With his hand he touches and strokes the moon and sun so mighty and powerful. He wields bodily mastery even as far as the Brahmā world."[24]

To achieve such powers, the mind must first be concentrated upon an object, and forty suitable objects of concentration are traditionally set forth. It is in these instructions that we find what most would consider some of the earliest practices of visualization. The first of the forty objects is the earth *kasina* (device). The meditator is to stretch a piece of leather or cloth across a wooden frame and then smear a disc of dawn-colored clay, the size of a saucer or a bushel, onto the surface, using a trowel to make it smooth. After sweeping the surrounding area and taking a bath, the meditator then sits down two and half cubits from the earth *kasina* and stares at the disc, mentally repeating the word "earth," opening and shutting the eyes until the disc appears just as clearly with eyes shut as it does with eyes open. At this point, the meditator is to return to his dwelling and concentrate on the mental image, only going back to look at the clay disc should the image fade. After focusing on the mental image for some time, it will be replaced by a bright light, "like a looking-glass disk drawn from its case, like a mother-of-pearl dish well-washed, like the moon's disk coming from behind a cloud, like cranes against a thunder cloud." This is the mark of the attainment of "access concentration" (*upacāra* samādhi), the precursor to *jhāna*.[25]

For the water *kasina*, the meditator stares at a bowl of clean water and thinks "water, water." For the fire *kasina*, the meditator makes a four-finger-breadth hole in a woven mat or a cloth or a piece of leather, hangs it between himself and a fire, and stares at the center of the flame through the hole, thinking, "fire, fire." For the air *kasina*, the meditator should notice the tops of trees moving in the wind or feel the breeze on his skin and think, "air, air." For the blue *kasina*, the meditator should stare at a tray filled with morning glorys or blue cloth and think "blue, blue." (There are also yellow, red, and white *kasina*s.) For the light *kasina*, the meditator should focus on a circle of sunlight or moonlight on the ground or circle of light cast on the wall by a lamp and think, "light, light." For the space *kasina*, the meditator is to look through a hole in the wall and think, "space, space."[26] In each case, therefore, a visual (or in

[24] Cited by ibid., p. 420.
[25] Ibid., pp. 126–31.
[26] Ibid., pp. 177–82.

the case of wind, a tactile) image provides the basis from which a mental image is formed and then visualized, augmented by mental repetition of its name.

Among the forty traditional objects for developing samādhi, the one that ostensibly seems the most obvious precursor to the visualization found in Dārikapa's sādhana is of a different type. This is the practice known as *buddhānusmṛti* (Pāli, *buddhānussati*), variously translated as "remembrance," "recollection," "commemoration," or "mindfulness" of the Buddha.[27] This practice, as generally described in the Nikāyas and as delineated by Buddhaghosa, is not predicated on sight. Instead, the meditator is instructed to call to mind the virtues of the Buddha through a formula of ten epithets, "Indeed this Bhagavān is the arhat, perfectly and fully enlightened, perfect in knowledge and deed, the Sugata, the knower of the world, the unsurpassed, the tamer of persons suitable to be tamed, the teacher of gods and humans, the Buddha, the Bhagavān."[28] Buddhaghosa comments on each of the epithets at great length, but his actual instructions on the practice of the mindfulness of the Buddha are quite sketchy, saying only that sustained attention to the Buddha's good qualities leads to happiness, which leads to bliss, which, in turn, leads to samādhi.[29] However, as with the case with the development of concentration through the *kasina*s, it is the "side effects" that are perhaps more interesting:

> When a bhikkhu is devoted to this recollection of the Buddha, he is respectful and deferential towards the Master. He attains fullness of faith, mindfulness, understanding, and merit. He has much happiness and gladness. He conquers fear and dread. He is able to endure pain. He comes to feel as if he were living in the Master's presence. And his body, when the recollection of the Buddha's special qualities dwells in it, becomes as worthy of veneration as a shrine room. His mind tends towards the plane of the Buddhas. When he encounters an opportunity for transgression, he has awareness of conscience and shame as vivid as though he were face to face with the Master.[30]

One of the earliest Mahāyāna sūtras (translated into Chinese in C.E. 179) derives its name from a practice designed to bring one face to face

[27] *Buddhānusmṛti* (with its possible precursors and descendants) has been usefully traced in two articles by Paul Harrison. See his "*Buddhānusmṛti* in the *Pratyutpanna-buddha-saṃmukhāvasthita-samādhi-sūtra*," *Journal of Indian Philosophy* 6 (1978): 35–57; and "Commemoration and Identification in Buddhānusmṛti," in Janet Gyatso, ed., *In the Mirror of Memory: Reflections on Mindfulness and Remembrance in Indian and Tibetan Buddhism* (Albany: State University of New York Press, 1992), pp. 215–38.

[28] *Majjhima Nikāya*, 1. 37.

[29] Buddhaghosa, *Path of Purification (Visuddhimagga)*, pp. 229–30.

[30] Ibid., p. 230.

with the Master. It is called the *Pratyutpanna-buddha-saṃmukhāvasthita-samādhi-sūtra*, "the sūtra on the samādhi of standing face to face with the buddhas of the present." As Paul Harrison has shown in his study of this sūtra,[31] this samādhi is clearly connected to *buddhānusmṛti* practices. Here, however, there is an explicit emphasis on vision and hearing. The meditator is to sit facing in the direction of a particular buddha, such as west in the case of Amitābha, and to visualize that buddha surrounded by disciples to whom he is teaching the doctrine. Through practicing this vision for seven days and seven nights, the meditator, in effect, joins the audience and receives the teachings of the buddha, guaranteeing rebirth in that buddha's pure land after death. Hence, to the earlier recollection of the Buddha's virtues are added two elements: the vivid imagination of the body of the buddha fully adorned with the thirty-two major and eighty minor marks, and the vivid imagination of the sound of the buddha's speech. According to the sūtra, a third element is also essential: "One does not objectify, one does not fixate on, does not falsely perceive, does not falsely imagine, does not falsely discriminate, and does not review the tathāgata: when in this way one obtains the samādhi of emptiness by concentrating on the tathāgata without objectification, that is known as the calling to mind of the buddha."[32] That is, the realization of emptiness is deemed essential to the vision.

By the eighth century at the latest, the visualization of the body of the Buddha, which had been but one of forty objects for the cultivation of samādhi in the Nikāyas, is praised as the supreme of all objects for the Mahāyāna version of "access concentration," the state called quiescence (*śamatha*), the state of meditative stability necessary for direct realization of emptiness. We find Kamalaśīla writing in his third *Bhāvanākrama*, for example: "The yogin at the outset should place his mind on the body of the tathāgata as it looks and sounds and then practice quiescence. Imagine that the body of the tathāgata is the color of refined gold, adorned with the major and minor marks, and seated in the middle of his retinue, constantly bringing about the welfare of beings through various methods. In order to produce the wish for his qualities and to pacify laxity, excitement, etc., you should concentrate as long as you can very clearly see him abiding before you."[33] According to Tsong kha pa, this visualization is developed through a technique very similar to that of the earth *kasina*. In this case, however, the meditator is to sit before a paint-

[31] Paul Harrison, *The* Samādhi *of Direct Encounter with the Buddhas of the Present*, Studia Philologica Buddhica Monograph series, no. 5 (Tokyo: International Institute for Buddhist Studies, 1990).

[32] Ibid., p. 38.

[33] Cited by Tsong kha pa, *Mnyam med tsong kha pa chen pos mdzad pa'i byang chub lam rim che pa* (mTsho sngon mi rigs dbe skrun khang, 1985), pp. 500–501.

ing or statue of the Buddha and study it intently, eventually producing a mental image of the Buddha that serves as the object of concentration.[34] Buddhas, then, seem to have come increasingly into focus under the meditator's gaze with the development of the Mahāyāna, where one finds a constellation of practices partaking of sight, sound, and emptiness.

Having very roughly sketched some of the antecedents of the practice of visualization represented in Dārikapa's sādhana, there remain a host of other questions, less accessible to historical and textual investigation, questions pertaining to what might be termed a poetics of visualization. It is here, taking Dārikapa's sādhana as the focus, that it is necessary to consider the usefulness of viewing visualization as an inscribed illusion, as a vision mediated by a text, as a scripted hallucination, as a dream read from a book.

We might begin by considering the role of the meditator in the process. If, at the outset, we consider the maṇḍala as a static scene, as a mental painting, is it more appropriate to consider the meditator as the artist or as the viewer? The meditator is instructed by the text to imagine the maṇḍala in the space before him, in front of him, laid out as if in panorama, with figures located at each of the cardinal directions. (Because the author to whom the sādhana is attributed was male, the reading assumes a male meditator for the sake of the interpretation.) There are no instructions as to the direction the meditator should be facing, nor is the direction of the goddess Prajñāpāramitā noted. One can assume from the lack of specificity that the usual orientation of a maṇḍala pertains, that is, with the central figure facing east and the meditator facing the central figure. The meditator would thus imagine Śākyamuni seated directly before him (in the east), with the Buddha's back turned to the meditator, Avalokiteśvara in front (west), behind Prajñāpāramitā, Śāriputra to his left (south), and Ānanda, to the meditator's right (north), the two śrāvakas opposite each other on the north–south axis.

The sādhana thus provides a grounding of the sūtra, a siting of the narrative within the space of the maṇḍala. To explore the iconology of the scene for a moment, we have in the maṇḍala a grouping of familiar figures, each with its own associations and meanings, who, when configured in the maṇḍala, give rise to further condensations. This network of signification operates both within the maṇḍala as well as intertextually, setting up a system of allusional relays, to both other images and other texts, a complex network of mutual implication. Three of the figures are mentioned in the sūtra, the fourth (Ānanda) is present as the rapporteur. And the fifth, the sole female figure surrounded by four males (three of whom are monks), is the central figure, the personification of the name of

[34] Ibid., p. 501.

the sūtra and the deification of the perfection of wisdom as the central figure. She is described as "the mother" appearing first in the maṇḍala before the meditator. Two of her four hands make the conventional gestures of teaching the dharma and bestowing protection; her two other hands hold a text (symbolizing the perfection of wisdom) and a *vajra*, which usually symbolizes the other essential element for the attainment of enlightenment, method (*upāya*). In tantric sexual imagery, the *vajra* is a symbol of the phallus. As the mother of the buddhas, she is the origin. As the knowledge of emptiness whereby buddhahood is attained, she is also the path. Finally, as the perfected state of wisdom, she is also the goal.[35] She is thus both the origin and the telos of the only proper desire, the desire for enlightenment, which she also represents. It is as such that the four surrounding figures behold her. She is therefore depicted as a beautiful and voluptuous woman, a vision of beauty to be looked at, a representation of the female form as "the locus of sexuality, site of visual pleasure, the lure of the gaze."[36]

Sitting facing her is Śākyamuni Buddha. He is closest to the meditator, indicating his importance as intermediary between the meditator and the goddess. Avalokiteśvara, the bodhisattva of compassion and the main speaker in the *Heart Sūtra*, sits behind Prajñāpāramitā. He sits with an unobstructed view of Prajñāpāramitā (at least of her back), Ānanda, and Śāriputra, but he cannot see Śākyamuni Buddha. To the left is Śāriputra, the wisest of all the śrāvakas, whose question occasions Avalokiteśvara to set forth the essence of the perfection of wisdom. Prajñāpāramitā's two right hands hold the *vajra* and bestow protection in his direction. Finally, to the right is the faithful Ānanda, the unnamed rapporteur of the sūtra, the "I" of "Thus did I hear." His presence is required so that the sūtra might be remembered. Perhaps suggesting this role as compiler and preserver of the word, Prajñāpāramitā's two left hands hold a sūtra and make the gesture of teaching the dharma in his direction.

The meditator thus sits as the observer of a scene, occupying a particular perspective before which the actors of the *Heart Sūtra* take their places. It is not an entirely panoramic view, since the gaze of the meditator is not unobstructed. Nor is it the aerial view adopted by painters of maṇḍalas in which the walls of the palace are laid flat in schematic representation. It is, instead, a painting from ground level, but a painting in

[35] Indian and Tibetan commentators outline three meanings of *prajñāpāramitā*: (1) a buddha's final knowledge of all aspects (*sarvākārajñāna*), (2) a path leading to that state, and (3) the sūtras that set forth those paths. For a discussion of various Indian and Tibetan delineations of the meaning of the term, see my *The Heart Sūtra Explained: Indian and Tibetan Commentaries* (Albany: State University of New York Press, 1988), pp. 21–24.

[36] Teresa de Lauretis, *Alice Doesn't: Feminism, Semiotics, Cinema* (Bloomington: Indiana University Press, 1984), p. 37.

which what E. H. Gombrich called "the beholder's share" is great, for what the meditator sees is the product not of paint on canvas, but of the visualization, the conscious representation of an alternative world, a world of fantasy in which nothing is invented, where fantasy remains bound to iconographically familiar, yet overdetermined images, a vision in which textuality interferes.

Unlike painting, these images, although textual, are not ostensibly graphic, and they appear not on a canvas but on another type of screen. According to E. H. Gombrich, one of the conditions necessary for the mechanism of projection is that the beholder "must be given a 'screen,' an empty or ill-defined area onto which he can project the expected image."[37] In the case of the sādhana, it is emptiness that provides the screen. After the preliminary offerings and supplications, the meditator is to dissolve everything into emptiness and then create the alternative universe of the maṇḍala out of this void. It is upon this emptiness that the four elements, then Mount Meru, then the palace, and then the throne of Prajñāpāramitā rest. And, as we will consider in more detail below, it is into this emptiness that the everything is once again absorbed. The degree to which the meditator remains conscious of this emptiness during the visualization remains in question. For Tsong kha pa, it is only when the meditator retains cognizance of emptiness in the midst of the most baroque of visualizations that the practice is truly "deity yoga" (*lha'i rnal 'byor*), which for him is the distinguishing feature of tantric practice.[38] Such a skill would seem to be akin to watching a film while remaining aware of the screen.

To call the residents of the maṇḍala actors in a scene is to evoke not painting but theater. The scene is set by the creation of the maṇḍala, after which the five actors take their places. The actors remain static, as in a *tableau vivant*. The visualizing gaze of the meditator provides the scenic setting, constructing the maṇḍala as an ideal spectacle, as a refuge from a less symmetrical world, a spectacle that remains on this side of "that delicate boundary which the dream image must not overstep lest it have a pathological effect (in which case mere appearance would deceive us as if it were crude reality)."[39] But the mere witnessing of the scene is not enough. For this spectacle to be truly Apollonian in Nietzsche's sense, it must provide "redemption through illusion" in which the dreamer has "completely lost sight of waking reality and its ominous obtrusive-

[37] E. H. Gombrich, *Art and Illusion: A Study in the Psychology of Pictorial Representation*, Bollingen series, no. 35.5 (Princeton: Princeton University Press, 1969), p. 208.

[38] Tsong-ka-pa [sic], *Tantra in Tibet: The Great Exposition of Secret Mantra*, trans. Jeffrey Hopkins (London: Allen and Unwin, 1977), pp. 114–28.

[39] Friedrich Nietzsche, *The Birth of Tragedy and the Case of Wagner*, trans. Walter Kaufmann (New York: Vintage, 1967), p. 35.

ness."[40] The meditator is to be this dreaming spectator, "the beholder of the visionary world of the scene."[41]

For the maṇḍala to function as drama, however, it is necessary for the meditator to not only have a view, like the audience in a Greek amphitheater, overlooking the scene, but to also see himself transformed into one of the actors on the stage, one of the figures in the maṇḍala. If we examine the topography of the visualization more closely, however, we see that this cannot take place. The meditator sits in the east facing the west, facing Prajñāpāramitā. His view of her is blocked, however, by Śākyamuni Buddha, also sitting in the east, facing the mother. The perfect, symmetrical world of the maṇḍala, in one sense the visualizer's creation, seems to have no place for him; the position of the Buddha even prevents him from seeing the central figure. It is as if the visualizer arrives after the maṇḍala is already complete, after all the seats are occupied. His belated arrival requires that he remain outside and take his place behind the Buddha, facing the Buddha's back, an ambivalent position of subordination to his ideal. As the latecomer, the visualizer must get in line behind the Buddha, who stands in his way. To stand behind is to be obstructed visually and restricted physically, but it is also to be protected, as a father situates his child behind him to guard the child from danger, a danger that may be physical or visual, something that the child should not see. The visualizer thus finds himself against a barrier, which prohibits his vision of and his access to Prajñāpāramitā. He will have to somehow shift his position, somehow find a substitute, in order to see.

Tantric sādhanas are divided by Tibetan exegetes into those in which the meditator remains outside the maṇḍala, visualizing the deities "in front" (*'dun bskyed*), and those in which the meditator imagines himself or herself as the central deity in the maṇḍala (*bdag skyed*). Here, however, something else seems to take place: the spectator joins the maṇḍala not in the center but on the periphery, as Śāriputra. (This is intimated by the fact that the visualizer and Śāriputra share the same seed syllable, *maṃ; mama* and *mām* are, respectively, the genitive and accusative forms of the personal pronoun *aham*, "I.") Having entered into another body, another character, through this magical transformation, the visualizer can now take his place in the drama. It is through this entry that the spectator becomes part of the spectacle, moving from his position in the east, where his view of the mother was blocked by Śākyamuni, in a clockwise direction (the proper direction of circumambulation) to the southern position, from which his view is unobstructed. It is only after this metamorphosis that he beholds another vision of Prajñāpāramitā. Al-

[40] Ibid., pp. 44–45.
[41] Ibid., p. 62.

though the meditator acting as Śāriputra remains a spectator, it is from this position that the drama now unfolds before his wide-open eyes.

The actors are only animated when the "actual" wisdom-beings (*jñānasattva*) are caused (whether they are invited or coerced, their presence is demanded by the omnipotence of the meditator's thought) to enter and to animate the pledge-beings (*samayasattva*). Now the action can begin, with (once again), Prajñāpāramitā in the center, facing Śākyamuni, who sits in the east. In the east, on Prajñāpāramitā's left, is Ānanda; on her right, the visualizer's double, Śāriputra; behind her, Avalokiteśvara.

> Imagine that the Conqueror [Śākyamuni] is drawn to the heart of the Mother and enters into samādhi. [Avalokiteśvara] gives answers to [Śāriputra's] question about the meaning of emptiness for all those surrounding.

From the southern seat, the visualizer as Śāriputra now witnesses Śākyamuni move from his throne on the periphery into the center, into the mother Prajñāpāramitā, the sādhana thus glossing the line of the sūtra, "At that time, the Bhagavan entered into a samādhi on the categories of phenomena called 'perception of the profound.'" That is, the sādhana tells us where Śākyamuni goes when he goes into samādhi. In describing Śākyamuni's movement as being drawn to "the heart of the mother," the author names the sūtra, for the heart of the mother is the heart of the perfection of wisdom (*prajñāpāramitāhṛdaya*). What is unusual, however, is that at this point in the sādhana, only Śākyamuni moves to the center. Movement in maṇḍalas is most often one of symmetrical expansion or contraction, with the residents of the maṇḍala being drawn inward or sent outward on beams of light. But here something unnatural occurs as the Buddha alone moves to the center, upsetting the balance of the maṇḍala. It is this unnatural act that prompts Śāriputra's question and Avalokiteśvara's answer, that is, that prompts the exposition of the sūtra, in which the riddle of saṃsāra—that there is no self, that everything is empty—is solved.

"There is a tremendously old popular belief," Nietzsche tells us, "that a wise magus can only be born from incest."[42] He interprets this to mean that it is only "an enormously unnatural event—such as incest" that breaks the spell of the rigid law of individuation, which is the primal cause of evil, with a restorative knowledge of the oneness of everything. It is wisdom that causes nature to surrender her secrets by means of an unnatural act. Wisdom, he says, "is an unnatural abomination."[43] If a taboo is to be broken, it is often preceded by a certain renunciation that

[42] Ibid., p. 68.
[43] Ibid., pp. 68–69, 74.

serves as a countermeasure to the transgression about to be committed.[44] From this perspective, the preliminary practices that precede the creation of the maṇḍala—confession of faults, taking of refuge, cultivation of virtue, and dedication of merit—can be seen as something more than an appended formula, rather as a propaedeuctic to the vicarious submission to instinct that occurs in the maṇḍala. The unnatural act here is also an act of incest, in which the Buddha unites with the mother from whom he was born, and it is this destabilizing act that at once causes a break in the perfect symmetry of the maṇḍala and allows the perfection of wisdom to be enunciated, a speech not produced naturally, through separation from the mother, but through reunion with her. And this speech announces that it is this oneness in emptiness that is the true nature of reality, that the individuated self that seems so natural is an artifice and the cause of sorrow. It is this same emptiness that serves as the foundation for the creation of the maṇḍala, for the fabrication of an imaginary world that can be mastered.

This act of incest is witnessed by the visualizer from his place as Śāriputra. No longer blocked by the Buddha, he can see, at least obliquely, from the overdetermined southern seat, what is for him both a vision of incest and the primal scene of parental intercourse. For Śākyamuni is not only the son of Prajñāpāramitā; he is also the guru and hence father of Śāriputra. And Śāriptura, as declared in the *Lotus Sūtra*, is a bodhisattva, also known as a *jinaputra*, a son of the Conqueror. Śākyamuni predicts in the *Lotus* as well that Śāriputra will one day become the buddha Padmaprabha. And when he is a buddha, Prajñāpāramitā will, perforce, have been his mother. Hence, by moving from the position behind Śākyamuni to the seat of Śāriputra, the visualizer not only gains an unobstructed perspective, but moves from a position of linear descent (from Prajñāpāramitā to Śākyamuni to himself) to a position of an Oedipal triangle from which he witnesses the primal scene. In moving from the position of overseer and creator of the maṇḍala to a site within the maṇḍala (by identifying with Śāriputra), the visualizer is displaced from the position of the lucid dreamer to that of a character in the dream, a witness to and voyeur of the prohibited act of incest that is about to take place, rather than its creator. But this enhanced perspective also has its cost, for Śāriputra is a monk, celibate and shaven. That is, for the child to move into a position of unobstructed access to the mother, in order for him to see, he must have been castrated, symbolized by both his shaven head and the fact that, unlike Śākyamuni and Avalokiteśvara, he does not sit on a

[44] Sigmund Freud, "Totem and Taboo," in *The Standard Edition of the Complete Psychological Works of Sigmund Freud*, trans. James Strachey, vol. 13 (London: Hogarth, 1958), pp. 97–98.

moon disc, the moon associated in tantric literature with semen.[45] In order that he not forget, the mother holds a *vajra* toward him, a *vajra* that at once represents the castrated phallus of Śāriputra, the nonexistent phallus of the mother, and all that remains of the now absent Śākyamuni.

For the movement of Śākyamuni into the mother is also the Buddha's disappearance. It is upon the death of the father that Śāriputra is empowered to speak. Having witnessed what is both a primal scene and a union of mother and son, he asks, "How should a son of good lineage who wishes to practice the profound perfection of wisdom train?" Stated more simply, "How can a son of the Buddha enter the perfection of wisdom?" Stated even more simply, "How can I do what the Buddha just did?" That is, the death of the father releases the child to articulate his own Oedipal wish.

The time has now finally arrived for the sūtra to be spoken and all of the actors are in their places. The Buddha has disappeared. Prajñāpāramitā sits silently in the center. On either side of her sit the castrated sons, Śāriputra and Ānanda. Behind her sits Avalokiteśvara. His position has obstructed his view of the primal scene, such that he speaks of what he has not seen. Yet his answer begins with an injunction to see. The child who wishes to practice the profound perfection of wisdom must see that every thing is empty. As he speaks to Śāriputra "and all those surrounding," the mother, the Perfection of Wisdom, sits silently between them, the only resident of the maṇḍala who did not rise from a seed syllable, the only figure who has no letter, yet the only one who holds the phallus and the word in her hands. She is also the only female figure in the maṇḍala, the object of male gaze from the cardinal directions, the only figure who lacks the sign (*lakṣana, liṅga, nimitta*). Like emptiness, she is signless (*animitta*). This absence is the mark of castration, an absence that is not subject to identical representation. Instead, the absence circulates through the maṇḍala from the mother, to the Buddha, to Śāriputra, an "indefinite, incessant and often violent displacement of marks and traces never entirely reducible to a signified significance: a process of reference without ultimate or fundamental referent."[46] The absence at the same time remains with the mother, but it is an absence that cannot be faced directly; unlike the "face-to-face" (*mukhāmukha*) samādhi, Śāriputra and Ānanda glimpse the mother

[45] The Buddha is also portrayed here in his nirmāṇakāya form, wearing the robes, and therefore, keeping the monk's vow of celibacy. His head is not shaved, however. Indeed, countering any suggestion of castration, his head is adorned with the immeasurable crown protrusion. His monastic garb, therefore, simply adds to the transgression of the act of incest.

[46] See Samuel Weber, "The Sideshow, or: Remarks on a Canny Moment," *Modern Language Notes* 88 (1973): 1132.

only obliquely, from the side. The subject is confronted with the discovery that "the object of its desire is almost nothing, but not quite. . . . [W]hat is 'discovered' is the absence of the maternal phallus, a kind of negative perception, whose object or referent—perceptum—is ultimately nothing but a difference, although no simple one, since it does not refer to anything, least of all itself, but instead *refers itself indefinitely*."[47]

It is, therefore, not surprising that the remainder of Avalokiteśvara's answer, the rest of the sūtra, is taken up largely with negation, as each element of the world is denied. This disavowal of the real ("in emptiness there is . . . no eye, no ear, no nose, no tongue, no body, no mind . . . ") serves to protect the maṇḍala as a self-contained system and at the same time releases the subject as Śāriptura from the repression that would restrict the impending repetition of incest that takes place when the remaining residents of the maṇḍala will be drawn into the mother.[48] It is Avalokiteśvara who speaks and, as is clear from the Buddha's expressions of approval at the end of the sūtra, he is speaking for the Buddha, in his absence. He thus structurally takes the place of the father. The triadic relation has now been lost, however, in the new topography of the maṇḍala, an ambivalence that allows the visualizer to move from Śāriputra's seat in the south back to his position in the east. The subject from his uncastrated position as the visualizer in the east, no longer obstructed by the Buddha, sits directly across from Avalokiteśvara on the east-west axis of the maṇḍala, with the mother in between—father (substitute), mother, son. Avalokiteśvara's litany of negations is not the father's "no," the prohibition of incest. It is not the prohibition of desire but the elimination of the intersubjectivity that is desire's barrier, allowing the subject to be that sign which will complete the mother's body. The Buddha now absent and the mother standing in the way of his surrogate (Avalokiteśvara), the threat of castration is lifted and the act of incest can take place as Śāriputra (and the entire maṇḍala) is drawn into the mother. The answer to Śāriputra's question is a disavowal of the real, the declaration of the real to be illusory, allowing absorption of the subject into the imaginary. This denial, is also, however, situated in an instruction on how to see, on how to acquire the power of vision that results in the mastery that is buddhahood. It is a desire to see, a "compulsive curiosity" to penetrate through the illusions of the superficial world to a reality beyond. But the object of this vision is that absence of the mark that can hardly be seen.

[47] Ibid.

[48] See Sigmund Freud, "Negation," in *The Standard Edition of the Complete Psychological Works of Sigmund Freud*, trans. James Strachey, vol. 19 (London: Hogarth, 1958), pp. 235–36.

This absence of an essence results in a crisis of perception that takes the form of repetitive denial.[49]

If constrained to provide a diagnosis, Dārikapa's sādhana shows the signs of narcissistic fantasy. The object choice is here not the ego itself but the ego ideal in the form of the maṇḍala, that system whose balance and symmetry betray the work of secondary revision, that rearrangement of psychical material that both serves the purposes of its own premises (here, a visualized setting for meditation on the *Heart Sūtra*) and serves a concealed, and truly operative reason (here, the staging of the incest fantasy).[50] Visualization here functions as the perception of an idealized self, an ideal ego, as if in a mirror. In this reflection, the Buddhist subject that had been fragmented into five aggregates and twelve sources (*āyatana*) and eighteen elements (*dhātu*) (the very categories that the *Heart Sūtra* denies) finds wholeness in the symmetry and wholeness of the maṇḍala, "possessed of every perfection that is of value."[51]

Withdrawn from the external world, the ego becomes fixated on internalized objects. But in order for the fantasy to be anything more than a daydream, those objects must also become somehow externalized, made "real." This occurs when the wisdom-beings are invited or coerced to enter into the simulacra that the meditator has imagined. It is when the players in the Oedipal drama are present and the fantasy has been expelled into the external world, almost like a hallucination, that the repressed fantasy of murder of the father and the union with the mother can be staged in the mirror of narcissism. Estrangement from the mother is caused by the position of the Buddha, the most immediate ego ideal ("what he himself would like to be"[52]), and is resolved when he is first circumvented (through the move to Śāriputra's seat, at the cost of temporary castration) and then destroyed (through his own reabsorption into the mother).

It is in this regard that Dārikapa's sādhana functions as what in the vocabulary of psychoanalysis is termed a phantasy. Like a phantasy, the sādhana is a script of an organized scene that is dramatized visually. The subject, the meditator, is present in the scene, moving from the position of the audience to that of an actor, when he moves to Śāriputra's seat. As in phantasy, what is imagined is not so much an object but an entire sequence in which the subject plays his own part, capable of var-

[49] See Weber, "Sideshow," pp. 1132–33.

[50] Freud, "Totem and Taboo," pp. 95–96.

[51] Sigmund Freud, "On Narcissism: An Introduction," in *The Standard Edition of the Complete Psychological Works of Sigmund Freud*, trans. James Strachey, vol. 14 (London: Hogarth, 1958), p. 94. See also Samuel Weber, *The Legend of Freud* (Minneapolis: University of Minnesota Press, 1982), pp. 12–14.

[52] Freud, "On Narcissism," p. 90.

ious permutations and attributions. Although a primitive desire is articulated in the phantasy, the phantasy allows various defenses also to operate, in this case, negation and projection, among others. And finally, as Laplanche and Pontalis note, "Such defences are themselves inseparably bound up with the primary function of phantasy, namely the *mise-en-scène* of desire—a *mise-en-scène* in which what is prohibited (*l'interdit*) is always present in the actual formation of the wish."[53]

We are left to consider the further function of the sādhana, especially when it is noted that a sādhana is something to be repeated, sometimes to be practiced six times a day. What is the purpose of this repetition, when we recall that Narcissus died? It thus remains to be determined whether Dārikapa's sādhana is best regarded as the symptom of a narcissistic neurosis (a neurosis that Freud declared unconquerable[54]), whether it is to be regarded as that art which, like Apollonian tragedy, is "the joyous hope that the spell of individuation may be broken in augury of a restored oneness,"[55] or whether it is simply further evidence of the tantras' storied ability to transform the prohibited into the path, as poison nourishes a peacock.

[53] Jacques Laplanche and J. B. Pontalis, *The Language of Psychoanalysis* (New York: W. W. Norton, 1973), p. 318. The other characteristics of phantasy listed in this paragraph are drawn from the same page.

[54] See Sigmund Freud, "Introductory Lectures on Psycho-Analysis" (pt. 3), in *The Standard Edition of the Complete Psychological Works of Sigmund Freud*, trans. James Strachey, vol. 26 (London: Hogarth, 1958), p. 423.

[55] Nietzsche, *Birth of Tragedy*, p. 74.

Six

The Commentaries of Jñānamitra and Praśāstrasena

Explanation of the Noble Heart of the Perfection of Wisdom

Āryaprajñāpāramitāhṛdayavyākhyā

JÑĀNAMITRA

Homage to the Bhagavatī Perfection of Wisdom

Heart of the Bhagavatī Perfection of Wisdom Sūtra expresses the name of the sūtra. Therefore, it says, *Heart of the Bhagavatī Perfection of Wisdom Sūtra*. If the name were not designated at the very outset, one would not know which sūtra it was.[1] Therefore, the name is stated. However, it is not merely the designation of a name. There is nothing in any sūtra that is not contained here in this *Heart of the Perfection of Wisdom*. Therefore, it is called the sūtra of sūtras.

In that [title], *bhaga* means the destruction of *māras*. [*Māras*,] such as the *māra* of the aggregates,[2] are not found when sought with this meaning of the perfection of wisdom, and no *māras* abide [there.] Thus, it destroys (*bhaga*). *Vat* [means] endowed with the six fortunes.[3] That is, since all the good qualities of knowledge arise from the blessings of the perfection of wisdom, it is endowed (*van*) [with them]. *Vat* [also] means the unlocated nirvāṇa (*apratiṣṭhitanirvāṇa*). Because all minds, intellects, and consciousnesses are overturned by this meaning of the perfection of wisdom, that is, since it is free from all predispositions, it has passed beyond. With regard to [the feminine ending] *ī*, all the buddhas arise

[1] Peking mistakenly reads *gtol mang* instead of *gtol med.*

[2] Four *māras*, or demons, are commonly listed: the *māra* of the aggregates (*skandhamāra*), the mind and body of a being in saṃsāra; the *māra* of the afflictions (*kleśamāra*), negative emotions, such as desire and hatred, that motivate nonvirtuous action; the *māra* of death (*maraṇamāra*), the factor that brings about the termination of the life faculty; and the deity Māra (*devaputramāra*), the god who attacked the bodhisattva under the Bodhi tree. For various Indian and Tibetan opinions as to the nature of the four *māras* and when they are overcome on the path, see Donald S. Lopez, Jr., *The Heart Sūtra Explained: Indian and Tibetan Commentaries* (Albany: State University of New York Press, 1988), pp. 25–27.

[3] For a list and discussion of the six fortunes, see Mahājana's commentary, p. 190.

from practicing the meaning of the perfection of wisdom; they are given birth by the meaning of the perfection of wisdom. Therefore, since the perfection of wisdom comes to be the mother of all the buddhas, [the feminine ending] *ī* [is used].

Regarding *prajñā*, reality is known just as it is by the three wisdoms of hearing, thinking, and meditating.[4] Therefore, it says *wisdom* (*prajñā*). Regarding *pāramitā*, because wisdom does not perceive any phenomena whatsoever, it has passed beyond signs, the two extremes, and birth and death. Therefore, it is said to be transcendent (*pāramitā*). Regarding *hṛdaya*, there is nothing profound or sublime in the *Śatasāhasrikāprajñāpāramitāsūtra* (Perfection of Wisdom in 100,000 Stanzas) that is not contained in this small sūtra. Therefore, it is the essence (*hṛdaya*).

Regarding *Obesiance to the Bhagavatī Perfection of Wisdom*, [281b] it is said in texts such as the *Śatasāhasrikāprajñāpāramitāsūtra* that when one makes obeisance to the perfection of wisdom, it is like making obeisance to all the buddhas of the three times; it is obeisance for the purpose of worship and the accumulation of merit.

Now, to the text. With regard to this perfection of wisdom, the meaning from beginning to end is clearly explained in seven parts: the setting, the entry into wisdom, the defining characteristic of emptiness, the sphere of wisdom, the qualities of wisdom, the fruition of wisdom, and the dhāraṇī of wisdom. The setting is from *Thus did I hear* to *together with a great assembly of monks and a great assembly of bodhisattvas*. The entry into wisdom is through, *and saw that even the five aggregates are empty of intrinsic existence*. The defining characteristic of emptiness is through, *no attainment and also no nonattainment*. The sphere of wisdom is through, *because they have no attainment, they abide in and practice the perfection of wisdom*. The qualities of wisdom is through, *they go to the completion of nirvāṇa*. The fruition of wisdom is through, *fully awakened into enlightenment*. The dhāraṇī of wisdom is the concluding mantra and above.

The Setting

Thus did I hear: the noble Mañjuśrī heard all of the Mahāyāna sūtras. Because he compiled [the sūtra], it says, *did I hear*. *Thus* is the very expression of the extent of what occurs in the *Heart of Wisdom*. *Did I hear* means it was heard at the feet of the Bhagavan; that is, speech from the

[4] For a delineation of these three forms of wisdom, see Vasubandhu's *Abhidharmakośabhāṣya* commenting on 6.5cd. See P. Pradhan, ed., *Abhidharmakośabhāṣyam of Vasubandhu* (Patna: Jayaswal Research Institute, 1975), pp. 334–35.

throat of the Glorious One was heard directly with the ear sense organ. *At one time* [means] that the *Heart of Wisdom* was not explained at some other time; it refers to the time, only once, when the Bhagavan explained [the sūtra] to the audience on Vulture Mountain. Regarding [the section that begins], *the Bhagavan*, [282a] [it might be asked], who is the teacher, what is the place, what is the audience, what meaning did he explain, upon their assembly? The teacher was the Bhagavan Buddha. The place was Vulture Mountain in Rājagṛha. The audience was a great assembly of monks and a great assembly of bodhisattvas. What meaning did he explain, upon their assembly? He taught them this *Heart of the Perfection of Wisdom*; the explanation of the meaning of the words of which is like what appears above. *Vulture Mountain in Rājagṛha*: [Rājagṛha, "abode of the king"] is famous because of the virtues of King Bimbisāra; the city of the area was used as the general name [of the region]. *Vulture Mountain*: because the area [of the city] was very vast [Vulture Mountain is mentioned as a more specific location]; it is so-called because many birds gathered at the summit of Vulture Mountain. *Great assembly of monks*: [*great*] means great in power and many in number. *Great assembly of bodhisattvas*: they had all penetrated directly to the marvelous meaning of the perfection of wisdom, and, furthermore, there were many [such] bodhisattvas who had entered the perfection of wisdom. *Together with*: because there were many around the Bhagavan, they surrounded him, that is, they abided with him. The preceding is the setting.

The Entry into Wisdom

At that time the Bhagavan was absorbed in a samādhi on the enumerations of phenomena called "perception of the profound." The Bhagavan, out of mercy for and in order to bless those in the audience and all sentient beings, entered [into samādhi]. *Enumerations of phenomena called "perception of the profound"*: because [the Buddha] understands and teaches in this text that all phenomena have passed beyond all observation and the extremes, it says, perception of the profound. *Absorbed in samādhi* means being in equipoise on that very profundity.

Also at that time, the bodhisattva, the mahāsattva, the noble Avalokiteśvara[5] *was contemplating*[6] *this very practice of the profound perfection of wisdom* [282b] *and saw that even those five aggregates are empty of intrinsic existence. Also at that time*: at the time when the audience had

[5] In this commentary, Avalokiteśvara is rendered as *spyan res gzigs dbang po* rather than *spyan res gzigs dbang phyug*.

[6] The text reads *rnam par rtog* rather than *rnam par lta*.

assembled and [the Buddha] was absorbed [in samādhi]. *Avalokiteśvara saw the emptiness of intrinsic existence*: the noble Avalokiteśvara, out of mercy for the audience and all sentient beings, contemplated the profound perfection of wisdom itself and thought, "even those aggregates are empty of intrinsic existence and unobservable; there is nothing other than emptiness." *The five aggregates*: the form aggregate is like a ball of foam, feeling is like a water bubble, discrimination is like a mirage, conditioning factors are like a banana tree, consciousness is like an illusion. *Empty of intrinsic existence*: those five aggregates themselves are naturally just empty of their own defining characteristic; because they are beyond all extremes and without defining characteristic, they are just empty.

Then, by the power of the Buddha, the venerable Śāriputra said this to the bodhisattva, the mahāsattva, the noble Avalokiteśvara. Śāriputra, the wisest of the great śrāvakas, through the blessing of the Tathāgata, asked the noble Avalokiteśvara, *"How should a son of good lineage train who wishes to practice the profound perfection of wisdom?" A son of good lineage* is born from the Mahāyāna scriptures and becomes a child of the Tathāgata. *Who*: whosoever abides in the Mahāyāna. *Practice the profound perfection of wisdom*: by practicing the profound perfection of wisdom, one partakes of the inexpressible profound reality of all phenomena. *How should one train who wishes to practice?* One who wishes to practice the meaning of the perfection of wisdom must know what it is like and what to train in. This is the question.

He said that, [283a] *and the bodhisattva, the mahāsattva, the noble Avalokiteśvara said this to the venerable Śāriputra*: [introduces] the answer to the question. *Śāriputra, a son of good lineage or a daughter of good lineage should analyze in this way*: one who wishes to practice the perfection of wisdom should analyze according to the meaning explained below. *They should correctly view those five aggregates also to be empty of intrinsic existence.* The aggregates are empty of intrinsic existence, that is, because they are without defining characteristic, they are not produced in the past, they do not abide in the present, they do not cease in the future. That is, because at no time are they produced, do they abide, or do they cease, their unlocated nature cannot be expressed. Hence, they are emptiness. *View* means to view things in accordance with reality; they are not to be viewed in any other way. The preceding is the entry into wisdom.

The Defining Characteristic of Emptiness

Form is empty; emptiness is form. Form is a word that conventionally designates the form that is seen and conceived of by those whose minds are mistaken in that they have not understood the nature of emptiness.

Regarding *emptiness*, emptiness is the nature of form, therefore, because [form] is without characteristic in the past, it is unobservable, and it is without defining characteristic and unobservable in the present and the future. Thus, since it does not abide anywhere or in anything, it says *emptiness*. *Emptiness is form* conventionally designates with the word "form" that even emptiness [has] an unobservable nature [like] form. Because it does not abide apart from that [form], emptiness is form. *Emptiness is not other than form, form is not other than emptiness*: that very thing which is form is the inexpressible emptiness; [283b] [when] form is abandoned, emptiness is not to be found. Therefore, it says *emptiness is not other than form*. That which is the inexpressible emptiness itself does not exist and is not found apart from that which is conventionally designated with the word "form." Therefore, it says *form is not other than emptiness*.

In the same way, feeling, discrimination, conditioning factors, and consciousnesses are empty: just as it is was explained concerning form, so one should view the other aggregates in the same way. *Śāriputra, in that way, all phenomena are empty*. Śāriputra is a term of address [meaning], "Listen undistractedly and well." In that way, all phenomena are empty: just as it was explained with regard to the five aggregates, he should also know that all [mundane and] supramundane phenomena, from the six sources to the knower of all aspects (*sarvākārajñatā*),[7] are emptiness. *Without defining characteristic*: just as space is without defining characteristic, [phenomena] are without the defining characteristic of affliction as well as without the defining characteristic of purity. *Unproduced, unceased*: present production is the subsequent coming into existence from what did not exist before. Cessation is the subsequent becoming nonexistent of what existed before. Because emptiness is unobservable, it is not produced before. Since it is not produced, it does not cease later. *Stainless, not stainless*: "stain" is the activity of consciousnesses as object and subject. Since emptiness[8] transcends consciousness, it is stainless. *Not stainless*: because stains do not exist, the lack of the [stainless] is also nonexistent. *Not diminished, not filled*: the diminished is sentient beings. The filled is the Buddha. *Not* means that sentient beings and buddhas cannot be not found even when sought; there is nothing diminished and nothing filled.

Therefore, emptiness is not form: the defining characteristic of form is disintegration whereas emptiness is without characteristic. Therefore,

[7] This is a stock term for "all phenomena," referring specifically to a list of the 108 phenomena of the afflicted class and the pure class. For the list, see Jeffrey Hopkins, *Meditation on Emptiness* (London: Wisdom, 1983), pp. 201–12.

[8] Peking reads *spyod pa nyid* instead of *stong pa nyid*.

emptiness is not form. *Similarly, it is not feeling* [because] the defining characteristic of feeling is experience. [284a] *It is not discrimination* [because] the defining characteristic of discrimination is apprehension. *It is not conditioning factors* [because] the defining characteristic of conditioning factors is conditionality. *It is not consciousness* [because] the defining characteristic of consciousness is individually apprehending particulars whereas emptiness is unobservable. Therefore, it is not consciousness. It is not *those* [aggregates] because the defining characteristic of the five aggregates is contamination; emptiness is not the aggregates.

It is not the eye [because] the defining characteristic of the eye is sight, but because emptiness is without defining characteristic, it is not the eye. *It is* similarly *not the ear* [because] the defining characteristic of the ear is hearing. *It is not the nose* [because] the defining characteristic of the nose is smelling. *It is not the tongue* [because] the defining characteristic of the tongue is experiencing tastes. *It is not the body* [because] the defining characteristic of the body is touching. *It is not the mind* [because] the defining characteristic of the mind is distinguishing particularities, but because emptiness is without defining characteristic, it is not the mind. Thus, the defining characteristic of the six senses is apprehending, but because emptiness is without defining characteristic, it is not the six senses.

It is not form. The defining characteristic of form is color and shape, but because emptiness is without defining characteristic, it is not form. *It is* similarly *not sound* [because] the defining characteristic of sound is euphony or cacophony. *It is not odor* because the defining characteristic of odor is scent. *It is not taste* because the defining characteristic of taste is flavor. *It is not tangible objects* because the defining characteristic of tangible objects is being rough or smooth to the touch. *It is not phenomena* because the defining characteristic of a phenomenon is a particular aspect, but emptiness is without defining characteristic; therefore, it is not phenomena. Thus, objects have the defining characteristic of conditions that cause observation, but emptiness is without defining characteristic. Therefore, it is not objects.

It is not the eye constituent, the mental constituent, up to and including the mental consciousness constituent. The defining characteristic of the eighteen constituents is viciousness, but emptiness is without defining characteristic. Therefore, it is not the eighteen constituents. *It is not ignorance, it is not aging and death, it is not the extinction of ignorance, it is not the extinction of aging and death.* [284b] The defining characteristic of the twelvefold dependent arising from ignorance to aging and death is upholding saṃsāra, but because emptiness is without defining characteristic, it is not ignorance up to and including aging and death. The defining characteristic of the extinction of ignorance up to and including the extinction of aging and death is purification, but because emptiness is without defining characteristic, it is not the extinction of ignorance up to and including the extinction of aging and death.

It is not suffering, origin, cessation, or path. The defining characteristic of suffering is affliction, the defining characteristic of origin is appropriation, the defining characteristic of origin is peace, and the defining characteristic of the path is knowledge, but emptiness is without defining characteristic. Therefore, emptiness is not the four truths.

It is not wisdom. The defining characteristic of wisdom is that it brings about the direct perception of all phenomena, but because emptiness is without defining characteristic, it is not wisdom. *It is not attainment, it is not nonattainment. Attainment* is the unsurpassed, perfect, complete enlightenment. *Nonattainment* is the nonattainment of the unsurpassed by sentient beings. *Is not* [means] that the defining characteristic of emptiness lacks unsurpassed enlightenment and lacks sentient beings. Therefore, it is not attainment and it is not nonattainment. These enumerations teach the emptiness of intrinsic existence with regard to all phenomena, saying "emptiness is like that." The preceding is the defining characteristic of emptiness.

The Sphere of Wisdom

Śāriputra, in that way, bodhisattvas abide in and practice the perfection of wisdom without attainment.[9] Because there are those who think that they have entered what they had not entered [before] it is explained that if one is endowed just with this sphere of the perfection of wisdom alone, it is the sign of the practice of emptiness. It says *in that way* because all phenomena become emptiness. *Bodhisattvas practice the perfection of wisdom without attainment.* Bodhisattvas who have entered the Mahāyāna should understand that there is nothing to be attained, from the five aggregates to omniscience, and they should practice the perfection of wisdom without seeing even a particle of any phenomenon. All phenomena are empty and are naturally unlocated. [285a] However, because [beings] become benighted by the mistaken mind of ignorance, which does not understand that, they cycle and wander in the ocean of mundane existence. What is the nature of that mistaken mind? Because the mind is observable when it is analyzed by the three types of wisdom, the afflictions are not seen, purity is not seen, [everything] from the aggregates to omniscience is not seen.

[9] The text reads *Shā ri bu de ltar byang chub sems dpa' thob pa med par shes rab kyi pha rol tu phyin pa la gnas shing spyod de* rather than the more common *Shā ri bu de lta bas na byang chub sems dpa' thob pa med pa'i phyir | shes rab kyi pha rol tu phyin pa la brten cing* [or *nas*] *gnas te.*

Emptiness, signlessness, the unproduced, the unceased, and so on are also not seen. Even wisdom itself is not seen in reality; not to see anything is to see the nature of the mind. To see the nature of the mind in that way is to see enlightenment. One who sees enlightenment sees the Buddha through reality (*dharmatā*). One who sees the Buddha through reality is completely awakened into highest enlightenment.

At this point, a doubter speaks, "Since you have just explained that nothing whatsoever exists, do you not fall to the view of annihilation of the non-Buddhists (*tīrthika*) or into the quietistic cessation of the śrāvakas?" The answer is that this is not the case. There is no such fault[10] because one acts for the welfare of all sentient beings and dedicates that [merit] to highest enlightenment in the manner of nonobservation, and because one practices the six perfections, and so on in a manner of nonobservation. The preceding is the sphere of wisdom.

The Qualities of Wisdom

Their minds are without fear and without obstruction. Having passed beyond error, they go to the completion of nirvāṇa. Because they are not frightened by the meaning of the emptiness, which is the perfection of wisdom, when hearing, thinking, or meditating, all minds, intellects, consciousnesses, and predispositions are overcome. Therefore, their *minds are without obstruction.* Having passed completely beyond the activities of the childish and the sphere of non-Buddhists, śrāvakas, and pratyekabuddhas, all of the afflictive obstructions and the obstructions to omniscience are exhausted and they go to the great nirvāṇa. [285b] The preceding are the qualities of wisdom.

The Fruition of Wisdom

All the buddhas who have come[11] in the three times, abide[12] in the perfection of wisdom and are fully awakened[13] into unsurpassed, complete, perfect buddhahood. All the buddhas who have come in the three times from worldly realms in the ten directions have upheld this profound perfection of wisdom; have read it, recited it, meditated on it, and taught it to others, and through practicing the perfection of wisdom, have been fully awakened into unsurpassed enlightenment. All the buddhas of the

[10] Derge mistakenly reads *skyod da* instead of *skyon du*.
[11] The text reads *gzhegs* instead of *bzhugs*.
[12] The text reads *gnas* instead of *brten*.
[13] The text reads *sang rgyas* rather than *byang chub*.

three times are also created by the perfection of wisdom, they arise from the perfection of wisdom. Therefore, the perfection of wisdom comes to be the mother of all the buddhas. The preceding is the fruition of wisdom.

The Dhāraṇī of Wisdom

Therefore, the mantra of the perfection of wisdom is true, it is not false. Therefore refers to what was stated above, hence *therefore. The mantra of the perfection of wisdom is true, not false*: because the purpose of the perfection of wisdom is the practice of knowledge (*vidyā*), it is called a mantra. Because all the doctrines of the world become a great vehicle to unsurpassed enlightenment, and [because] oneself and others are awakened into unsurpassed enlightenment, it says *true, not false. Mantra of great knowledge*: the meaning of the perfection of wisdom is a knowledge-mantra because it teaches that all desire, hatred, ignorance, and sufferings of saṃsāra are inexpressible and without intrinsic existence. Thus, the perfection of wisdom is a mantra of great knowledge. *Unsurpassed mantra*: because the perfection of wisdom establishes one in unsurpassed enlightenment, it is the unsurpassed mantra. *Mantra unequaled and equal*: the perfection of wisdom is not equal to the practices of worldly beings, śrāvakas, or pratyekabuddhas, [286a] and it is equal to the wisdom of all the buddhas. Therefore, it is unequaled and equal. It should be known as the *mantra that completely pacifies all suffering*: upholding the perfection of wisdom, reading about it, reciting it, keeping it properly in mind, and explaining it to others destroys all diseases, such as diseases of the eye, and brings protection because one is protected by the buddhas of the ten directions, by gods, nāgas, and so forth. By practicing the perfection of wisdom, the unfortunate realms and the entire ocean of saṃsāra are overcome. Therefore, it is the mantra that completely pacifies all suffering. *The mantra of the perfection of wisdom is stated: tadyathā gate gate pāragate pārasaṃgate bodhi svāhā.*[14] This mantra of the perfection of wisdom naturally establishes the combined meaning of all sublime profundities. Therefore, it is said to be a mantra of blessing.

Śāriputra, a bodhisattva mahāsattva should practice the profound perfection of wisdom in that way. All the buddhas of the three times become buddhas through the practice of the perfection of wisdom. Therefore, bodhisattvas who have entered the Mahāyāna should practice the perfection of wisdom. *Then the Bhagavan rose from samādhi.* By the power of the Bhagavan's entry into samādhi on the profound, Śāriputra asked his question and Avalokita gave his explanation. Having fulfilled his pur-

[14] The text reads *paragate parasaṃgate* rather than *pāragate pārasaṃgate*.

pose, he rose from samādhi. *He said, "Well done" to the bodhisattva, the mahāsattva, the noble Avalokiteśvara. "Well done, Well done."* The statement of the meaning of the heart of the perfection of wisdom accords with the pronouncements of all the buddhas. Because it was unmistaken, he praised it, "Well done." *Child of good lineage, it is like that. Child of good lineage, it is thus: the profound perfection of wisdom should be practiced just as you have taught it.* [286b] What Avalokita has declared accords with the pronouncements of all the buddhas, therefore, it is so. Bodhisattvas who have entered the Mahāyāna should practice the perfection of wisdom just as it was taught by the noble Avalokita. *Even the tathāgathas admire this.* If the tathāgatas admire the explanation given by Avalokita, how could others have doubts? *The Bhagavan was pleased,*[15] and having said that: through the declaration of the perfection of wisdom, everyone in the audience understood the meaning of the perfection of wisdom. Because there were no obstacles in the Mahāyāna, he was pleased and said that. *The venerable Śāriputra, the bodhisattva Avalokiteśvara, the gods, humans, demigods, gandharvas, and all of the audience took delight in the statement of the Bhagavan.*

The commentary to the *Bhagavatī Heart of the Perfection of Wisdom* by the master Jñānamitra is complete.

Vast Commentary on the Noble Heart of the Perfection of Wisdom

Āryaprajñāpāramitāhṛdayaṭīkā

PRAŚĀSTRASENA

Homage to the youthful Mañjuśrī and [295b] to the noble Avalokiteśvara

In the explanation of this sūtra, the meaning will be elucidated in ten categories: the name of wisdom, the setting , the absorption, the opening, the entry into wisdom, the nature of wisdom, the sphere of wisdom, the qualities of wisdom, the effect of wisdom, and the dhāraṇī of wisdom.

The Name of Wisdom

If there were no name it would not be possible to know the thing. Therefore, in order to recognize the thing, the name is stated. Thus, it is the

[15] The text adds *dgyes shing.*

Noble Heart of the Perfection of Wisdom. Regarding *jña* [knowledge, as in prajñā], it is said that there is mundane knowledge, supramundane knowledge, and unsurpassed knowledge. The mundane knowledge is polluted; it conceives the impermanent to be permanent, the impure to be pure, the miserable to be pleasant, and the selfless to be self. The supramundane knowledge is the knowledge of śrāvakas and pratyekabuddhas [that knows] that persons are selfless, that is, which knows that the conditioned is impermanent, the conditioned is miserable, persons are selfless, and that peace is nirvāṇa. The unsurpassed knowledge is the knowledge of the tathāgatas that persons and phenomena are selfless; it is the knowledge of signlessness, wishlessness, and emptiness. This knowledge [in the title] is to be understood as the unsurpassed knowledge. Regarding *ārya* (noble), with this knowledge, one is far separated from sorrow and suffering. Regarding *pra* [of prajñā, an intensifier], the wisdom that is superior to the mundane and supramundane is the unsurpassed wisdom. Regarding *pāramitā*, the sufferings of birth and death are here [on this side], nirvāṇa is beyond [on the other side]. Sentient beings who are driven by the desires of saṃsāra are [caught] in the middle. This wisdom acts as a raft and ship and delivers them to the shore of nirvāṇa. Therefore, it goes to the other side. Regarding *hṛdaya* [heart or essence]: everything in the *Śatasāhasrikāprajñāpāramitā* (Perfection of Wisdom in 100,000 Stanzas) is included in this. Hence, it is called the essence. At the same time, among the teachings of the Tathāgata, this ultimate perfection of wisdom alone is said to be supreme. Hence, it is called the essence. [296a]

The Setting

If the setting is not set forth, one does not know the place where [the sūtra] was explained [or to whom]. Therefore, in order to indicate the place where [the sūtra] was explained and to whom, the setting is stated. *Thus* refers to the meanings that appear below whereby one abandons superimposition and deprecation. *I* indicates that it was heard directly; it indicates simply that the doctrine was heard directly, not that the meaning was [necessarily] understood. *Did hear* is a term meaning apprehended by the consciousness of an ear sense organ that is capable of hearing. *One time*: heard on one occasion, that is, the morning or the evening. *The Bhagavan* [is so-called] because he has abandoned the afflictions to be abandoned by [the paths of] vision and meditation. In order to explain where [the sūtra was taught], it says *Rājagṛha* because the particular city was called Rājagṛha. The city was very vast; so that there be no confusion about where he abided, it says *Vulture Mountain.* The summit of that mountain is shaped like a vulture. Because they have abandoned all afflictions, they are *monks*. Because they are not divided by opponents, they are an *assembly*. Because of a greatness of number and of good qualities, it is *great*. Because they proceed to the enlightenment that is unsurpassed in nature, they are *bodhisattvas*. Because they deliver all sentient beings in the state of the unlocated nirvāṇa, they are *mahāsattvas*. *Abiding* is to be understood as their posture. These indicate when, by whom, where, and to whom it was explained. When? It was explained at one time. By whom?[16] By the Bhagavan; this indicates the marvelous teacher. Where? On Vulture Mountain in Rājagṛha; this indicates the marvelous place. To whom? To monks and bodhisattvas; this indicates the marvelous audience.

The Absorption

Without going into absorption, the matter under analysis could not be clearly understood. Therefore, in order that the matter under analysis be clearly understood,[17] the absorption is stated. [296b] *At that time* refers to being absorbed in samādhi at the time when the Bhagavan was abiding in Rājagṛha. It might be asked in which samādhi he was absorbed when it says *samādhi*. Therefore, it says *[perception] of the profound [in] the enumerations of phenomena*. Regarding that, a *phenomenon* is that which bears its own specific and general characteristics. The *enumerations* of those phenomena refers to the categories of phenomena, that is, the five aggregates, the constituents, and the sources. The *profound* means the emptiness of intrinsic existence because it is unproduced and unceased. When absorbed in samādhi, one realizes the nonproduction and noncessation of phenomena such as the aggregates. Therefore, the name of the samādhi is *perception of the profound [in] the enumerations of phenomena*. *Perception* means realization. *Absorbed* is a term that means placing the mind continually and one-pointedly in samādhi.

The Opening

Without an opening, the words are confusing and unconnected. Therefore, in order that the words be connected and not confusing, the opening is stated. *Also at that time* refers to the fact that at the very time at which

[16] Derge, translated here, reads simply *gang gis gang du*. Peking reads *rtogs pas brtag pa'i dngos po gsal bar gang gis gang du*.

[17] The phrase *brtag pa'i dngos po gsal bar rtogs par bya ba phyir* is absent in Peking.

the Bhagavan was absorbed on Vulture Peak, the noble Avalokiteśvara was viewing the emptiness of inherent existence of the five aggregates. [In the term "bodhisattva"], *bodhi* refers to the sphere of the mind, reality, the limit of reality. Because he exerts himself and strives to achieve that, he is a hero contemplating enlightenment [bodhisattva]. Because he has left the two obstructions at a great distance, he is noble (ārya). *Avalokita*: because he looks on all sentient beings with compassion in the manner of nonobservation (*anupalabdhi*), from among the three types of compassion,[18] he is one looking down [*avalokita*]. Because he has found the power himself to dispel the sufferings of sentient beings, he is the powerful one [*īśvara*].

Wisdom [in *perfection of wisdom*] is of three types: there is the sword of wisdom that cuts through the nets of the five aggregates, there is the thunderbolt of wisdom that smashes the aggregates of suffering, and there is the lamp of wisdom that dispels the darkness of ignorance. In brief, the nonconceptual wisdom that realizes the emptiness of all phenomena in all ways is called *wisdom*. [297a] Because that wisdom takes one beyond to the other side, it is called *perfection* [etymologized here as, "gone beyond" (pāramitā)]. There are three types of perfection: mundane perfection, supramundane perfection, and supramundane ultimate perfection. The mundane perfection is the state of having abandoned the suffering of the three paths [of animals, ghosts, and hell-beings]. The supramundane perfection is the state of having abandoned the cycle of birth and death and attained the nirvāṇa that is one-sidedly quietistic. As for the supramundane ultimate perfection, the three realms are like a dream; there is thus no desire even for nirvāṇa. Sentient beings are like illusions; there is thus no hope even for the fruition of buddhahood. Because all phenomena are naturally passed beyond sorrow, one attains the unlocated nirvāṇa. This is the attainment of the ultimate perfection.

To [answer the question of] what the perfection of wisdom is, it says, *practice of the profound*. The *profound* is nonproduction and noncessation. *Practice* refers to the meaning. Nonproduction and noncessation is called the perfection of wisdom. *Contemplation*[19] is to observe the meaning of nonproduction and noncessation. Not only is the meaning of nonproduction and noncessation observed, but the five aggregates, such as form, are also seen to be empty.

Emptiness is of two types: the emptiness of unconditioned space and the emptiness that is the lack of subject and object that is specifically understood by a noble's wisdom of the ultimate. The [sūtra] means that

[18] The three types of compassion are discussed by Candrakīrti in commenting on *Madhyamakāvatāra* 1.3–4abc. See *Heart Sūtra Explained*, p. 46.

[19] The text reads *rnam par rtog pa* rather than *rnam par lta ba*.

he was viewing the emptiness that is absence of subject and object in the aggregates. There are three kinds of views: the views of common beings and non-Buddhists (*tīrthika*), the views of śrāvakas and pratyekabuddhas, and the views of bodhisattvas and tathāgatas. Common beings and non-Buddhists view the five aggregates as a living being, a self, and a person. Śrāvakas and pratyekabuddhas view the five aggregates as origins and sufferings [among the four truths]. Bodhisattvas and tathāgatas view the five aggregates and see that they are empty of intrinsic existence.

The Entry into Wisdom

Because [Śāriputra] does not know the method of entry, the words of the question are set forth. What are they? [297b] *Then. . . .* Why did the noble Śāriputra[20] ask the bodhisattva Sarvālokiteśvara[21] and not another bodhisattva? To that this is said: when this perfection of wisdom is explained, among the assembly of countless hundreds of thousands in the audience, that bodhisattva is the chief. Therefore, by the power of the Buddha, the noble Śāriputra asks about the points that appear below in order to eliminate the doubts of himself and others. *Then* means after what was explained above.[22] *By the power of the Buddha* means by the blessing of the Tathāgata. *Śāriputra* is named Śāriputra because he was named after his mother, Śārika. *Said this* means that he asked what is explained below. *Who* is a term for whosoever. *Perfection of wisdom*: there are two wisdoms, the wisdom that understands the conventional and the wisdom that understands the ultimate. The wisdom that understands the conventional understands that all phenomena are like an illusion, a mirage, and a dream, and the wisdom that understands the ultimate understands that all phenomena are inexpressible and inconceivable, like the surface of the sky. Because that wisdom takes one to the unlocated nirvāṇa, it is called the wisdom that goes to the other side [i.e., the perfection of wisdom]. In fact, the profound meaning of non-production and non-cessation is called the perfection of wisdom.

The *one who [wishes to] practice* is the person, the bodhisattva. The *practice* is the doctrine, the perfection of wisdom. *How should one train* means how one should enter into the meaning of the perfection of wisdom through hearing, thinking, and meditation. In a second way, one should train in four kinds of practice: the practice of the ultimate, which

[20] The text reads *Shā ri'i sras po* instead of *Shā ri'i bu.*

[21] The text reads *Kun tu spyan res gzigs.*

[22] Derge mistakenly reads *gang du* instead of *gong du.*

is the nonconceptual knowledge; the practice of the elements of the category of enlightenment (*bodhipakṣa*) because the afflictions do not exist; the practice of bringing sentient beings to complete fruition without adherence; [298a] and the practice of bringing the teaching of the Buddha to complete fruition without attachment. *How should one train* is a term for how one should practice such practices. On this point, if someone does not understand the nature of wisdom, they are unable to grasp the meaning. Therefore, the words of the answerer are indicated by *bodhisattva mahāsattva* [to emphasize the authority of the speaker]. *Said this to Śāriputra* is a term meaning that he said that which appears below. *Should analyze in this way* is a term meaning that one should practice the perfection of wisdom in this way. He was asked how [one should practice]. Therefore, he says one *should view the aggregates to be empty of intrinsic existence*. The five aggregates are form, feeling, discrimination, conditioning factors, and consciousness.

Empty of intrinsic existence: there are five types of emptiness: the emptiness of what did not exist before, the emptiness of what does not exist after being destroyed, the emptiness of the utterly nonexistent, the emptiness of one not existing in the other, and the emptiness of intrinsic entity.[23] The absence of yogurt in milk is the emptiness of what did not exist before, the absence of milk in yogurt is the emptiness of what does not exist after being destroyed, the absence of horns on the lower part of a rabbit's head is the emptiness of the utterly nonexistent, the absence of an ox in a horse is the emptiness of one not existing in the other, and the nonintrinsic existence of all phenomena is the emptiness of intrinsic entity. Among the five types of emptiness, the five aggregates are empty in the sense of being without intrinsic entity; they should therefore be analyzed as empty.

Form is empty: form refers to earth, water, fire, and wind. Emptiness is the ultimate, the *dharmadhātu*. Because of the defining characteristic of emptiness, those forms are emptiness. The defining characteristic of emptiness is that it is nondual, beyond enumerator and enumerated; it is the state of having abandoned the view of I and mine. It is free from object and subject. Therefore, nonduality is the nature of reality (tathatā). Phenomena are not the composite of many empty characteristics. Therefore, even the four—earth, water, fire, and wind—are without defining characteristic, without entity, without self, without principal (*pradhāna*). [298b] It is not that things become emptiness when they are smashed to pieces; they are naturally empty. Therefore, *form is empty*. That very thing which is the natural emptiness of form is the ultimate emptiness itself; the ultimate emptiness does not exist apart from the natural empti-

[23] See *Heart Sūtra Explained*, pp. 53–56.

ness of form. Therefore, *emptiness is form*. The words mean that the ultimate emptiness is itself form's empty nature.

What is the evidence that the emptiness of form is the ultimate emptiness? The *Akṣayamatinirdeśa Sūtra* (Teaching to Akṣayamati) says, "Bodhisattvas, [when one speaks of] the wisdom that enters into the *dharmadhātu*, the *dharmadhātu* is the elements of earth, water, fire, and wind. However, the *dharmadhātu* is not the defining characteristics of hardness, moisture, heat, and motility. The *dharmadhātu* and all phenomena are similar. Why? They are similar because they are similar in emptiness." Thus, it should be known that the emptiness of form is the ultimate emptiness.

[There is] a second way in which *form is empty*. The three types of form are imaginary form (*parikalpitam rūpam*), imputed form (*vikalpitam rūpam*), and the form of reality (*dharmatā rūpam*).[24] Childish common beings' imputation of the defining characteristic of hardness to earth, and so forth is imaginary form. The form that is the object of engagement by a correct consciousness is imputed form. The nature of reality free from imaginary form and imputed form is the form of reality. Since there is no imaginary form and imputed form in the form of reality, it is said that *form is empty*. To those who wonder whether the reality of form—emptiness—is something that exists apart from imaginary form and imputed form, it is said that *emptiness is form*, meaning that the form of reality—emptiness—has the same nature as imaginary form and imputed form.

That very thing which is form is emptiness. Emptiness is also form. [299a] *Emptiness does not exist apart from form*.[25] The emptiness that is the defining characteristic of form and the ultimate emptiness are not different but one. Therefore, *emptiness does not exist apart from form*. Why are they not different? Because there is no difference in the defining characteristic of emptiness, which is the nature free of augmentation, diminishment, and is the state of having abandoned the two extremes. Saying that that which is form is empty is a way of saying that that which is the defining characteristic of form is also the defining characteristic of emptiness. Saying that that which is emptiness is form is a way of saying that that which is the defining characteristic of emptiness is also the defining characteristic of form.

Therefore, this is taught: sentient beings, debased and childish, cycle in the five evil paths in the cycle of birth and death without beginning. Through acquaintance with the five aggregates and familiarity with the eighteen elements, they become attached and attracted to them and be-

[24] See ibid., pp. 63–64.

[25] The text reads *gzugs las stong pa nyid gud na med do*.

lieve them to be real and solid. If, based on the fact that the Tathāgata teaches that they are naturally empty [they mistakenly conclude that], the defining characteristic of form is destroyed in emptiness, they will believe that the antidote, emptiness, exists apart. [Consequently] they are attached to the nirvāṇa of a śrāvaka, who is one-sidedly quietistic. Thus, *that which is form is emptiness* is set forth as an antidote that prevents them from falling into the extreme of saṃsāra due to their attachment to form. *That which is emptiness is form* is set forth as an antidote to falling into the extreme of nirvāṇa for śrāvakas who enter into the selflessness of persons and who create signs of emptiness, [thinking] that form is destroyed in emptiness.

If form and emptiness are to be abandoned because they do not exist, when emptiness is taught so that [sentient beings] will abandon the belief that form has signs [of intrinsic existence], they think that emptiness has signs. Hence, both form and emptiness are to be abandoned. Signs is the observation of signs [of intrinsic existence] anywhere. Therefore, because it obstructs the realization of reality, the belief that emptiness is real is a sign. For example, a person with cataracts was traveling. Along the right side of the path were thorns and ditches. [299b] Along the left side of the path were ravines and precipices. If a person with faultless vision said, "There are thorns and ditches [on the right]," the person would fall into the ravines and off the precipices. If he said, "There are ravines and precipices [on the left]," the person would fall into thorns and ditches. Rather, [a person with faultless vision] indicated that only the middle of the path was pleasant and without the slightest obstacle. [The person with poor vision] arrived home. As in that example, the person with cataracts is the common being impeded by the afflictive obstructions and the śrāvaka impeded by the obstructions to omniscience. The thorns and ditches are attachment to the signs of persons, forms, and so forth, that is, falling to the extreme of saṃsāra. The ravines and precipices are attachment to the nirvāṇa of the śrāvakas, that is, falling to the extreme of emptiness. The person with vision is the Tathāgata. Because he sees with the clear eyes of wisdom that form is naturally empty, he does not abandon saṃsāra because birth and death are like an illusion. Because [he sees that] the three realms are like a dream, he does not even seek the qualities of nirvāṇa. Because he enters the middle path with signlessness, wishlessness, and emptiness, he arrives at the location of the unlocated nirvāṇa. Therefore, because he taught that conceiving of signs is a precipice and a fault, signs are not to be held regarding existence or nonexistence.

In the same way, feeling, discrimination, conditioning factors, and consciousness are empty. Earlier, it said that [Avalokiteśvara] saw that the five aggregates are empty. The emptiness of form was stated, it was taught that form is empty, and it was taught that emptiness and form are not different. Those statements can be applied to three types of explanation, providing six types. The first of the three types of explanation, the emptiness of intrinsic existence, is the explanation of sameness. The middle, which applies to the three types of imputation, is the explanation of one taste. The last brings about entry into the middle path, the state of having abandoned abiding in both the extreme of true existence, the state of common beings in saṃsāra, and the extreme of emptiness, the nirvāṇa of the śrāvakas. Applying these three individually to the pair, *form is empty; emptiness is form* makes six. [300a] Similarly, it is to be explained in this way with regard also to the five aggregates or the four [other] aggregates. The five kinds of mutual emptiness[26] are explained. In the same way, feeling, discrimination, conditioning factors, and consciousness are explained by the five kinds of mutual emptiness.

Those phenomena are the continuum of one's mind. The mind is formless, with a nature of emptiness; it is based on the form aggregate upon the maturation of predispositions. It is similar to the example of an empty vessel; [what it contains] depends on the vessel. If the vessel is destroyed , there is no place for the supported; it is not different from the great void [of space]. In the same way, by analyzing the form aggregate and [finding it to be] empty, there is no place for the mental aggregates; they are not different from the ultimate, the *dharmadhātu*. What is the evidence that the five aggregates are empty of intrinsic existence? The *Akṣayamatinirdeśa Sūtra* says:

> The form aggregate is like a ball of foam; it cannot withstand being grasped and held. The feeling aggregate is like a water bubble; because it is momentary, it is impermanent. The aggregate of discrimination is like a mirage because it is mistakenly apprehended by the thirst of attachment. The aggregate of conditioning factors is like the stalk of a lotus; when it is destroyed it has no core. The aggregate of consciousness is like a dream; it is mistakenly conceived. Therefore, the five aggregates are not a self, not a person, not a sentient being, not a life, not a nourisher, not a being. The five aggregates are naturally like this: empty of I and mine, unproduced, unarisen, nonexistent, the sphere of space, unconditioned, and naturally passed beyond sorrow.

Because it is understood that the four great external [elements] are empty, it is said that form is empty. Because it is understood that the four internal minds [feeling, discrimination, conditioning mental factors, and consciousness] are empty, it is said that [they are] empty. Thus, it says *empty*; by abandoning signs of the identity of form and emptiness, one is free from the duality of object and subject. Therefore, it is called the body of complete freedom. This is the sphere of wisdom. If the sphere is not un-

[26] Peking mistakenly reads *ston pa* rather than *stong pa*.

derstood, it is unsuitable to mediate upon it. Therefore, it is explained so that yogins may enter into meditation.

Śāriputra, it is thus [300b] [means] it is like what was explained above. *All phenomena are empty*: *all phenomena* refers to that which is based on the aggregates, that is, the sense powers, their objects, the constituents, the sources, dependent arising, and so forth. By understanding that the aggregates are empty, it is also known that the defining characteristic of their branches is emptiness. For example, if one understands that the primary part of the body is empty, one will implicitly know that the feet, arms, and so on [are empty]. *Without defining characteristic*: because all phenomena [have] signs and are beyond signs, they are without defining characteristic. *Unproduced and unceased*: the subsequent existence of what did not exist before is production. The subsequent nonexistence of what existed before is cessation. The buddha-nature, the *dharmadhātu*, is the ultimate emptiness. Because this has no beginning, its end is not to be found. Therefore, it says *unproduced and unceased.* Even when sentient beings cycle on the five paths [of rebirth], the buddha-nature does not become stained. Therefore, it is *pure.*[27] Even the buddhahood that is unsurpassed and perfect complete enlightenment is not purer than the buddha-nature. Therefore, it is *not pure.*[28] Because the buddha-nature exists even in the bodies of ants and beetles without shrinking, it is *undiminished.* Because it exists even in the dharmakāya without expanding, it is *unfilled.* Why? Because it is beyond thought and expression; it is not encompassed by measures. Because the *dharmadhātu* is not produced in the two ways, by actions or afflictions, it is *unproduced.* If it is not produced, it is not destroyed. Therefore, it is *unceased.* Because the *dharmadhātu* is naturally pure, it is without purity. Therefore, it is *not pure.* Although it is naturally pure, the adventitious afflictions do not make it impure. Therefore, it is *pure.* Because it is the state of having abandoned the completely afflicted class, the *dharmadhātu* is undiminished. Hence, it is *undiminished.* Because the *dharmadhātu* does not increase when purity increases, it is *unfilled.* [301a]

It was taught above that the individual divisions of the five aggregates are empty. Consequently, if the five aggregates, which are [mistakenly] thought to have signs, are empty, it is unsuitable to designate them with names such as "form," because they are indivisible from emptiness. Thus, in order to dispel signs that are conceptions about the names, it says [*when there is*] *emptiness, form is not, feeling is not,*[29] and so forth.

[27] The text reads *rnam par dag pa* rather than *dri ma med pa.*

[28] The text reads *rnam par dag pa med pa.*

[29] The text reads *stong pa nyid ni gzugs ma yin tshor ba ma yin* rather than the more familiar *stong pa nyid la gzugs med tshor ba med.* I have translated it as I have because to

The five aggregates are empty of intrinsic entity, that is, their defining characteristic is indivisibility [from emptiness] beyond names and designations. Therefore, because the signs imputed to form and so forth do not exist, it says *form is not, feeling is not*; the words mean, *no form, no feeling*. Furthermore, the words mean that in emptiness, "form" is not expressed as a name and "feeling" is not expressed.

Not eye, not ear, not nose, not tongue, not body, not mind. This is the six senses. The six senses depend on the five aggregates. Therefore, if the five aggregates do not exist neither do the six senses because they are not other than the five aggregates. Therefore, it says *no*. *Not form, not sound, not odor, not taste, not touch, not phenomena*. This is the six objects. They are the fructifications of predispositions due to the power of ignorance. A polluted mind holds that that which is established as [these] conditioned effects exists. Because ultimately they are empty of intrinsic entity, [they] *do not exist*. *Not the eye constituent to not the mental constituent*. This is the eighteen constituents. If the six internal senses do not exist, the bases of the six consciousnesses do not exist. Therefore, because the six external objects do not exist, the abodes of the six consciousnesses do not exist. Because nothing arises, the six consciousnesses also do not exist. Therefore, the eighteen constituents do not exist.

Ignorance is not, the extinction of ignorance is not, aging and death are not, the extinction of aging and death is not. [301b] This is the sphere of those who have entered the vehicle of pratyekabuddhas. Saying *ignorance* conveys in brief the teaching [of the eleven other branches] up to and including aging and death: from [action] conditioned by ignorance are seen consciousness, name and form, the six sources, contact, feeling, attachment, grasping, existence, birth, aging and death. Ignorance arises from the view of self. The conception of self arises from that which does not exist. Therefore, ignorance also does not exist. For example, by lighting a single lamp in a house that has long been dark, [the darkness] becomes nonexistent in an instant and the nonexistence is not perceived to be something real. Similarly, investigation with the lamp of wisdom makes nonexistent in an instant the thick darkness of ignorance [that has benighted] sentient beings beginninglessly. The nonexistence is not perceived to be something real. What is called "knowledge" is nothing more than the mere designation for the opposite of ignorance; because ignorance does not exist, not even the name of knowledge is established. Therefore, *ignorance is not and the extinction of ignorance is not*. Because the entity of ignorance does not exist, ignorance does not exist.

read the line simply as "emptiness is not form, not feeling" would directly contradict what has just been said.

Because its nonexistence does not appear as something real, its extinction also does not exist.

Suffering, origin, cessation, and path are not. This is the four truths, the sphere of those who have entered the vehicle of śrāvakas. The truths are of three types: the mundane, the supramundane, and the ultimate supramundane truths. Regarding that, the mundane truths are the understanding that the five aggregates are origins and are sufferings of aging and death. The supramundane truths are understanding suffering, origin, cessation, and path. Regarding the [ultimate] supramundane noble truths, the understanding that the five aggregates are not produced is the understanding of the truth of suffering. The understanding of the truth of origin is that by which mundane existence is destroyed. The understanding that ignorance and the insidious defilements (*anuśaya*) are without intrinsic entity is the understanding of the truth of cessation. [302a] Not making superimpositions about anything due to the scope[30] of the equality of phenomena is the understanding of the truth of the path. Thus, because the truths also are ultimately without intrinsic entity, [the sūtra says they] *do not exist.* What is the evidence that the truths lack intrinsic entity? The *Akṣayamatinirdeśa Sūtra* says:

> Which bodhisattva is skilled in the truths? These aggregates are suffering. The understanding of how [the aggregates] are empty of the signs of suffering is called the noble truth of suffering. The origin of the aggregates are the cause of attachment and the cause of [wrong] view. That which does not grasp and does not superimpose the cause of attachment and the cause of [wrong] view is called the noble truth of origin. The understanding that the aggregates do not arise earlier and do not depart later and do not abide in the present is called the noble truth of cessation. That which is placed in equipoise on the nondual wisdom and understands that the four truths are emptiness is the noble truth of the path.

Wisdom is not, attainment is not, nonattainment is not. This is the sphere of one who has entered the great vehicle of the bodhisattva. *Wisdom* is the nondual wisdom that is the state of having abandoned the afflictive obstructions and the obstructions to omniscience. Because it is not wisdom ultimately, it says, *wisdom does not exist. Attainment* is the attainment of what did not exist before. If attainment exists, it also was absent [at some prior point]; if there is fruition, it will disintegrate. Therefore, the buddha-nature abides equally in all sentient beings and is not absent in the beginning or attained in the end. Even the levels of the ten stages that are mentioned are nothing more than just the gradual

[30] Derge reads *chos mnyam pa nyid du ring bas.* Peking reads *chos mnyam pa nyid du reng bas.* The translation is tentative.

purification of the predisipositions of ignorance on the *ālayavijñāna*; upon purifying the predispositions of ignorance, the *dharmadhātu* that is the mirror-like wisdom of a buddha [is attained]. Regarding [the *dharmadhātu*], there is nothing to be called attainment or nonattainment. Therefore, *no attainment, no nonattainment.* The *Saptaśatikāprajñāpāramitā* (Perfection of Wisdom in 700 Stanzas) says, "To practice no signs is to practice the perfection of wisdom." [302b]. To have no attainment whatsoever is to attain unsurpassed enlightenment.

The Qualities of the Perfection of Wisdom

Although the unsurpassed enlightenment of yogins has the nature of emptiness, it is not the case that there are no effects of the perfection of wisdom; there are. In order to create joy [its] good qualities are explained. *Therefore, Śāriputra, because bodhisattvas have no attainment, they abide in the perfection of wisdom.* This is said: *Therefore*: in accordance with what was explained above. *No attainment*: there is no attainment of the fruition, unsurpassed, perfect enlightenment. *Abide in and rely on the perfection of wisdom*: they do not abide in any sign. *Their minds are without obstruction*: they have abandoned all internal predispositions and external signs; they do not exist. *Without fear*: because their minds are without obstructions in that way, they have no fear of birth in saṃsāra and the bad realms and no fear of the profound doctrine, the meaning of no production or cessation. *Passed completely beyond error*: error is seeing nonexistent external objects as various objects due to predispositions of ignorance on the *ālayavijñāna*. Having come to understand that persons and phenomena are selfless, they abandon the afflictive obstructions and the obstructions to omniscience and pass beyond error. *Go to nirvāṇa*: it is said that ignorance is the afflicted *ālaya*; because it acts as the cause of saṃsāra among the twelve branches of dependent arising, it comes to include only the suffering aggregates in the end. When one knows that ignorance does not exist, all the suffering and afflictions also become nonexistent. Therefore, *they go to nirvāṇa.*

The Fruition of the Perfection of Wisdom

If there were no fruition, [one might think] that practice has no purpose. Therefore, the fruition is explained. *All the buddhas who abide in the three times rely on the perfection of wisdom.* This is said: [303a] the times are the different times of the past, future, and present. *Who abide*: those who come [or go] in the three times. *Buddhas*: because they have attained the eye of wisdom free from the contamination of the triple-realmed saṃsāra, they are called buddhas. In fact, having become the dharmakāya, that which is the marvelous and limitless qualities, such as wisdom, knowledge, samādhi, the major marks, the minor marks, and the unshared qualities, is called a buddha. *Rely on the perfection of wisdom*: they abide in the absence of all signs. Because all of the buddhas of the three times are similar in that they arise from the perfection of wisdom, the perfection of wisdom is called the mother of the buddhas. *Unsurpassed, perfect, complete enlightenment*: this is said: *unsurpassed*: beyond the three realms. *Perfect, complete*: the final quality of unmistaken reality. *Enlightenment*: the *dharmadhātu* of unmistaken[31] reality. *Awakened*: fully awakened, having practiced the perfection of wisdom nonconceptually. This is in no way different from the buddhas of the past and refers to similar qualities.

The Dhāraṇī *of the Perfection of Wisdom*

It is stated to prevent downfall. *It is true; it is not false.* Because it is not spoken with words, it is wishless. Therefore, it is verbally true.[32] Because it is not practiced with the body, it is signless; it is physically true. Because it cannot be conceived by the mind, it is emptiness;[33] it is mentally true. Thus, it does not contradict the three doors of liberation of nobles. The perfection of wisdom accords with the meaning of the nonconceptual door that clears away all mental signs and causes simultaneous entry into the ultimate.[34] Therefore it is true; it is not false. Because it completely clears away all the predispositions of internal consciousness, it is *the mantra of the perfection of wisdom*. Because it naturally understands and clears away all signs of external[35] objects, [303b] it is *the mantra of great knowledge*. Because it clears away all signs of the internal and external, it is *the unsurpassed mantra*. Because it brings about the fruition of buddhahood, it is *the mantra equal to the unequaled*. Because it effects the abandonment of the unfortunate realms and fulfills the welfare of sentient beings, it is *the mantra that pacifies all suffering*. *It is to be known*: the words mean that the perfection of wisdom is to be known as the

[31] Derge omits *ma nor ba'i*.

[32] Derge reads *de dag gir bden pao'*. Peking reads *de dag gis bden pao'*. I have followed neither, reading it (to be consistent with what follows) as *de ngag gi bden pao'*.

[33] Derge reads *stong pa nyid las* instead of *stong pa nid pas*.

[34] This may be a reference to the *Sakṛtprāveśikanirvikalpabhāvanārtha*, attributed to Vimalamitra. On this work, see Giuseppe Tucci, *Minor Buddhist Texts*, pts. 1–2 (Delhi: Motilal Banarsidass, 1986), pt. 2, pp. 115–21.

[35] Peking mistakenly reads *spyi* instead of *phyi*.

cause of going to buddhahood. *The mantra of the perfection of wisdom is stated: tadyathā gate gate pāragate pārasaṃgate bodhi svāhā.* This mantra of the perfection of wisdom serves as the cause of mundane and supramundane merit. Mundane merit is effectively able to prevent harm and protect one from afflictions, demons, and obstacles. Regarding supramundane merit, relying on this dhāraṇī serves as a cause of wisdom and knowledge.

Then the Bhagavan rose from samādhi. This is said: Without the Tathāgata, others were not able to explain and hear the meaning of the perfection of wisdom. Thus, the noble Avalokiteśvara's explanation and Śāriputra's hearing are the blessings of that samādhi. Because the explanation and hearing had taken place, he rose from samādhi. Seeing the pure cause and the pure effect, the Bhagavan said *Well done* to the noble Avalokiteśvara. Seeing the pure cause and effect, the Buddha said *Well done*. The gods, humans, and so on were delighted by and admired the Bhagavan's statement.

This concludes the *Vast Commentary on the Heart of the Perfection of Wisdom*, clearly set forth in ten points,[36] composed by the master Praśāstrasena.

[36] The phrase *don bcus gsal bar bstan pa slob dpon* is absent in Peking.

Seven

The *Heart Sūtra*'s Mantra

HOW ARE WE TO UNDERSTAND ritual speech? Some conceive ritual language as an Austinian speech-act, others as a magical instrument, others as a constituent of a language game, still others as not language at all. But, as if with one voice, the students of ritual speech proclaim the preeminence of sound and of context, the situation of the utterance in time and space. One specimen of ritual speech is the most widely repeated of Buddhist mantras, the mantra that occurs at the end of the *Heart Sūtra*: *gate gate pāragate pārasaṃgate bodhi svāhā*. Unlike other mantras, the *Heart Sūtra*'s mantra seems to occur first not as sound but as writing. And although mantras are commonly identified as a fundamental constituent of tantra, both Hindu and Buddhist, this mantra occurs in a work that calls itself a sūtra. It seems to be a text without context, injected as if from nowhere into the most compact of Buddhist scriptures.

It is, nonetheless, possible to situate the mantra provisionally in the sūtra. Avalokiteśvara has announced that all the buddhas of the past, present, and future rely on this perfection of wisdom in order to gain enlightenment. Next, with a "therefore" that can only strike us as a non sequitur, he says, "Therefore, the mantra of the perfection of wisdom is the mantra of great knowledge, the unsurpassed mantra, the mantra equal to the unequaled, the mantra that completely pacifies all suffering. Because it is not false, it should be known to be true. The mantra of the perfection of wisdom is stated thus: *[oṃ] gate gate pāragate pārasaṃgate bodhi svāhā*."

The Indian commentators on the *Heart Sūtra*, all writing at a time when tantric Buddhism was in full flower, find varying degrees of significance in the mantra. In what follows, we will have occasion to consider the views of these ancient interpreters and those more modern in an effort to phrase the question of the meaning of this mantra, a case of ritual speech without a ritual setting, of ritual speech as text. It is necessary first, however, to determine in what sense, if any, these Sanskrit syllables are a mantra.

It may seem foolish to ask whether these syllables in the *Heart Sūtra* are a mantra when the sūtra itself calls it "the mantra of great knowl-

A previous version of this essay appeared as "Inscribing the Bodhisattva's Speech: On the *Heart Sūtra*'s Mantra," *History of Religions* 29 (1990): 351–72.

edge, the unsurpassed mantra," and so forth. However, the mantra lacks many of the characteristics identified by scholars who have attempted to define the term. These scholars generally agree that mantras are sacred syllables, transmitted from master to disciple, often ostensibly unintelligible, which are recited in a strictly controlled ritual context from which they derive their esoteric meaning.[1] Although the *Heart Sūtra* has certainly been employed in a variety of rituals over its long history in many parts of Asia,[2] the sūtra is not traditionally (although, as we have seen, not unequivocally) regarded as secret but rather as part of the Buddha's exoteric teaching, the *prajñāpāramitā* corpus of Mahāyāna scriptures, and its mantra is part of a text, not an initiation ritual or a daily meditation rite (sādhana). Although a sublime power is suggested for the mantra by its epithets ("the mantra of great knowledge," etc.), the *Heart Sūtra* differs from other important Mahāyāna sūtras like the *Lotus* or the *Laṅkāvatāra* that contain mantras and dhāraṇīs (condensations of texts that often function as mnemonic aids or as substitutes) in that it contains no instruction as to how the mantra is to be used, or to what end; its instrumental quality, the activity it performs (which all mantras are presumed to possess), remains unspecified. If it is true, as André Padoux maintains, that "a mantra has a use rather than a meaning,"[3] then perhaps the *Heart Sūtra*'s mantra is not a mantra at all.

There is, furthermore, no deity to be propitiated, counter to Jan Gonda's claim that a mantra "is identical with the aspect of the god which is invoked with or by means of it."[4] Among other purposes of the repetition of mantra, according to a traditional fourfold division, are the pacification of negative circumstances, the multiplication of what is

[1] On mantra theory, see the classic article by Jan Gonda, "The Indian Mantra," in J. Gonda, *Selected Studies*, vol. 4, *History of Ancient Indian Religion* (Leiden: E. J. Brill, 1975), pp. 248–301. Gonda's definition of mantra occurs on p. 253. See also Agehananda Bharati, *The Tantric Tradition* (Garden City, N.J.: Anchor, 1970), chap. 5. Bharati's definition of mantra occurs on p. 111. A more recent volume is Harvey Alper, ed., *Understanding Mantras* (Albany: State University of New York Press, 1989). The hardback edition of this book contains the most complete bibliography of Western-language works on mantra available.

[2] On its use in modern Japan, see Michael Pye, "The Heart Sutra in Japanese Context," in Lewis Lancaster, ed., *Prajñāpāramitā and Related Systems* (Berkeley: Berkeley Buddhist Studies Series, 1977), pp. 123–33. In the Tibetan Buddhist tradition, it is often recited before a religious discourse as a means of dispelling obstacles. The sūtra was put to a related used in the summer of 1988 when, prior to his address before the European Parliament in Strasbourg, in which he offered a new proposal for bringing an end to the crisis in Tibet, the current Dalai Lama instructed the monks of the exile monasteries in India to recite the *Heart Sūtra* several million times.

[3] André Padoux, "Mantras—What Are They?" in Alper, ed., *Understanding Mantras*, p. 302.

[4] Gonda, "Indian Mantra," p. 283.

deemed desirable, the acquisition of a particular power, and the wrathful destruction of opponents. But the commentator Vajrapāṇi does not categorize the mantra as any of these, instead putting it in a class by itself, suggesting that we moderns are not alone in being at a loss as to what to make of this mantra. He writes, "This mantra of the perfection of wisdom is the heart of the meaning of all secret mantras. . . . The mantra of the perfection of wisdom is not a mantra for pacification, increase, power, or wrath. What is it? By merely understanding the meaning of this mantra, the mind is freed."

But Frits Staal argues that meaning is not the issue, because mantras are not language; they lack two of four properties that characterize language: they are phonological and pragmatic, but lack the syntactic and the semantic.[5] Indeed, Staal discerns parallels between mantras and the presleep monologues of babies. (His example of "go go go go all gone all gone all gone all gone good luck" is particularly evocative of the *Heart Sūtra*'s mantra.[6]) Yet the *Heart Sūtra*'s mantra, as we shall see, can be rather easily construed to have both syntax and semantics. Harvey Alper has postulated that there is a correlation between the linguistic intelligibility of a mantra and its purpose: mantras uttered to achieve some worldly goal are what he calls "linguistic" while mantras used for a more transcendent or redemptive goal are "alinguistic," that is, they cannot be understood as ordinary language.[7] Yet the *Heart Sūtra* mantra is linguistically intelligible (as will be considered below) despite being proclaimed in the sūtra itself as having a redemptive effect; it is "the mantra that completely pacifies all suffering."[8] It violates Alper's correlation by being both "linguistic" and redemptive.

Modern scholars of mantra seem to agree that, unlike children, mantras should be heard but not seen, that is, they are to be spoken but not read. Andre Padoux, noting the privileged position held by speech in the Indian tradition, writes that "Mantra is sound (*śabda*) or word (*vac*); it is never, at least in its nature, written."[9] And Frits Staal declares, "No mantras may be learned from books."[10] But the *Heart Sūtra*'s mantra is writ-

[5] See Frits Staal, "Vedic Mantras," in Alper, ed., *Understanding Mantras*, p. 70.

[6] See Frits Staal, *Rules without Meaning: Ritual, Mantras and the Human Sciences* (New York: Peter Lang, 1993), p. 272.

[7] Alper, *Understanding Mantras*, pp. 9–10.

[8] Bharati writes, "These meaningful mantras, then, derive from specific doctrines: they have, like the *dhāraṇīs*, simultaneous but distinct functions, to impress the essence of the doctrine *in nuce* on the mind of the votary as a didactic device and a mnemonic aid, and to work as *mantras* proper, as alleged power-vehicles in the manner previously discussed." See *Tantric Tradition*, p. 114.

[9] Padoux, "Mantras," p. 297.

[10] Staal, "Vedic Mantras," p. 69.

ten and, as such, must be readable after the disappearance of its intended recipient.

Nor was Vajrapāṇi the only Indian commentator on the *Heart Sūtra* who was deterred by the mantra. Two others, Jñānamitra and Praśāstrasena (whose commentaries precede this chapter), seem to see the mantra as anomalous to the rest of the sūtra, something that they are unable to integrate into their explications. They cursorily refer to it as the dharaṇī of the perfection of wisdom and ascribe to it the qualities of blessing and protection that are commonplace in descriptions of the powers of Hindu and Buddhist mantras. Jñānamitra provides no interpretation of the meaning or function of the mantra itself, focusing rather on the five epithets, each of which he glosses in terms of the general category of the perfection of wisdom itself, rather than of the mantra. For example, it is the mantra that completely pacifies all suffering because reciting the perfection of wisdom, bearing it in mind properly, and explaining it to others destroys all maladies and brings one under the protection of buddhas and supernatural beings, while practicing the perfection of wisdom turns one away from rebirth in the unfortunate realms and the ocean of saṃsāra. There is nothing new here to indicate the specific use-value or meaning of the mantra; such advertisements abound in the Perfection of Wisdom sūtras.

Four of the other Indian commentators—Śrīsiṃha, Kamalaśīla, Atiśa, and Śrīmahājana—bring a different agenda to their reading of the mantra. As we have already seen, the *Heart Sūtra* presents the Buddhist scholastic with the following dilemma. The Perfection of Wisdom sūtras are traditionally considered to set forth two central topics: first, the ultimate nature of reality, emptiness (śūnyatā), and, second, the structure of the path to enlightenment, the complex of realizations (*abhisamaya*) that bodhisattvas must gain along the long path to buddhahood. It is to be presumed that the *Heart Sūtra*, as the quintessence (*hṛdaya*) of the Perfection of Wisdom sūtras, would contain pithy expositions of both themes. And indeed much of the text is devoted to emptiness. Yet there is no mention of the path, except to say that it does not exist: "There is no suffering, no origin, no cessation, no path, no wisdom, no attainment, and also no nonattainment." Therefore, these commentators take it as their task to discover in the sūtra an exposition of the structure of the path, an exposition that is ostensibly absent. In their efforts thus to decode the sūtra, they turn to the mantra, both because of its inherently cryptic nature (as a mantra) and because of what the mantra seems to say.

Although it does not appear in all editions, the Indian commentators agree that the mantra should begin with *oṃ*, whose wealth of meaning need not detain us here, other than to note that *oṃ* seems to mark the threshold of some sacred verbal space, while *svāhā* marks its closure. It is to the *gate* that we must proceed. *Gata* is a past passive participle from the root *gam*, which means both "go" and "understand." Hence, *gata* is used as an adjective meaning "gone" or "understood" and often appears as the final member of a compound, where it means "gone to" or "related to." Why the mantra says *gate* rather than *gata* is a source of some puzzlement. Conze notes two possible readings. The first, which is not supported by the Indian commentaries, is to read it as a feminine vocative, which he translates, "O, you (feminine) who have gone." The other possibility is to read it as a locative absolute: "he is gone" or "she is gone," or simply, "gone."[11] Since "gone" could have been more clearly communicated by *gata*, the *e* ending may provide the "coefficient of weirdness" that Malinowski deems essential to magical language.[12] Thus, the mantra seems to say, "Gone, gone, gone beyond, gone completely beyond, enlightenment, *svāhā*."[13] The term *pāragate* "gone beyond" evokes both *prajñāpāramitā* (the most frequently used term in the sūtra apart from "no" [*na*]) as well as the popular but false etymology of pāramitā ("perfection") as pāram-ita, "gone beyond."[14] The mantra thus seems to connote progression, movement toward a goal amid the static series of negations that constitute the body of the sūtra.

The commentary by the tantric master Śrīsiṃha sees such a progression, with the syllables alternating between the perfection of one's own welfare and the welfare of others, culminating in *svāhā*, which connotes a spontaneous and natural liberation. He writes:

> *Gate* [gone] beyond to the fruition is gone for one's own welfare. The [second] *gate* means gone also for the welfare of others. *Pāragate* [means] that one has gone to the supreme state of one's own welfare and there is nothing to hope for elsewhere. *Pārasaṃgate* [means] that one has [gone] to the supreme state or perfected the welfare of others and the compassion observing disciples arises; the appearance to disciples of pure karma is a nirmāṇakāya, the appearance to [disciples] of pure nature is a saṃbhogakāya. Bodhi is uninterrupted compas-

[11] See Edward Conze, *Buddhist Wisdom Books* (New York: Harper and Row, 1972), p. 106.

[12] Bronislaw Malinowski, *Coral Gardens and Their Magic*, vol. 2, *The Language of Magic and Gardening* (Bloomington: Indiana University Press, 1965), pp. 221–23.

[13] Admittedly, *svāhā* resists translation. A common ejaculation at the end of mantras, it is probably derived from *su* ("good") and the verbal root *ah* ("say"). It is often translated as "hail" or even "amen." The Indian commentator Vajrapāṇi reads it creatively as the imperative "become," so that *bodhi svāhā* is "become enlightened," *byang chub tu gyur cig* (P 5219, vol. 94, 291.4.3).

[14] On the meaning of *pāramitā*, see Etienne Lamotte, *Le Traite de la grande vertu de sagesse de Nāgārjuna (Mahāprajñāpāramitāśāstra)*, tome 2 (Louvain: Institut Orientaliste, 1967), p. 1058; and Donald S. Lopez, Jr., *The Heart Sūtra Explained: Indian and Tibetan Commentaries* (Albany: State University of New York Press, 1988), pp. 21–22.

sion arising as the meaning of the perfection of wisdom for disciples. *Svāhā* means the self-liberation of the minds [of disciples]; this is the meaning of liberation of itself by itself.

Recognizing that for the late Indian Buddhist scholastic, the more standard progression of the course to enlightenment was in terms of the five paths (the paths of accumulation, preparation, vision, meditation, and no further learning, the latter synonymous with enlightenment), we can anticipate Kamalaśīla's attempt to find an exposition of the path in the *Heart Sūtra*: "The five paths are set forth from the standpoint of the benefits [provided] by the five words of the mantra. These five paths are the meaning of the perfection of wisdom." He contends that the five paths constitute the very meaning of the perfection of wisdom while projecting them onto the five words of the mantra: *gate gate pāragate pārasaṃgate bodhi (svāhā)*. Thus does Kamalaśīla find the position for which he is best remembered, the defense of the gradual path to enlightenment, expounded even in the *Heart Sūtra*'s mantra.

Atiśa, writing over two centuries later, is also compelled to find the path in the sūtra but takes a somewhat different tack: he apportions the sūtra up to the point of the mantra under the headings of the five paths. But if the entire path has been presented to that point, why is the mantra necessary, why is it not superfluous? In a move that is not entirely unexpected, he accounts for the presence of the mantra by explaining that everything in the sūtra up to the mantra has been the teaching for those of dull faculties, whereas the mantra is the exposition of the five paths for bodhisattvas of sharp faculties, suggesting that the entire structure of the path to enlightenment becomes clear to these bodhisattvas of more acute intellect simply upon hearing Avalokiteśvara's invocation of the mantra. By identifying a specific audience for the two sections of the sūtra (the section preceding the mantra and the mantra itself), he anticipates the view of some modern scholars who see the presence of the mantra in the sūtra as indicating the confluence of exoteric and esoteric elements in Mahāyāna Buddhism. More important for our purposes, however, is that, as he introduces an audience into his reading of the mantra, Atiśa not only opens the question of what is being communicated by the mantra, but also plays the commentator's key role: he provides context.

The last of the four commentators to be considered, Śrīmahājana, makes the correlation between the words of the mantra and five paths more explicit. (Note that he reads *gate* in the present rather than the past tense.) He says:

Gate gate pāragate [teaches] the state of having abandoned the six types of rebirth, the path of vision, because one has gone beyond from going on the

> path of great desire by going on the path of accumulation. One has gone beyond from going on the path of accumulation to going on the path of preparation. Thus, going is *gate gate pāragate*, the path of vision. *Pārasaṃ* [means] abide on the path of meditation. *Gate* means abide on the special path and the path of no more learning. *Bodhi* is the fruition. *Oṃ* and *svāhā* are terms of blessing for the purpose of achieving the effect of the repetition.

It seems from this statement that, for Śrīmahājana, the first "going" (*gate*) marks the progression from the state of a worldly being, involved in great desire, to the path of accumulation, the first of the bodhisattva paths. The second going (*gate*) refers to moving from the first path to the second, the path of preparation. "Going beyond" (*pāragate*) indicates the movement from the path of preparation to the path of vision. It is with the attainment of the path of vision that emptiness is seen directly for the first time, freeing the bodhisattva from powerless future rebirth as an animal, ghost, or hell-being. Because of the special qualities of this path, it merits "going beyond" (*pāragate*) rather than a simple "going" (*gate*). *Pārasaṃgate* means "going completely beyond." Śrīmahājana chooses to divide the word into two with *pārasaṃ* ("completely beyond") suggesting the fourth path, the path of meditation, and the final *gate* evoking the final path, the path of no more learning, synonymous with buddhahood. Thus, he says, the final *gate* does not mean "going," apparently because there is no place further to which to go, but rather "stay." *Bodhi* means "enlightenment."[15]

We see here that Śrīmahājana does something rather rare; he "translates" a mantra, raising the questions of translation and translatability, questions that can be approached on a number of levels. On the most practical, a mantra is often untranslated simply because, measured against the model of classical Sanskrit as the perfected language, the mantra has suffered sufficient deformation as to render it grammatically illegible. Further, as an element of ritual discourse, a mantra is as much an event as a denotative statement and as such, resists translation or transference from its structural moment. And from the Indian perspective, a mantra can only be in Sanskrit and must remain so in order to retain its potency as speech (*vac*), with its traditional originary primacy over the derivations of script. Indeed, not only should a mantra not be translated from Sanskrit into another language; it should also not be

[15] Later Tibetan commentators arrived at a somewhat more straightforward correspondence, following Śrīmahājana's gloss through the path of seeing, but then explaining that "going completely beyond" refers to the path of meditation and "bodhi" to buddhahood, the path of no further learning. This reading of the mantra appears to be derived from Kamalaśīla.

transferred from its natural medium to some other, from sound to writing. A mantra, writes Padoux, "is never, at least in its nature, written."[16]

Yet the mantra of the *Heart Sūtra* seems to confound these issues of writing and translation as a mantra that *is* written, but written as the representation of sound. First, it is only mildly deformed. It should say "*gata gata pāragata* . . ." instead of "*gate gate pāragate*. . . ." But this *a* to *e* shift does not render the words incomprehensible. As we have just seen, it seems to say, "Gone, gone, gone beyond, gone completely beyond, enlightenment, *svāhā*." And the Sanskrit reader's reading of the mantra is ambiguously enhanced by knowing that the root *gam* means not only "go" but "understand": "understood, understood, understood what is beyond, completely understood what is beyond, enlightenment, *svāhā*."

So the mantra could almost be translated, but it is not. Buddhism, which, unlike Hinduism, spread far beyond the confines of the Indian subcontinent, was faced with the task of translating its scriptures. Yet the translators of the *Heart Sūtra*, into Tibetan, into Chinese, into Japanese, did not translate the mantra but transliterated it, in an effort to duplicate and thereby preserve the sound of Avalokiteśvara's voice. They translated the rest of the sūtra but left the mantra, in sound if not in form, in Sanskrit. We must recognize, then, that the experience of reciting the *Heart Sūtra* would be very different for a Tibetan monk than it would be for an Indian monk. The Indian monk, reciting the sūtra in Sanskrit, would intone a Sanskrit mantra. The Tibetan monk, reciting in Tibetan, would come to a phrase marked by its incomprehensibility, reading a transliteration to produce sounds that were clearly not Tibetan. This, apparently, was the intention of the translators and indeed of those Indian interpreters who collaborated in the translation of their commentaries on the *Heart Sūtra* into Tibetan, all of whom render the mantra in transliteration and only two of whom (Śrīmahājana and Vajrapāṇi) then go on to provide a translation.[17]

[16] Padoux, "Mantras," p. 297.

[17] Śrīmahājana, who wrote his commentary in Tibet and oversaw its translation into Tibetan, used the present form of the verb "go" (*'gro*) to translate *gate*, (P 5223, vol. 94, 303.5.4–7). He translates the mantra as "goes, goes, goes beyond, goes completely beyond, abide [in] enlightenment." Vajrapāṇi translates it using the simple past, "gone," *phyin* (P 5219, vol. 94, 291.3.6–4.3). The Tang Dynasty master Fazang translates it into Chinese as *chu*, "go" and *tu*, "pass over" (see *Taishō Shinshū Daizōkyō* 1712, 555a). A nineteenth-century Tibetan exegete translates it with the imperative *songs zhig*, "proceed" (see Gung thang dKon mchog bstan pa'i sgron me, *Shes rab snying po'i snags kyi rnam bshad sbas don gsal ba sgron me* in *Collected Works of Gun-thaṅ dKon-mchog-bstan-pa'i-sgron-me*, vol. 1 [New Delhi: Ngawang Gelek Demo, 1971], p. 682). Thus, the commentators, whether they knew Sanskrit or not, seemed little concerned with the tense of the verb, preferring instead

Translating the sūtra into Tibetan or Chinese or Japanese but leaving the mantra in Sanskrit (intact) inevitably alters the mantra, beyond the changes of time or setting, changes that in themselves are weighty enough as evidenced by Pierre Menard's version of *Don Quixote*.[18] The Sanskrit mantra in a translation is no longer continuous with the sūtra but is strange and disjunctive, a disjunction, it might be suggested, which can only add to its power. Hence, whereas the sūtra, as a representation of the Buddha's wisdom compassionately dispensed to the ignorant world, must be translatable, the mantra cannot be; it can only be transferred. The sūtra must be translatable because the content of the Buddha's wisdom, its truth and meaning, are above and before language. It is as if all of the developments of Buddhist philosophy across Asia have, in this sense, seen themselves as attempts to articulate the silent substance of the Buddha's enlightenment under the tree at Bodhgaya; meaning is central to this philosophical endeavor. As a contemporary pundit of speech and writing comments, "Meaning has the commanding role, and consequently one must be able to fix its univocality or, in any case, to master its plurivocality. If the plurivocality can be mastered, then translation, understood as the transport of a semantic content into another signifying form, is possible."[19]

But the mantra is not translated but rather transferred, representing neither the meaning of the words (the semantic content) nor their Sanskrit orthography, but their sound. The transliteration of the mantra marks the transportation of the original to another time and another place, offering an image of the timeless, bringing the past into the present, with that presence valued for its form rather than its content, allowing the original to survive, to persist in presence. The mantra is transported so that it may remain pure and original, so that it may survive.[20] The task of the translator here is not communication but rather evocation, to preserve the sacred text as event, for, as Benjamin writes, the

---

to note the element of progression that the mantra clearly embodies, going, going, going beyond, going completely beyond, enlightenment.

[18] In Borges' short story, the French author set out in 1934 to write *Don Quixote*. His "aim was never to produce a mechanical transcription of the original; he did not propose to copy it. His admirable ambition was to produce pages which would coincide—word for word and line for line—with those of Miguel de Cervantes." Menard produces an exact copy of Cervantes' text, which the reviewer finds more subtle than the work of Cervantes. See Jorge Luis Borges, "Pierre Menard, Author of Don Quixote," in his *Ficciones* (New York: Grove, 1962), p. 49.

[19] Jacques Derrida, *The Ear of the Other*, trans. Peggy Kamuf (Lincoln: University of Nebraska Press, 1988), p. 120.

[20] Ibid., pp. 121–22.

sacred text does not require translation because it translates itself via its pure transferability.[21] The translators of the *Heart Sūtra* thus opt for transference rather than translation, leaving the mantra untouched by translation and the apparent limitation that that would entail, leaving the mantra unreconciled with the tongue of the reader but protected as event, an event that communicates nothing.[22] That is, leaving the mantra untranslated stills the possibility of the identification of signifier and signified promised by "meaning." We cannot say what the mantra means in and of itself, imagining that the sound could have meaning independent of grammar and syntax; meaning is derived from context. The translators, in choosing not to translate, joyfully abandon meaning in favor of the power of the event; for the Tibetan, or Chinese, or Japanese reader, the Sanskrit mantra is in a language "entirely freed of the illusion of meaning."[23] Without translation, there is "only the letter, and it is the truth of pure language, the truth as pure language,"[24] the pure language, called *saṃskṛta*. Untranslated, "language and revelation are one without any tension."[25]

Although the magic/religion/science trichotomy that so obsessed anthropologists of past generations no longer preoccupies us, we nonetheless find it difficult to avoid occasionally bumping our heads on the low-hanging *Golden Bough*.[26] And it is indeed the case that in the study of Asian religions in the West from the past century until the present, the term "mantra" is commonly translated as "spell."[27] So let us turn next to anthropological theories of magical speech, focusing on the work of Mal-

[21] See Walter Benjamin, "The Task of the Translator," in *Illuminations*, edited with an introduction by Hannah Arendt (New York: Schocken, 1969), pp. 69–82.

[22] On translation and transferability, see Jacques Derrida, "Des Tours de Babel," in Joseph F. Graham, ed., *Difference in Translation* (Ithaca: Cornell University Press, 1985), pp. 200–205.

[23] Paul de Man, *Resistance to Theory* (Minneapolis: University of Minnesota Press, 1986), p. 84. Freed from meaning, it would seem that the possibility of interpretation is closed off (and thereby opened wide). Of the *Heart Sūtra*'s mantra, Kūkai writes, "If each word, however, should be interpreted from the point of view of its ultimate meanings, immeasurable significances . . . would be revealed." See Yoshito Hakeda, *Kūkai: Basic Writings* (New York: Columbia University Press, 1972), p. 273.

[24] Derrida, "Des Tours de Babel," p. 204.

[25] Benjamin, "Task of the Translator," p. 82.

[26] For anthropological critiques of the category of magic, see Hildred Geertz, "An Anthropology of Religion and Magic I," *Journal of Interdisciplinary History* 8 (1975): 71–89; Dorothy Hammond, "Magic: A Problem in Semantics," *American Anthropologist* 72, no. 6 (1970): 1349–56; D. F. Pocock's foreword to Marcel Mauss, *A General Theory of Magic*, trans. Robert Brain (London: Routledge and Kegan Paul, 1972), pp. 1–6.

[27] See, for example, David Snellgrove, *Indo-Tibetan Buddhism*, vol. 1 (Boston: Shambala, 1987), p. 122.

inowski, in an effort to determine what he might do with the *Heart Sūtra*'s mantra.

Malinowski is an extreme pragmatist in his theory of meaning. In the second volume of *Coral Gardens and Their Magic*, he defines meaning as "function within the context of situation."[28] He argues that an expression is only intelligible when one has understood the *context*, by which he means the culture and the environment in a general sense, and the *situation*, the specific "real-life" setting of the utterance.[29] He rejects the view that meaning is contained in the utterance itself and rails against the philologists who attempt to glean linguistic theory from dead languages while ignoring the direct and real approach of the ethnographer who observes firsthand "winged words, passing from man to man."[30] Language, for Malinowski, is a practical pursuit, a mode of vital action, and not some reflection of thought. It is hardly necessary, then, to deconstruct Malinowski's essay to reveal his logocentrism, for he is quite clear on the question of the spoken versus the written word: "the manner in which the author of a book, or a papyrus, or a hewn inscription has to use it, is a very far-fetched and derivative function of language."[31]

Malinowski's visceral conception of meaning as the creative function of words ("ultimately all the meaning of all words is derived from bodily experience"[32]), of language as something that acts, produces, achieves, his conception of words as an invisible appendage that grips that which is beyond the speaker's grasp, extends also to his view of magical language. For magical language also has its pragmatics. Just as the meaning of a word, sentence, or phrase "is the *effective change* brought about by the utterance within the context of situation in which it is wedded,"[33] so the meaning of magical spells is the effect their words have within the ritual context of their utterance.

For Malinowski, magical language is an extension of ordinary expressions of the hopes of the individual, hopes that are frustrated against the wall of reality. In his classic essay, "Magic, Science, and Religion," Malinowski writes his own cosmogonic myth on the origin of magical speech as he recounts how man in the course of practical activities comes to a gap—the hunter loses the track, the lover yearns for the absent beloved. The confrontation with this gap creates frustration and anxiety to which

[28] Malinowski, *Coral Gardens and Their Magic*, vol. 2, p. 233.

[29] Bronislaw Malinowski, "The Problem of Meaning in Primitive Languages," in C. K. Ogden and I. A. Richards, eds., *The Meaning of Meaning* (New York: Harcourt, Brace, 1923), pp. 465–67.

[30] Ibid., pp. 466–68.

[31] Ibid., p. 474.

[32] *Coral Gardens and their Magic*, vol. 2, p. 58.

[33] Ibid., p. 214.

he must respond with some activity, as his mind imagines the absent goal. Overwhelmed by emotion and desire, he spontaneously "breaks out" into words that give vent to his passions.

> When passion reaches the breaking point at which man loses control over himself, the words which he utters, his blind behavior, allow the pent-up psychological tension to flow over. But over all this outburst presides the image of the end. It supplies the motive-force of the reaction, it apparently organizes and directs words and acts towards a definite purpose. The substitute action in which the passion finds its vent, and which is due to impotence, has subjectively all the value of a real action, to which emotion would, if not impeded, naturally have led.[34]

He later labeled this phenomenon "the creative metaphor of magic,"[35] by which he seems to have meant little more than the belief that the repetition of certain words brings a desired result, in short, Frazer's homeopathic magic.[36]

Malinowski's derivation of magical speech cited above again demonstrates his fixation on context of situation as the prime determinant of meaning. Because the first evidence of the *Heart Sūtra*'s mantra occurs as written words rather than speech, it is difficult to imagine how one might construe its meaning using Malinowski's approach. It embodies all of the qualities that he apparently eschews: written words in a dead language whose sound and "meaning" have been approximated by transliteration and, rarely, by translation into other dead or dying languages, like classical Chinese and classical Tibetan. Furthermore, the sūtra seems to suggest that Avalokiteśvara is attempting to transmit some noetic content to Śāriputra through speaking the mantra. But Malinowski claims that the conception of language, magical or otherwise, as "a means of transfusing ideas from the head of the speaker to that of the listener" is a false one.[37]

[34] Malinowski, *Magic, Science and Religion and Other Essays* (Garden City, N.Y.: Doubleday, 1954), pp. 80–81. D. T. Suzuki, in his rather desultory commentary on the *Heart Sūtra*, provides an uncannily Malinowskian reading of the origin of the mantra. "Utterly exhausted intellectually and emotionally, he [Avalokiteśvara] made a final leap. The last tie which held him to the world of relativity and 'self-power' completely snapped. He found himself on the other shore. Overwhelmed with his feelings, he could only keep uttering the '*Gate!*'" See his *Essays in Zen Buddhism*, 3rd ser. (London: Rider, 1985), pp. 235–36.

[35] *Coral Gardens and Their Magic*, vol. 2, p. 238.

[36] However, whereas Frazer believed that the practice of homeopathic magic derived from a natural human tendency to animate things, Malinowski here attributes its "origin" to some primal scene, some ur-magician, in a manner not unlike Freud's approach in *Totem and Taboo* (a comparison at which Malinowski would surely balk).

[37] *Coral Gardens and Their Magic*, vol. 2, p. 9.

The major questions that remain concern how, if at all, the context of the mantra can be determined and whether the mantra qualifies as magical speech. To take up this second question first, let us examine the mantra not as extraordinary language but as ordinary language, as represented in J. L. Austin's vexing little book.

For those few readers who have yet to commit *How to Do Things with Words* to memory, Austin's argument can be briefly summarized. He makes an initial distinction between constative utterances (descriptive statements) and performative utterances (certain statements the utterances of which constitute the performance of some action). Austin's High Church examples of the latter include the statement, "I do" in a marriage ceremony and the statement, "I name this ship *Queen Elizabeth*" as one smashes a bottle of champagne against the hull of an ocean liner. As is evident from these examples, we will be confronted here once again by the problem of context. Austin argues that unlike constatives, which can be judged true or false, performatives are either happy or infelicitous, based on the presence or absence of a number of factors. These include the following: "(A.1) There must exist an accepted conventional procedure having a certain conventional effect, that procedure to include the uttering of certain words by certain persons in certain circumstances, and further (A.2) the particular persons and circumstances in a given case must be appropriate for the invocation of the particular procedure invoked."[38]

In later chapters he refines his vocabulary. Thus, uttering noises is a phonetic act; uttering words in a certain construction and conforming to a certain grammar is a phatic act; using those words with a more or less definite sense and reference is a rhetic act.[39] All rhetic acts are phatic acts, but the converse is not true because, Austin writes (as if he had mantras in mind), "we may repeat someone else's remark or mumble over some sentence, or we may read a Latin sentence without knowing the meaning of the words."[40] He also introduces the terms "locutionary act," "illocutionary act," and "perlocutionary act." The distinctions here are ones of emphasis. Hence, a locutionary act is a sentence uttered with a certain sense and reference that can be judged either true or false. An illocutionary act is one that carries a certain conventional force by its utterance. A perlocutionary act is the achieving of certain effects by saying something—the consequence the words of the speaker has for the listener. Austin devotes most of the rest of the book to discussing illocution-

[38] J. L. Austin, *How to Do Things with Words* (Cambridge: Harvard University Press, 1975), pp. 14–15.

[39] Ibid., pp. 92–93.

[40] Ibid., p. 97.

ary acts, what we do in saying something, the salient factor of which is not their consequences or truth or falsity, but the force that bears on the circumstances of the statement. An illocutionary act is either happy or not, and this depends not on its correspondence with facts but on whether its effect is achieved by the audience hearing what is said and understanding it in the way the speaker intended. This Austin names the securing of "uptake."[41]

Let us see what any of this might have to do with the *Heart Sūtra*'s mantra,[42] taking up the question of the mantra as performative utterance, specifically as an illocutionary act. We can begin by saying that the mantra is predicative in that it seems to signify some kind of progression that culminates in an end, using a form of the verb "to go" and ending with the word "enlightenment." Next, one must determine whether it performs anything, and here one must look to the commentaries. For Austin, the tense and voice of the utterance are significant, although not determinative in establishing a statement as a performative; he notes that most commonly performatives take the grammatical form of the first-person singular present active indicative or the imperative. Here the commentators are of little help; as noted above, *gate* is variously read as present, past, and imperative. For the sake of argument, let us adopt the fanciful reading of the mantra as an imperative, provided by the influential Tibetan exegete Gung thang (1762–1823), who translates the mantra as "Proceed, proceed, proceed beyond, proceed completely beyond, be established in enlightenment."[43] Let us also entertain the explanation of Atiśa that the mantra is intended for those listeners seated on Vulture Peak, the traditional setting of the *Heart Sūtra*, who are endowed with sharp faculties, the smarter bodhisattvas. With these suppositions, we have construed a context within which to analyze the mantra.

It will be recalled that illocutionary acts carry what Austin calls "a certain conventional force" that the speaker is seeking to convey, while

[41] Ibid., p. 117.

[42] I am by no means the first to apply Austin to religious or magical language. See, for example, Ruth Finnegan, "How to Do Things with Words: Performative Utterances among the Limba of Sierra Leone," *Man*, n.s., 4 (1969): 537–52; Stanley J. Tambiah, *Culture, Thought, and Social Action* (Cambridge: Harvard University Press, 1985), pp. 77–80; Philip L. Ravenhill, "Religious Utterances and the Theory of Speech Acts," in William J. Samarin, ed., *Language in Religious Practice* (Rowley, Mass.: Newbury House, 1976), pp. 26–40; Anders Jeffner, *The Study of Religious Language* (London: SCM, 1972); Roy A. Rappaport, *Ecology, Meaning, and Religion* (Berkeley: North Atlantic Books, 1979), pp. 173–221; Frits Staal, *Rules without Meaning: Ritual, Mantras and the Human Sciences* (New York: Peter Lang, 1993), especially pp. 237–51; and the articles by Findly, Staal, Wheelock, Taber, and Alper in Harvey P. Alper, ed., *Understanding Mantras* (Albany: State University of New York Press, 1989).

[43] See n. 17.

the perlocutionary effects are what is brought about in the listener by the speaker's statement. The illocutionary force of the mantra, if it has one, will become evident by adapting several principles outlined by Searle.[44] With the help of Atiśa's commentary, we can fairly easily imagine a purpose in Avalokiteśvara's statement of the mantra, as well as an appropriate relationship between the speaker and hearers, a commitment on the speaker's part, a propositional content to the statement as well as difference in the speaker's and hearers' relation to that proposition,[45] and a balanced psychological state of the speaker, all necessary criteria for identifying illocutionary force. Searle's last question is how the statement relates to the rest of the conversation. This is, of course, the most difficult point, for Atiśa's implication is that the mantra serves as an encoded summary of the preceding sūtra and, by extension, of the entire Perfection of Wisdom corpus. If bodhisattvas of sharp and dull faculties sit together on Vulture Peak to hear the discourse, what purpose is served by delivering the same content in two versions?

The perlocutionary effect of the mantra must be measured for the two groups of listeners, those of sharp and those of dull faculties. The mantra is not true or false, but happy or infelicitous. Again, following Atiśa, it is happy for those of sharp faculties: they understand what it is that Avalokiteśvara intends for them to understand. They fulfill Austin's criterion that "the particular persons and circumstances in a given case must be appropriate for the invocation of the particular procedure invoked."[46]

[44] See John R. Searle, *Speech Acts* (Cambridge: Cambridge University Press, 1969), p. 70.

[45] The propositional nature of the mantra, and hence its illocutionary force, is clarified by prefixing *tadyathā* ("It is thus:"). This phrase is read as part of the mantra in the tantric sādhana on the *Heart Sūtra* ascribed to Nāgārjuna (see P 3464, vol. 77, 30.34.1–2) and is transliterated rather than translated in the Tibetan, indicating that the translators deemed it part of the mantra. It functions in relation to the rest of the mantra as what P. F. Strawson calls a "subjoined quasi-comment," acting as a force-elucidating comment on the mantra. See P. F. Strawson, "Intention and Convention in Speech Acts," in J. R. Searle, ed., *The Philosophy of Language* (London: Oxford University Press, 1971), pp. 31–32.

[46] Austin, *How to Do Things*, p. 15. Bourdieu emphasizes the importance of the speaker and the source of his authority:

> If, as Austin observes, there are statements whose role is not only to "describe a state of affairs or some fact," but also to "execute an action," this is because the power of the words resides in the fact that they are not pronounced on behalf of the person who is only the "carrier" of these words: the authorized spokesperson is only able to use words to act on other agents and, through their action, on things themselves, because his speech concentrates within it the accumulated symbolic capital of the group which has delegated him and of which he is the *authorized representative*.

See Pierre Bourdieu, *Language and Symbolic Power*, trans. Gino Raymond and Matthew Adamson (Cambridge, Mass.: Harvard University Press, 1991), pp. 109, 111.

Understanding the meaning and force of the locution, they secure "uptake." But for the members of the audience whose faculties are less acute, the mantra is an infelicity; they do not understand it. It is in this sense, according to Atiśa, that the mantra is secret; the meaning is hidden to those who are incapable of understanding it. As he notes, "Whether something is secret or not secret is a matter of awareness; in fact there is no difference in what is taught. The Teacher does not have a closed fist."

His comment is useful in indicating one way in which *gate gate pāragate pārasaṃgate bodhi svāhā* might fulfill one of the common criteria of mantras: it is secret, that is, incomprehensible to the uninitiated. But here we must seek to identify in Austin's terms the difference between bodhisattvas of sharp and dull faculties as the audience of the mantra. They are not to be distinguished by linguistic competency in any conventional sense but rather in their ability to comprehend language that is somehow symbolic. Atiśa's reading suggests that the dull bodhisattvas would be, for Austin, not "appropriate for the invocation" of the mantra. Unlike the śrāvakas who walked out before the Buddha delivered the *Lotus Sūtra*, they sat and listened to something that they did not understand, something that was unsuitable for them. The situation of the sharp bodhisattvas is no less problematic for the principle of *upāya* (the Buddha's pedagogical skill) in that, if we follow Atiśa, they had to listen to the full exposition of the sūtra before being told the mantra, a capsule-version of what they had just heard. For them, the mantra would be but a poetic redundancy. The mantra does not seem entirely felicitous for either group.

Failing thus far to find a satisfying reading of the mantra in the approaches of Malinowski and Austin, we may be forced back to a time when the magic/science dichotomy was acknowledged, but the members of the hierarchy were transposed. We have noted that the *Heart Sūtra*'s mantra inscribes temporality by implying movement toward a goal. Atiśa and other commentators have argued that the mantra communicates the instructions necessary for that movement. If the mantra is thus a code for the entire path to enlightenment, a representation of the path that is somehow symbolic, might we not draw on the richly theological reading of the symbol by Romanticism? In one of his many pronouncements on the symbol, Goethe declared that "True symbolism is where the particular represents the more general, not as a dream or a shadow, but as a living momentary revelation of the inscrutable,"[47] whereby the symbol participates in the reality of the symbolized, enunciating while remaining unified with that which it represents.

The symbol partakes of a principle of imitation marked by autonomy, totality, immediacy. Natural and innate, it is not conventionally referen-

[47] Goethe, *Maximen und Reflexionen*, 1112.

tial but rather is at once signifying and intransitive in that the symbol is somehow the thing it symbolizes without being it, laconically revealing the signified only later in an experience that is epiphanic, unified, inexpressible. The symbol is ever alive, inexhaustible, accomplished in itself. To the exalted symbol is contrasted the allegory, which is contingent and transitive, transparently and reflexively pointing to its referent. Unlike the symbol, the allegory is merely functional, with no identity beyond the transfer of its meaning; having done its job, it dies. Whereas the symbol can be sensed by all those with intuition, the allegory is wholly arbitrary, its code learned by rote.[48]

We are tempted, then, to see the mantra as a symbolic enactment of the path, where the literal and the metaphoric are conflated, while allowing the mantra as symbol to remain inscrutable, poetic, inexhaustible by interpretation. Yet such a reading attempts to ascribe to the mantra the same panaceaic power that the Romantic poets saw in the symbol. The symbol was seen as that which unified and resolved the oppositions of subject and object, the material and the spiritual, in the unity of its organic substance. There are similar conflicts that we yearn for the mantra to resolve in a nostalgic desire that it embody the reconciliation of signifier and signified, the simultaneity of speech and enlightenment, that it be, indeed, enlightenment in sound, marking not the movement but the moment in which language and reality, the semantic and the representative, the image and the substance it intimates coincide, "uniquely alive because it participates in a higher order of existence . . . coextensive in matter and form; resistant to explication; largely independent of intention, and of any form of ethical utility."[49]

For those who recite the transliterated sound, the mantra offers this promise of the symbol, representative of the strangely atemporal priority of sacred speech and of the origin. The mantra as such a symbol is superior to the mantra as allegory, "a sign that refers to one specific meaning and thus exhausts its suggestive potentialities once it has been deciphered."[50] But the Indian commentators who attend to the sense of the words read the mantra—with its intimation of movement toward a goal, with its hint of the future and its promise of completion amid the litany of apophasis which is the sūtra ("In emptiness, there is no eye, no ear, no nose, no tongue, no body, no mind . . .")—as an allegory. The mantra simulates the path by providing an encoded narrative, with a beginning,

[48] This characterization of symbol and allegory is drawn from Tzvetan Todorov's discussion of Goethe in *Theories of the Symbol*, trans. Catherine Porter (Ithaca: Cornell University Press, 1982), pp. 198–207.

[49] Frank Kermode, *The Romantic Image* (New York: Macmillan, 1957), p. 44.

[50] Paul de Man, *Blindness and Insight*, 2nd ed., rev. (Minneapolis: University of Minnesota Press, 1983), p. 188.

middle, and sense of an ending, employing highly evocative terms like *pārasaṃgate* and bodhi, all described in the past tense ("gone, gone, gone beyond . . . "), providing the comfort that what must be done has been done before. For the Indian commentators like Śrīmahājana, the allegory is indeed transparent as they move to make the mechanical correspondence: *gate* = going to the path of accumulation, and so forth.

However, for Paul de Man (if not for Goethe) an allegory is not merely dogmatically substituted for its referent; in allegory time intervenes. He writes, "It remains necessary, if there is to be allegory, that the allegorical sign refer to another sign that precedes it. The meaning constituted by the allegorical sign can then consist only in the *repetition* . . . of a previous sign with which it can never coincide, since it is of the essence of this previous sign to be pure anteriority."[51] Thus, for de Man the allegorical relationship is not one of signifier to signified but signifier to signifier, and this latter relation is never of unity but always spaced by time. For those who see in the words of the mantra an allegory for the five paths, the reference is to yet another category, and one must go, go, go beyond along a path that is gradual, but is also endless, a path backward and forward through time along a "chain of signifiers" that moves relentlessly in an effort to encompass all of the myriad categories of Buddhist scholasticism, the very categories that the *Heart Sūtra* takes as its task to negate.

We must finally turn from text to context, recalling its absolute centrality for the analysts of mantras and to Malinowski's and Austin's theories of language. André Padoux reminds us that "mantras, even in their higher, supposedly redemptive forms, are always part of a precise and compulsory ritual context, outside which they are useless and powerless" without efficiency, without value, without significance, without meaning.[52] For Malinowski, it is only with an understanding of the vital, present, "pragmatic setting" of utterance that meaning can be determined. And in speech-act theory, as Searle has noted, "since meaning is always derived from intentionality, contextual dependency is ineliminable."[53] For Austin there must be a certain utterance for a certain audience in a certain circumstance. And it is a context that the commentators seek to supply, attempting to integrate the eruption of the mantra into the sūtra by retrojecting onto its syllables the structure of a fivefold path, a structure that historically may have developed after the sūtra's composition, or by accounting for the mantra's apparent unintelligibility with the use-

[51] Ibid., p. 207.

[52] Padoux, "Mantras," p. 308.

[53] John R. Searle, "The Background of Meaning," in John R. Searle, ed., *Speech Act Theory and Pragmatics* (Dordrecht: D. Reidel, 1980), p. 231.

ful device of the elusive disciple of sharp faculties, who always understands what others cannot. Atiśa rewrites the sūtra, centuries after its composition, for those of sharp and dull faculties, making the mantra's simulacrum of the path explicit. It is this alone that provides the mantra with any perlocutionary effect, albeit an effect felt only by those mythic beings of Buddhist scholasticism, the disciples of sharp faculties.

But what of the sūtra itself, at the imaginary moment before commentary? We are often entranced by the illusion of speech that pervades the sūtras: Ānanda begins the *Heart Sūtra*, as he does every sūtra, by testifying to what he heard at one time; then the Buddha, surrounded by monks and bodhisattvas on Vulture Peak, enters samādhi; Śāriputra asks the bodhisattva how a son or daughter of good lineage should practice the perfection of wisdom; Avalokiteśvara answers; then Avalokiteśvara tells how the mantra is spoken (*ukto*); the Buddha rises from samādhi to praise Avalokiteśvara's words. But this is a dramatic setting, not a pragmatic setting, devoid of the emotional and social context that Malinowski deems essential in the determination of meaning. The sūtra and the mantra it contains are written words, inscribed, composed, isolated, lacking the spontaneity of speech. Even within the oral conceit of the sūtra, Avalokiteśvara's words are already a repetition, an iteration, spoken "by the power of the Buddha"; in Austin's terms, the "utterance-origin" of the words is absent. They are words that are only read and recited, the kinds of words that Austin cast out of the garden of locution. A performative utterance spoken by an actor on a stage, he argues, or appearing in a poem, or quoted by someone else is hollow and void; it is not a serious use of language but an etiolation, parasitic on language's normal use.[54] The context is fabricated, lacking the authenticity provided by the speaker, and hence the force of the utterance is lacking. A mantra is phatic and (presumably) not rhetic; it is devoid of determinate meaning because it can be repeated out of context. Austin's suspicion of that which can be cited thus extends to texts, which lack the immediacy of the presence of the speaker and hearer, leaving the possibility of interpretation ever open; the putative purity of the performative—where that which did not exist before is made fully present through speech in total context—is violated. Hence, Austin would applaud the importance invested by the tradition (and its students) in the secret oral transmission of the mantra from guru to disciple.

In his essay "Signature Event Context," Jacques Derrida discerns in Austin's concern an obsession with the self-presence of speech over writing. Derrida notes the "iterability" of performatives, that they can effectively be transferred from one context to another, that they are forms of

[54] Austin, *How to Do Things*, pp. 22, 104.

utterance that continue to function outside of their original context. They cannot be confined to a single, unique moment of self-presence but, like all language, in the play of linguistic convention, they always already precede and exceed the intention of the speaker through the arbitrariness of the sign.[55] Derrida argues that it is the very structure of the written that it always breaks with its context, "the collectivity of presences organizing the moment of its inscription."[56] He catalogues the absences inherent in writing. There is the absence of the addressee; one writes to those who are absent. And there is the absence of the writer "from the mark that he abandons, and which cuts itself off from him and continues to produce effects independently of his presence and of the present actuality of his intentions, indeed even after his death."[57] Turning to the *Heart Sūtra* and its mantra, we see absence multiply. Considering the sūtra as a fabrication of an event, a context, we see that the Buddha is absent; in the sūtra he remains in samādhi. The audience is absent. The author of the sūtra, whoever he may have been, is absent, as are his own context and audience. Even his tongue is dead, resuscitated only in repetition. This does not turn the sūtra and its mantra into some empty container to be filled with meaning supplied from outside by commentators. Rather, the Buddhist exegetes endlessly attempt to recover the context of the sūtra, tracing back its "original" meaning as they write over the sūtra and the isomorphic mantra inscribed on a bottomless page. The meaning of the mantra, then, must remain elusive/illusive, as long as text is devoid of context and context is but a construct.

Atiśa's purpose in interpreting the mantra is to supply it with the context that it so clearly lacks. This freedom from context is not a mystical quality unique to this mantra; it is simply one of the consequences of being written. Only with this context so prudently recreated does the mantra become capable of satisfying the interpreters', both ancient and modern, expectations of what a mantra should be: not read from a book, but learned by eligible students from an eligible teacher, secret in that it remains unintelligible to the unqualified. Nonetheless, we have seen that

[55] See Jacques Derrida, *Limited Inc* (Evanston, Ill.: Northwestern University Press, 1988), pp. 13–19. On iterability, see also pp. 61–63, 71, 119, 123. The translation of the essay by Samuel Weber is the same that appeared in *Glyph* 1 (1977). A translation of the same essay by Alan Bass appears in Jacques Derrida, *Margins of Philosophy* (Chicago: University of Chicago Press, 1982), pp. 307–30. On Derrida's critique of Austin, see also Christopher Norris, *The Deconstructive Turn* (London: Methuen, 1983), pp. 59–84; Gayatri Chakravorty Spivak, "Revolutions That as Yet Have No Model: Derrida's *Limited Inc*," *Diacritics* 10 (December 1980): 29–49; and, especially, Henry Staten, *Wittgenstein and Derrida* (Lincoln: Nebraska University Press, 1984), pp. 111–30.

[56] Derrida, *Limited Inc*, p. 9.

[57] Ibid., p. 5.

attempts to codify the mantra and thereby enclose it in context have failed, that the contexts remain the most tenuous grafts in the pursuit of meaning. This is not to suggest that such attempts should be abandoned or that we should seek for some pristine meaning outside of context, because there are only contexts. As Derrida writes, "if the structural limit and the remainder of the simulacrum which has been left in writing are going to be taken into account, the process of decoding, because this limit is not of the sort that circumscribes a certain knowledge even as it proclaims a beyond, must be carried to the furthest lengths possible."[58] But what lengths are possible?

Gabriel Garcia Marquez describes a parchment that a generation of sons seeks to decipher over a hundred years of solitude. Finally, the last of the family line, Aureliano, breaks the code. The words are written in Sanskrit, with the even lines encoded in the private cipher of the emperor Augustine and the odd lines in Lacedemonian military code. As Aureliano finally is able to read what is written on the parchment, he finds the entire history of his family recorded one hundred years ahead of time. However, the account was not an ordinary chronology, "but had concentrated a century of daily episodes in such a way that they coexisted in one instant." As he read along, "he began to decipher the instant that he was living . . . as if he were looking into a speaking mirror."[59] This is the fantasy of the *Heart Sūtra*'s mantra. It is imagined as a supplement to the sūtra, augmenting it by adding a path to the proclamation of emptiness, by fulfilling emptiness, while at the same time displacing the sūtra (in Atiśa's reading) by offering a superior substitute for the wise bodhisattvas, those who need only hear the mantra to understand the entire path in all its fullness and complexity. In this sense, the mantra is Malinowskian magic, serving as a supplement to the relentless rigor of emptiness set forth in the sūtra up to that point.

In this fantasy, the Sanskrit mantra, preserving the anteriority of sacred speech, seems to precede speech, to be prelinguistic, pointing "backwards to the source of language, which is the source of all creation itself."[60] Since the mantra is written, it is a representation that supplants the presence of speech. But in this fantasy, the mantra is unlike other writing in that its reading restores presence as the sūtra moves from exposition to manifestation, with form prevailing over meaning, but in such a way that reading makes it so, that to read the mantra to its conclusion is simul-

[58] Jacques Derrida, *Spurs* (Chicago: University of Chicago Press, 1979), p. 133.

[59] Gabriel Garcia Marquez, *One Hundred Years of Solitude* (New York: Avon, 1971), pp. 382–83.

[60] Wade T. Wheelock, "Mantra in Vedic and Tantric Ritual," in Alper, ed., *Understanding Mantras*, p. 120.

taneously to complete the path. The mantra would be that wondrous moment of speech that is consubstantial with enlightenment, the fulfillment of intention: to read bodhi is to be enlightened. But there is danger here. As Aureliano discovered as he read, swept up in a whirlwind, this fulfillment is death. The goal must be sought but it must not be attained. Thus, the grace of Śrīmahājana's description of the mantra as "the perfection of wisdom to be repeated," for it is repetition that makes idealization possible through the intimation of the full and singular presence of the original object—the imitation of identity with that which it repeats—while at the same time preventing the attainment of the ideal, because repetition is also other than that which it repeats.

Eight

The Commentaries of Mahājana and Vajrapāṇi

Complete Understanding of the Meaning of the Heart of the Perfection of Wisdom

Prajñāpāramitāhṛdayārtha[1]*parijñāna*

MAHĀJANA

Homage to the youthful Mañjuśrī

> Without relying on the explanations of others, I will distinguish the paths using reasoning. Those who strive to give up preconceptions do not follow the literalists.

In the earlier history, the stages of entry into the excellent doctrine were heard in this way. Having first turned the wheel of doctrine of the four truths at Vārāṇasī, the Sugata then turned the wheel of doctrine of signlessness, the mother of the conquerors, in order to overcome the conception of a self of phenomena. Regarding the process of compilation by the rapporteur after the Bhagavan had passed beyond sorrow, Dignāga and so forth assert that the rapporteur was Vajrapāṇi in the Abode of Controlling Others' Emanations (*paranirmittavaśavartin*);[2] Vimuktisena and so forth, following the *parīndanā* chapter [of the *Aṣṭasāhasrikāprajñāpāramitā*], assert that it was the noble Ānanda, and Ratnākaraśānti and so forth assert that it was the noble Ānanda, who had been blessed by the Bhagavan. In order to properly protect the teaching, the rapporteur entrusted [the teaching to those] in harmony with it: Nāgānandin and Upānanda [received] the *Śatasāhasrikā* (Perfection of Wisdom in 100,000 Stanzas); the king of gods, Śakra, [received] the *Pañcaviṃśatisāhasrikā* (Perfection of Wisdom in 25,000 Stanzas); the noble protector Ajita [Maitreya] [received] the *Aṣṭadaśasāhasrikā* (Perfection of Wisdom in 18,000 Stanzas), the *Daśasāhasrikā* (Perfection of Wisdom in 10,000 Stanzas), and the *Saṃcayagāthā* (Condensed Verses of the Perfection of Wisdom); and Kubera [received] the *Aṣṭasāhasrikā* (Perfection of Wisdom in 8,000 Stanzas).

[1] Peking omits *artha*.

[2] The highest of the six heavens of the realm of desire (*rūpadhātu*).

Then, regarding the stages of the composition of commentaries by the commentators, this was prophesied by the perfect, complete Buddha [in the *Mañjuśrīmūlatantra*]:

> In the city of Seng-ge-gar-gnas (Siṃhapura) a monk known as Asaṅga who understands the meaning of the śāstras will differentiate the many aspects of the definitive and provisional sūtras. By nature he will be a composer of texts that will fully express the reality to be known by the beings of the world. He will speak through achieving the female messenger Sala;[3] by the power of her knowledge mantra, he will create the awareness of certainty and in order that the teaching may long remain, he will gather the essential meaning of the sūtras. He will live for 150 years. When he gives up his body, he will go to the land of the gods and will long experience bliss. Having cycled long in saṃsāra, this great being will eventually attain enlightenment [304b].

The noble Asaṅga, who had attained the samādhi of the stream of doctrine, went to Tuṣita and beseeched the noble Maitreya. The noble Maitreya had realization of the *Abhisamayālaṃkāra*, the commentary derived from the unique sūtras, discipline (vinaya), and knowledge (*abhidharma*), and kept it for this world. Later, the noble Nāgārjuna went to the land of the nāgas and took the *Śatasāhasrikāprajñāpāramitā* (Perfection of Wisdom in 100,000 Stanzas). Based on its view, he composed a commentary on it, analyzing it with his awareness of the middle way.

Thus, from among the vast, middle [length], brief, and very brief Perfection of Wisdom sūtras, this *Heart of the Perfection of Wisdom* was intended for the audience of inferior awareness. It has three parts: the setting, the actual [sūtra], and the summation. The setting has two parts: the common and uncommon [settings]. The uncommon setting has five parts: the opening that removes [false] assumptions about the rapporteur, the marvelous time, teacher, place, and audience.

Regarding the removal of certain assumptions, it says, *thus*.[4] Being incapable of making the teaching manifest because of not having the complete compilation [results] in the assumption that the words compiled are mistaken. This is eliminated by *did I hear*, which implies that memory was manifest. There are also the two assumptions that (1) it was heard without attention [and so] was not [actually] heard and that (2) even if it was known to be as it is at the time it was compiled, if it was not

[3] On female messengers, see Alex Wayman, "Messengers, What Bring Ye?" in Tadeusz Skorupski, ed., *Indo-Tibetan Studies: Papers in Honour and Appreciation of Professor David L. Snellgrove's Contribution to Indo-Tibetan Studies*, Buddhica Britannica, Series Continua 2 (Tring, U. K.: Institute of Buddhist Studies, 1990), pp. 305–22.

[4] Peking reads *'di skad bdag*.

done with attention, it is not without mistakes. Those two assumptions are removed by *I*, which implies the [presence] of attention that specifically understands with the body [i.e., the ear] and the mind. *Hear* [means] it is of a nature that was not completely imagined by him. Furthermore, *did I hear* [means] that it was not heard indirectly. Thus, four points are set forth in the opening. The complete purity[5] of this is [implied] by the admiration by the tathāgatas [at the end of the sūtra]. It refers to *thus did I hear.* [305a] What the compiler did at that time was connect a collection of words that were not understood. Otherwise, if they were connected[6] gradually [i.e., passed down from others], he would have to hear even things that he would have had to have seen [earlier], like [the fact that the Buddha and the assembly of monks and bodhisattvas were] *abiding together*. In that case, it would absurdly follow that it was *heard indirectly*, and this is contradicted by renown. Our assertion is that not only is [the possibility that it was heard indirectly] eliminated [by] merely being contradicted by renown; it is eliminated by the refutation expressed by the words. Also, at the compilation,[7] the complete and perfect Buddha advised that when one hears a compiled stanza, even if it is a compiled word of context [such as the name of the site], it is not made by the compiler [but should be regarded as the word of the Buddha]. Therefore, because everything is heard, there is no fault. This very point was made by Ratnākaraśānti, who said that the compiler was the noble Ānanda, blessed by Bhagavan. Then what purpose does the compiler have? He is merely the questioner.

At one time is marvelous. It is not at some other time because when the complete and perfect Buddha turned the wheel of doctrine in consideration of other disciples, he introduced the heart of the perfection of wisdom to the noble Avalokiteśvara. Therefore, the simultaneous hearing establishes that it is marvelous. In terms of those who are not disciples, the complete and perfect Buddha appeared to have entered into samādhi, but ultimately, he turned the wheel of doctrine without interruption in whatever way was appropriate. Also, *at one time* means at the time of [the disciples] not having been tamed by the Buddha. Otherwise, the noble Avalokiteśvara would have had no opportunity to teach.

The Bhagavan is the marvelous teacher. One might ask why the Bhagavan is the marvelous teacher if the noble Avalokiteśvara is the teacher here. It said that Śāriputra asked [his question] by the power of the Bhagavan and asked [it] due to the Bhagavan himself [305b] being absorbed in samādhi. This also characterizes the context of the answer.

5 Derge reads *dag*; Peking reads *ngag*.

6 Derge reads *'brel ba na*; Peking reads *'bral pas na*.

7 Peking reads *sdud pa'i dus*; Derge reads *sdud pa po dus*.

Therefore, there is not the slightest fault in saying that just the Bhagavan is the marvelous teacher. "The marvels of complete lordship, of qualities, of fame, of glory, of wisdom, and of effort; these six are called fortunes." This means that because he has fortune (*bhaga*), he is endowed with it (*bhagavan*). Lordship is his outshining of others; he abandons the afflictive obstructions and the obstructions to omniscience, through the power of which he destroys the four *māra*s. Thus, he attains power. Quality is his natural virtue, such as the ten powers. Those two [lordship and quality] have the nature of the wisdom[8] of the utterly pure *dharmadhātu*. Fame is the quality of his *rūpakāya*, the cause of his fame; it has the nature of the mirror-like wisdom. Glory[9] is the wisdom of equality because he has attained the sky treasury of all phenomena.[10] Wisdom is his specific understanding. Effort is earnest action. Some say that the place of "quality" is "auspicious form." That is mirror-like. If it is [explained] in that way, "glory" has the nature of teaching the doctrine. Therefore, it is attentive action.

Pile of Vultures Mountain in Rājagṛha is the marvelous place. Because there are differences in what is appropriate in food and requisites, two abodes of the nirmāṇakāya are set forth in terms of the audience. Or, because Rājagṛha is suitable in general, Vulture Mountain provides specificity. In reality, the basis of the nirmāṇakāya is the dharmakāya [and not one of these two places]. Regarding that, the term *rāja* means "benefit" and "destroy" because the qualificand illustrates the quality. There are five abodes of the king's knowledge;[11] their abode (*gṛha*) is the meaning of dharmakāya. *Vulture* implies not knowing satisfaction; to enter into that which is without limit. *Pile* means inexhaustible. Therefore, it should be understood that [Vulture and Pile] mean having the quality of the limitless collection of good qualities and to be without diminution, respectively. Thus, it is like the statement that the *dharmadhātu* is not known to diminish, [306a] nor is it known to increase. The term *mountain* implies that it abides on the earth and makes its abode there. Therefore, the dharmakāya is the lord of the earth. Thus,[12] the dharmakāya that is implied by these three terms [Rājagṛha, Pile of Vultures, and mountain] is the abode of the nirmāṇakāya; it abides in reality.

Because of possessing fearlessness, one is free from all fear. Therefore, one enters into bliss. [This is the meaning of] *together*. *Was abiding* is in the past tense; one should know that how it is taught is nondeceptive in

[8] Peking omits *ye shes*.

[9] Derge mistakenly reads *dang la* instead of *dpal*.

[10] On the five wisdoms, see Donald S. Lopez, Jr., *The Heart Sūtra Explained* (Ithaca, N.Y.: State University of New York Press, 1988), pp. 28, 194–95 (n. 44).

[11] Derge reads *rgyal po'i rig pa'i gnas lnga*; Peking reads *rgyal po ni rig pa'i gnas lnga*.

[12] Peking reads *de ltar na*; Derge reads *shing ltar na*.

the two types of compilation. *A great assembly of monks* is the marvelous retinue. It should be known that there are three divisions, the low, intermediate, and superior. It should be known that the low are gods and humans. The intermediate is the assembly of monks. The superior is the bodhisattvas.

Because they are ordained through four petitions, they are called monks. However, that is not necessary here. Or because they seek virtue[13] in order to be fulfilled through being taught, they are called monks. It means one who seeks the marvelous wealth of virtue from others. They are called an *assembly* because they are worthy of unsurpassed worship due to their creation of the aspiration to enlightenment. The *Maitreyavimokṣa* (Liberation of Maitreya) says:

> It is said that even though a diamond has been broken, it outshines in all ways the most excellent of gold ornaments; a broken diamond does not lose the name[14] [diamond] and it completely clears away poverty. Child of good lineage, in exactly the same way, although one has not fulfilled the diamond creation of the aspiration to omniscience, it outshines the gold ornaments of the good qualities of all śrāvakas and pratyekabuddhas; [that person] does not lose the name "bodhisattva" and the poverty of saṃsāra is overturned.

The term *great* is used to express specifically that the assembly of monks are suitable as vessels by virtue of their creation of the aspiration [to enlightenment] because they have attained the capacity to hear about the profound. [Regarding *bodhisattva*], *bodhi* is the knowledge of cessation (*kṣayajñāna*) and of nonproduction (*anutpādajñāna*). *Sattva* is aspiration; it means approaching in application and so forth. The term *mahāsattva* indicates a bodhisattva who is irreversible [on the path]. [306b] Because the assembly of monks are of intermediate [importance], it is suitable that they be mentioned after the assembly of bodhisattvas. However, it should be understood that they are mentioned first in order to indicate the correct view for those who have newly entered the vehicle. Regarding the bodhisattvas, because it is clearly set forth that they create the aspiration [to enlightenment] through the power of lineage, it is not necessary that they sit very close [to the Buddha], like a child that needs the words of its mother.

It is said that śrāvakas who have created the aspiration to enlightenment are like children just born; they are to be protected through guarding the wish that creates the aspiration. Thus, it is fitting that it should be set forth as it is [with the monks mentioned before the bodhisattvas]. Because the number is not set forth, it is to be understood that the audi-

[13] Peking reads *dge ba slong bas na*; Derge reads *dge ba slong ba na*.

[14] Peking reads more prolixly *ming yang 'dor bar byed pa ma yin te*.

ence was beyond enumeration; otherwise, it would have been suitable to mention the number.

The uncommon setting has two parts: the context of the question and the actual question. The context of the question has two parts: the action of the Bhagavan and the action of the noble Avalokiteśvara. [The former is discussed] first, because if the Bhagavan had not entered samādhi, it would not be correct to request [teaching] from another without depending on him. The Bhagavan is permanently in equipoise. Therefore, "The nature body is held to be the cause of equality, subtlety, and what is connected with those; [the cause] of all happiness, of resources, of teaching, and of the enjoyment [body]."

Since it is not correct for it to be otherwise,[15] the nirmāṇakāya is not endowed with wisdom. Therefore, although it is not correct that after teaching the enumerations of phenomena, the perception of the profound, he [i.e., the Buddha] was [actually] absorbed in samādhi, the category of disciples who are not vessels for entering into the wheel of doctrine through him [i.e., the Buddha] are disciples who, due to their belief in the noble Avalokiteśvara, are taught by him [i.e., Avalokiteśvara].

They did not enter into the teaching of the perfect and complete Buddha [because] he *was absorbed in samādhi.* The meaning of the term "samādhi" is well known in the world; it says *samādhi* here. Therefore, because samādhi is the word for absence here, it indicates the absence of [the Buddha] engaging in explanation. [307a] Also, being absorbed in samādhi suggests that he remained without saying anything. Therefore, it means that no words were spoken. Here it should be known that the thing called *perception of the profound* is not expressed by the samādhi. It is said to be *profound* because it is not understood by common beings, śrāvakas, and bodhisattvas who have newly entered the vehicle because their minds are distracted from emptiness, and it is said to be perception because it has the quality of being praised as that which removes ignorance and darkness. *Enumerations of phenomena* is a term enumerated in the śāstras. Regarding that, *phenomena* is the mode of being of things that are free from being an expression or an object of expression. Because its enumeration teaches through conventions that are taught subsequently, it is a śāstra. Therefore, it is called an enumeration of names.

Regarding, *also at that time*, because the teaching of the Buddha was being compiled, it was a time [for the use of] the [ear] sense organ; except for listening to the noble Avalokiteśvara, it is not suitable to contemplate. *Noble* means gone far beyond the two obstructions. He is called *Avalokita* because he looks at sentient beings with great compassion. He is

[15] Derge reads *bzhin* instead of *gzhan*.

called *īśvara* because he possesses the fruition of compassion due to his great power.

With consciousness (*jñā* of *prajñā*) one understands the things of the world. It is *wisdom* (*pra* of *prajñā*) because it understands their mode of being, such as their momentary nature. It is *beyond* (*pāram*) because it is the understanding of the two truths. It is *gone* (*itā*) because there is nothing higher. *Viewing* means contemplating. Thus, his excellence in entering fully [into the perfection of wisdom] in mere contemplation [rather than deep samādhi] serves as an occasion for the noble Avalokiteśvara to be petitioned [by Śāriputra]. Otherwise, because he would be moving into absorption, it would not be the occasion to petition him. For that very reason, it says *then*, [meaning] that after the noble Avalokiteśvara's contemplation, he was in a state of ease. The [untranslated] term *sma* expresses what is known as the nature of noncontradiction; it means that when there was the ease to teach, it was not contradictory [for Śāriputra] to ask. *Venerable* [literally, "endowed with life"] is known as a way of addressing the young. [307b]

Others may have[16] the great courage of the bodhisattva that seeks the welfare of sentient beings and act accordingly. However, only Śāriputra, without understanding those, has the fortune to be empowered by the Buddha to ask. Among the sphere of disciples, those with confidence in śrāvakas have inferior understanding. Therefore, they believe that his question and the answer will be a cause of benefit to themselves as well. Thus, they enter into attainment. If the questioner had been a bodhisattva, even though it would be a cause of benefit, it would not cause confidence because they [i.e., bodhisattvas] have great courage and understand the answer. Except through empowerment by the Bhagavan, even Śāriputra could not fathom the depths of the behavior of sentient beings; he knew their thoughts [through the Buddha's empowerment] and did not [have to] strive independently in order to fully apprehend them. Thus, through the blessing of the Buddha, having understood the thoughts of others, it was appropriate for him to ask this. The people of the world do not believe that Śāriptura is free [to elucidate] the profound intention [of the Buddha]; because he is a śrāvaka, they understand that he is of inferior awareness. Therefore, the Bhagavan did not bless Śāriputra to teach. The people of the world believe, however, that only the noble Avalokiteśvara, because of his great intelligence and great compassion, is able to set forth the mother of the conquerors [the perfection of wisdom] in a way that accords with the wisdom of the inferior; the noble Avalokiteśvara is the object of the question.

[16] Peking reads *yod med* instead of *yod mod*.

Whoever means those who abide on the path of accumulation or those who abide on the path of preparation, and so forth. Or, it can be known [to mean those] of the three times; there is no difference in meaning between *ask* and request. By the combination [of the terms] *son and daughter* one is to understand the nature of females and males who are distinguished by being suitable as vessels [of the teaching]. However, the term that distinguishes their *lineage* indicates that they abide only on the path of accumulation. It is like this: the lineage is the bodhisattva lineage; sons and daughters of those endowed with the tathāgathagarbha or who have listened to them. By the power of lineage they have the aspiration that wishes to be protected from suffering and to attain nirvāṇa. [308a] They have the aspiration that wishes to fully cultivate [the path] through the stages of the establishments of mindfulness, and so on [and thereby] to be protected from suffering, accordingly, to find refuge following the Mahāyāna, the cause of abandoning suffering, and to attain nirvāṇa. They thereby create the aspiration to enlightenment, having a nature of wisdom and compassion, are endowed with the cultivation of the five perfections of merit [through] compassion [i.e., giving, ethics, patience, effort, and concentration], and, through wisdom, have the wisdom that is put to use in the cultivation of hearing and thinking. [Such persons] are called sons and daughters of good lineage. This provides an answer for understanding the path of accumulation, as before. This teaching applies primarily to the close disciples, and so forth, within that audience. It is not the stage of [someone] attaining the capacity to abide in the audience of the Sugata, such as a beginner who has not amassed the collections. *This* [perfection of wisdom] [means that] although the *Śatasāhasrikā*, and so forth have been taught in sequence, they have not been understood. For that very reason, it is called *profound.*

Practice, [according to the *Madhyāntavibhāga* V.9] is, "Writing, making offerings, giving gifts, listening, reading, study, explaining, recitation, contemplation, and meditation." *The wish to practice* is through the practice of the dharma subsumed within activities of body, speech, and mind. Here, the practice of the dharma is the nature of the accumulation of merit of the eight branches. It is said that purification through the collection of wisdom is of the nature of thinking and meditation. *How should one practice* means "Which is fundamental, the collection of wisdom or the collection of merit?"; "Which should one train in during subsequent attainment?" Here, the answer is given that first one should primarily follow wisdom. Later, there is what is known as that which accords with the collection of merit. Therefore, in order to answer accordingly, that which is fundamental is twofold: the practice of what is fundamental and the practice of the subsequent attainment.

The practice of what is fundamental is sevenfold: the occasion, the path of preparation, the path of vision, [308b] the path of meditation, the special path,[17] the *vajra*-like samādhi of the path of no more learning, and the fruition of that. The occasion is *Śāriputra, a son of good lineage or.* . . . The path of preparation is, *these five aggregates . . . consciousnesses are empty*. Regarding the path of preparation, heat (*ūṣma*) and peak (*mūrdha*) have a nature of capacity and forbearance (*kṣānti*), and supreme mundane quality (*laukika-agra-dharma*) have a nature of power. There is capacity because of possessing the capacity to abandon that which is antithetical to faith and so forth. There is power because of having abandoned the antithetical. These are not divisions of the respective objects of those [mental states]; the contemplation through belief and the contemplation of suchness[18] are distinguished by the accompanying [mental factors]. According to some, it should be understood that what is referred to as contemplation through belief and contemplation of suchness during heat are types of persons, the followers of faith and the followers of doctrine. The followers of faith, due to their belief and confidence, enter into what is and what is not real. The followers of doctrine, without relying on the person, understand the reality of things and enter into it; those are the differences. Therefore, without there being a difference in object, it is said that an object is taken by contemplation through belief and an object is taken by the contemplation of suchness.[19]

Regarding that statement, *Form is empty; emptiness is form* is the brief teaching. *Emptiness is not other than form, form is not other than emptiness* is the extensive explanation. Regarding that, some assert that emptiness is the destruction of form. The answer to that is that form is empty. It is said that emptiness is not other than form because dependent natures and unreal imaginaries are empty of the nature of duality[20] that is imputed [by ignorance]. The nature of form is the emptiness of duality[21] in the manner of an affirming negative. Some say that form and so forth turn into the nature of the *dharmadhātu*, like an illusion. In response to that it said that only emptiness is form. *Form is not other than emptiness* [309a] [means] that dependent forms are only emptiness, that is, they have the nature of the *dharmadhātu*.

It might be said that if blue and so forth had a nature of not losing their entity and exceeding the *dharmadhātu*, then blue and so forth and that [*dharmadhātu*] would be in direct and mutual contradiction, like the mottle of a butterfly. In that case, even the *dharmadhātu* would be dam-

[17] Peking omits *khyad par gyi lam dang*.

[18] Peking reads *de go na*.

[19] Peking reads *de kho na*.

[20] Peking reads *grtags pa'i gnyis kyi rang bzhin gyi stong pa*; Derge reads *btags pa'i gnyis kyis rang bzhin gyis stong pa*.

[21] Derge reads *gnyis kyis*; Peking reads *gnyis kyi*.

aged by the contradiction of singularity and plurality and would thereby become deceptive (*samvṛti*). However, blue and so forth do not attain this status. Thus, it is said that *form is not other than emptiness. Other* means that blue and so forth would be endowed with a mode of existence whose entity was not included by the luminous and clear nature of the mind. Therefore, if having lost its entity, [blue] appeared to be similar to that [*dharmadhātu*], the contradiction of being related to its own entity would not apply to the *dharmadhātu*. It is said, "Because the varieties, such as blue, [that appear] to consciousness are consciousness, they are not other. Those who are not able to see engage in the discrimination of objects." Because the way in which this is the case is examined in the lesser *Pratibandhasiddhi* and in the *Pramāṇaviniścaya*,[22] I will not expand on it here.

Therefore, this directly indicates the character of emptiness that is free from superimposition and denial. The superimposition of existence onto form, the superimposition of a nature of negating that onto emptiness, and the imagined nature of objects are eliminated by the first, *Form is empty. Emptiness is not other than form.* The denial of the existence of the ultimate by asserting that the *dharmadhātu*, like form, is a conventionality or denial through asserting nonexistence, that is, that because it is not correct that its entity is a conventional entity, the final nature does not exist, entails the superimposition of apprehending form to be endowed with a mode of being [leading to the position] that it is correct [to hold] that the *dharmadhātu* is not the nature of form and so forth. [309b] This is dispelled by the latter, *Only emptiness is form and form is not other than emptiness.*

Therefore, it should be understood that the state of abandonment of misconceptions concerning subjects and objects in accordance with the respective antidotes to superimposition and denial is taken as the object through contemplation by belief on heat and peak and [it should be understood] that the state of having abandoned misconception concerning objects on forbearance and the state of having abandoned misconceptions concerning subjects on [the level of] supreme mundane quality are taken as the object by the contemplation of suchness. This is because the Mādhyamikas say to the proponents of apperception (*svasaṃvedana*) that it is correct that apperception does not ultimately exist because it would contradict oneness from the point of view of [apperception] ap-

[22] The translation here is uncertain. The Tibetan reads *'brel pa grub pa chung ngu'i yongs su shes pa dang rnam par nges pa'i yongs su shes par dpyad pa. 'Brel pa grub pa* is presumably Śaṃkarānanda's *Pratibandhasiddhi*, but *chung ngu* does not appear in the title and the meaning of *yongs su shes pa* (*parijñā*) is unclear. *rNam par nges pa* is usually Dharmakīrti's *Pramāṇaviniścaya* (or the commentary of Dharmottara or Jñānaśribhadra), but again, *yongs su shes pa* does not appear in the titles.

prehending blue and so forth directly. [That is, to have an apperception that directly apprehends blue would mean that it would have to be the same as the eye consciousness apprehending blue; this contradicts oneness.] Otherwise, the reason would not be established because their assertion would not be established. Therefore, even though it is asserted that they do not ultimately exist, it is asserted that subjects exist conventionally. However, some assert that conventionally apperception is an aspect of object and subjects. They dispute the reality of the object that is asserted by the Mādhyamikas to exist conventionally in that way.

The path of vision is set forth by *Śāriputra, it is thus . . . unfilled.* In that, it should be known that what is fundamental is the simultaneous understanding of the eight profundities. From among the sixteen moments having the nature of forbearance and knowledge observing the four truths,[23] the eight forbearances are concomitant with the uninterrupted path. The moments of knowledge that are concomitant with the path of liberation can be known in the extensive teaching here because the cause [the forbearances] is understood through the effect [the knowledges]. Furthermore, they do not occur in a different order; the initial knowledge is the doctrinal knowledge and that which comes at the end through the power of the doctrinal knowledge is called the subsequent knowledge. Regarding that, the complete knowledge that the truth of suffering is empty of intrinsic existence is the doctrinal knowledge of suffering. The subsequent knowledge of suffering is the realization that it is without character through realizing that it is empty of intrinsic existence. The knowledge that the truth of origin is not intrinsically produced [310a] is the doctrinal knowledge of origin. The subsequent knowledge of origin is the realization that it is not ceased because it is not feasible that that which is not produced could be otherwise. The complete knowledge that the truth of cessation is not intrinsically connected with the stains is the doctrinal knowledge of cessation. The subsequent knowledge of cessation is the realization that it is not stainless because of it not being intrinsically mixed with stains, that is, the purity that is free of stains is adventitious. Regarding the truth of the path, because the objects of abandonment are adventitious, they do not intrinsically exist. Therefore, the discordant class not being diminished due to the power of the antidote is the doctrinal knowledge of the path. The subsequent knowledge of the path is [the understanding that] because there is nothing that is not included in the *dharmadhātu*, then just as [the objects of abandonment] do not diminish, it is not feasible that the antidotes have a nature that increases.

Therefore, here, the moments of forbearance and knowledge abide

[23] See *Heart Sūtra Explained*, pp. 133–35.

even in the application to [conventional] things; what is fundamental on the path of vision is surrounded by the seven branches of enlightenment (*bodhyaṅga*). Therefore, because the eight moments of knowledge are taken as the object by the branch of enlightenment of correct mindfulness, this progression is to be known [to apply also] to subsequent attainment.

Having set forth the path of vision in that way, on the path of meditation the thirty-six conceptions concerning subject and object, each with nine individual aspects, are abandoned through the divisions based on the discordant class and the antidotal class.[24] Therefore, here, the path of meditation sets forth the stages of the abandonment of objects of abandonment, *Śāriputra, it is thus . . . and also no nonattainment. It is thus* means "meditate on that very object which was actualized by that very path of vision; the thirty-six conceptions concerning the aggregates and so forth are abandoned."

Regarding that, from among the conceptions that conceive of that which has an imputed base [to be real], the conception of the aggregates is up to [*no*] *eight consciousnesses.*[25] The antidote to the conception of the sources is up to *no phenomena.* The antidote to conception of the constituents is up to *up to and including no mental consciousness constitutent.* [310b] The antidote to dependent arising is up to *up to and including the cessation of aging and death also does not exist.* The antidote to conception is up to *no path.* The antidote to the conception about the path of vision is *no wisdom*; this includes the doctrinal knowledge and subsequent knowledge. The antidote to conceptions about the path of meditation is *no attainment*; because it is attained by this, it is attainment. The path of meditation is comprised by the supramundane and mundane wisdoms. The antidote to conceptions about the special path and the path of no more learning is *also no nonattainment.* Because there are no thoughts of the object of attainment or the means of attainment, *no nonattainment* expresses the special path [i.e., the *vajra*-like samādhi] and the path of no more learning.

The antidote to the conception conceiving [things] having a substantial basis [to be real] is set forth here through elimination. However, specifically, with the exception of the antidote to the conception of an autonomous self, the other antidotes are set forth in sequence through the aggregates and so forth: the antidote to the conception of unity, agent, seer, the basis of the affliction,[26] the basis of separation from desire, of vision,

[24] See Eugene Obermiller, *Analysis of the Abhisamayālaṃkāra* (London: Luzac, 1933), pp. 76ff.

[25] Both Derge and Peking read *rnam par shes pa rgyad* instead of *rnam par shes pa med.*

[26] Peking reads *nyon mongs pa'i rten*; Derge reads *nyon mongs pa dang rten.*

meditation, and having a basis of function. Similarly, the antidote to the conception that takes [things] with a basis [that bodhisattvas should] pursue [to be real] is set forth with the conception of the aggregates, and so forth. Specifically, regarding the incomplete conception of emptiness and the perfections, the conception of the four truths is additional. *No attainment* explains just the path of no more learning. From among the conceptions that take [things] that have a basis [that bodhisattvas should] turn away from [to be real], ignorance, adherence to names, and forms, and the conception that is attachment to the two extremes are not included here. The rest are set forth explicitly in this way: the conception of the aggregates by the meaning of *aggregates*; conception, by *wisdom*. That which is included in the conception of self, and so forth due to the nature of the independence of the imputed object [is explained] by *attainment*. [311a] The others, included from the point of view of antidote, are like this: no attainment is the expression of nonproduction; therefore it is [the antidote to] the conception of nonproduction. [The antidote to the] conception that misunderstands the afflicted and the pure [is indicated] by *ignorance and cessation of ignorance, aging and death, and the cessation of aging and death*. [The antidote to] the conception of not abiding on the noble path [is indicated] by the conception of the four truths.

The special path, the path of no more learning, and the fruition are set forth by *Therefore, Śāriputra . . . complete buddhahood*. By *therefore* the thirty-six conceptions are abandoned. *Because there is no attainment* is the purification of the three cycles of conceptions about attainment and nonattainment. *Rely on the perfection of wisdom* fulfills the special path. *Practice* is the practice of the special path. *Abiding in the observation of the mind*[27] is what is fundamental in the special path. Having set forth the special path, the teaching of the path of no more learning is *without fear*, and so forth. Having abided in what is fundamental on the special path, without observing[28] the object that is the mind, nonobservation is set forth. Fear is interference of the afflictions. Therefore, having overcome that, it says *without fear*. Nonfear refers to the tenth stage. Therefore because one has *passed completely beyond the error* of the afflictions and of objects of knowledge, it is irreversible. It is connected to *All the buddhas of the three times who have passed beyond sorrow relying on the perfection of wisdom and have fully awakened into unsurpassed, complete, perfect enlightenment*. Because of being the nature of completion and having nothing more to learn, *nirvāṇa* and *relying on the perfection of wisdom* are the meaning of the nature of the path of no more

[27] This phrase *sems kyi dmigs pa la gnas te* does not appear in other versions of the sūtra.

[28] Derge reads *ma dmigs par*; Peking reads *ma dmigs pas*.

learning. *All the buddhas who abide in the three times* [311b] are the persons who are the foundation. Without relying on the past, there would be qualms about the existence of other paths. Without the present, there would be no nondeceptive achievement. Without the future, there would be no cause of entry [into the path]. Therefore, it says *abiding in the three times*. Thus, this sets forth the proof of a single vehicle.

Having set forth the path of no more learning, the fruition is set forth by *unsurpassed*, and so on. It is *unsurpassed* because knowledge and liberation are of the same taste. Regarding *complete and perfect*, an awakened one is fully complete; enlightenment [itself] is not complete and perfect. Regarding this, complete and perfect enlightenment is the wisdom of nonextinction[29] and the wisdom of nonproduction. Some assert that *without fear*, and so on is the path of no more learning, *go to the completion of nirvāṇa* is the fruition, and *abide in the three times*, and so on is the proof that the path is one.

Thus, having set forth how to practice what is fundamental in that way, the practice of the subsequent attainment is, *Therefore*. This has four parts: the exposition of the cause of undoubtable entry, the preparation of the practice of the perfection of wisdom whose repetition has the nature of the collection of merit, the actual perfection of wisdom to be repeated, and the summation. *Therefore* is the cause of marvelous abandonment and wisdom. *Perfection of wisdom* means that which accords with liberation through the accompanying establishments of mindfulness and so forth on the path of accumulation. *Great knowledge* is that which accords with emergence [i.e., the path of preparation] through the practice of capacity and power. It is *unsurpassed* because it is equal to the Buddha through comprehending the fundamental abiding on the path of vision. Regarding *equal to the unequaled*, the unequaled is the special path and the path of no more learning. [312a] That which is equal to those in abandoning obstructions is the path of meditation. It *completely pacifies all suffering* because on the special path and the path of no more learning, respectively, it is particularly distant and is the cause of comprehending the perfected purity, self, permanence, and bliss.[30] *Because it is not false* [means] because of marvelous abandonment. What is it? It is the mantra that possesses the perfection of wisdom. *Mantra* means protection and wisdom because it abandons the respective discordant factors on all the paths and because it possesses the respective understanding. Having set forth how it is to be known, it teaches what is to be known; *tadyathā* [means] "having made manifest these meanings, recite." This

[29] Both editions read *zad pa med pa*, but this may be excessive apophasis for *kṣayajñāna*.

[30] See *Heart Sūtra Explained*, pp. 83–86.

sets forth the stages of practice. Birth is abandoned on the path of vision in this way: "Even though he has transcended birth through seeing reality as it is, the Compassionate One teaches birth, aging, sickness, and death."

Gate gate pāragate [teaches] the state of having abandoned the six types of rebirth, the path of vision, because one has gone beyond from going on the path of great desire by going on the path of accumulation. One has gone beyond from going on the path of accumulation to going on the path of preparation. Thus, going is *gate gate pāragate*, the path of vision. *Pārasaṃ* [means] abide on the path of meditation. *Gate* means abide on the special path and the path of no more learning. *Bodhi* is the fruition. *Oṃ* and *svāhā* are terms of blessing for the purpose of achieving the effect of the repetition.

Thus, it is explained that one practices what is fundamental for the collection of wisdom and practices in subsequent attainment for the collection of merit. Here, also, the perfection of wisdom that is to be repeated is implied. Therefore, it is taught that at the time of rising, [312b] one should train in all eight collections of merit, the nature of the letters, and so forth.

Now, the summary of the answer to the statement, "How does one practice?" is *Śāriputra . . . should practice in that way*. Thus, having delineated what is fundamental, the reception [of the teaching] is *Then . . . praised the teaching of the Buddha*. There are two parts: the reception by the Buddha and the reception by the audience. In terms of the reception of the Buddha, the statement is, *Then, at that time. . . . Then* [means] the noble Avalokiteśvara having completed his teaching. *At that time* means at the time of establishing as the word [of the Buddha] this teaching for the sake of the entry of future sentient beings. It is not for the sake of the entry of present sentient beings because if they believe in the noble Avalokiteśvara, they are without qualm. *Rose from samādhi* is an action taken from the perspective of others. Regarding *well done, well done*, the speaker is joyful; it is a term that turns away praise and blame and disturbance due to fear. Saying it [means] there is no fault. In this way, the repetition *well done, well done* is special praise and has the effect of indicating special praise. In the future, admiration [will cause] entry into the teaching [and show] the undeceptive nature of the path when the fruition is attained. Therefore it says, *All the tathāgatas admire this*. The reception by the audience: the noble Avalokiteśvara [praises the Buddha because] his courage was created by the power of the Buddha. The statement of demigods, and so on after gods and humans sets forth the special vessels of the training and the lesser [vessels]. The praise by the gods and so forth should be understood to be of the nature of their assent to enter the training. This teaching is called the heart of the perfection of wisdom because it teaches the stages of realization through summarizing what is explained in the great detail. [313a]

> Obeisance to you who, through the method of teaching various sūtras, directs those inclined toward nirvāṇa to enter the perfect practice.
>
> I have written this commentary empowered by joy relying merely on the dust at the feet of the glorious excellent being.
>
> One who does not benefit others is not a great being. Because of the power of evil, beings cannot strive for the benefit of others.
>
> This commentary was composed by a seeker who is surrounded by scholars in the center of the supreme land.
>
> The essence of the mother is like medicine. May this medicine-like [wisdom] remove the miserable sickness of the sick and afflicted world.

This completes the *Complete Understanding of the Heart of the Perfection of Wisdom* written by the *paṇḍita* Śrīmahājana. It was revised by the Indian abbot himself and the translator, the monk Seng ge rgyal mtshan. *Ye dharmā hetu prabhavā hetun teṣān tathāgato hyavadat teṣāñca yo nirodha evaṃ vādī mahāśramanaḥ.*[31]

Commentary on the Bhagavatī Heart of the Perfection of Wisdom Sūtra, Lamp of the Meaning

Bhagavatīprajñāpāramitāhṛdayārthapradīpanāmaṭīkā

VAJRAPĀṆI

Homage to the Bhagavatī Perfection of Wisdom

Homage to the basis, the wisdom that knows all aspects without mindfulness, to the path, the consciousness of the path, which is unproduced, and to the fruition, the knowledge of all aspects, which is beyond awareness. Homage to the perfection of wisdom is homage to the omniscient wisdom.

Thus did I hear at one time: these four syllables *evam mayā* are the source of the 84,000 collections of doctrine [and] the basis of all that is marvelous. The four doctrines concerning the identity of the mind and reality, that is, mindfulness, unmindfulness, [287a] nonproduction, and beyond

[31] The mantra occurs only in the Peking.

awareness, are heard at one time in two ways—profound and manifest. The profound is beyond hearing, thinking, and meditation. It is an appellation (*adhivacana*) that denotes abiding in one instant in the equality that is the nondifference of the entity of the *dharmadhātu* in the buddhas of the three times and in all sentient beings of the three realms. The manifest is the aspect of mindfulness, sentient beings' attachment to their actions. The *Bhagavan* has destroyed all of the afflictive obstructions and obstructions to omniscience and passed beyond sorrow to the dharmakāya. *Rājagṛha* is the best of all afflicted abodes because, since all phenomena are like illusions and dreams, a variety of worldly miracles were performed there. *Pile of Vultures Mountain* is the best abode of pure phenomena and is heaped with the brilliance of birds—the beings who abide in emptiness. The *great assembly of monks* are those who avoid the [ocean of] afflictions and stay on dry land by their own choice. The *great assembly of bodhisattvas* are those who, being equally free of consciousness and the objects of consciousness, understand everything exactly as it is. *Was abiding together* [means] together with those who are vessels of the profound reality who know the varieties of mindfulness to be expedient, are not tainted by mindfulness, and are not bereft of the three types of knowledge.

At that time, the Bhagavan [was absorbed in a samādhi called] perception of the profound. The profound is that which is not tainted by any type of mindfulness, knowledge, or awareness. Although it cannot be illustrated with examples and signs, it is like space, reality without ends or middle. *Perception* is temporary mindfulness, the contemplation of the unreal—that which is impermanent and changing, like bees moving in the sky at the onset of autumn. The *enumerations of phenomena* are the profound and the vast. The profound and vast are not mixed into one; for example, it is rare to see the reflection of the sky in clear water, but is quite common to see the reflection of the sun, moon, and stars. [287b] In the same way, a person who is acquainted with and believes in the teachings on the profound—without mindfulness, unproduced, and not within the sphere of awareness—is extremely rare whereas there are many who are attached to and believe in the various types of mindfulness, the teachings on the vast. *Absorbed in samādhi*: the profound and the vast are not different in the *dharmadhātu*. For example, when the sky is reflected in a clear lake, the reflections of the sun, moon, and stars are the same as the entity of the water. In the same way, the contemplation of the buddhas of the three times is the same.

Also at that time, the bodhisattva: [who is so-called] because he contemplates the profound reality that is contemplated by the Buddha himself and abides in the appearance of method for the welfare of sentient beings. *Mahāsattva* [is so-called] because he abides in the contemplation of the buddhas of the three times and acts for the welfare of limitless realms of sentient beings. *The noble Avalokiteśvara* [is so-called] because having surpassed the mundane and supramundane, he sees with the eye of nonconceptual wisdom and is endowed with the compassion of nonobservation. The *perfection of wisdom* [means] knowledge of the unmistaken wisdom. *Perfection* [means] beyond the sphere of awareness. *Beheld the practice of the profound and* [means] that, through not being tainted by mindfulness, he saw the uncertainty of practice that perceives diversity. *Those five aggregates* are those that are contaminated, such as the form aggregate and the five uncontaminated aggregates, such as the aggregate of ethics. *Saw them to be empty of intrinsic existence* indicates that the contaminated aggregates that [beings] seek to abandon and the uncontaminated aggregates that they wish to appropriate are not intrinsically established.

Then by the power of the Buddha, Śāriputra [means] that through the profound contemplation of the buddhas of the three times, [Śāriputra] was blessed, [allowing him] to perceive and be mindful of the sentient beings of the three realms, creating boundless courage. [288a] *To the bodhisattva,*[32] *the mahāsattva, the noble Avalokiteśvara* [means that] considering the welfare of persons who have interest only in the profound contemplation of the buddhas of the three times, [Śāriputra] thought, "I will ask." Having considered that, he said this: *A son or daughter of good lineage*. These are those who have the Mahāyāna lineage. Among them, [it refers to] those who have interest in the profound meaning, the perfection of wisdom, and who seek it. Furthermore, the mind itself is one; it appears to be different, as in a dream. [Hence] there is male and female. *Who* [refers to the fact] that there are some who have no interest in the profound meaning and who become frightened, fearful, and terrified [by it]. Some, through merely hearing of the profound doctrine become joyful and exultant and, through merely creating the aspiration [to enlightenment], attain unsurpassed enlightenment. *Those who wish to practice the profound perfection of wisdom*: he asks how one should practice such that self and other are not observed. *He said this* means that he thought, "I will answer the question." Who thought that? The bodhisattva, the *mahāsattva*, the noble Avalokiteśvara contemplated the profound doctrine just as it is and said this to the venerable Śāriputra for the welfare of sentient beings. *Śāriputra, a son of good lineage or a daughter of good lineage* [means that Avalokiteśvara] observed Śāriputra, the captain of those who seek the profound meaning, [and saw] that it is as if other sūtras were essenceless and meaningless, that some have faith in provisional sūtras and some have faith in definitive sūtras.

[32] Derge mistakenly reads *byang chub sems dga'*.

This perfection of wisdom is the essence of the minds of the buddhas of the three times and, therefore, the profound meaning is not within the sphere of awareness.

Thus, *those who wish to practice the profound should view things in this way*, that is, they should delight[33] in practicing with an awareness of the profound reality; by practicing with the factor of appearance, one does not encounter the essential quality. Therefore, as long as one has not purified these appearances of mindfulness, it is difficult to understand the meaning of the *Heart of the Perfection of Wisdom.* [288b] Hence, *one should correctly view even those five aggregates to be empty of intrinsic existence.* However, outsiders who have not encountered the unmistaken profound reality view it as self and view it as non-self. Furthermore, those who view it as self assert that awareness (*rig pa*) exists in reality. Those who have faith in selflessness hold that consciousness is empty and without duality. In order to accustom one's mind to viewing persons and phenomena as selfless, one accustoms the mind to not finding the self by investigating and examining the minute particles of all internal and external phenomena. Having done that, when [the mind] is placed in equipoise, it does not observe anything or conceive of anything. When one takes as his object of attainment the placement of the mind there for a prolonged period, it is meditative equipoise in which the mind is observed to be clear and joyful. At the time of subsequent attainment, all phenomena are mentally arisen, observed to be like illusions, like dreams, like mirages, like echoes, like a moon in water, like rainbows, like a city of the *gandharvas*, like the wheel of a firebrand, like falling hairs [seen by a person with cataracts], like Indra's net, and an emanation. For the sake of persons who, having done that, become discouraged and have an interest in the union of the varieties and emptiness, it says, *Form is empty, emptiness is form. Emptiness is not other than form, form is not other than emptiness.*

As is the form aggregate, so also are feeling, discrimination, conditioning factors, and consciousnesses empty. Because [consciousness] is in the plural, the eight collections of consciousness are also emptiness. Among these it is not good to seek the profound and subtle *ālayavijñāna*. What does this indicate? The illusion-like samādhi, which takes the varieties of appearance as its object through mindfulness of them, is based on the mindfulness of the union of all phenomena, which [in turn] is ascertained through sense direct perception. [This] is the doctrine that has been taught to common beings. Now, that which is based on the profound reality, which is not within the sphere of common beings, is without mindfulness, unproduced, [289a] and beyond the sphere of awareness. Regarding that, the three samādhis of emptiness, signlessness, and wishlessness are the

[33] Derge mistakenly reads *dka'* rather than *dga'*.

three types of wisdom, free from the three conditions, through nonabiding emptiness, nonabiding equanimity, and not abiding interruptedly, these being [ascertained through] mental direct perception, self-knowing direct perception, and yogic direct perception [respectively].

Regarding the instructions for these, the samādhi of emptiness, the nirmāṇakāya, is indicated by, *Śāriputra, therefore, all phenomena are empty. . . . In that* [*emptiness*], *there is no form, no consciousness . . . no aging and death.* The samādhi of signlessness, the saṃbhogakāya, is indicated by, *without characteristic, unproduced, unceased, no suffering, origin, cessation, and path.* The samādhi of wishlessness, the dharmakāya, is indicated by, *stainless, not stainless, undiminished, unfilled, no attainment, no nonattainment.*

To clarify this, emptiness is untainted by mindfulness and not taken to mind. Furthermore, in the emptiness that is not taken to mind, there is *no form, no feeling, no discrimination, no conditioning factors, and no consciousness.* That in which there is no consciousness is without mindfulness. In the emptiness that is not taken to mind, there is *no eye, no ear, no nose, no tongue, no body, and no mind.* That in which there is no mind has nothing to take to mind. That which is without mindfulness and has nothing to take to mind is mindful of the Buddha, mindful of the dharma, and mindful of the saṃgha. That which is mindful of the three jewels is the supreme mindfulness. That which is without mindfulness and has nothing to take to mind is mindful of giving, mindful of ethics, and mindful of the deity. It is mindful of giving without observing subject and object. It is mindful of ethics without observing production and disintegration. [289b] It is mindful of the deity without observing the three bodies. In the emptiness that is without mindfulness and has nothing to take to mind there is *no form, no sound, no odor, no taste, no object of touch, no phenomena.* In that in which there is no phenomena, there is no conditioned phenomena and no unconditioned phenomena, no virtuous phenomena, no nonvirtuous phenomena, no scripturally specified phenomena, no scripturally unspecified phenomena. In the emptiness that is without mindfulness and has nothing to take to mind, there is *no eye constituent, no eye consciousness constituent up to and including no mental consciousness constituent.* In the emptiness that is without mindfulness and has nothing to take to mind, there is *no ignorance, no extinction of ignorance, up to and including no aging and death and no extinction of aging and death.* That which is not born does not grow old and die. That which is not gathered is not separated. That which is not found is not lost. That which is not made is not destroyed. That which is not remembered is not forgotten. That which is not permanent is not annihilated. This indicates the samādhi of emptiness of the nonabiding emptiness, ascertained by the mental direct perceiver.

Now, one does not abide in the defiled phenomena or the pure phenomena of the four truths. Therefore, the samādhi of signlessness of the nonabiding equanimity should be ascertained by the self-knowing direct perceiver. Regarding that, equanimity is equality. That which is equal does not observe the three times. Furthermore, equality, because it is not tainted by any observation, is a mere name. Therefore, regarding signlessness, the sign of the afflicted is this mindfulness. The sign of the pure is the sphere of nonmindfulness. If those two do not move, if there is not an atom of mindfulness, how could it become nonmindfulness? The factors of mindfulness do not move, nor do the factors of nonmindfulness move. Therefore, they are not produced and do not cease. Moreover, the mindfulness arising from ignorance of the profound reality is the origin [the second of the four truths]. Because [beings] see that which does not exist to exist, there is suffering. [290a] Because they do not understand that neither existent nor nonexistent phenomena exist, the aspects of the path are what is to be purified and the purifier. Through cultivating the aspects of the path one passes beyond the domain of attainment and attainer [to] the cessation that makes manifest the dharmakāya, the fruition. Therefore, [the sūtra] says, *No suffering, no origin, no cessation, no path*. Therefore, because the purified and the purifier are not established, it is said that all phenomena are like illusions and dreams. What is to be purified is only this mindfulness.

Morever, because of being imputations, that which is like an illusion and a dream is self-arisen and self-pacifying. However, when the lamp of bliss, knowledge, emptiness, and compassion is blazing, meditation should be known to be just a sign indicating the essence of method. Being indicated thereby, mindfulness does not move from that; that should be known to be just an aspect of wisdom. That which is not produced from something other than those two [method and wisdom] should be known to be just a perfection. Not being aware of anything other than that is called the essence of the perfection of wisdom. Therefore, the instructions on the meaning of the essence is that all mindfulness is like an illusion. Not being tainted by mindfulness is the meaning of emptiness, not being tainted by mindfulness or nonmindfulness is the meaning of signlessness, not being tainted by nonproduction is the meaning of wishlessness. This indicates the concentration of uninterrupted instruction. There are beings who recognize the concentration of abiding in that way and there are beings who do not know it.

For example, the element water, gold, and the sky are naturally pure; they are not tainted by adventitious defilements. When the moon is full and is unobscured by clouds[34] and mist, upon seeing it reflected in a clear

[34] Peking mistakenly reads *spyin* rather than *sprin*.

lake, some feel enjoyment and delight and become attached; some do not think of anything. Similarly, although the basic mind is naturally pure, [some] feel enjoyment and delight in the arising of different appearances [when] in the illusion-like samādhi, thereby creating attachment and desire. Excellent beings who have encountered the basic mind experience the illusion-like samādhi [290b] but do not think of anything. Some find the gold color that is the nature of gold to be beautiful and make ornaments, wealth, etc. Moreover, [when] tarnish temporarily forms, they see it as ugly and become angry. Because the wise have seen, they know that the tarnish can be removed, because it is temporary, and they do not see it as ugly.[35] In the same way, beings who have not encountered the basic mind cherish the mind in equipoise and see subsequent consciousness as ugly and create hopes and fears. Excellent beings who have encountered[36] the basic mind know that equipoise and subsequent attainment are like illusions and like dreams and do not love or hate. The sky is just a name and does not exist in actuality. However, due to the power of conditions, various things appear in it, such as shades of darkness; days and nights, months, years, and aeons are counted and [beings] think that the earth and sky are very distant [from each other]. The wise, because they have seen, do not see even a place to put one-hundredth of a hair between the earth and sky. In the same way, beings who have not encountered the basic mind are not freed from the swamp of birth, aging, and death until countless aeons of many types of hardships [have been endured]; the fruition that one wishes to attain is difficult to attain. When the excellent beings who have encountered[37] the basic mind realize the profound reality, the mind is liberated; therefore, they do not see anything between sentient beings and the dharmakāya.

Therefore, for the sentient beings of the three realms who have not encountered the profound reality, the basis, nonmindfulness, the path, nonproduction, and the fruition, that which is beyond awareness, are transformed through the twelve links of dependent arising, such as ignorance, into the aggregates, constituents, and so on. Regarding that, the I and mine are the appropriated aggregates. From ignorance, one becomes attached to adventitious knowledge.[38] This serves as the cause of all suffering. Furthermore, there is the suffering of pain, the suffering of change, and the suffering of conditioning. [291a] Some, who wish to be liberated from those sufferings, seek to actualize cessation in order to attain nirvāṇa, the fruition, through cultivation of the aspects of the

[35] Derge mistakenly reads *mi sdug par ltao'* rather than *mi sdug par mi ltao'*.
[36] Peking mistakenly reads *sems dangs ma dang ma phrad.*
[37] Peking mistakenly reads *sems dangs ma dang ma phrad.*
[38] Peking reads *rigs* rather than *rig.*

paths of the noble. By understanding the way things are, that all of these are like dreams and illusions [they come to know] the signs of saṃsāra—suffering and origin—and the signs of nirvāṇa—cessation and path—such that there is nothing to adopt or discard. By not conceiving any of these to be real, they ascertain the signless samādhi of equanimity.

Now, I will teach the wishless samādhi that does not abide interruptedly, which is not within the sphere of awareness [but] of yogic direct perception. Because none of the stains of consciousness or object arise, it is *stainless*. It is also *without stainlessness*. The dharmakāya is beyond thought and meditation. Therefore, an attitude of pride in the wisdom that knows all aspects does not exist. [This is the meaning] of *no wisdom*. Furthermore, regarding *no wisdom*, it is not a case of nonexistence in relation to existence; it refers to the nature body (*svabhāvikakāya*) that is free from existence, nonexistence, and so on, and does not differ in entity from the unchanging *vajra*-like samādhi. Furthermore, regarding the divisions, the three bodies are spontaneously established.

Regarding the purpose, having understood the meaning of the profound, the mind is liberated. The purpose of purposes[39] is the effortless arising of the welfare of all sentient beings. With regard to the etymology, no-wisdom is the dharmakāya. Furthermore, the dharmakāya is not an effect that arises from a cause; it is not a fruition that arises from karma. In the same way, there is *no attainment* because it is not an object of awareness, mind, sentience,[40] or consciousness. There is *no nonattainment* because it is not encompassed by being beyond awareness, mind, sentience, or consciousness. *Therefore, Śāriputra* [is said] just because it is beyond being the object of expression of collections of stems, collections of words, collections of letters. *Bodhisattvas* are bodhisattvas who understand and comprehend that the mind, awareness, sentience, and consciousness that come from the actions and afflictions of the sentient beings of the three realms as well as the wisdom that comes from consciousness and object of consciousness are adventitious. [291b] *Because they are without attainment* means that there is no attainment even through actualizing the stages and paths. Wisdom is of three types. The wisdom of hearing arises from stems, words, and letters. The wisdom of thinking is the unerring contemplation of their meaning. The wisdom of meditation is one-pointedness of mind. *Perfection* is passing beyond those. *They rely and abide in the profound*: when one goes beyond hearing, one has no thought whatsoever. This is being without mindfulness.

[39] For a discussion of this term, see F. Th. Stcherbatsky, *Buddhist Logic*, vol. 2 (New York: Dover, 1962), pp. 1–2 and Michael M. Broido, "A Note on Dgos-'brel," *Journal of the Tibet Society* 3 (1983): 5–19.

[40] Derge reads *ming* instead of *yid*.

When one goes beyond thinking, one has no thought whatsoever. This is nonproduction. When one goes beyond meditation, one has no thought whatsoever. This is passing beyond being an object of awareness. Because they rely and abide in such a manner of nonreliance, *their minds are without obstruction*. The utterly pure basic mind is not tainted by actions, afflictions, or the obstructions to omniscience. *Without fear*: having heard about the profound reality, they are not frightened, do not panic, and do not become afraid.

Error is not to have confidence in reality and to see the factors of mindfulness as real, thinking that sentient beings of the three realms exist ultimately. Those who are mistaken about error are sentient beings of the three realms; the happiness and suffering of the sentient beings of the three realms are like, for example, seeing a magician's illusion in a dream or seeing a rope as a snake in a dream or a virgin seeing the birth and death of a son in a dream. *Error* is mistakenly seeing the unmistaken as ultimate truth. For example, some people on ships see mountains and cliffs move and tremble. In the same way, people without a virtuous friend mistakenly see the profound and unmistaken reality. For example, young lions drink lion's milk that, if drunk by others, will split the body and poison them. Similarly, the profound meaning of the perfection of wisdom is to be taught to those of the Mahāyāna lineage with very pure minds. If it is taught to those of the Hināyāna lineage, they will be frightened with terror and fear. For example, [292a] if a person with a phlegm [disorder] is given milk to drink, it will not dispel the malady and will poison him. In the same way, the profound reality is not to be taught to those who are not vessels. However, when that milk[41] is made into yogurt and whey and given to the person with a phlegm [disorder], it will prove beneficial. In the same way, when the profound reality that is the perfection of wisdom is mixed with the [other] five perfections, such as giving, and is taught to Hīnayānists, it will be beneficial. For example, suppose that many blind people are separated from their hometowns and from their mothers and wander in cities and towns. Upon returning, although they encounter their hometowns and their mothers, they do not recognize them. Similarly, Hināyānists become separated from the city of omniscience and from the mother, the perfection of wisdom, and wander through the cities of saṃsāra. Upon returning, although they encounter the city of omniscience and the mother, the meaning that is the heart of the perfection of wisdom, they do not recognize them. They will [only] understand the heart of those through examples and meanings taught by the virtuous friend endowed with method and wisdom. For example,

[41] Peking mistakenly reads *'o na* rather than *'o ma*.

some people who wished to take jewels from a jewel mine were told by a mistaken person that the footprint of an ox was the source of jewels. If they believed what they heard,[42] they would be impeded. In the same way, those of the Mahāyāna lineage who cast aside the meaning of the *Heart of the Perfection of Wisdom* are impeded if they look at and believe other sūtras.

Therefore, excellent persons who rely completely and in all ways on the instructions on the meaning of the *Heart of the Perfection of Wisdom* bring together the meanings of the four: actions, view, meditation, and fruition. Repeatedly viewing the meaning of the unmistaken essence of the Buddha's word and being mindful by mixing the mind with that [essence], without being separated from emptiness, is the meaning of action. The actual teaching of abiding continually in emptiness, supreme and not taken to mind, is the meaning of meditation. [292b] Nonproduction and noncessation, upon freeing oneself by not seeing thoroughly afflicted phenomena and pure phenomena[43] as real, is the meaning of the view. Because buddhas have no object of meditation and sentient beings have no object of awareness, the stains of objects of knowledge do not exist and the nonconceptual wisdom does not exist. Therefore, there is nothing to attain and nothing to be lost. This is the meaning of fruition. It is suitable that the meaning of the *Heart of the Perfection of Wisdom* that is completely encompassed by these [four] be greatly cherished.

Due to its qualities, one goes to *the completion of nirvāṇa. Completion of nirvāṇa*: the limit of the three worlds are the three nirvāṇas. The completion that is nirvāṇa is beyond expression, thought, and meditation. With regard to the activities of that [state], [the sūtra says], *All the buddhas of the three times*. The buddhas of the past, in reliance on this profound doctrine, see appearances like illusions and act for the welfare of unobservable sentient beings. The buddhas of the present, in reliance on the profound reality, view that which appears to and is remembered by sentient beings to be like illusions and, in order to liberate them from that, they bring to fulfillment good qualities and actions and teach the three doors of liberation. The buddhas of the future, in reliance on this profound perfection of wisdom, view the phenomena that sentient beings remember to be adventitious and, in order to liberate them from that, teach sentient beings the samādhi without thought. That which is the samādhi without thought is the perfection of wisdom. In dependence on that, they were fully awakened into unsurpassed, complete, perfect enlightenment, they are fully awakened, they will be fully awakened.

[42] Following the Peking, which reads *de la yid ches zhing nyan na*. Derge simply says *zer zhing nyan na*.

[43] In both Derge and Peking the phrase *rnam par byang ba'i chos rnams* appears twice.

Many tantras were taught[44] for the sake of those of sharp faculties who have interest in the secret Mahāyāna. The outer secret[45] mantra teaches such things as pacification and increase and the inner mantra teaches the bliss of body and mind through reliance on the channels, winds, and so forth. [293a] Having been taught through secret mantra to abide for a long time in samādhi, buddhahood occurs in one instant or in one lifetime or in the intermediate state or after seven lifetimes.

Someone may have doubts concerning whether this instruction on the meaning of the *Heart of the Perfection of Wisdom* is of the Definition Vehicle (*lakṣanayāna*) or the Mantrayāna. What appears to the minds of sentient beings seems to be different, but there is no differentiation in the profound reality. Therefore, this mantra of the perfection of wisdom is the heart of the meaning of all secret mantras. The realization of that is called the *mantra of great knowledge. Knowledge* is mindfulness, perception, and experience. *Great* is like the sky. The identification of the profound is the mantra of the illusion-like samādhi. *Unsurpassed mantra*: that which is not tainted by mindfulness, knowledge, perception, or experience is not subdued. Therefore, the *unsurpassed mantra* is the mantra of the samādhi on emptiness. *The mantra equal to the unequaled*: it is without mindfulness and because it does not arise, it is not produced. Because it is not produced, it is not equal to anything. That which is *equal to the unequaled* is the mantra of the signless samādhi. *The mantra that completely pacifies all suffering*: there is nothing that even the wisdom of the mind of the Buddha meditates on; it is neither conceptual nor nonconceptual. Therefore, the *mantra that completely pacifies all suffering* is the mantra of the wishless samādhi. This is the meaning of the four.

Those who look at and think about different pronouncements and texts see the joy and misery of the sentient beings of the three realms and feel sorrow, or hear about the qualities of greatness of buddhas and bodhisattvas and feel joy. When they analyze conventional truths to be like illusions, they are joyful. Therefore, *it is not false*. Furthermore, sorrow is anger and joy is desire. Because one does not recognize these as being one's own mindfulness, it is obscuration. For example, someone who delights in desire has sexual intercourse with a beautiful woman in a dream or a woman created by a type of potion or [293b] a woman made of a variety of woods. After that, by investigation and analysis, [he sees] that those women do not exist and the experience arising from that also does not exist. So it is for the mind of joy; by analyzing the pleasant and blissful, it is not true. For example, a skillful painter can paint a picture of a frightful demon on a piece of cloth such that when he looks at it, he

[44] Read *bstan* rather than *brten*.

[45] Derge omits *gsang*.

himself becomes alarmed and very frightened. Such is the mind of sorrow. Therefore, for the purposes of persons who believe in sorrow and joy, it is said that cause and effect or past actions and the fruition of actions *are not false*. For the purposes of excellent beings who see the truth, even action does not exist ultimately; it is said in the pronouncements, "even the fruitions of actions do not exist." Therefore, in the lineage of instructions [it is said] that the phenomena of which we are mindful appear like illusions; [their] nature does not exist. The phenomena of which we are not mindful are profound and do not appear; [their] nature exists. Therefore, the phenomena of which we are mindful function as mere illusions; they are *not false*.

The profound reality, untainted by mental activity, points to[46] the three doors of liberation. Therefore, *it should be known to be true*. For example, there was a person who wished to cross a great river that [in reality] was a mirage. He came to the bank of the great mirage river and called to a ferryman with a boat, and said, "Man, free me from this great river. I will give you whatever fee you wish." The ferryman said, "I will take the fee" and came [across]. Then the ferryman opened the person's eyes and made the mirage river disappear. In the same way, beings who wish to cross the great river of the three types of saṃsāra, created by actions and the fruitions of actions, approach virtuous friends endowed with method and wisdom and ask to be freed from the great river of the sufferings of saṃsāra, [promising], "I will do what you say." The virtuous friend cites many passages from the sūtras and causes them to feel sorrow and joy. Then [he shows them that] even that sorrow and joy [294a] is this mindfulness of their own minds. What is the method for crossing over this mindfulness? The phenomena of which we are mindful are to be known as the method, and the state of being untainted by mindfulness is the threefold profundity. Therefore, as long as the profound reality, the perfection of wisdom, is not understood, [the world] is like a mirage river. The phenomena of which we are mindful are true *because they are not false*. When we encounter the profound reality, it is as if the mirage river were destroyed; the state of being untainted by mindfulness *is known to be true*.

The mantra of the perfection of wisdom is stated. The mantra of the perfection of wisdom is not a mantra of pacification, increase, power, or wrath. What is it? By merely understanding the meaning of this mantra, the mind is freed. The first four syllables of this mantra [*tadyathā oṃ*] are the arising of action, the meaning of the middle four syllables [*gate gate*] is to teach clearly, and the end summarizes the meaning of the mantra in four aspects. What are the four meanings? The illusion-like, emptiness,

[46] Peking reads *bstad*; Derge reads *bstan*.

signlessness, and wishlessness. *Tadyathā* means "like this." *Gate, gate*: "gone, gone"; all mindfulness has gone [to be] like illusions. *Pāragate*: "gone beyond"; beyond mindfulness, one goes beyond to emptiness. *Pārasaṃgate*: "gone completely beyond"; beyond the illusion-like and emptiness, one goes beyond to signlessness. *Bodhi svāhā*: "become enlightened"; having purified the afflictions and all objects of knowledge, one transcends awareness. These set forth the four nonabidings, the four direct perceptions, and the four samādhis. If one takes such instructions, one should do so attentively.

Śāriputra, a bodhisattva mahāsattva should practice the perfection of wisdom in that way means "be attentive." *Then the Bhagavan rose from samādhi*: he [in fact] neither rose from the profound samādhi or entered into the absorption, but he displayed the equipoise and subsequent attainment for the perception of sentient beings. [294b] *To the bodhisattva, the mahāsattva, the noble Avalokiteśvara*: because he [Avalokiteśvara] unmistakenly set forth the thought of the buddhas who abide in the three times, the meaning of the profound perfection of wisdom just as he [the Buddha] intended it, he was pleased. Thus, it was seen by the eye of the Buddha, and he said, *Well done*. Furthermore, because he was contemplating the samādhi called "perception of the profound" he said it twice, *Well done, well done. Child of good lineage, it is thus* is said for the sake of those with confidence in the manifest reality, the Mahāyāna lineage. The continuative [*te*] is a term meaning, the mind is not freed by the phenomena which appear. *Son of good lineage, it is thus*: is a term [meaning], when one understands the profound reality, the mind is liberated. *Just as you have taught it*: as long as one remains in the world, one must rely on illusion-like appearances. Having been awakened into the unsurpassed enlightenment that is beyond the world, one considers the welfare of sentient beings and must rely solely on the profound reality. *Practice the profound perfection of wisdom*: those who seek the path to liberation must rely only on the profound. Thus it is said many times, over and over again. The virtuous friends who cause confidence in the meaning of the profound *are admired even by the tathāgatas of the three times.*

The Bhagavan having so spoken, the venerable Śāriputra, the bodhisattva, the mahāsattva, the noble Avalokiteśvara, and all those surrounding and those of the world, the gods, humans, demigods, and gandharvas were filled with admiration and praised the words of the Bhagavan. This is easy to understand so I will not explain it. This completes the commentary on the *Sūtra on the Heart of the Bhagavatī Perfection of Wisdom* called "Lamp for the Meaning." [295a]

In the past, some Tibetan virtuous friends asked for teaching from the excellent venerable guru Vajrapāṇi at Lalitapattana in Nepal. One day before the time for the excellent guru to teach the doctrine had arrived, the Tibetan virtuous friends recited a sūtra. The excellent guru asked the translator, "What was that they recited?" The translator said, "The *Heart of the Perfection of Wisdom*." [Vajrapāṇi said], "Oh, if the *Heart of the Perfection of Wisdom* has spread to Tibet, the Buddha's prophecy is true." He asked whether they knew the instructions on the meaning of the *Heart Sūtra*. The translator answered that they had not sought them. "Well then," he said, "I will give you the instructions." They carefully memorized and wrote down the instructions on the meaning of the *Heart Sūtra*.

> Who has drunk the intoxicating water, the honey from the lotuses at the guru's feet? Who shall listen at the mouth of the bee, drunk on the uncreated great bliss? Who thinks there may be truth in the drunken words? Though they may not be true, please think about them, agreeable friends.
>
> If emptiness were the method, then buddhahood could not be. Since there could be no fruit other than this cause, the method is not emptiness. The conquerors teach emptiness to overcome the conception of self in those who have turned away from views and in those who seek the view of self.[47]
>
> I bow down again and again with faith and respect to the mother of the conquerors of the three times, the equality of mundane existence and peace, to the jewel-like nature of the texts, teaching the skillful methods for bringing bliss to transmigrators.
>
> This commentary was written with enthusiasm and a wish to be of benefit. My prayer is that the lineage and teaching will pass from hand to hand of excellent persons. Because reality is true, may it be so established.

The Indian abbot himself and the translator, the monk Seng ge rgyal mtshan, revised the text.[48]

[47] This is a quotation from the first chapter of the *Vajrapañjara Tantra*, P 11, vol. 1., 223.4.4–6.

[48] This sentence is absent in the Peking.

Nine

The *Heart Sūtra* as Exorcism

> It is as if ritual practices were wishes or supplications of collective distress, expressed in a language that is (by defintion) collective (in which respect they are very closely related to music)—forlorn attempts to act on the natural world as one acts on the social world, to apply strategies to the natural world that work on other men, in certain conditions, that is strategies of authority and reciprocity, to signify intentions, wishes, desires or orders to it, through performative words or deeds, which make sense without signifying intention.
>
> —Pierre Bourdieu, *The Logic of Practice*

IN THE EARLY SPRING of 1976 the Tibetan monk and scholar Lati Rimpoche was in residence at the University of Virginia. He was living with Professor Jeffrey Hopkins in a faculty apartment and I, a second-year graduate student in the Buddhist Studies program, was staying in a small room next to that of Lati Rimpoche in order to assist in attending to his needs. He was a prominent incarnate lama who had never traveled outside of Tibet or India before and he spoke no English. In an apartment down the hall lived Anne Klein, Harvey Aronson, and Elizabeth Napper, who also helped care for Lati Rimpoche, especially in the preparation of his evening meal. The early months of his stay in Charlottesville were understandably difficult for Rimpoche. Apart from Professor Hopkins, he had no one to talk to; I initially understood very little of what he said. Our daily afternoon walks were passed in silence for many days, a situation that only improved in the spring when we would walk to a nearby park to watch people playing softball. Rimpoche found it uproariously funny when someone swung and missed and he would laugh loudly, often drawing menacing glances from the assembled teams from Albemarle Appliance and Shiflett's Farm Supply, glances that only became more menacing when they saw that the laughter emanated from a shave-pate Oriental in flowing red robes sitting on a picnic table. I would smile weakly and wave, trying to communicate my wish that they not harm us.

In the early spring, Rimpoche seemed preoccupied. I knew that he had not been sleeping well because he kept me awake almost every night with a terrible cough. He had apparently had disturbing dreams. And in retrospect, I would not be surprised to learn that his diet of a boiled lamb chop, boiled frozen green beans, and boiled egg noodles that he ate for lunch and dinner every day for eighteen months had sent him into clinical depression. When I would take him his afternoon tea on a beautiful sunny day, I would often find him with the shades drawn in his room, wearing some strange green crystal glasses (like those worn by Dorothy in the Emerald City of Oz), ringing his bell, beating his *damaru*, and chanting. One day while shopping in a health food store I came across something that I thought might lift his spirits. It was an exorbitantly priced bag of roasted barley powder, *tsampa*, the famous staple of the monastic diet in old Tibet. I took it into his room and presented it to him. By that time I had learned enough Tibetan to understand what he said: "I don't like *tsampa*."

I was surprised a few weeks later to find Lati Rimpoche in the kitchen with the package of *tsampa* emptied into a bowl. He had a large cardboard box on the table and was making the *tsampa* into a dough. He first made four cones about eight inches high (which I recognized from books as *torma*, a form of ritual offering) and placed them in the four corners of the box. He then set about making a human figure, embedding toothpicks to provide stability. He worked with great speed and skill, beautifully forming the hands and fingers. Soon it became clear that this was the figure of a monk and when he finally finished the head, it was also apparent that the monk bore an uncanny resemblance to Lati Rimpoche. He took the box back into his room, where he arranged some bowls with meat and beer on the bottom. He then told me to return an hour later. When I came back, he was seated with a text open before him. He told me that upon his signal I was to pick up the box and then, when he clapped his hands, I was to take the box outside and set it next to a stream. I was then to return quickly home without looking back. When he clapped, I picked up the box and left the apartment, but before performing my task, I could not resist taking the box down the hall to show some of my fellow graduate students. We all admired his skill and wondered what this could possibly mean. With this brief detour completed, I followed my instructions, walking down Rugby Road carrying the box, trying to think of where the closest stream might be. Not wanting to draw any more stares than I already had, I crossed Beta Bridge and walked down to the railroad tracks where there was a dirty trickle of water in some woods behind a church. I set down my burden and ran.

What follows is a discussion of the most common use to which the *Heart Sūtra* is put in Tibet, as part of a rite for (literally) turning away demons (*bdud bzlog*), what I render loosely as "exorcism."[1] The discussion that follows is not of the performance of a ritual but rather of the contents of a ritual text, a manual that explains how the rite of exorcism is to be performed. The work is entitled *The Procedure for Repelling Demons Based on the Heart Sūtra, the Summation of the Vast, Intermediate, and Condensed Mothers* (*Yum rgyas 'bring bsdus gsum gyi don bsdus shes rab snying po'i sgo nas bdud bzlog gi rim pa*)[2] and it is attributed to Kumārabuddha, who states in the colophon that his work is based on a handbook by one dBu dkar ba of [s]Kyi ljang. The ritual set forth in the text is prescribed as a cure for a wide range of calamities, misfortunes, dangers, and afflictions, including epidemics, possession by demons, sick livestock, loss of wealth or property, dying under a bad star, false accusations, and bad dreams. The assumption in each case is that a malevolent force has intruded into the human domain. That force must be brought under control and expulsed, to return to its proper realm.

The text begins with two histories: the history of the lineage and the history to inspire belief. The first is simply a lineage list of the transmission of the practice, designed to establish the Buddhist pedigree, beginning of course with the perfect Buddha, and then moving to Avalokita,

[1] For discussions of related exorcism rites practiced in modern Nepal, see Sherry B. Ortner, *Sherpas through Their Rituals* (Cambridge: Cambridge University Press, 1978), pp. 91–127; and Stan Royal Mumford, *Himalayan Dialogue: Tibetan Lamas and Gurung Shamans in Nepal* (Madison: University of Wisconsin Press, 1989), pp. 140–64.

[2] The version of the text I have used is a badly worn blockprint from the Library of Tibetan Works and Archives in Dharmsala, India, a photocopy of which was kindly provided to me by Hubert Decleer. This edition contains no information on the place or date of publication. I have subsequently found three other versions of the text, each of which contains minor additions and elaborations on the basic ritual. The first, a dGe lugs version with the same title, is found in the fourth volume of an eleven-volume set, published in India, of ritual texts of the rGyud smad tantric college, entitled *gSang chen dpal ldan smad rgyud grva tshang gis nyams bzhes chos skor gyi rim pa*, pp. 309–31. The second, kindly provided to me by Professor Yael Bentor, is a Sa skya work by Thar rtse mKhan chen Byams pa nam mkha' 'chi med, entitled *Yum rgyas 'bring rnams kyi don bsdus pa shes rab snying po'i sgo nas bdud bzlong gi cho ga bar chad kun sel* in Dpal ldan Sa skya gsuṅ rab series, no. 5 (New Delhi: Ngawang Topgay, 1974), pp. 87–165. A third version (also kindly provided by Professor Bentor) is by the great *ris med* master 'Jam mgon kong sprul blo gros mtha' yas (1813–99), entitled, *bKa' 'khor bar pa'i yang bcud shes rab snying po'i mdo la brten pa'i bdud zlog bar chad kun sel lag len*, in Rgya chen bka' mdzod: *A Collection of the Writings of 'Jam-mgon Koṅ-sprul Blo-gros-mtha'-yas*, vol. 13 (Paro, Bhutan: Ngodrup, Kyichu Temple, 1976), pp. 59–99. A close comparison of these texts remains a desideratum. See also a work by the dGe lugs polymath Sum pa mkhan po Ye shes dpal 'byor (1704–76) that brings together a number of sūtric and tantric practices connected with the *Heart Sūtra*, entitled *Shes rab snying po'i sgrubs thabs las byor bcas pa mun sel sgron ma*, in *Collected Works of Sum-pa-mkhan-po*, vol. 3 (ga), Śata-piṭaka series 216 (New Delhi: International Academy of Indian Culture, 1975), pp. 627–62. Unfortunately, this edition is very difficult to read and is entirely illegible in places.

Mahākaruṇa, a Nepalese *paṇḍita* and translator who taught Rva Lo tsa ba rdo rje grags and 'Gos Lo tsa ba rta nag khug pa lhas btsas, then [Dharmakīrti of] Suvarṇadvīpa, Atiśa (982–1054), who brought it to Tibet and transmitted it to his disciple, 'Brom ston pa (1005–64), who in turn gave it to Po to ba rin chen gsal (1031–1105), who passed it on to the translator [Tshul khrims] 'Byung gnas rdo rje of sTong (sTeng) (1107–90), then dBu dkar ba of [s]Kyi ljang, and Kumārabuddha.

The other history, the history to inspire belief, comprises two stories illustrating the efficacy of the exorcism ritual. In the first story, the ritual is used to defeat an evil magician.

> The lineage was received by dBu dkar of [s]Kyi ljang. He performed [the practice of its] protective deity and gained faith in it. In that area lived dBu dkar of [s]Kyi ljang and someone called Ku lo. Ku lo was performing black magic of [deities] such as red and black Yama and red and black Dark One (*Mun pa*) and had liberated [i.e., killed] many people with his power. One day, dBu dkar of [s]Kyi ljang offered Ku lo something to drink, gave him some clothing, and offered him counsel, "Your power works quickly, but afterward there will be certain [negative karmic] effects." [Ku lo] was hurt by what he said and became enraged, swearing an oath, "You will not live [another] week." Ku lo left. Then, because dBu dkar practiced this [rite], in a week Ku lo's own power was deflected back upon him and he died. He [dBu dkar then] surpassed [everyone] in repelling curses.

In the second story, the ritual is used to exorcise a malevolent spirit of an evil king or unethical lama, known simply as "the king" (*rgyal po*), which I translate below as "spirit king."

> A Chinese named Pha 'tsho was being afflicted by the spirit king. An astrologer made a horoscope and said, "If you perform a rite for removing obstacles with the corpse of a young child, place it in a clay pot and get rid of it in [the central province of] dBus, it will help." He did that, and took it to dBus where it was purchased by dGe ser in Phan yul. The spirit king attacked dGe ser, and all of his horses and donkeys were destroyed. The spirit king appeared [then] to dGe ser, who asked him, "Whom do you fear?" "I fear dBu dkar of [s]Kyi ljang, no one else." dGe ser then tricked him, saying, "Tell me where he is and I will kill him. Then you will fear no one." He [the spirit king] told him what had happened and gave him directions. dGe ser went to the place of dBu dkar and explained the situation. He was given this very sādhana and with it dGe ser repulsed the demon. From that point on, the harm of the spirit king was pacified and [dGe ser] was able to use his mind for the dharma. Then the spirit king returned to the Chinese Pha 'tsho. Pha 'tsho said, "Whom do you fear that you have come back?" "I returned in fear of dBu dkar of Kyi ljang and dGe ser; up until now I have been staying at dGe ser's place." Pha 'tsho said, "I will go to

> dBus again. You guide me. The two of us will go to dGe ser's place and will stay there." dGe ser and Pha 'tsho met and he explained to him what had happened before and gave him an auspicious gift. He asked for the method of getting rid of the spirit king and was given this [rite]. By practicing it he was freed from the harm of the spirit king. In the same way, if you make effort at this, whatever you wish for, such as the supreme achievements, will be quickly attained.

The remainder of the text is devoted to instructions for the performance of the rite of exorcism. The person performing the rite (whom we will call the officiant) first places either a painting or statue of the Buddha in the center of a white cloth and arranges offerings in front of it. To the east (i.e., in front of the Buddha image) he places seven images of dough stamped with the impression of the divine demon Māra, in the form of a white human on a white horse, with flowers in his right hand (the flowers of desire that Māra shoots at his victims) and a noose in his left. Behind the images of Māra the officiant places a line of seven draught animals, seven dogs (perhaps substitutes for animals sacrificed in a previous age), seven thin tubes of dough (*chang bu*), seven small pieces of meat, seven buttons of dough (*mtheb kyu*). In the south he places seven images of the Demon of the Afflictions (*nyon mongs, kleśa*) in the form of a yellow human on a yellow horse. In his right hand is a sword, in his left a noose. In the west, the officiant places seven images of the Demon of the Aggregates (*phung po, skandha*) in the form of a red human on a red horse. In his right hand is a spear, in his left a noose. In the north, the officiant places seven images of the demon who is the Lord of Death in the form of a black human on a black horse. In his right hand is a club, in his left a noose. For each of the others, the officiant also lays out the five rows of draught animals, dogs, and so on. He then prepares individual offering bowls for the Buddha and the four demons with something to eat and three kinds of *torma*.

It is then necessary to prepare the *ngar mi*[3] (usually translated as effigy) of the person who has commissioned the performance of the rite, the patron (*yon bdag*). The officiant makes a dough statue of the patron after having the patron breathe on and spit on the dough. The effigy is then dressed in a garment made from clothing belonging to the patron and is placed in front of the Buddha image with its face turned toward the Buddha and its back toward the officiant. In this position, the effigy stands as both a substitute and a protector for the patron, acting as his surrogate before the demons.

The officiant then visualizes himself as the Buddha, seated in the midst

[3] The term *ngar mi* can be read literally either as "powerful human" or as "human as I [am]." For a discussion of the term *ngar*, see Samten G. Karmay, "L'Homme et le boeuf: Le rituel de glud («rançon»)," *Journal Asiatique* 279, nos. 3–4 (1991): 330, n. 14.

of the four demons. This is a position of both danger and power, from which the long process of exorcism is executed, with the officiant, as the Buddha, playing the role of first host of the demons, then as the agent who enters into a contract with the demons, and finally as their conqueror. The text instructs the officiant to recite:

> From the nature of emptiness [appears] a cushion of jewels, lotus, and moon [upon which sits] the chief of teachers, the complete and perfect Buddha Śākyamuni. His body is gold, with one face and two arms. His right hand touches the earth, his left is in the gesture of equipoise. On his head is the crown protrusion. He is adorned with the thirty-two auspicious marks and eighty auspicious minor marks, such as wheels on the soles of his feet. He emanates boundless light and beams of light. A retinue appears; the pledge and wisdom-beings nondual. He is attended to the right by the noble Avalokiteśvara and to the left by the eight dear bodhisattva sons[4] and the eight supreme śrāvakas,[5] such as Śāriputra. At his heart on a lotus and moon is the great mother surrounded by her sons, the buddhas of the ten directions. At the heart of the great mother is a moon maṇḍala. At its center is the letter *āḥ*. At the edge appear the letters of the *Heart Sūtra*. They radiate beams of light together with their own sound, making an offering that delights the conquerors and their children. All the blessings and powers gather and touch those gathered for the rite, as well as all sentient beings, purifying all sins and obstructions and pacifying all sickness, demons, and obstacles; the meaning of the eighteen emptinesses is created in your mind.

Here, rather than visualizing the Buddha and the residents of the maṇḍala as arrayed before the meditator, as in Dārikapa's sādhana, the officiant visualizes himself as Śākyamuni Buddha, adorned with the major and minor marks. Instead of sitting in the middle of a maṇḍala, he is surrounded by a retinue, with Avalokiteśvara on the right and eight bodhisattvas (among whom Avalokiteśvara appears again) and eight śrāvakas on the left. As in Dārikapa's sādhana, the visualized pledge-beings fuse with the actual wisdom-beings. The meditator next visualizes the goddess Prajñāpāramitā seated on a moon disc, surrounded by buddhas and bodhisattvas. Moving to an even smaller scale, the meditator imagines that there is a moon disc in the center of her heart, upon which stands the letter *āḥ*.[6] At an even more minute level, the officiant

[4] Mañjuśrī, Vajrapāṇi, Avalokiteśvara, Kṣitigarbha, Sarvanīvaraṇaviskambhin, Ākāśagarbha, Maitreya, and Samantabhadra.

[5] Śāriputra, Maudgalyāyana, Mahākāśyapa, Ānanda, Rahula, Aniruddha, Subhūti, and Upāli.

[6] Rather than the long *ā*, one might expect here instead the short *a*, the symbol of the perfection of wisdom and subject of the *Perfection of Wisdom in One Letter Sūtra* (*Ekākṣarīprajñāpāramitā*).

is instructed to visualize the letters of the *Heart Sūtra* standing upright around the edge of the moon disc at the goddess's heart, not simply the letters of the mantra, but the entire sūtra, for as we will see below, the entire sūtra functions as a mantra in this ritual. The letters of the sūtra radiate both light and their own sound, serving as offerings to the buddhas and bodhisattvas, who in turn alleviate the sufferings and purify all those gathered for the performance of the rite (and all sentient beings) as the officiant contemplates the meaning of emptiness. Here, as in Dārikapa's sādhana, emptiness appears to function as the water of the Vedic sacrifice, lustrating the officiant for his imminent task.

The officiant is then instructed to recite the *Heart Sūtra* as much as possible and then make the standard offerings of flowers, incense, lamps, perfume, and so on with the appropriate mantras followed by verses praising Śākyamuni and Prajñāpāramitā. He then moistens the images and offerings with water and invites the four actual demons to come from their abodes, the four formless absorptions,[7] and dissolve into their molded images. For example, to the Demon of the Afflictions, he says: "O yellow Demon of the Afflictions, abiding in the realm of neither existence nor nonexistence.[8] Afflicted sentient beings wander in saṃsāra. Assembled army of the Demon of the Afflictions, so that the afflictions of sentient beings might be removed, when I, the mantra holder, invite you, I beseech you to come here for just a little while and abide in your image. *Jaḥ hūṃ baṃ hoḥ.*" This is the same mantra that is used to cause the wisdom-beings, the actual buddhas and bodhisattvas, to merge with their visualized doubles (the pledge-beings) to bring the beneficent deities into the presence of the meditator. Here, however, something else seems to be at work. The four demons are believed to be invisible, perniciously invading the human domain undetected but for the harm they inflict. In order that the demons be placated and turned back, they must be made visible and brought into physical presence. Hence, dough images are made for them, which they are then invited to enter and animate; "the making and existence of the artifact that portrays something gives one power over that which is portrayed."[9]

[7] The four demons are presumably said (in this text) to reside in the formless absorptions (*arūpyasamāpatti*) because they are invisible. The deity Māra is generally said to abide in the realm of desire (*kāmadhātu*), for example, as Nandikeśvara in the Heaven of Controlling Others' Emanations (*paranirmittavaśavartin*).

[8] The fourth of the four formless absorptions, also known as the realm of neither discrimination nor nondiscrimination (*'du shes med 'du shes med min skye mched, naivasaṃjñānāsaṃjñāyatanaṃ*).

[9] Michael Taussig, *Mimesis and Alterity: A Particular History of the Senses* (New York: Routledge and Kegan Paul, 1993), p. 13.

The text then provides the *Heart Sūtra* in full, with the instruction that it is to be repeated nine times. After each set of nine repetitions, the officiant claps and turns one of the seven rows of demons, draught animals, dogs, tubes of dough, pieces of meat, and buttons of dough so that it faces outward. The sūtra is then recited nine more times and another row is turned, until the seven rows in the east have all been turned around, requiring sixty-three recitations of the sūtra. The same procedure is repeated for the demons in the other three directions, such that the sūtra must be repeated 252 times to complete the process. The four demons and their retinues have been turned away (*bzlog*) from the Buddha by the power of the *Heart Sūtra* so that they now face outward, toward the effigy of the patron.

If the rite is being performed for a sick person, the officiant is then instructed to say:

> *Namo*. I bow down to the lama. I bow down to the Buddha. I bow down to the dharma. I bow down to the saṃgha. I bow down to the great mother, the perfection of wisdom. Through bowing down to them, may these, our true words, be effective. Just as in the past the lord of gods, Śakra [Indra], contemplated the profound meaning of the perfection of wisdom and, through reciting the words, repelled all opposing forces such as the sinful demons, so in the same way, may I also contemplate the profound meaning of the great mother, the perfection of wisdom, and through reciting the words repel all opposing forces such as the sinful demons and for this [sick person] so and so. May those obstructing demons who led in the disease in the beginning, who took up residence [literally, "build a nest"] in the middle, and who provide no benefit in the end all now be repulsed [clap], destroyed [clap], pacified [clap], and completely pacified by the performance of this repelling of demons with the *Heart Sūtra* and by the words of truth of the noble three jewels. May he [or she] be freed from the 84,000 types of obstruction and the conditions of discord and harm, and may he [or she] be enriched by the good fortune that brings harmony. May there be happiness and goodness here today.

Here, a further connection to the Perfection of Wisdom sūtras is drawn with what Stanley Tambiah calls a "primeval precedent,"[10] an allusion to an incident that occurs in (at least) the *Aṣṭasāhasrikāprajñāpāramitā* (Perfection of Wisdom in 8,000 Stanzas)[11] and the *Aṣṭadasasāhasrikā-*

[10] Stanley J. Tambiah, *Culture, Thought, and Social Action* (Cambridge, Mass.: Harvard University Press, 1985), p. 152. Tambiah's discussion of a Sinhalese exorcism rite (pp. 146–53) provides useful points of parallel with the Tibetan *Heart Sūtra* exorcism. See also John Halverson, "Dynamics of Exorcism: The Sinhalese Sanniyakuma," *History of Religions* 10, no. 4 (1971): 334–59.

[11] See P. L. Vaidya, ed., *Aṣṭasāhasrikā Prajñāpāramitā*, Buddhist Sanskrit Texts, no. 4 (Darbhanga, India: The Mithila Institute), p. 39, ll. 11–25. For an English translation, see

prajñāpāramitā (Perfection of Wisdom in 18,000 Stanzas) in which Māra conjures a fourfold army and approaches the Buddha. Śakra recognizes him and turns him and his host away by calling to mind and repeating the perfection of wisdom.

If the rite is being performed in order to destroy an enemy, the officiant is instructed to say, "By the power of the words of truth of the noble three jewels, may our enemy so and so today be summoned, liberated [i.e., killed], and his flesh and blood eaten by the gods and demons of the world. May his consciousness be led into the *dharmadhātu*."

Offerings of food and the *torma* are then made to the demons, with requests that they refrain from further harm. The demons, now residing physically in their dough images and facing toward the officiant, are further brought under control by bringing them into a social relation, the position of the guest, to be offered hospitality in the form of food and gifts by the officiant, acting as host. For example, to the divine demon Māra the officiant is instructed to say, "I offer this biscuit, endowed with a hundred flavors and a thousand potencies, to the assembled armies of the child of gods. May it turn into enjoyments, their exhaustion unknown, that agree with their individual thoughts. Having delighted and satisfied them all, I pray that all of the harm unleashed by the four demons will be cast aside."

The gift to be offered to the demons is the *ngar mi*, the effigy of the patron. First, the person whom the effigy represents cleans the effigy with water that has been in his or her mouth. The officiant then blesses the effigy. Once again, lustration is provided by emptiness:

> From the nature of emptiness, *oṃ āḥ hūṃ svāhā*. The effigy arisen from the melting [of those letters] comes to have all of the aggregates, constituents, and sources complete, is endowed with the qualities of the desire realm, and has a treasure of wealth of resources whose exhaustion is not known. *Hūṃ*. This beautiful effigy of a human I offer today as ransom for the patron. As to its cause, it is made from jewels. It is adorned with colored silk. Its ornaments sway. I have put turquoise in his mouth and I send gold in his hands, [all] offered into the hands of the four demons. [If, hereafter, the patron] meets them in a pass, they turn around in the pass; [if he] meets them in a valley, they turn around in the valley. His [i.e., the effigy's] skill in speech is clarity, his skill in movement is grace. What is greater than the beautiful fillet on his head? His auspicious body is adorned with ornaments; this auspicious person has great power. I have no attachment to him [and offer him freely]. In order to purchase the patron [from the demons], I send this ransom today. May it remain as

Edward Conze, *The Perfection of Wisdom in Eight Thousand Lines and Its Verse Summary* (Bolinas: Four Seasons Foundation, 1973), pp. 110–11.

> ransom for the great lords of ransom [i.e., the demons]. This is a ransom for his eight collections of consciousness [eye, ear, nose, tongue, body, and mental consciousnesses and the afflicted mind (*nyon yid*, *kḷṣṭamanas*), and the foundation consciousness (*kun gzhi rnam shes*, *ālayavijñāna*)], five elements [earth, water, fire, wind, space] and his [twelvefold] dependent origination, a ransom [for] his [eighteen] constituents (*khams*, *dhātu*) and [twelve] sources (*skyed mched*, *āyatana*), a ransom for his six collections of sense organs. A great person of grain with clothes of the five types of precious substances [gold, silver, turquoise, coral, pearl]. In his right hand a bannered spear that turns back the onslaughts of saṃsāra, in his left a pliant rope. His right foot is wisdom—copper, his left foot is great method—iron. I offer such a great person made of dough as a ransom for this patron to the assembled armies of the four demons together with their retinues. Because this ransom is more auspicious than the person [the patron], this beautiful ransom is received by all the assembled armies of the four demons. May they now prepare to go to their own abodes. Do not break the words of the three jewels . At the request of Śakra [Indra], the king of gods, the Bhagavan Śākyamuni summoned the four demons and gave them a ransom.[12] Remember your promise to follow his instructions; do not harm those assembled here. Go, demons, to your own abodes. By satisfying the demons with the ransom, may harm by the four demons be pacified.

The *ngar mi* is called a ransom (*glud*)[13] and is repeatedly praised; it is described as being superior to the patron of whom it is a replica. This is the key moment in the ritual, in which the demons, in attendance at a feast as guests of the officiant, in the form of the Buddha, are asked to

[12] This is the second point in the text in which reference is made to Indra to suggest the ancient (read, "Indian") origin of the practice. In the first case, Indra is said to have called to mind and recited the Perfection of Wisdom in order to repulse Māra and his hosts. And, as noted above, this is indeed related in the *prajñāpāramitā* sūtras. In this case, the Buddha is said to have offered the demons a ransom (*glud*). To my knowledge, this story does not occur in the *prajñāpāramitā* corpus. However, it is not uncommon for Tibetan ritual texts to attribute the origin of a rite to a request made by Indra to the Buddha. For example , the *brGya bzhi'i cho ga legs mdzes 'phreng ba* by rMor chen Kun dga' lhun grub, a ritual text in which the *Heart Sūtra* is also recited, begins, "In the past, the lord of gods Śakra was afflicted with a virulent disease. Upon being asked by the gods, the Bhagavan thought that the lord of gods was possessed by a demon. He composed this 'rite of the four hundred' as a result of which he was liberated from the four demons and freed from the disease." See rMor chen Kun dga' lhun grub (1654–1726), *brGya bzhi'i cho ga legs mdzes 'phreng ba*, ed. Sa skya Gon ma Kun dga's blo gros (New Delhi: Ngawang Topgay, 1974), 1b4–2a2. See also 28a4-b1. I am grateful to Dan Martin for providing me with a copy of this text. For a discussion of the *brgya bzhi* rite, see Anne-Marie Blondeau, "Questions préliminaires sur les rituels *mdos*," in F. Meyer, ed., *Tibet: civilisation et société* (Paris: Éditions de la Fondation Singer-Polignac, 1990), pp. 97–99.

[13] The most thorough discussion of the concept of *glud* is that of Karmay, "L'Homme," pp. 327–81.

participate in an exchange. In return for releasing the patron from their power, they will be given something of greater value, the *ngar mi*. This does not seem to be a case of confusing the demons into thinking that the *ngar mi* is the patron; rather, the officiant's task is to convince the demons that the *ngar mi* is more desirable than the patron. The assumption, of course, is that they cannot but agree to the bargain. As a result, the person represented by the *ngar mi* will eventually come to possess the wealth and beauty of his dough double. Referring to the gift, Mauss writes, "Invested with life, often possessing individuality, it seeks to return to what Hertz called its 'place of origin' or to produce, on behalf of the clan and the native soil from which it sprang, an equivalent to replace it."[14]

Once the offering of the effigy has been made to the demons, the next step is the dispatching of the demons and the removal of the *torma*. The demons, as guests, have been fed and offered a gift. It is now time for them to depart. The officiant says:

> *Hūṃ*. I am the Bhagavan Śākyamuni. I am the great and glorious Guhyapati. I am the opponent of demons and obstructions. Great demons, gods, nāgas, evil spirits of the night, hungry ghosts, flesh eaters, demonic lady of disease, may you not transgress my words. By receiving this ransom *torma*, the sickness, demons, and impediments of myself and the donor, lord of the offering, are pacified, the grip is broken, the bonds are released, the knots are loosed, the suppression is lifted. If the deeds that are requested are not established, the punishment [decided by] the Sugata in the past is that [you] sentient beings will be reborn in the hells again and again and will experience great suffering. Therefore, may we not be harmed. Four demons, prepare to return to your abodes. The true and infallible words of the Buddha are achieved accordingly and bliss is attained. I and the patron, lord of the offering, are freed from the four great demons and the impediments, sickness, and demons are quickly pacified; the aims of our intentions are achieved. Assembled armies of the four demons, do as you have been instructed and go to your abodes in the four realms. Demon Child of Gods [the *devaputra* Māra] and your hosts of white, go to the abode of nothingness. Yellow Demon of the Afflictions, go to limitless consciousness. Red Demon of the Aggregates, go to the abode of neither existence nor nonexistence. Lord of Death and your hosts of black, go to the realm of limitless space. Demon Child of Gods, Demon of the Afflictions, Demon of the Aggregates, Demon Lord of Death [all of whom] arise from the obstructions to omniscience and the afflictive obstructions, assembled demonic armies of the four demons, receive this offering of *torma*. Completely abandon the intention to do harm and mischief to the patron, lord of the offering, and myself. Remain in your respective beautiful palaces, endowed with a mind of

[14] Marcel Mauss, *The Gift*, trans. W. D. Hall (New York: W. W. Norton, 1990), p. 13.

> bliss; do not harm those assembled here. Go blissfully to your own abodes. *Samaya prabeśaya phaṭ.*

Here the demons are both cajoled and threatened, invited to return with the gifts they have received to their palaces in the formless realm. The patron, in order to save himself, gives up something of himself by pressing precious substances into the body of his effigy. This is what allows the officiant to deceive the demons into accepting the effigy, believing the mannequin of dough to be more desirable than his human double. The offering of the effigy is thus a gift given in order to receive; in effect the demons and the patron (with the officiant acting as his agent) enter into a contract. The demons are to understand that any breach of this contract carries with it a penalty; should they not keep their part of the bargain, the officiant, through his surrogate, the Buddha, will, in Maurice Bloch's phrase, transform "prey into hunter" and visit them with punishment.

The next step is to take all of the images and offerings (with the exception of the Buddha image) to a safe distance and then place them facing away from the place where the rite was performed. The location, however, depends on the purpose for which the rite is performed. For example, if the rite is for the welfare of a sick person, they are to be put in a cemetery. If a horoscope predicts that danger is approaching as a result of the "fourth-year executioner," the inauspicious year that occurs four years after one's birth animal in the twelve-year cycle, or as a result of the "conjunction of the seven," the ill fortune that results from a relationship with someone seven years apart in age, they are to be placed in the direction the harm is predicted to come from. If it is for bringing happiness, it is placed either above or below a crossroads. If a curse is being deflected, they are placed in the direction of the curse. If one is making a curse, they are placed in the direction of the enemy. If one has been harmed by the spirit king, they are placed at the base of a temple or a stūpa. If one has been harmed by a female devil, it is placed outside the town. If one has been harmed by a nāga, they are to be placed at a lake or a spring. "In brief, it is said that wherever the harm comes from, deliver it there."

Before going, however, it is important to make an offering of golden elixir (*gser skyems*) to all the other demons who might do harm. This is a long section. Here is part of what it says:

> *Bhyo.* Sole mother, lady of pestilence together with your retinue, in the left hands of each of you is the x of a demon. If an x [meaning death] should fall on the patron, officiant, or those surrounding, please erase the x. Sole mother [*dPal ldan lha mo*], in your left hand are the dice and black and white fortune-telling stones of a demon. When I and the patron, the lord of the offering, cast our fortunes, separate the black and white dice now. When you gather the red

> lots [with the names] of those you will harm, remove ours now. In your left armpit is the black bag of disease tied with five hundred snakes [and] a multitude of spirits are then released [from the bag]. Cast out the army of spirits now. In order to purchase the lord of the offering the exorcism is offered. I am not mistaken in making the offering. Receive it and revel in delight. Repel the ritual weapons of Buddhist and Bon priests now. Repel nāgas, plagues, and curses now. Repel enemies, brigands, and thieves now. Repel evil gossip now. Repel the loss of property and animals due to accident now. Repel the death of family members now. Repel epidemics and plagues now. Repel false accusation of the innocent now. Through the repelling rite of the *Heart Sūtra*, may all classes of disrupting harm be repelled right now. Through blessings together with the *Heart Sūtra* [exorcism], evil fortune [connected with] earth, water, fire, and wind are repelled. Through the formation of the ransom effigy, offerings, and so forth, evil omens are pacified in my land. I pray that loss [due to] sickness and epidemic be repelled. Thus, wherever there is danger, may all the damage of the four demons be repelled to their own abode by the compassion of the three jewels, the blessings of the *Heart Sūtra*, and my power as a mantra holder. May they be turned back right now. *Samaya prabeśaya phaṭ*.

At this point, everything is carried away as music is played. According to the text, it is not necessary for the officiant himself to carry the *torma* to the appointed place, unless he is placing a curse on someone or unless the purpose of the rite is "very important." The text does not specify who should go under ordinary circumstances, but we know from other sources that a person of low social class, such as a beggar or a corpse cutter, will be hired for the purpose.[15] (This was apparently the role I played for Lati Rimpoche).

The rite then concludes with a blessing, calling upon the five buddhas and a sixth deity, perhaps suggesting the chtonic concerns of the exorcism ritual, the goddess of the earth:

> *Hūṃ* The good fortune from the center, the good fortune of Vairocana, the good fortune of an auspicious body, *Jaya*! bestow them on this patron today. By this good fortune may he have happiness. *Hūṃ*. The good fortune from the east, the good fortune of Vajrasattva, the good fortune of stability, *Jaya*! bestow them on this patron today. By this good fortune may he have happiness. *Hūṃ*. The good fortune from the south, the good fortune of Ratnasambhava, the good fortune of the granting of all wishes, *Jaya*! bestow them on this patron today. By this good fortune may he have happiness. *Hūṃ*. The good for-

[15] Réne de Nebesky-Wojkowitz, *Oracles and Demons of Tibet: The Cult and Iconography of the Tibetan Protective Deities* (London: Oxford University Press, 1956), pp. 511–13.

tune from the west, the good fortune of Amitābha, power, wind, fame, and good fortune, *Jaya*! bestow them on this patron today. By this good fortune may he have happiness. *Hūṃ*. The good fortune from the north, the good fortune of Amogasiddhi, the good fortune of spontaneous deeds, *Jaya*! bestow them on this patron today. By this good fortune may he have happiness. *Hūṃ*. The good fortune from the downward direction, the good fortune of the earth goddess Dṛḍha, the good fortune of life-bearing grains, *Jaya*! bestow them on this patron today. By this good fortune may he have happiness. May good fortune arise in the day, *la la*; may good fortune be stored up at night, *li li*; By whatever good fortune occurs in the three times, may we be happy here today.

The usual offerings, prayers, and dedications are then made, with the officiant reminded to keep in mind throughout that both he and the patron are by nature empty. The text concludes with a final testimony to the rite's potency:

Specifically, harm from evil spells cast by Buddhist and Bon priests, curses, destroying an enemy who harms with disease, the spread of an epidemic that moves up gradually into one's country, sickness and accidents befalling animals, having the spirit king in the home, dying under an evil star [and thus bringing ill fortune to one's family], false accusation, abusive people, children who do not grow up, depletion and loss of wealth, bad omens and bad dreams, rough years and horoscopes, curses, spells, and so on, one is immediately freed from these by doing this exorcism. As long as one lives, when you repeat it one, three, or nine times in proportion to the size of obstacle, there is no doubt that it will eradicate the obstacle. Thus is the essence of the minds of the scholars and adepts of India, the personal deity of the glorious Atiśa, and the unerring practice of geshe sTon pa, Po to ba rin chen gsal, Ri mos gsung rdo rje, Kyis ljang dbu dkar, and so forth.

There is then a concluding dedication that ends with the words, "By coming under the power of the four in this existence, one is bereft of happiness and tormented by millions of sufferings. Until one attains the *vajra*-like samādhi [the final moment of meditation before the achievement of buddahood], this rite is an amazing method of exorcism."

There are obviously many questions that can be asked about this text and about the rite it prescribes. Is it fruitful, for example, to consider this rite as a sacrifice? Hubert and Mauss, in their classic essay on the subject, define sacrifice as "a religious act which, through the consecration of a victim, modifies the condition of the moral person who accomplishes it or that of certain objects with which he is concerned."[16] One of the

[16] Henri Hubert and Marcel Mauss, *Sacrifice: Its Nature and Function*, trans. W. D.

"primordial components" of sacrifice, for them, is "the expulsion of a sacred spirit, whether pure or impure,"[17] resulting in the transformation of the person for whom the sacrifice is performed, whom they call the "sacrifiant" (which the English translator renders with the neologism "sacrifier"). Some form of mediation is required, an intermediary between the sacrifiant and the god, and this central function is provided by the sacrificial object, the victim. It is through the victim that communication between the sacred and profane is established; some time in the course of this communication, the mediator is destroyed.[18]

They divide sacrifices into two types, depending on the direction of the movement of the sacred presence. In rites of "sacralization," the sacred characteristic is transmitted from the victim to the sacrifiant. In such sacrifices, rituals connected to entry predominate. The other type of sacrifice is that of expiation, in which some form of impurity is to be removed from the sacrifiant. The movement of the sacred here is in the opposite direction, from the sacrifiant to the victim. In such cases, it is rituals of exit that are emphasized. In either case, the victim is, at some point in the ceremony, more sacred than the sacrifiant. Even in sacrifices of expiation, the victim is not merely the repository of the sacrifiant's sins, but is also a consecrated being.[19] For both types of sacrifices, another mediator is often required. This is the priest. "He bears the name, the title, or the robe of his god. He is his minister, even his incarnate presence, or at very least the repository of his power. He is the visible agent of consecration in the sacrifice."[20]

If we can bracket the categories of the sacred and profane that we associate so strongly with Durkheim and his nephew, it is easy enough to match elements of the *Heart Sūtra* exorcism rite to Hubert and Mauss's scheme. An individual or community has been invaded or fears invasion by a malevolent force. The victim of this force (or, in the case of an afflicted community, their representative) takes the role of sacrifiant and pays for the performance of a ceremony in which the malevolence will be expiated. The entire ceremony is officiated over by a ritual master who at the beginning of the ceremony is sanctified by visualizing himself as

---

Halls (Chicago: University of Chicago Press, 1981), p. 13. Their study is based largely on Biblical and Sanskrit sources. For an evaluation of the usefulness of their theory for understanding Vedic sacrifice, see Madeline Biardeau and Charles Malamoud, eds., *Le Sacrifice dans l'Inde ancienne* (Paris: Presses universitaires de France, 1976), pp. 19ff. For a survey and critique of theories of sacrifice, see J. van Baal, "Offering, Sacrifice, and Gift," *Numen* 23 (1976): 161–78.

[17] Hubert and Mauss, *Sacrifice*, p. 6.

[18] Ibid., p. 97.

[19] Ibid., pp. 50–60.

[20] Ibid., p. 23.

Śākyamuni Buddha, retaining this identity throughout. The role of mediation between the sacrifiant and the demons is performed by the *ngar mi*, an adorned dough effigy of the sacrifiant, whom the demons are requested to take (and, presumably, destroy) in the place of the sacrifiant, as a ransom (*glud*). Because the ultimate purpose is to lift the affliction from the sacrifiant, consecration, and hence value, move from the sacrifiant to the victim. The effigy, having first been magically identified with the sacrifiant in ways that Frazer would call both imitative and contagious[21] (it is a representation of the patron dressed in his clothes and is breathed upon by him), is then exalted above the patron with the embedding of gold and jewels into his body and the singing of songs of praise. The demons, having been convinced that the person they possess is less valuable than the one being offered to them by the Buddha, agree to a trade, releasing their hostage in exchange for the ransom. And, as further evidence of a sacrifice of expiation, we note elaborate and lengthy rites of exit, as the effigy is carried beyond the bounds of the community and an elixir (*gser skyems*) is offered to the demons.

Theorists of sacrifice generally agree that the destruction of the victim is part of what makes a given ritual a sacrifice. J. C. Heesterman argues that sacrifice is a complex composed of three major elements: killing, destruction, and food distribution. Among these three, destruction is the key. Food simply excluded from human use and left out for the gods does not qualify as sacrifice; "it is this element of destruction, not the killing or the meal, that is the distinctive feature setting off sacrifice from the gift."[22] In his study of Greek sacrifice, Marcel Detienne argues that sacrifice as a universal category should be allowed to go the way of "totemism." He is sharply critical of Hubert and Mauss's emphasis on identification with the victim, seeing in it evidence of annexation by a pernicious Christian mentality that has dominated theories of religion from Robertson Smith to Cassirer.[23] For Detienne, the key element in Greek sacrifice is not some movement between sacred and profane, but the butchering of the animals, roasting their flesh, and distributing the meat as a meal.

In the *Heart Sūtra* exorcism, however, the *ngar mi* is neither eaten nor destroyed. He is certainly made of food, "a great man of grain," but

[21] For a recent discussion of these categories and their mutual implication, see Taussig, *Mimesis and Alterity*, especially pp. 44–58.

[22] J. C. Heesterman, *The Broken World of Sacrifice: An Essay in Ancient Indian Ritual* (Chicago: University of Chicago Press, 1993), p. 14.

[23] Marcel Detienne and Jean-Pierre Vernant, *The Cuisine of Sacrifice among the Greeks*, trans. Paula Wissig (Chicago: University of Chicago Press, 1989), pp. 13–20. See also Maurice Bloch, *Prey into Hunter: The Politics of Religious Experience* (Cambridge: Cambridge University Press, 1992), pp. 27–31.

during the ritual he is consumed by neither the officiant, the patron, nor the demons. Nor is the effigy destroyed. It is, instead, left out, often at a crossroads, outside the perimeter of the community, at a dangerous place unprotected by the Buddha, where it is presumably taken and eaten by demons. But that eating is not a ritual meal and plays no part in the ceremony. The exorcism, then, at least by the criteria of Heesterman or Detienne, is not a sacrifice.

If the *glud*, the ransom, is not ritually destroyed but is ceremonially taken outside the protection of the community, might it be considered a scapegoat? The *glud* sometimes took the form of a dough figure but was sometimes played by a living human, as in the *glud 'gong* ceremony performed as part of the New Year celebrations in Lhasa since the time of the fifth Dalai Lama. This is the only Tibetan ritual mentioned in the 1890 edition of *The Golden Bough*, where it is described in the chapter "Killing the God" in the section on "Scapegoats."[24] Two men, one drawn from the servant staff of the government offices in Zhol, were allowed to help themselves to whatever they wanted, receiving money and gifts from the residents of the city in return for not bringing them bad luck. On the twenty-ninth day of the second month they participated in a short ceremony in the Jokhang and, after losing a rigged game of dice with a representative of the Dalai Lama, left the city as part of an elaborate procession, their faces painted half-black and half-white. The two *glud* then departed to their respective destinations, Phan po and bSam yas. At the latter, the human *glud* deposited a dough *glud* of the Dalai Lama in a sealed room of the temple, said to be the storehouse of the breath of the dead, and remained there for seven days; the place was so horrific that some were said to have died of fright.[25] Those who survived were then allowed to sell the things they had gathered in the city and eventually to return to Lhasa. There is some disagreement as to their subsequent fate. According to Nebesky-Wojkowitz, most *glud* died shortly after completing their journey,[26] whereas Waddell reports, "It is said that in former times the man who performed this duty died at Chetang [rTses thang, near bSam yas] in the course of the year from terror at the awful images he was associated with; but the present scape

[24] James G. Frazer, *The Golden Bough: The Roots of Religion and Folklore*, 2 vols. in one (New York: Avenel, 1981), vol. 2, p. 197.

[25] The best account of the *glud 'gong* is to be found in Hugh Richardson, *Ceremonies of the Lhasa Year* (London: Serindia, 1993), pp. 61–71. See also Nebesky-Wojkowitz, *Oracles and Demons*, pp. 508–11. Karmay ("L'Homme," p. 348) states that the man himself is considered as a *sku glud* ("ransom of the body") of the Dalai Lama.

[26] Nebesky-Wojkowitz, *Oracles and Demons*, p. 511.

goat survives and returns to reenact his part the following year."[27] In addition to Nebesky-Wojkowitz and Waddell, many scholars and travelers, such as Alexandra David Neel, Giuseppe Tucci, Snellgrove and Richardson, and Ferdinand Lessing,[28] either translate or describe *glud* as "scapegoat." But as Samten Karmay has recently argued, based on a careful analysis of texts associated with the *glud 'gong* ceremonies celebrated in Lhasa annually, one finds there no evidence of what appears to be definitive to the Hebrew festival of Yom Hakipurim or the Greek *pharmakos*, that is, the transfer of the community's sins onto a surrogate.[29]

In both the *glud 'gong* and the *glud* described in the *Heart Sūtra* exorcism, we see a strange version of mimesis at play, in which a double is created, endowed with the qualities of beauty, strength, and power that one has so long desired, and then expelled outside the boundary, of the body or the city, to be consumed by demons. It is as if in order to repel threats to the inside from the outside, all of the desired qualities from the inside are placed outside in the form of the *glud*. The *glud* then becomes the agent by which the boundary between inside and outside, self and other, is traced.[30] In his essay, "Ambiguity and Reversal: On the Enigmatic Structure of *Oedipus Rex*," J. P. Vernant draws a distinction between the *pharmakos* and the ostracized. In the person of the *pharmakos*, like the scapegoat, the city expels what is most vile about itself, "what incarnates the evil that menaces it from below." The ostracized, on the other hand, is expelled from the city because it is that which is too exalted, "what incarnates the evil which can come to it from above."[31] The *glud*, clearly not the scapegoat, seems closer to the ostracized, representing in the beauty of his form and the splendor of the jewels embedded in his body all that is envied by the community and hence what is also envied by the demons. By expelling that which it itself exalts, the community protects itself from the envy of the demons, who, despite the vileness of their deeds, descend from above, from the formless realm.

[27] L. Austine Waddell, *The Buddhism of Tibet, or Lamaism* (London: W. H. Allen, 1956), p. 513.

[28] Ferdinand Lessing, "Calling the Soul: A Lamaist Ritual," *Semitic and Oriental Studies* 11 (1951): 281–82, n. 17. For the other references, see Karmay, "L'Homme." The English-language reference for Tucci (Karmay provides the German) is Giuseepe Tucci, *The Religions of Tibet*, trans. Geoffrey Samuel (Berkeley: University of California Press, 1980), p. 177.

[29] Karmay, "L'Homme," pp. 327–81.

[30] See Derrida's essay, "Plato's Pharmacy," in Jacques Derrida, *Disseminations*, trans. Barbara Johnson, (Chicago: University of Chicago Press, 1981), p. 131.

[31] J. P. Vernant, "Ambiguity and Reversal: On the Enigmatic Structure of *Oedipus Rex*," trans. Page du Bois, *New Literary History* 10, no. 3 (1978): 491–92. Cited in Derrida, *Disseminations*, p. 131.

Is there anything to be gained by considering the function of the *glud* as somehow magical? As we recall, Sir James Frazer declared all magic to be sympathetic magic, rites that act upon their object directly without any mediation by a spiritual agent and whose effect is immediate. These rites operate either through homeopathic (or imitative) magic in which there is an association of similarity between the objects used in the rite and the "real object" to be affected (voodoo doll), or through contagious magic in which the desired effect is achieved through physical contact (protective amulet). (As noted above, the effigy used in the exorcism appears to employ both the imitative and the contagious: it is a representation of the patron dressed in his clothes.) But the *Heart Sūtra* exorcism ritual is fraught with mediations and spiritual agents, suggesting that rather than magic, it might better be described as sorcery, what Freud defined as "the art of influencing spirits by treating them in the same way as one would treat men in like circumstances."[32]

After Frazer, other theorists, notably Marcel Mauss, attempted to shift the focus away from the mechanics of magic to its social function, explaining that magical rites are generally performed in privacy and secrecy rather than public ceremony, for the benefit of an individual rather than a community, for a specific and immediate purpose rather than a generalized goal, by a reclusive professional rather than a public priest; in short, the act and the actor are mysterious, leading Mauss to define a magical rite negatively as "any rite which does not play a part in an organized cult."[33] Given the variety of strategies employed throughout the *Heart Sūtra* exorcism text to signal its Indian Buddhist origins, it would be difficult to construe it as magical in Mauss's sense.

But the term "magic" carries very little weight until we place it in contrast to its two nineteenth-century opponents, religion and science. In both the religion and magic and the magic and science dichotomies, it is magic that is the debased member of the pair, associated consistently with the Other, whether it be the primitive past, the present-day peoples of other cultures, or the ignorant members of one's own society. This is not the occasion to trace the vicissitudes of the various magic-religion-science dyads.[34] However, it may be of some use to mention briefly the special place of Tibet, that storied domain of magic and mystery, in the designation of Buddhism as a "world religion."

[32] Sigmund Freud, "Totem and Taboo," in *The Standard Edition of the Complete Psychological Works of Sigmund Freud*, trans. James Strachey, vol. 13 (London: Hogarth, 1958), p. 78.

[33] Marcel Mauss, *A General Theory of Magic*, trans. Robert Brain (New York: W. W. Norton, 1972), pp. 23–24.

[34] This task has been performed recently in Stanley Jeyaraja Tambiah, *Magic, Science, Religion, and the Scope of Rationality* (Cambridge: Cambridge University Press, 1990).

With the rise of the colonial powers in the eighteenth and nineteenth centuries, the list of the "world's religions" slowly grew, admitting first Islam and then Confucianism for its ethics and Hinduism, or at least "classical Hinduism" for its mystical philosophy, and finally Pāli Buddhism for its rationality and individualism. But the religion of Tibet, a country that never came under colonial domination by European powers, remained largely unknown except from outside. Catholic missionaries accepted the Chinese view that the religion practiced at the Manchu court was not Confucianism, not Daoism, and not Buddhism, but rather was the *lama jiao*, the sect of the lamas, or "lamaism." The term entered Western usage, such that we find Huc and Gabet writing of "Lamanesque" practices and L. Austine Waddell entitling his 1895 masterpiece, *The Buddhism of Tibet or Lamaism*. For Waddell and other British scholars of the Victorian period, the religion of the Tibetans was not authentically Buddhist: "the Lamaist cults comprise much deep rooted devil worship, which I describe in some fulness. For Lamaism is only thinly and imperfectly varnished over with Buddhist symbolism, beneath which the sinister growth of poly demonist superstition darkly appears."[35]

It is, of course, anathema to Tibetans to suggest that their religion is not Buddhism and it may seem ridiculous to us that whereas all forms of Buddhism outside of India contain within them the inevitable admixture of indigenous cultural forms, it is only the Buddhism of Tibet that somehow does not deserve the name. The reasons for this lie in a history of Orientalism that remains to be written. It is also important to note that, although not couched in the offensive terms Waddell employed, the claims of certain Tibetan Buddhists that there is not a single Buddhist practice in Tibet that does not derive directly from an Indian master is equally misleading. But the objection to the term "lamaism" is neither misplaced nor anachronistic. At a highly acclaimed exhibition at the National Gallery in Washington, "Circa 1492: Art in the Age of Exploration" (a show both dazzling and incoherent), there was a gallery among the four devoted to Ming China, called "Lamaist Art." The exhibition brochure provides the following definition: "Lamaism was a combination of the esoteric Buddhism of India, China, and Japan with native cults of the Himalayas." Among the many things that could be said about this sentence, let us simply note that the verb is in the past tense and that the signifier "Tibet" occurs nowhere in the definition.

It is this legacy of religion and magic, India and Tibet, Buddhism and Lamaism that has perhaps caused the current generation of scholars of

[35] Waddell, *Buddhism of Tibet*, p. xi. For a fuller discussion of the use of the term "lamaism," see my "'Lamaism' and the Disappearance of Tibet," *Comparative Studies in Society and History*, 38, no. 1 (January 1996).

Tibetan Buddhism generally to shy away from texts like the *Heart Sūtra* exorcism because they tend to raise those old issues so rudely. It is almost as if in these days after the diaspora, Tibetan culture has suffered enough. Do we really need to remind ourselves and our readers of the existence of the kinds of practices that Waddell found so repellent and by which we, in our pre–history of religions Frazerian moments, are also repulsed? So let us show "the other side," the side of *lam rim* and *mtshan nyid* and *grub mtha'*, to demonstrate to the world that Tibetan Buddhism also has texts, has ethics, has philosophy, has logic, has hermeneutics. Why is it that there has not been a book-length study of this "other side" of Tibetan Buddhism since 1956 (which one should note is before 1959) with the publication of René de Nebesky-Wojkowitz's *Oracles and Demons of Tibet*? It is not simply because Nebesky-Wojkowitz died prematurely of mysterious causes shortly after its publication. Rather, there seems something unseemly about returning to materials the study of which is so closely associated in our minds with an ethnocentric analysis of Tibetan culture that was so openly motivated by the wish to justify and promote the colonial order. It would seem to be the task of the current generation of scholars, then, to challenge the characterization of Tibetan Buddhism that has so long tainted their field of study—not by defensively concerning themselves exclusively with those texts and practices and persons who most easily fit into our conceptions of what is legitimately "philosophy" or "religion" (a fit achieved only through the most violent decontextualization), but by attempting to move beyond an ethnography in which "aversion serves to transform behavior and material substances into the objects of representation and interpretation."[36]

It is in this sense that the study of Tibetan ritual might allow us to break down the opposition that we imagine to exist between thought and action, which makes it difficult for us to think that Bu ston also did choreography, that dKon mchog 'jigs med dbang po also made pills, that Tsong kha pa wrote so profoundly on the role of reason while experiencing visions of Mañjuśrī, that the Nobel laureate does not make a major decision without asking a semiwrathful deity to take possession of the body of an oracle.

Having thus dispensed, however inadequately, with the categories of gift versus sacrifice, ostracism versus scapegoat, magic versus religion, Lamaism versus Buddhism, as they might pertain to the *Heart Sūtra* exorcism text, there is one further opposition to consider, the only opposition taken up also by Tibetan scholars: the opposition of Bön versus Buddhism. Is it Bön po or is it Buddhist? It is certainly widely practiced by Buddhist monks and that, it would seem, would be enough to make it

[36] Stephen Greenblatt, "Filthy Rites," *Daedalus* 111, no. 3 (1982): 4.

Buddhist. But for modern scholars as much as for traditional exegetes, identity is a function of origin. For the rite to be Buddhist, it must have come from India. One might consider the claim of its transmission lineage: that this exorcism ritual is of Indian origin, brought to Tibet by Atiśa himself, that most authentic of Indian masters in the Tibetan historical imagination. Atiśa transmitted it to his disciple, 'Brom ston pa (1005–64), who in turn gave it to Po to ba rin chen gsal (1031–1105), who passed it on to the translator [Tshul khrims] 'Byung gnas rdo rje of sTong (sTeng) (1107–90). If the dates in the *Blue Annals* are correct, however, the bKa' gdams pa master Po to ba rin chen gsal died in 1105 and the disciple to whom he transmitted this practice, the translator Tshul khrims 'byung gnas rdo rje, was born in 1107, two years after Po to ba's death. This problem might lead some to suspect that the lineage was fabricated. The structure of the rite, nonetheless, is certainly familiar enough from Indian tantra, with the invitation of deities, the presentation of offerings, the request for boons, and the entreaty for the gods to depart, a structure that probably is traceable to Vedic structures.

But as we have seen, despite a supererogatory recitation of the *Heart Sūtra*, what seems to be the real heart of this rite is that doughboy, described as *ngar mi* and *glud*. These are terms that, as far as I know, do not appear in Indian sādhanas. They are, however, common in the Bon po literature that Snellgrove[37] and Karmay,[38] for example, trace to the pre-Buddhist period, and they are common as well as in present-day Bön po rites, such as the death ritual documented by Per Kvaerne.[39] We also find evidence of the use of offering of effigies as substitutes for humans among Tibeto-Burman tribes such as the Lahu in northern Thailand and Yunnan province of China.[40] There would seem to be good reason to believe, then, that what we are dealing with here is a pre-Buddhist rite "legitimized" for use by Buddhist officiants through the addition of a transmission lineage, a tantric format, and the *Heart Sūtra*, which functions here as nothing more nor less than a long mantra.

The issue, however, is not whether the ritual is actually Buddhist or Bön po, for it clearly contains Buddhist and pre-Buddhist elements. The text is, in that sense, a hybrid. But Buddhism and Bon are also hybrids, the latter emerging in the eleventh century as both a reflection of and in

[37] David Snellgrove and Hugh Richardson, *A Cultural History of Tibet* (Boston: Shambhala, 1980), pp. 55–56.

[38] Karmay, "L'Homme," pp. 363–69.

[39] Per Kvaerne, *Tibetan Bon Religion: A Death Ritual of the Tibetan Bonpos* (Leiden: E. J. Brill, 1985).

[40] See, for example, Anthony R. Walker, "*Jaw te meh jaw ve*: Lahu Nyi (Red Lahu) Rites of Spirit Exorcism in North Thailand," *Anthropos: International Review of Ethnology and Linguistics* 71 (1976): 377–422.

opposition to the "new" (*gsar ma*) sects of Sa skya, bKa' gdams, and bKa' rgyud. Renouncing the quest for origins, we can nonetheless strive to identify the Indian and Tibetan elements in a work like the *Heart Sūtra* exorcism text, in an effort to trace the lines of convergence, overlap, and divergence. Marcel Detienne's comments about the study of Greek sacrifice can be applied, *mutatis mutandis*, to the Tibetan situation: "Expressed in actions and carried out since time immemorial in eating habits, the sacrificial system eludes clear and explicit analysis. It depends on shared knowledge, the various terms of which the Greeks felt the need to formulate only in marginal milieus where the voices of protest were raised and heard. The denials and distortions found there enable us to trace, as if in a broken mirror, the outlines of a secret, implicit system."[41] The *Sher nying bdud bzlog*, the "turning back of demons [with] the *Heart Sūtra*," provides one such mirror, perhaps reflecting more clearly a paradigm of Tibetan ritual knowledge and praxis than would a text more "purely" Buddhist or Bön po. The various attempts to refract an Indian lineage need not be regarded as merely distortions, but as components of a strategy of legitimation for the practice. The foremost of these strategies is the transformation of a work exalted for its philosophical profundity into a long mantra, repeated beyond the point of comprehension, in an effort to bring about a most quotidian effect.

[41] Detienne and Vernant, *Cuisine of Sacrifice*, p. 5.

Ten

Commentators Ancient and Postmodern

IN DISCUSSING the Indian commentaries on the *Heart Sūtra*, Alex Wayman found that "The writers seemed to be experiencing some difficulty in exposition, as though they were not writing through having inherited a tradition about this scripture going back to its original composition, but rather were simply applying their particular learning in Buddhism to the terminology of the sutra."[1] Without pausing to consider the criteria by which one would come to such a judgment, we can nonetheless note an important assumption that underlies Wayman's claim: that the value of a commentary derives largely from its link to the original that is being commented upon, the root text. It is difficult for us to speculate, much less determine, what it was about the *Heart Sūtra* that warranted so many commentaries deriving from (in terms of the history of Indian Buddhism) a relatively limited period of time. We can assume, at least, that the sūtra was widely known during the Pāla period (c. 750–1155 in Bengal and c. 750–1199 in Bihar). But it is difficult to say precisely what it is about the text that elicited such interest, a text that strikes us today, even in its brevity, as a redundant litany of negations.[2] The *Heart Sūtra* was probably used in Pāla India, as it would be elsewhere in Asia, as a long

[1] Alex Wayman, "Secret of the Heart Sutra," in Lewis Lancaster and Luis O. Gómez, eds., *Prajñāpāramitā and Related Systems: Studies in Honor of Edward Conze* (Berkeley: Berkeley Buddhist Studies, 1977), p. 136. Wayman concluded that the Indian commentaries, "while helpful on this or that phrase, still were not really explaining the sutra." This apparently moved Wayman to write his own commentary. In a similar vein, Edward Conze found Vimalamitra's commentary "none too helpful. Laboured, over-elaborate and unsystematic, it does not always represent the main stream of Buddhist thinking. A lay Tantric, with often strange views, Vimalamitra could not maintain himself in Tibet against the orthodoxy of Kamalaśīla and had to leave for China." See his "Praśāstrasena's *Ārya-Prajñāpāramitā-Hṛdaya-Ṭīkā*," in L. Cousins, A. Kunst, and K. R. Norman, eds., *Buddhist Studies in Honour of I. B. Horner* (Dordrecht: D. Reidel, 1974), p. 51.

[2] We need not, however, concur with the view of Winternitz, who wrote of the *prajñāpāramitā* sūtras, "Nevertheless, it is very difficult for us to imagine that the immense sanctity which is attributed to these texts, can really be due to a valuation and an understanding of the metaphysical doctrines which they propound. It is more probable that it is precisely the dark and incomprehensible element in the doctrines taught by these texts, which has attributed to make them sacred. *Omne obscurum pro magnifico*." See Maurice Winternitz, *A History of Indian Literature*, vol. 2, *Buddhist Literature and Jaina Literature*, trans. V. Srinivasa Sarma (Delhi: Motilal Banarsidass, 1983), p. 311.

mantra, something that was merely repeated.[3] This very quality may have posed an irresistible challenge to the commentatorial skills of the Indian Buddhist scholastic. As we have seen, most of the commentators were concerned to derive much from the sūtra (in most cases, an elaborate taxonomy of the path) that was not ostensibly there, both emboldened and constrained by the two roles of commentary:

> On the one hand, it permits us to create new discourses ad infinitum: the top-heaviness of the original text, its permanence, its status as discourse ever capable of being brought up to date, the multiple or hidden meanings with which it is credited, the reticence and wealth it is believed to contain, all this creates an open possibility for discussion. On the other hand, whatever the techniques employed, commentary's only role is to say *finally*, what has silently been articulated *deep down*. It must—and the paradox is ever-changing yet inescapable—say, for the first time, what has already been said, and repeat tirelessly what was, nevertheless, never said. The infinite rippling of commentary is agitated from within by the dream of masked repetition: in the distance there is, perhaps, nothing other than what was there at the point of departure: simple recitation. Commentary averts the chance element of discourse by giving it its due: it gives us the opportunity to say something other than the text itself, but on the condition that it is the text itself which is uttered and, in some ways, finalised. . . . The novelty lies no longer in what is said, but in its reappearance.[4]

The *Heart Sūtra* commentators, therefore, are not concerned to say anything new; innovation is one of the great sins of Buddhist letters. Instead, they are concerned to reveal its hidden meaning, and the traditional hidden meaning of the Perfection of Wisdom sūtras is the sequence of realizations (*abhisamaya*) that constitute the bodhisattva's path. Among the cults of the book that came to be called the Mahāyāna there appears to have been the notion that one's chosen sūtra was the perfect expression of reality, of the world as it truly is, a notion that persisted in China and Japan where schools and sects were organized around a single sūtra. This ideology of the plenum compelled the commentators to demonstrate how the *Heart Sūtra* is complete, how it contains everything. If the Perfection of Wisdom sūtras contain the complete path to enlightenment, and if, as Jñānamitra says, "There is nothing in any sūtra that is not contained here in this *Heart of the Perfection of Wisdom*. Therefore, it is called the sūtra of sūtras," then it must be demonstrable that the *Heart Sūtra* contains

[3] Winternitz claims that the *Heart Sūtra* and the other short Perfection of Wisdom sūtras were "only used as magical formulas." Ibid., pp. 303–4.

[4] Michel Foucault, *The Archaeology of Knowledge and the Discourse on Language*, trans. A. M. Sheridan Smith (New York: Harper and Row, 1972), p. 221.

everything, even those doctrines that, from our perspective, may have developed after the composition of the sūtra.[5] They must "say, for the first time, what has already been said."

But to do so requires a method. The articulation of what, to the untrained ear, seems absent in the sūtra, must be heard in the sūtra's own voice, what is invisible to the untrained eye must be discerned in the sūtra's own letters. The commentator's task, therefore, is the discovery, the identification, the elaboration, even the manufacture, of allusion. And for the manufacture of allusion, one of the commentator's favorite tools is the delineation of multiple levels of meaning. Thus, Praśāstrasena sets forth the mundane, supramundane, and unsurpassed meaning of this or that term and Śrīsiṃha speaks of the outer, inner, and secret meanings, of, for example, Vulture Peak: "The outer place is the mountain that is [shaped] like a pile of jewels or like a round stūpa in the eastern part of the land of Magadha, the abode of King Bimbisāra, where the buddhas abide, the special place among all mountains. The inner place is the [pure land of] Akaniṣṭha, where one does not go to the depths of form, signs, or apprehension. The secret place is the awareness [and] *bodhicitta* that abide throughout saṃsāra and nirvāṇa."

Foucault observes that "to comment is to admit by definition an excess of the signified over the signifier; a necessary, unformulated remainder of thought that language has left in the shade—a remainder that is the very essence of thought, driven outside its secret—but to comment also presupposes that this unspoken element slumbers within speech (*parole*), and that by a superabundance proper to the signifier, one may, in questioning it, give voice to a content that was not explicitly signified."[6] To find multiple levels of meaning in the words of the sūtra is to admit to the excess of the signified over the signifier. However, the Indian commenta-

[5] Of course we do not know the date of the sūtra. Conze places it around C.E. 350, Nakamura places it two centuries earlier, and Nattier suggests the possibility that it is a Chinese apocryphon translated into Sanskrit in the seventh century. See Jan Nattier, "The *Heart Sūtra*: A Chinese Apocryphal Text," *Journal of the International Association of Buddhist Studies* 15, no. 2 (1992): 153–223. Regardless, the authors of the commentaries would presumably have been oblivious to the chronology of Buddhist thought, at least as it pertained to the sūtras they had inherited. It is noteworthy that modern Buddhist commentators continue to find what they seek in the sūtra. See, for example, Mu S. Sunim, *Heart Sutra: Ancient Buddhist Wisdom in Light of Quantum Reality* (Providence, R.I.: Primary Point, 1992) and Thich Nhat Hanh, *The Heart of Understanding* (Berkeley: Parallax, 1988), who derives an environmental message from the text. The *Heart Sūtra* also figured prominently in Bernardo's Bertolucci's 1993 film *Little Buddha*, with the Sanskit *rūpaṃ śūnyatā śūnyataiva rūpaṃ* ("form is emptiness, emptiness is form") sung as an aria during the closing credits.

[6] Michel Foucault, *The Birth of the Clinic: An Archaeology of Medical Perception*, trans. A. M. Sheridan Smith (New York: Random House, 1973), p. xvi.

tors make use of another tool to manufacture allusion, one that is powered by the superabundance of the signifier. This is the tool of etymology. Consider, for example, the first word in the title of the sūtra, *bhagavatī*. *Bhaga* means "fortune" and *vat* indicates possession. *Ī* is the feminine ending, in the feminine because the word that it modifies, *prajñāpāramitā*, is in the feminine; the adjective and noun agree in gender. *Bhagavatī* could be translated as "fortunate" (feminine). Thus, Mahājana says that the Buddha is called *bhagavan* because he is endowed with six fortunes, etymology providing, as it so often does for the commentators, an occasion for a list. But few of the etymologies are so straightforward. In order to mine a wealth of doctrine from so brief a sūtra, the commentators make extensive use of so-called folk etymologies, etymologies that rely less on semantics than phonology, less on derivation than evocation, using what appear to be capricious coincidences of sounds. Hence, *bhaga* (fortune) sounds like *bhaṅga* (destroy), such that the Bhagavan is the destroyer. What he has destroyed is (in another list) the four demons or *māra*s: the *māra* who is death, the *māra* who is the afflictions (*kleśas*), the *māra* who is the aggregates, and the deity Māra—the one who attacked Prince Siddhārtha under the Bodhi tree. *Van* (the possession indicator) sounds like the *vāṇa* of nirvāṇa (meaning "passing away"). Jñānamitra writes, "*Van* means the unlocated nirvāṇa (*apratiṣṭhitanirvāṇa*). Because all minds, intellects, and consciousnesses are overturned by this meaning of the perfection of wisdom, that is, since it is free from all predispositions, it has passed beyond."[7] The monks (*bhikṣu*) of "a great assembly of monks" in the sūtra are so-called, according to Mahājana, because they seek the marvelous wealth of virtue, deriving bhikṣu from *bhikṣ*, "beg." But Praśāstrasena says that they are monks because they have abandoned all afflictions, seeing in bhikṣu *bhid* ("cut") and *kṣudh* ("hunger").[8]

The irony, of course, is that because the Indian commentaries are lost in the original Sanskrit and preserved only in Tibetan, all of the homonymy is also lost on the reader and can only be guessed at by the English translator. How then to translate *bhagavan*, for example? The convention is to translate *bhagavan* as "lord," such that Bhagavad Buddha is "Lord Buddha." But some might object that "lord" has excessively Christian overtones. There is the added difficulty that the term as it appears in the title of the sūtra is in the feminine, leaving us with "The Lady (-like?) Heart of the Perfection of Wisdom Sūtra." Others have rendered *bhagavat* as "blessed," but who blessed the Buddha? Still others have

[7] For this and other etymologies of *bhagavan*, see Étienne Lamotte, *Le Traité de la grande vertu de sagesse*, tome 1 (Louvain: Institut Orientaliste, 1949), pp. 115–26.

[8] See Ibid., p. 201.

expressed the desire to translate terms not from their Sanskrit "originals"[9] but from the Tibetan in which they are preserved, in that way attempting at least to represent the term as it may have been understood by a Tibetan reader. The most common and contested case is the question of how to translate arhat. In Indian commentaries, arhat is subjected to the same etymological play as *bhagavan*. Hence, a term that means "worthy one" is made to mean also *ari* + *han*, "enemy killer," one who has destroyed the enemy of the afflictions, and so on. When it came time for the Tibetan translation teams (which often included visiting Indian *paṇḍitas*) in the eighth century to render arhat into Tibetan, they sometimes chose "worthy of offering" (*mchod 'os*), but settled on "enemy killer" (*dgra bcom pa*) as the standard translation. Should arhat be rendered as "enemy killer" (or the apparently more poetic "foe destroyer") when a Sanskrit text preserved only in Tibetan is rendered into English? Is the translator more justified in such a rendition when the work being translated is an autochthonous Tibetan work, under the assumption that this is how the term would have been understood by a Tibetan reader?[10] Nietzsche's oft-cited statement from the *Genealogy of Morals* perhaps deserves to be quoted here:

> There is for historiography of any kind no more important proposition than the one it took such effort to establish but which really *ought to be* established now: the cause of the origin of a thing and its eventual utility, its actual employment and place in a system of purposes, lie worlds apart; whatever exists, having somehow come into being, is again and again reinterpreted to new ends, taken over, transformed, and redirected by some power superior to it; all events in the organic world are a subduing, a *becoming master*, and all subduing and becoming master involves a fresh interpretation, an adaptation through which any previous "meaning" and "purpose" are necessarily obscured and even obliterated.[11]

For the Tibetan translation teams to standardize arhat as *dgra bcom pa* (enemy killer) is to authenticate the "folk etymology," which is further authenticated by rendering the Tibetan in English as "foe destroyer (arhat)." The point is, however, not to bemoan the loss of an earlier and, therefore, a somehow more original and authentic meaning, but instead

[9] K. R. Norman notes the possibility that bodhisattva is a back-formation in Sanskrit from the Pāli bodhisatta, where *satta* is not *sattva* but *śakta*, such that bodhisattva would mean "one who is capable of enlightenment." See his "Pāli Philology and the Study of Buddhism," in Tadeusz Skorupski, ed., *The Buddhist Forum*, vol. 1 (London: School of Oriental and African Studies, 1990), p. 36.

[10] For a defense of the translation of arhat as "foe destroyer," see Jeffrey Hopkins, *Meditation on Emptiness* (London: Wisdom, 1983), pp. 871–73.

[11] Friedrich Nietzsche, *On the Genealogy of Morals and Ecce Homo*, trans. Walter Kaufmann (New York: Random House, 1967), p. 77.

to consider what system of purposes and what superior power (in Nietzsche's terms) are served by this new interpretation in the history of the Tibetan language. That is, it is necessary to acknowledge that etymologies and the texts in which they occur are embedded in changing contexts, and that these etymologies and texts are always understood from a particular position within a particular interpretative community, such that an entirely stable identity is not to be found.

In the case of arhat, the translator at least has the luxury of dealing with a Tibetan term that is not a neologism in Tibetan. This is not the case with *bhagavan*. The translators who rendered *bhagavan* into Tibetan took *bhaga* not as "fortune" but as "destroy." When it came to *van*, they immortalized the dilemma of the translator by indicating both its meaning of "possession" and its sense of "passage." That is, as they did with buddha (*sangs rgyas*, "awaken-expand") and bodhisattva (*byang chub sems dpa'*, "purify-complete-mind-hero"), the translators rendered bhagavan with a neologism intended to convey multiple meanings: *bcom ldan 'das*, "destroy-possess-pass beyond." How should *bhagavan* then be rendered into English by a translator who is not attracted to the old choices of "lord" or "blessed one"? In the past, in an attempt to give some sense of how the term is understood in Tibetan, I have translated *bhagavan* as "Transcendent Victor," deriving "transcendent" from *van* (*'das*) and "victor" (rather than the perhaps hyperviolent "destroyer") from *bhaga* (*bcom*). Under this approach the title of the sūtra would be the "Transcendent and Victorious Heart of the Perfection of Wisdom Sūtra." What such a triumphant rendering occludes is the presumed fact that for a Tibetan unfamiliar with Sanskrit and with the elaborate etymologizing of Buddhist terms, *bcom ldan 'das* would mean about as much in Tibetan as "destroy-possess-pass beyond" means in English. Presented with such a state of affairs, rendering *bhagavan* as "Bhagavan" becomes increasingly attractive, not simply as yet another concession to the Sanskrit hegemony of Buddhist Studies, but in recognition of the traditional power ascribed to the sound of Sanskrit, that, just as buddha seems somehow more appropriate than "Awakened One" and bodhisattva seems certainly more appropriate than the problematic "Enlightenment Being" or "Awakening Hero," so *bhagavan* might best simply be left in the Sanskrit. (The implications of taking such a decision to its logical conclusion need not be articulated.)

To return to the more general issue of etymology, however, we see the appeal of the folk etymology to the *Heart Sūtra* commentators. Folk etymology serves as a tool for elaborating on this most condensed of sūtras by physically expanding it: by changing vowels and adding and deleting letters, more meanings can be extracted without contravening the ideology of the plenum. The sūtra contains everything in potential; its letters need only be properly manipulated for the hidden meaning to come forth. In this sense, the activity of the commentators might more accurately be regarded not as etymologizing but as paronomasia, as wordplay or punning, the device in which "two similar-sounding but distinct signifiers are brought together, and the surface relationship between them is invested with meaning through the inventiveness and rhetorical skill of the writer."[12] But this is play that can never be depicted as ludic or random because it operates within a transhistorical view of the text, for the *Heart Sūtra* is being shown to contain within its syllables all that is essential to the Buddhist path, but nothing that is inessential. Hence, Vimalamitra, who is quite content to use the "folk etymology" of bhikṣu as "one who has destroyed the afflictions," objects to the folk etymology of pāramitā (endorsed by the other commentators) as "gone beyond" rather than "perfect" or "excellent": "Etymologies other than that are not correct and the joining of sounds is difficult; it would contradict the etymology [provided] by the Bhagavan."[13] This wordplay gives the sūtra an identity across time and history, the discovery of any point of doctrine subject only to the limits of the commentator's ingenuity. The obvious point, of course, is that the meaning of the sūtra is the meaning that the commentator manufactures. But it does not follow that these "folk etymologies" are "the quaint misunderstanding by the ill-educated but imaginative 'folk'";[14] they are the product of a long and sophisticated scholastic, although no less imaginative, tradition, one of whose aims is to complicate the familiar rather than to simplify the unfamiliar, as folk etymology is often purported to do.[15]

A folk etymology works on the principle of homonymy, an association based on sound. Association is also central to psychoanalytic practice, referring to a bond between elements of the psyche. The term derives from Freud's earliest clinical practices, described in the 1895 *Studies on Hysteria*. Here, Freud (and Breuer) followed the "free associations" in their patients' discourse in order to trace back to a single event that had

[12] Derek Attridge, *Peculiar Language: Literature as Difference from the Renaissance to James Joyce* (Ithaca: Cornell University Press, 1988), p. 108. Elsewhere (p. 119) Attridge refers to etymology's status as "imaginative storytelling," a function suggested long ago by Max Müller in his dictum of mythology as a disease of language, where the crucial factor in the mythologizing process is the faulty etymology or pun. On Müller, see Tomoko Masuzawa, *In Search of Dreamtime: The Quest for the Origin of Religion* (Chicago: University of Chicago Press, 1993), pp. 58–75.

[13] Vimalamitra thus anticipates the objection of Winternitz, who translates the *Heart Sūtra*'s mantra as "O Enlightenment, which hast gone, gone, to the other shore, completely gone to the other shore, gone hail" and comments in a note, "This is nothing but a false etymology of *pāramitā*." See Winternitz, *History of Indian Literature*, vol. 2, p. 368.

[14] Attridge, *Peculiar Language*, p. 112.

[15] See ibid., pp. 112–13.

either been forgotten or fended off. Freud describes the associations as organized simultaneously according to a number of principles; there are chronological linear sequences, strata organized thematically, and irregular routes of thought-content, which move along logical lines but jump illogically when they near the pathogenic nucleus.[16] Associations, thus, are like a system of archives that is organized according to a number of classificatory systems, and thus may be approached from a number of routes.[17]

In the case of commentary on Buddhist texts, the chronology of associations is a long one, stretching far into the past, long before the Pāla commentators, and into the present, where a metaphorical homonymy has been central to the practitioners of comparative philosophy, for whom something in Nāgārjuna "sounds like" something in Wittgenstein, for example. Here, what is in fact a psychological association, a subjective recollection of similarity, is often turned into a historical association through recourse to some theory of influence, diffusion, or borrowing on the one hand, or to some theory of deep structure on the other. But the recourse to one or another theory is never unmotivated nor untainted by social and political factors.

The question of what it can possibly mean to do comparative philosophy in the age of historical contextualization has begun to be considered by others.[18] The most obvious problem with comparative philosophy as

[16] Sigmund Freud, *The Standard Edition of the Complete Psychological Works of Sigmund Freud*, vol. 2 (London: Hogarth, 1955), pp. 288–91.

[17] Jacques Laplanche and J. B. Pontalis, *The Language of Psychoanalysis* (New York: W. W. Norton, 1973), p. 41.

[18] There is, for example, Gerald Larson's introduction in Gerald James Larson and Eliot Deutsch, eds., *Interpreting across Boundaries: New Essays in Comparative Philosophy* (Princeton: Princeton University Press, 1988), a volume that contains essays by many of the more prominent practitioners of comparative philosophy of the last generation. Andrew P. Tuck, in *Comparative Philosophy and the Philosophy of Scholarship: On the Western Interpretation of Nāgārjuna* (New York: Oxford University Press, 1990), provides, in effect, a useful Gadamerian update of Guy Richard Welbon's *The Buddhist Nirvāṇa and Its Western Interpreters* (Chicago: University of Chicago Press, 1968). Finally, see especially the trenchant comments of Wilhelm Halbfass in his *India and Europe: An Essay in Understanding* (Albany: State University of New York Press, 1988), pp. 419–33.

Of some historical interest are two articles published by Edward Conze in *Philosophy East and West* in 1963. One is entitled "Spurious Parallels to Buddhist Philosophy." These parallels (he focuses on those to Kant, Bergson, and Hume) "often originate from a wish to find affinities with philosophers recognized and admired by the exponents of current academic philosophy, and intend to make Buddhist thinkers interesting and respectable by any current Western standards. Since this approach is not only objectively unsound, but has also failed in its purpose to interest Western philosophers in the philosophies of the East, the time has now come to abandon it." Reprinted in Edward Conze, *Thirty Years of Buddhist Studies* (Oxford: Bruno Cassirer, 1967), p. 229. Yet in the other essay, "Buddhist Philosophy and Its European Parallels," Conze draws comparisons between Buddhism and

it has been practiced, in both Asia and the West, is its ahistorical nature, portraying the concerns of certain types of Asian texts as manifestations of perennial philosophical forms. To the extent that history is evoked, it is a history of ideas, a transindividual, transcommunal, transcultural, and transtemporal movement, often toward a particular telos. Whether this comparative philosophy is being practiced by an Asian or Euro-American scholar, that telos is generally represented as the ultimate position of a particular Asian thinker—the Advaita Vedānta of Śaṃkara, the Madhyamaka of Nāgārjuna, the Zen of Dōgen. Comparative philosophy is ahistorical in the sense that it neglects the complex of social, political, and material forces that modify the individual (whether it be Dōgen or the comparative philosopher) and the community (whether it be the community of Buddhist clerics in thirteenth-century Japan or the community of academics in an American institution of higher learning) "in a succession of experienced presents."[19] What comparative philosophy neglects is the historical situatedness of both the text and its interpreter, a lesson that should have been learned from Gadamer long ago.

Wilhelm Halbfass suggests that the term "comparative philosophy" may have been coined not in Europe but in India by the Bengali scholar Brajendranath Seal (1864–1938) in his 1899 *Comparative Studies in Vaishnavism and Christianity* and later in his 1915 *The Positive Science of the Ancient Hindus*. In the former work, he writes: "Chinese, Hindoo, Mohamedan culture-histories, therefore, require to be worked out on a general historic plan, and in obedience to a general law of progress. . . . This will furnish new and comprehensive material for more correct generalisations,—for the discovery of general laws of the social organism. . . . It will bring new influences, new inspirations, new cultures to Europe. It will infuse new blood, the blood of Humanity, and bring on the greater European Renaissance of the coming century."[20] We find two arguments for comparative philosophy being made here, arguments that remain current almost a century later. The first is that to truly understand the development of philosophy, the cultures of Asia cannot be neglected; it is only when they have also been accounted for that it will be possible to trace accurately the ways in which cultures and philosophies develop and progress according to general laws. Here, we see the European influence of morphology that occasioned the development of comparative

the Greek skeptics; the "wisdom-seeking mystics," among whom he includes the Neo-Platonists, Eckhart, and Schopenhauer ("It is only on two points that he differs from Buddhism"; *Thirty Years*, p. 223); and the monists, such as Parmenides and F. H. Bradley. See *Thirty Years of Buddhist Studies*, pp. 210–28.

[19] Attridge, *Peculiar Language*, p. 105.

[20] Cited in Halbfass, *India and Europe*, p. 423.

philology and comparative mythology earlier in the nineteenth century, which in turn had developed under the influence of comparative physiology and anatomy in the previous century. Seal's book was used by Paul Masson-Oursel, perhaps the first European to use the term "comparative philosophy" (in his 1923 *La philosophie comparée*), to develop a Comtean systematic in which "developmental schemas and repeatable structural relationships should be worked out, while the specific contents are of secondary importance."[21] Thus, for Seal, Asia offers important data that cannot be ignored if truly comprehensive "laws of the social organism" are to be discovered.

But side by side with this plea for Asia in a generalized scheme of human culture is a prediction of Asia's unique contribution to Europe. The terms he used echoed those of Schlegel almost a century before, who wrote in 1808, "The Renaissance of antiquity promptly transformed and rejuvenated all the sciences; we might add that it rejuvenated and transformed the world. We could even say that the effects of Indic studies, if these enterprises were taken up and introduced into learned circles with the same energy today, would be no less great or far-reaching."[22] But even at the time that Schlegel made his prediction, the European portrayal of India as the abode of spirit had begun to be displaced and India had begun to be represented as a corrupt and, later, as a racially inferior civilization.[23] This shift in perception occurred as the European powers were undertaking their conquests of Asia. (In light of the prominence of these racial theories by the end of the nineteenth century, Seal's prediction of an infusion of new blood is striking.) For Seal, the Asian tradition that would bring its inspiration to Europe was Hinduism, described in terms similar to those used by British missionaries to explain what Christianity would do for India: "The speculative ardour, the metaphysical genius, the science of the Absolute of the Hindus are exactly fitted to infuse a new blood into European philosophy, and to rouse its dormant activity."[24] In one of the networks of exchange so evident in the history of colonialism, it is only after the enthusiasm for the European Renaissance predicted by Schlegel had largely

[21] Ibid., p. 427.

[22] Friedrich Schlegel, *Über die Sprache und Weisheit der Indier*, cited in Raymond Schwab, *The Oriental Renaissance: Europe's Rediscovery of India and the East, 1680–1880*, trans. Gene Patterson-Black and Victor Reinking (New York: Columbia University Press, 1984), p. 13. See also Mary Helms, *Ulysses' Sail* (Princeton: Princeton University Press, 1988).

[23] Much of the disenchantment with India and China was fully formed by 1800. See P. J. Marshall and Glyndwr Williams, *The Great Map of Mankind: Perceptions of New Worlds in the Age of Enlightenment* (Cambridge: Harvard University Press, 1982), pp. 169–82.

[24] Quoted in Halbfass, *India and Europe*, p. 307.

faded in Europe and India had come under European domination that the prediction of such a renaissance was declared in India.[25]

There are, then, two apparently contradictory assumptions that underlie Seal's program, assumptions that remain evident in later comparative philosophy. Each of the assumptions is, in its own way, apologetic. The first holds that a truly universal history of ideas cannot be written until the ideas of Asia have been given their due. Whether it be the mind–body problem or the mechanics of the syllogism, Asian formulations deserve a rightful place alongside the formulations of the European tradition, where they can be evaluated, compared, and ranked in the evolution of philosophy. (Despite the fact that the appeal of such an argument appears to be to the merely morphological, it continues to have strong institutional implications, especially in the United States, where the absence of positions in Eastern philosophy in departments of philosophy is often bemoaned with similar arguments.)[26] The second assumption is also apologetic and also subscribes to an evolutionary model of the history of philosophy. Here, however, the apologia carries with it a pronounced triumphalism, for not only are Asian thinkers and their thoughts to be given their rightful place in the continuum; one or another of those thinkers and his thoughts is declared to occupy the end-point, the telos, of that continuum. In the previous generation, pride of place was most commonly given to Śaṃkara, under the formidable influence of a tradition that can be traced back from Radhakrishnan, to Vivekananda (whose famous dictum that all religions are one seems to have meant that all religions are Hinduism), to Ramakrishna.[27] In the Kyoto School in Japan, Nietzsche and Heidegger are surpassed only by Dōgen.[28] It is im-

[25] Enthusiasm for Indian thought continued into the late nineteenth century in Germany, largely under the influence of Paul Deussen, one of whose concerns was to find in Indian texts confirmations of the philosophy of his teacher, Arthur Schopenhauer. On Deussen, see ibid., pp. 128–33.

[26] Gadamer would apparently not be sympathetic. He wrote in 1949:

> Although in the meantime the research in Eastern philosophy has made further advances, we believe today that we are further removed from its philosophical understanding. The sharpening of our historical awareness has rendered the translation or adaptations of the texts . . . fundamentally problematic. . . . We cannot speak of an appropriation of these things by the Occidental philosophy. What can be considered established is only the negative insight that our own basic concepts, which were coined by the Greeks, alter the essence of what is foreign.

Cited in Halbfass, *India and Europe*, p. 164.

[27] On this Neo-Hinduism and its "inclusivism," see ibid., pp. 217–46.

[28] See Nishitan Keiji, *Religion and Nothingness*, trans. Jan Van Bragt (Berkeley: University of California Press, 1982). For some of the antecedents of this position, see Robert H. Sharf, "The Zen of Japanese Nationalism," in Donald S. Lopez, Jr., ed., *Curators of the*

portant to note that this latter tendency is a product of late colonialism, in which European-educated elite males of the colony read Western philosophical works, found affinities with their native philosophies (which they sometimes encountered for the first time in European translation), and eventually came to proclaim the priority (both temporal and hierarchical) of an Asian thinker, who had anticipated (often by over a millennium) and superseded a particular development of European philosophy. Hence, an Asian, usually the Buddha or Nāgārjuna or Dōgen, was already a pragmatist or a phenomenologist or an existentialist or a deconstructionist long before the term was even coined in the West.

To digress for a moment, it is significant that no Tibetan names come to mind when we list modern Asian contributors to the field of comparative philosophy. One of the reasons for this is that, unlike most of the other Buddhist societies of Asia, Tibet neither came under direct European imperial control nor did it make any real attempt to "modernize" (despite certain failed attempts by the thirteenth Dalai Lama) by establishing European-style universities, importing European technologies, or sending elites for education in Europe. There are many reasons why the European powers were deterred, one of which is the fact that in 1792, the Manchu emperor Qianlong had declared imperial control over all Tibetan communications with foreign countries. This did not sever Tibet's long-standing relations with Inner Asia and China. Instead, from that point until the twentieth century, further relations of Europeans with Tibet had to be positioned from the borderlands. In the nineteenth century, Tibet became a cherished prize in the Great Game played by the two great European powers of the region, Britain and Russia. It was during this period that Tibet came to be consistently portrayed as "isolated" or "closed," characterizations that meant little except in contrast to China, which had been forcibly "opened" to British trade. Tibet was thus an object of imperial desire, and the failure of the European powers to dominate Tibet politically only increased European longing and added to the fantasy about life in the land beyond the Snowy Range. In the process, highly romanticized portrayals of traditional Tibet emerged, many of which continue to hold sway.

At the same time, the absence of Western colonial institutions in Tibet prevented Tibetan scholars from participating in the production of Western forms of knowledge. Among the many institutions established by the colonizer are schools and universities in the colony and departments and archives devoted to the study of the colony in the metropole. When the

Buddha: The Study of Buddhism under Colonialism (Chicago: University of Chicago Press, 1995), pp. 107–60.

colony is granted independence, these institutions generally remain in place, with native faculty trained in Europe often assuming positions of authority. Eventually, as in the case of the Subaltern Studies collective in India, an oppositional historiography may emerge. This turn of events never took place in Tibet, although a similar process has been undertaken by the current colonial administration, of whose products we must also be aware.

The two assumptions of this Asian version of comparative philosophy (in which Tibetans have yet to participate) are obviously inextricable: there must be a global and teleological history of philosophy for an Asian philosopher to occupy the end-point. The Asian comparativist thus, in a move that is at once belated and preemptive, assumes, as if by necessity, a European model of philosophy but then places an Asian philosopher at its pinnacle before he can be incorporated into yet another Western totalizing ideology at some point below the pinnacle.

The writings of these Asian comparativists (such as Radhakrishnan and Nishitani) have determined the agenda of much "comparative philosophy" in Europe and, especially, the United States.[29] Just as Vajrapāṇi could find *mahāmudrā* in the *Heart Sūtra*, although *mahāmudrā* probably developed in India after the Perfection of Wisdom sūtras, so more recent commentators have participated in a similarly ahistorical ideology of the plenum, such that the elusive master Nāgārjuna, or at least his *Mādhyamikakārikās* (Verses on the Middle Way), could be read as Kantian at the beginning of this century, as Wittgensteinian in its middle, and as Derridian at its end.[30]

Candrakīrti, for example, has lately been portrayed as a deconstructionist par excellence. One reason for this portrayal is the historical accident of the preservation in Sanskrit of his commentary to the *Mādhyamikakārikās*, a work devoted largely to negation. However, just as we gain a more complete picture of Nāgārjuna by reading the *Ratnāvalī* (Garland of Jewels), the *Suhṛllekha* (Letter to a Friend), the *Śūnyatāsaptati* (Seventy Stanzas on Emptiness), and the *Catuḥstava* (Four Hymns)

[29] In the case of Buddhism, there may be something else at work: the strange perception that "Buddhism, perhaps even more so than other religions, is built around a set of concepts which seem always to be on the verge of disappearing into the realm of what can no longer be conceptualized, and which therefore can lend themselves to such unlimited exegesis that they can be made to agree with one's particular philosophical and ideological commitments." See Gustavo Benavides, "Giuseppe Tucci or Buddhology in the Age of Fascism," in Lopez, ed., *Curators of the Buddha*, p. 162. Discussions of "Buddhism and Science," for instance, and for reasons that deserve scrutiny, remain as common today as they were in the nineteenth century.

[30] On modern philosophers' fascination with Nāgārjuna, see Richard P. Hayes, "Nāgārjuna's Appeal," *Journal of Indian Philosophy* 22 (1994): 299–378.

alongside the *Mādhyamikakārikās*,[31] so we gain a different picture of Candrakīrti by reading the moral tales that he tells to comment on Āryadeva's *Catuḥśataka* (Four Hundred), the *other* nine chapters of the *Madhyamakāvatāra* (Entrance to the Middle Way), and his *Triśaranasaptati* (Seventy Stanzas on Refuge). Such readings show both Nāgārjuna and Candrakīrti to be first and foremost Indian Buddhist thinkers of their times, committed to the effective exposition of enlightenment and to the path to it, with all that that entails. There appears to be little reason to call Nāgārjuna or Candrakīrti deconstructionists.[32]

But what is perhaps more important is to consider what is at stake in asking the question, "Was Nāgārjuna a deconstructionist?" As already noted, the strategy of legitimation through association is a common element of late colonial discourse, where the long oppressed and demeaned colonized demonstrates superiority over the colonizer by showing that they (the colonized) have the same things that the colonizer values, and that the colonized had them first. Thus, from the eighteenth-century Hindu renaissance until the present day, we continue to hear conservative Hindus claim that everything from the locomotive to interstellar travel is to be found in the Veda, that the withering light that Śiva emits from his brow is a laser. We find Theravādins reminding us that the Buddha was a pragmatist long before William James; T. R. V. Murti finds Hegel's dialectic foreshadowed in Mādhyamika; the Kyoto School proclaims that its rather idiosyncratic version of Zen anticipates and surpasses Nietzsche.

However, European and American scholars have also attempted to demonstrate that the texts and authors that they study anticipate philosophical issues in the West. It is certainly laudatory on one level that they attempt to identify with the concerns of the oppressed cultures that they

[31] The attribution of the *Ratnāvalī* and the *Suhṛllekha* to Nāgārjuna has been challenged recently by Tilmann Vetter and Sieglinde Dietz. See Tilmann Vetter, "On the Authenticity of the Ratnāvalī" *Asiatische Studien Études Asiatiques* 46, no. 1 (1992): 492–506; and Sieglinde Dietz, "The Author of the *Suhṛllekha*," in E. Steinkellner and Helmut Tauscher, eds., *Contributions on Tibetan and Buddhist Religion and Philosophy* (Vienna: Arbeitskreis für Tibetische und Buddhistische Studien Universität Wien, 1983), pp. 59–72.

[32] Some of the more problematic uses of deconstruction in this regard include works such as Harold Coward's *Derrida and Indian Philosophy* (Albany: State University of New York Press, 1990) and Robert Magliola, *Derrida on the Mend* (West Lafayette, Ind.: Purdue University Press, 1984). A useful response to Magliola's claims is found in Roger R. Jackson, "Matching Concepts: Deconstructive and Foundationalist Tendencies in Buddhist Thought," *Journal of the American Academy of Religion* 57 (1989): 561–89. Jackson states, however, that "Buddhism includes both deconstruction and foundationalism" (p. 567) and appears to have no qualms about the question of whether Nāgārjuna was a deconstructionist; he simply answers in the negative. He concludes, "The spiritually agile Buddhist walks a difficult tightrope, balancing two truths, holding a pole weighted deconstructively on one end and foundationally on the other, knowing that if her equilibrium is lost, the fall will be a long one" (p. 585).

study rather than with the oppressive cultures of their birth. Yet it is not simply sympathy that motivates the desperate measure of showing that Buddhism had deconstruction first, a position the advocacy of which effectively demeans the Buddhist tradition with the tacit suggestion that in order for its literature to be legitimate, it must have deconstruction. In some cases, these claims are the remnants of a Romantic Orientalism, in which Asia provides what the West lacks. As discussed at the end of the previous chapter, colonialist legacies have contributed to much of the focus on Tibetan Buddhist "philosophy."

There are also institutional concerns. Scholars of Asian philosophy in Britain and America often find themselves as the sole scholar of Asia in a department of Religion or Religious Studies with strong historical links to the tradition of Christian seminary education. Marginalized, as in a colony, the Asianist often is compelled to demonstrate the value of his or her scholarly commodity by a claim to philosophy, that discipline which has always carried the greatest cachet among the humanities (and for whom Religious Studies has always been something of a poor relation). In order for that claim to carry any weight, it must be cast in terms of comparison. Once a comparison has been made under such circumstances, the compulsion to evaluate the Asian text as somehow superior to its Western counterpart is difficult to resist. In a certain sense, then, the European or American scholar of Asian religion shares much in common with the Asian colonized elite, both seeking to challenge the Christian hegemony of Europe and the West and to establish legitimacy through recourse to the enterprise of comparison.

This is not to suggest that comparison is undesirable or, for that matter, avoidable. Kant noted that "since human reason has been enraptured by innumerable objects in various ways for many centuries, it cannot easily fail that for everything new, something old can be found which has some kind of similarity to it."[33] Twentieth-century Westerners, or at least denizens of Western society, are not sixth-century Indian monks. How are they to understand and make understandable to others texts from which they are doubly alienated, by time and by culture? And so it seems in some ways perfectly appropriate and indeed desirable that they be familiar with what has become the common vocabulary of academic discourse in the humanities and that they in fact read Derrida and other theorists. And it is also not inappropriate should they endeavor to bring the considerable insights of these authors to bear on their own work and on their own texts. But to say that Derrida may help us interpret Buddhist texts is something very different from saying that Nāgārjuna does what Derrida does. To call Nāgārjuna a deconstructionist or to translate this or that

[33] Cited in Halbfass, *India and Europe*, p. 112.

Sanskrit or Chinese term as "deconstruct" is to take a name for a specific approach to the reading of literature derived from an individual lineage of twentieth-century continental philosophy and to deprive that name of any meaning.

On the role of theory, Jonathan Z. Smith has noted:

> Having persuaded ourselves that, whatever else it is, religion is ultimately important (or, important because it is ultimate), we illicitly use that claim to justify anything we happen to study as being self-evidently significant. But significance is not a matter of peacock-like self-display, nor is it guaranteed by something merely being "there." Theory, and its attendant operations (such as comparison) are disciplined exaggerations in the service of knowledge. They provide both the grounds and the means by which we re-vision phenomena as our data, as significant in that they address our theoretical problems.[34]

Far too often the agenda of scholarship in the study of Asian texts is set by the tradition, with scholars examining whether the Yogācāra critique of Mādhyamika is justified, taking sides in sectarian disputes, repeating what the masters say and acting as their advocates. Perhaps more important than mimicking the moves of the masters is to consider how and why they made those moves. There are certain hard-won skills that are essential prerequisites for this work; one must know how to read the languages and must learn the allusions. It is important also, however, to become conscious of the presuppositions and prejudices that motivate the manipulation of those skills, skills that are to be employed in the service of an argument, not simply to provide an illustration of an unquestioned assumption.

One of the pitfalls in the appropriation of theory is a pitfall of comparative philosophy—the reduction of complex texts to a crude ideology ignoring the historical, cultural, and social perspectives of their production, viewing them as simply speaking to a canonical set of philosophical questions and themes. Even the most abstract systems (with which Buddhism is replete) cannot be regarded merely as bodies of propositions. They must also be treated as located utterances, the rhetorical purposes of which one must seek to determine if they are to be understood. This is not a claim about authorial intention but rather about recontextualization, not just of the history and political climate of the text's composition, but of one's own reading as well. And once the decision is made to recontextualize Buddhist philosophies, one must guard against the tendency to reconstruct their intellectual context too narrowly. Hence, before one spins off in poststructuralist flights on Nāgārjuna's famous dic-

[34] Jonathan Z. Smith, "Connections," *Journal of the American Academy of Religion* 58, no. 1 (1990): 10.

tum that he has no thesis, one might attempt to understand this statement in light of his rather prosaic advice to a king, that one read what his commentators in India and Tibet and China have said about it. That is, rather than engaging in a compulsive and reflexive analysis borne on the heady vapors of omnipotent theory, what Freud called "wild psychoanalysis," one might take stock of all the resources provided by the tradition; commentaries are there to be read, without naively assuming that the commentary is going to determine what the text "really means."

In the end, then, there may be some sense of commonality between the commentators ancient and postmodern. After we try to see as clearly as possible how we differ from Vimalamitra or Vajrapāṇi, we might also see how we are the same, how we simultaneously share with them both a dilemma and a challenge. The dilemma is that we never begin from nowhere, we never begin anew, but are always bound tightly to the text. As already noted, in commentary, "the top-heaviness of the original text, its permanence, its status as discourse ever capable of being brought up to date, the multiple or hidden meanings with which it is credited, the reticence and wealth it is believed to contain, all this creates an open possibility for discussion." So the commentator needs the text. But, as Gershom Scholem has noted, the text also needs the commentator; revelation needs commentary, which he calls, "a prime example of spontaneity in receptivity." And lest we fear that what we say is somehow unfaithful to our chosen text, we might take some comfort in the Jewish belief that the revelation of the law to Moses at Sinai contained within itself as sacred tradition all future commentary on the law. Or, as the third-century Palestinian rabbi Joshua ben Levi wrote, "Torah, Mishna, Talmud, and Aggadah—indeed even the comments some bright student will one day make to his teacher—were already given to Moses on Mount Sinai."[35] We must also note, however, that it is precisely this notion of commentary, as the sanctified eternal plenitude, already complete at the beginning, which is the target of deconstruction.

In the study of Buddhist texts, we might, then, adopt a tripartite procedure that has become generally accepted in other disciplines in the humanities over the past decade or so, during which the attention of scholars in the humanities has been directed toward the contexts of the works they study, not so much in hope of arriving at historical reconstruction, but in an effort to identify and understand the complex of influences—social, political, artistic, philosophical—at play in the production of a text. The first requirement is that we examine our chosen

[35] Gershom Scholem, "Revelation and Tradition as Religious Categories in Judaism," in *The Messianic Idea in Judaism and Other Essays on Jewish Spirituality* (New York: Schocken, 1971), p. 289.

text or topic within as broad a historical context as possible. This entails situating our subject; in the case of a text it is necessary to consider the relationships at work among the various Buddhist textual practices in a specific time and place as well as their relations to non-Buddhist textual practices. This would involve attempting to determine the circumstances of the text's production and the history of its circulation, for whom it was written and how and by whom it was used. A careful examination of the conditions of the production of knowledge requires that we transfer our expectations for the source of meaning *away* from the origins of the tradition to local circumstances, such as the technologies, practices, and institutions that made the production and persistence of a given text possible.[36] All of this involves a good deal of hard-nosed historical research into the social and political factors at play. This is not to suggest that the intricacies of a certain author's *pramāṇa* theory can be accounted for by a simple appeal to social history. It is necessary as well to make an attempt to discern the contours of the particular rules of discourse under which the text was composed, to place it within what some would call its archive, what others would call its *doxa*. Such an investigation might entail, for example, an ideological critique of a Tibetan society in which the minds and bodies of intellectually elite males were engaged in the production of a highly stylized and hermetic scholastic discourse, what some would term "scribalism."[37]

The second requirement is that we examine not only our text or topic but the history of its study, not only in Asia but also in the West, again attending to the circumstances that led to a particular text coming under Western scrutiny or remaining hidden from the Buddhological gaze. The investigation of the history of a text's study also entails the examination of the modern reproductions of a text or textual practice, in both Asia and the West. Aijaz Ahmad has warned that these various networks of exchange have created "such a wilderness of mirrors that we need the most incisive of operations, and the most delicate of dialectics, to disaggregate their densities."[38] But this is a wilderness into which we have already wandered.

The third requirement is the scholar's critical estimation of his or her own situation in the entire process; an examination of the position from which we speak, the historical conditions from which we emerge as scholarly agents. One of the possible conclusions of such contextualiza-

[36] See Charles Hallisey, "Roads Taken and Not Taken in the Study of Theravāda Buddhism," in Lopez, ed., *Curators of the Buddha*," pp. 49–53.

[37] See Jonathan Z. Smith, *Map Is Not Territory: Studies in the History of Religions* (Leiden: E. J. Brill, 1978), pp. 70–71.

[38] Aijaz Ahmad, *In Theory: Classes, Nations, Literatures* (London: Verso, 1992), p. 184.

tion is a radical historicism that holds that a text from which the interpreter is abstracted by time and culture must remain utterly beyond the understanding of the interpreter. Few would claim that it is possible to retrieve fully one of the Pāla commentators' understanding of the *Heart Sūtra*, especially when we concede that his understanding is not identical to what is represented in his commentary. The danger of radical contextualization (to the extent that it is even possible in the case of Indian scholastic literature) is an essentialism that portrays such works as the product of "the Indian mind," itself one of the more lamentable fruits of comparative philosophy. Should it be possible, then, to navigate between the multiheaded Scylla of comparative philosophy and the all-swallowing Charybdis of incommensurable difference, this third requirement may prove to be of some import.[39]

[39] Of the "differend" Jean-François Lyotard writes:

> The stakes of a genre are often set by the phrase of canonical value. This phrase may be formulated in the interrogative regimen. What about this? What should I do? Have you understood? Shall we judge that to be beautiful? If this is so, what can we do? Do you agree? Do you want to? Is it legitimate to . . . ? What happened? What will happen? What follows from this? How much is this worth? Success comes from giving an "answer" to the key-phrase. The "answer" is a phrase that suspends the question contained in the key-phrase. It is then asked whether this suspension is legitimate, and the answer to this last question becomes the object of new differends, whose various parties question the said answer on the basis of key-questions which set the stakes for their respective genres.

See Jean-François Lyotard, *The Differend: Phrases in Dispute*, trans. Georges Van Den Abbeele (Minneapolis: University of Minnesota Press, 1988), p. 137.

Halbfass's conclusion on the question of comparative philosophy also warrants citation here. He writes:

> "Comparative philosophy," if it is possible at all is still in a nascent stage, and it requires much critical reflection and hermeneutic awareness. Western partners in the comparative enterprise and the East-West "dialogue" have to be aware of their historical background and of some long-standing biases in the European approach to non-European traditions—as well as an inherent bias and one-sidedness in the "comparative" approach as such: They have to recognize that their allegedly neutral, purely theoretical, and objective approach is itself the result and expression of peculiar historical and cultural developments, and that the very openness of comparative, cross-cultural "research" is conditioned by an implicit European parochialism, by one peculiar, almost idiosyncratic manner of understanding reality. On the other hand, Indians in many cases still have to find the necessary freedom for a kind of comparison which is not primarily apologetics and cross-cultural self-defense against the Western challenge, which does not amount to hastily reinterpreting or readjusting their own traditional concepts and ways of thinking, and which at the same time does not simply extrapolate and perpetuate the traditional schemes of inclusivism by subordinating all other world views to Advaita Vedanta.
>
> . . . And, of course, in applying the term and concept of philosophy cross-culturally and beyond the sphere in which it was created and originally used, we cannot

The Pāla commentator can say that the Buddha is called *bhagavan* because he has destroyed the afflictions for the reason that, in his language, *bhaga* (fortune) sounds like *bhaṅga* (destroy). The reason that I can suggest in chapter 5 that the tantric sādhana on the *Heart Sūtra* is about incest is that, in my language, the statement in the sādhana, "Imagine that the Conqueror [Śākyamuni] is drawn to the heart of the Mother and enters into samādhi," sounds Oedipal. My reading of the maṇḍala is the articulation of an association, an association whose causal chain leads back not (only) to a pathogenic nucleus, but to another reading. The association then, is never free, but is determined by what has been read, and that, in turn, is determined largely by an institution, by a community that has a history. What distinguishes the ancient commentator from the postmodern, then, is the historical consciousness available to the latter and its attendant demand to historicize not only the root text but the very act of commentary itself.

If there is a sense of dis-ease at the disciplined exaggeration of a Freudian reading of an Indian maṇḍala, it may perhaps be traced to a source beyond that of the quite justified discomfort that a textual scholar experiences when his or her translation is made to illustrate some facile comparative point or to confirm a Jungian theory.[40] To regard such a reading as an intrusive intervention betrays the assumption of the text (or Buddhism, for that matter) as a natural object that is not to be interfered with, but only described. However, Buddhist texts and theories about Buddhist texts are always in a state of mutual interchange, making a neutral and merely descriptive theory of textual interpretation impossible. It is ostensibly simpler to concentrate on the nature of the object, whether it be the *Heart Sūtra* or Buddhism, than it is to consider the problem of one's relation to the scholarly object. A singular focus on the object remains possible as long as the founding conventions that have established the object remain either unacknowledged or are regarded as unproblematic. The most important of these conventions is that the larger object, in this case Buddhism, does indeed constitute a self-identical and self-contained

be sure whether we are indeed comparing philosophies, or whether we are comparing the Western tradition of philosophy with other traditions which, in spite of all analogies, are ultimately not philosophical traditions. But this might be a deeper challenge to self-understanding than merely dealing with what is explicitly referred to as philosophy, i.e., with the history of philosophy under the secure and thoughtless guidance of the word "philosophy."

Halbfass, *India and Europe*, p. 433.

On such constructs as "the Indian mind," see G. E. R. Lloyd, *Demystifying Mentalities* (Cambridge: Cambridge University Press, 1990).

[40] On Jung's relation to Asia, see Luis O. Gómez, "Oriental Wisdom and the Cure of Souls: Jung and the Indian East," in Lopez, ed., *Curators of the Buddha*.

entity. As long as the basic premises that underlie the institution of interpretation are not called into question, the institution can maintain its stability while encouraging progress, which in Buddhist Studies has largely been measured by the number of texts edited and translated. However, when changes both inside and outside the institution call into question those conventions that provide it with its particular identity, when the founding assumptions of the discipline are challenged, the very notion of what constitutes progress within the institution is also challenged. It is at such moments that the process by which the unity of the institution is established, maintained, and disrupted becomes discernible. As Samuel Weber notes, "The self-identity of an interpretation will depend on what it attacks, excludes, and incorporates—in short, on its relation to and dependency on that which it is not, other interpretations."[41] Hence, in interpreting a Buddhist text, it is not necessarily the case that the interpreter be limited by those interpretations previously certified by the institution; it is possible to make use of interpretations deriving from other institutions, which may or may not challenge the fundamental assumptions of Buddhist Studies.[42]

In his December 6, 1896 letter to Fliess, Freud wrote, "As you know, I am working on the assumption that our psychical mechanism has come about by a process of stratification: the material present in the shape of memory-traces is from time to time subjected to a rearrangement in accordance with fresh circumstances—is, at it were, transcribed."[43] This is an early formulation of his central notion of *Nachträglichkeit* (translated often as "deferred revision"), that experiences, impressions, and memo-

[41] Samuel Weber, *Institution and Interpretation* (Minneapolis: University of Minnesota Press, 1987), p. 137.

[42] The passage from Nietzsche cited above may be cited again here: "[W]hatever exists, having somehow come into being, is again and again reinterpreted to new ends, taken over, transformed, and redirected by some power superior to it; all events in the organic world are a subduing, a *becoming master*, and all subduing and becoming master involves fresh interpretation, an adaptation through which any previous 'meaning' and 'purpose' are necessarily obscured or even obliterated." But in the same book of the *Genealogy of Morals*, Nietzsche argues that there is also a debt owed by the present to the past, and consciousness of this debt emerges as the sentiment of guilt. Interpretation is agonistic in the sense that in order to affirm itself it must in some sense deny what has come before. Thus, the inevitable indebtedness of the interpreter to the past is easily transformed into a guilt that most commonly manifests itself as a humility of the interpreter before the text. "The construction of the good, meaningful text which the critic simply *serves*, together with the bad critic who *betrays* the text, would be the guilt-ridden attempt of criticism to avoid or evade a debt that is impossible to repay." See Weber, *Institution and Interpretation*, p. 39. This point is derived from Weber's comments on pp. 38–39.

[43] Sigmund Freud, *The Origins of Psychoanalysis: Letters to Wilhelm Fliess, Drafts and Notes 1887–1902*, ed. Marie Bonaparte, Anna Freud, and Ernst Kris; trans. Eric Mosbacher and James Strachey (New York: Basic Books, 1954), p. 173.

ries from the past are sometimes revised at a later date in accordance with new experiences or with the movement to a new stage of psychical development. Freud meant by this term something more than the idea that the past is reinterpreted according to the needs of the present; he seems also to have meant something more specific than Borges' observation that each writer creates his own precursors.[44] For Freud, not all experience is subject to deferred revision, but only those experiences (most notably traumatic events) that could not be fully assimilated into a meaningful context in the first instance. Further, deferred revision does not occur constantly, but is occasioned by specific events or situations, especially moments of maturation "which allow the subject to gain access to a new level of meaning and to rework his earlier experiences."[45] Without implying on the one hand that the study of Buddhist texts is moving to ever higher levels of maturation, toward some distant goal, nor on the other, that the commentary of a given era is nothing more than a mere reflection of the peculiar concerns of its day, I would suggest that there may be some value in reading commentators, both ancient and postmodern, as deferred revisers, aiming ever at reworking and rewriting into a meaningful context those textual traces that seem most resistant to incorporation.

[44] Jorge Luis Borges, "Kafka and His Predecessors," in Emir Rodriguez Monegal and Alastair Reid, eds., *Borges: A Reader* (New York: E. P. Dutton, 1981), p. 243.

[45] Jacques Laplanche and J. B. Pontalis, *The Language of Psychoanalysis* (New York: W. W. Norton, 1973), p. 112.

Index

The index covers historical figures and titles of works mentioned in the body of the text and in the notes. Tibetan names are alphabetized by root letter.

About the Author

DONALD S. LOPEZ, JR., is Professor of Buddhist and Tibetan Studies in the Department of Asian Languages and Cultures at the University of Michigan. He is the editor of Princeton Readings in Religions, which includes *Religions of China in Practice, Buddhism in Practice,* and *Religions of India in Practice.*